CONFESSIONS
of a
CLOSET YOGI

Hi Jeremy,

Once you finish this
book then
you won't be able to
pick it up again

Cheers,

Larry

CONFESSIONS
of a
CLOSET YOGI

Larry Wardwell

www.closetyogi.com

Confessions of a Closet Yogi
by Larry Wardwell
© 2011

For information please contact www.closetyogi.com

Front cover design by Gene Avery North www.medicinehorsestudio.com

Book design by Kai Crozer

For Linnea

CONTENTS

Introduction   1

1. Visions of Golden Light and Cold Beer   3

2. The Air Force for Dummies   14

3. Dreaming in German   47

4. Exiled to Cleveland   74

5. Lower Education in Texas   77

6. Auspicious Encounter at the Columbus Airport   101

7. Intelligence School: Classified Clowns   118

8. Top Secret Acid Heads   146

9. It Happened One Night!   162

10. Polish Sausage and Hungarian Light Bulbs   168

11. The Search Begins   179

12. Homecoming   190

13. Retreat to the Mountains   214

14. A Month with Maharishi   237

15. Mediterranean Meditations   252

16. Bible Belt Meditators   269

17. Master's Degree from the Master   304

18. Frat House Ashram   315

19. Higher Consciousness at Higher Altitudes   327

20. The Accidental Ashram   360

21. Island Paradise   380

22. New Delhi and the Sacred Industrial Park   388

23. Midnight Monster in the Closet   410

24. A Taste of Utopia   425

25. Back to Washington, Again!   437

26. Golden Dome in the Hill Country   452

27. Lost on the Mountain   461

    Epilogue   466

INTRODUCTION

When I decided to call this book *Confessions of a Closet Yogi*, I wasn't sure if the word *confessions* was appropriate, since it is usually associated with scandalous or criminal behavior. While my youthful activities weren't serious enough to warrant a long prison sentence, they certainly weren't something that I would put in a résumé. I felt that by recounting these stories of my life before I became a "seeker of truth," I could provide a frame of reference for the narrative of my transformation from an intellectually anesthetized hell-raiser to a dedicated and curious consciousness-raiser. It wasn't until I had the opportunity to meet Timothy Leary at Millbrook House in New York, and have my first LSD "trip" while working as an intelligence analyst at the Defense Intelligence Agency, that I realized that human consciousness has the capacity to experience a blissful oneness with the entire universe. This was my first step on a path of seeking enlightenment through meditation and Vedic knowledge. A few months after this experience in the spring of 1968, I left my job in Washington, D.C. and headed out to Berkeley, California, the epicenter of the counterculture, in search of a higher state of consciousness.

Although this is a true story, it is written from my subjective memory without spending a lot of time on research and checking for accuracy. Therefore, some of the dates and details might be out of sequence, exaggerated, or interpreted differently by others. For the most part, it provides candid insight into the Transcendental Meditation movement from my uniquely goofy perspective. As a matter of fact, the most bizarre events are the most accurately described. Also, I have changed most of the names of the characters in the story to protect their privacy and have changed the names of a few locations for the same reason. My only agenda is to tell an entertaining story that includes the ancient wisdom of the Vedas. I like to describe myself as a "closet yogi" because even though I spend two to three hours a day in blissful silence, I still enjoy normal things like cutting firewood, hiking and sailing. I believe that meditation has resulted in immeasurable bliss and serenity for both Linnea, my beloved wife of forty years, and me. Who knows, maybe if we had never learned to meditate, it would have turned out the same. But we doubt it!

— Larry Wardwell

1

VISIONS of GOLDEN LIGHT and COLD BEER

Now that we were hopelessly lost and trapped in a raging blizzard, I felt like kicking myself for not having paid more attention to the uneasy premonitions I'd had as we'd been climbing the mountain. I am always amazed at how suddenly a seemingly modest adventure can turn into a nightmare. A delightful day hike in the springtime Arizona sun with my wife, Linnea, and our eight-year-old son, Devan, was now an urgent struggle to stay alive in a sudden mountain snowstorm with no warm clothes, shelter, or food.

As the pitch-black night descended upon us, we quickly gathered pine needles and logs for a makeshift lean-to shelter that faced our campfire, so that Linnea and Devan could get some relief from the driving snowstorm. I realized I would need to keep awake all night in order to keep the fire going, so I decided to meditate for a half-hour to gain some rest, then add more wood to the fire, then go back into meditation. As I sat facing the fire, my face and hands were fairly warm, but my back was drenched with the cold, wet snow, so I turned my back to the fire to dry it out. After about ten minutes I noticed that the smoke from the fire had a strange odor. I soon realized that the back of my jacket was burning, so I quickly lay down in the snow to put out the fire and then turned around to face the fire again. This time I noticed my hiking boots were smoldering.

After long hours of alternating between facing the fire and then drying my back, I mastered the technique of keeping fairly dry by switching from front to back just as the steam from my clothes would change to smoke. As the interminable night wore on, I began drifting in and out of consciousness. Suddenly I found myself enveloped by an extremely comfortable, brilliant golden sunlight. I had a vague feeling of being in the past rather than the present. Then some past events began to manifest. I thought, *Maybe I am dead, and this is the video of my life that is supposed to play before I pass over to the "other side."* As the golden light began to transform into a clear image, my awareness was drawn toward a brilliant summer sun radiating light and warmth, illuminating what appeared to be a shining golden and reddish mountain. I shifted my attention to the mountain and it became clearer. It now resembled a huge mound of beer cans piled three stories high—glinting in the blinding sunlight. This visual sensation of a specific place now became supplemented by a growing sense of time. Then, like a computer turning on, I realized this was my own past. It was 1958 outside a dump in a small town about twenty miles from Boston, Massachusetts. My consciousness continued to contract from a transcendental state of universal oneness to a progressively more localized and focused awareness, until I was sitting in my 1949 Ford with three of my high-school buddies. Now I was reliving a memory stored on my mental "hard drive" for more than thirty years.

We had just finished our high-school classes the day before and had a day off to raise hell before the graduation ceremony that evening. Along with cars and girls, drinking alcohol was a very important teenage activity in the late 1950s. The fact that it was illegal to drink or buy alcohol if you were younger than twenty-one presented an exciting challenge that added to the thrill of drinking. When a major beer producer decided to locate its new brewery in our small town, it became the focal point of a multitude of rumors and tall tales for beer-hungry teenagers. One of the stories floating around was that whenever they ran a fresh batch of beer through the system, the first five to ten thousand cans of beer were considered "green" and did not meet the taste specifications for the brewery. So these cans were run through a machine that punched holes in the tops of the cans, which allowed the defective beer to run out. The hole-punching machine had a defect, however, that caused it just to dent every fourth can instead of punching a hole in it. The cans would then be loaded into dump trucks and hauled to the landfill. I don't remember how we'd found this out, but we knew that if we could get into the dump and go through the mountain of beer cans, we could find thousands of full ones. After having cased the dump, we located the huge pile of beer cans behind a chain-link fence. We noticed two dump attendants who kept an eye on every activity there. Every day from 12 to 1 PM, however, they locked the dump and went to lunch. So we came back the next day and scaled the fence as soon as the attendants had left. The temperature was over ninety degrees, and as we approached the mountain of shiny, sticky, dripping beer cans with our burlap bags, the stench of decaying, stale beer and the roar of millions of flies became overwhelming. After a brief moment of fearful hesitation, we charged forward and attacked the hill, slipping, sliding and stumbling, sometimes up to our waists in the putrid garbage heap of discarded beer cans. The attendants were due back soon, so we feverishly clawed our way through the cans in search of the heavier ones that were mostly full of beer. It didn't take long for us to fill our bags and get back to the car. Though we were drenched with old beer and smeared with bits of disgusting garbage, we had our beer.

The town lake was the center of our social universe. A small beach at the end of a residential road was where we hung out, had parties, parked and planned stupid pranks on one another and the adults in the neighborhood. After having jumped in the car, the four of us instinctively headed for the lake without even discussing it. By the time we got there, we were hot, smelly and covered with a variety of sticky foreign substances. We burst from the car and jumped into the lake without taking our clothes or shoes off. After ten minutes of joyful splashing in the cool water, we looked triumphantly back at the car and its precious booty. In our world this was a supreme accomplishment, on a par with winning a gold medal in the Olympics or a scholarship to Harvard. We dumped the filthy cans of beer in the lake and proceeded to scrub each one meticulously. Then the moment of truth had arrived: it was time to taste the beer. It was the most wretched, foul-tasting brew imaginable. This, however, didn't seem to bother us that much. We were so elated about the carload of free beer and the excitement of our raid on the dump that taste was a minor consideration.

After having drunk as much of the beer as we could stomach, we had the brilliant idea of securing the bags of beer on the bottom of the lake. This would provide us with free cold beer every time we returned to the lake. Then one of us looked at his watch and let out a big "Uh-Oh!" It was 6:30 PM, and we were supposed to have been at the high school at five to put on our caps and gowns for the graduation ceremony, which was to begin right now. So we piled into the car and roared off to the high school, about fifteen minutes away.

As we approached the school, we could see a long line of students wearing caps and gowns, with faculty members running around like border collies barking to keep them in line. As we pulled up, a large group of mortarboards and tassels with heads below them turned toward us. Someone pointed in our direction and yelled something that triggered a response in our homeroom teacher, Mr. Gleason. He charged out of the school as we were staggering out of the car and grabbed me by the collar. We were feeling no pain at the time, so when he started screaming at us, we started laughing at him. The poor guy was livid! Not only were we late and holding up the graduation procession, but he'd found out that we had hidden Jerry Monroe's cap and gown, and he had spent the last hour looking for them. We grabbed our gowns, along with Jerry's, and jumped in line just as the procession into the auditorium began.

After the ceremony was over, everyone threw their caps and gowns into a heap and headed off to various parties. There were two major groups in our high school: the "Joe College" kids and the "Shop" kids. The "Joe College" kids were on the college-preparatory track and were full participants in school activities: sports, clubs, newspaper, theater and so on. They wore button-down shirts and chino pants with a little strap and buckle on the back, and they sported crew cuts. The "Shop" kids wore more rebellious clothes, looked like Elvis Presley, and didn't participate much in school activities. They were ready to learn a trade and start working right after graduation and were more interested in cars than college. I didn't really belong to either group. Though I took college-preparatory courses, I was out of the loop when it came to school activities. Most of my friends were industrial arts students and were dedicated to having fun and not thinking about the future. Life for them was a series of parties and crazy stunts. I was tired of school and didn't want to go to college, yet I wasn't ready to join the working class and be trapped in some boring job. Some of the guys in our "gang" had joined the Navy and come home with tales of travel to exotic places like Cuba. So why not join the service, I thought, have some adventures, maybe learn a skill and then go to college or get a job?

In 1958 there were no wars—Korea had ended in 1953, and Vietnam was a sleepy French colony called "Indochina." There was also an economic recession, and because there were few jobs available, there was actually a long waiting list to get into the military. A few days after graduation in June, I paid a visit to the Air Force recruiter and was told that I would have to wait until October or November to enlist. I thought, *Oh, well, I can continue working at my part-time job as a sales-clerk and enjoy the New England summer.* I worked in a high-quality men's clothing store in what was called the "men's furnishing" department: shirts, ties, pants and so on. One slow afternoon a group of us sales-clerks were hanging around talking, and I mentioned that I was joining the Air Force. A few of my fellow employees were college students and advised me to go to college first. Bob, the kid in the shoe department who had also just graduated from high school, said that he had been accepted to college in the fall and was planning a career in accounting. I mentioned that I would probably go to college eventually, but I wanted to enjoy a few "wild years" before going back to school. Bob gave me a surprised look and said, "Gee, I never thought of that!" He had a very "straight-arrow" appearance, with a crew cut and a dark business suit with black wingtip shoes. Bob seemed as if he needed to get in touch with his inner party animal, so I invited him to join a group of us on a weekend trip to Cape Cod. He got very excited and said he would love to go if his parents would let him.

Just before picking up Bob at his parents' house, we loaded four cases of beer into my weird bronze and green 1948 Plymouth. Beer and bathing suits were all we needed—no toothbrushes, towels, extra clothes, or food. We pulled up in front of Bob's house, and he came running out to the car with a big suitcase, dressed in expensive slacks and his black wingtips. We could see his worried parents peering out the windows as Bob jumped in the car and yelled, "Quick, let's get going!" By the time we got to Provincetown, at the end of Cape Cod, it was midnight, and the five of us had finished two cases of beer. We were all so drunk we could hardly see, so we drove onto the sand dunes about two hundred yards off the road until we got stuck, and all of us piled out of the car. We staggered a few feet onto the dunes and promptly passed out. I woke up a few hours later and remembered there were hundreds of firecrackers in the car. Jim and I set the firecrackers off next to the rest of the guys, who were sleeping under a pitch-pine tree. As the explosive flashes of light and flying sand erupted all around them, they awoke in a state of total confusion, then staggered around and convulsed with each explosion. By the time the barrage had ended and the smoke had cleared, they could hear Jim and me rolling in the sand and laughing so hard we were crying. Pete and Joe weren't really mad (we were always pulling pranks on one another): they just vowed revenge and went back to sleep. Poor Bob, however, was not doing too well; he was in a state of shock from the terrifying onslaught of explosions. Some of the firecrackers had gone off too close to his ears and he had temporarily lost his hearing and balance. His glasses were missing, and he groveled around looking for his missing shoe for ten minutes before passing out.

When the sun came up the next morning, it quickly beamed such intense heat and light on our bodies, strewn about the sand dunes, that we could no longer sleep. I looked around at the clothes, beer cans and other debris scattered across the dunes and tried to figure out where we were. There were no houses nearby—just sand dunes in every direction. The car was half buried in the sand a few dunes over from where we'd slept and the sound of the ocean came from the opposite direction about a half mile away. Two of the guys volunteered to go back to the car and retrieve the cooler full of beer so we could have some "breakfast." When they returned about twenty minutes later, the sun was high and it was getting very hot. The ice-cold beer hit the spot and energized us for an expedition across the dunes to the ocean. This was the ultimate minimalist camping--no sleeping bags, tents, or camping gear whatsoever. All we had were the clothes on our backs, bathing suits and beer. For us this was the good life; who could ask for more? We were all so happy that we sang our favorite rock-and-roll songs as we struggled across the dunes toward the sea. Occasionally we would stumble upon shallow tide pools with water heated by the sun, and we'd lie there and soak while drinking a cold beer—what joy! After a few hours we reached the remote beach near Provincetown and plunged into the surf. The cool, foamy salt water felt wonderful on our sunburned and tired bodies, and we frolicked and horsed around in the waves until most of us lay exhausted on the sand unable to move or even laugh. The intense sun, lack of sleep and excessive beer drinking were taking their toll on us. We staggered back across the hot dunes to the car, picked up most of our clothes, and, without a thought, left the empty beer cans and other trash on the dunes.

Before driving onto the main highway leaving the Cape, we stopped at a fast-food drive-in and loaded up on burgers, fries and milkshakes, or "frappes" as they were called in New England. As we drove along the highway, Bob, who was operating on only one shoe, leaned out the window while drinking his chocolate milkshake. Apparently he had never done anything like that before and was ignorant of certain laws of physics, which caused the sixty mile-per-hour wind to remove the milkshake from its container and spray it all over his face and expensive dress shirt. This was the highlight of the day. We all laughed (including Bob) until it was too painful to continue. When we pulled up to Bob's house to drop him off, Bob thanked us profusely for the great time. He seemed really happy, but he didn't look very good. His hair was matted with chocolate milkshake, which was also splattered on his face and shirt. He still had only one shoe, and far fewer clothes and accessories than when he'd started. As he hobbled up to the house, his parents, who must have heard our loud exhaust system, were on their way out to greet him. You could tell by the stunned look on their faces that they had never seen Bob like this before. When they looked over at us in the car, we decided to leave before they invited us in to discuss the details of Bob's great weekend.

About a week later I invited Bob to one of our parties. He fit right in with our group of friends and began dating one of the girls. One day at work Bob announced that he wasn't quite ready for a career in accounting and that he thought joining the Air Force would be more fun. I said, "Great, we can join on the buddy system and go through basic training together." By the end of the summer we were both ready for our new adventure in the Air Force, but we had to wait until November.

Early in September I moved with my family to Ohio, where my father had been transferred with his job at Ford Motor Company. Moving from the charm and beauty of New England to the grimy industrial suburbs of Cleveland was a real culture shock. The entire landscape was dominated by ugly steel mills, auto plants and shipbuilding facilities. The smokestacks of the steel mill, which towered over the landscape for miles, belched a foul-smelling, rust-colored cloud twenty-four hours a day. The sky was lit with an orange glow all night, and in the morning everything was covered with a coarse, reddish metal dust. This was around the time that the Cuyahoga River in Cleveland, which was full of industrial chemicals, actually caught on fire! My three younger sisters, who were still in school, seemed to adapt to this new world, but I was in a gruesome limbo—not going to school and not going to work because I would be leaving in a month for the Air Force. After a few weeks I called Bob and told him how miserable life was in Ohio, and he suggested that I come back to Massachusetts and live at his house until we joined the Air Force. This sounded great, but I wasn't sure his parents would approve after our little excursion on the Cape, and given that Bob was joining the Air Force with me instead of going to college. I was shocked when his folks, who I assumed regarded me as an evil influence on Bob, said OK, and I was on a flight back to Massachusetts in less than a week.

The next month was a blur of parties and hanging out with friends—a lot more fun than Ohio—but Bob and I were still in limbo. Everyone else had either started school or had a job, so we had a lot of free time during the day. We both realized that our free time could be spent more creatively, so one day we encouraged a couple of young ladies to skip their beauty school classes and join us in a daytime party at Bob's house. Both his parents worked, so we had the house to ourselves. The girls arrived at 8:30 AM, a little earlier than expected, so Bob entertained them over breakfast while I took a bus to the closest liquor store and picked up a case of beer. We started drinking right after breakfast, and by noon the case was polished off. Bob and Sally were sort of comatose in the living room with the TV blasting away. Beth and I were splashing around in the bathtub and ended up frolicking around on Bob's parents' bed. Suddenly the bed collapsed with a sickening sound of cracking wood and twisting metal. Bob snapped out of his stupor and came running down the hall toward the bedroom. As he passed the bathroom, his feet went out from under him, and he landed in a pool of water on the floor. When he got back up on his feet, his face turned a sickly white as he realized that his parents' house was sustaining serious damage. The bathtub was overflowing into the hall; beer bottles, wet clothes and cigarette butts were strewn about; and his parents' bedroom looked like a crime scene. Bob, usually a laid-back guy, was clearly distressed. As he began surveying the damage, he suddenly realized that his mother would be home from work any minute.

Bob and Sally panicked, shut off the overflowing tub, and began mopping up the water with towels and mops. Beth and I were soaked.

I found some dry clothes in my suitcase, and Beth fortunately had her white nurse's uniform in her school things. She didn't have any dry underwear, however, so she reluctantly borrowed a bra and panties from Bob's mother's dresser. While Bob and Sally worked on the rest of the house, we worked on the bedroom. The box spring was cracked, and the frame was bent, but we propped it up so that it looked normal.

As we were picking up the wet underwear, towels and bedding, Bob's mother came walking up to the house. Now we all panicked! Beth and I grabbed the wet clothes and soaked towels and sheets, threw open the cellar door and heaved everything down the stairs. Bob and Sally chucked all the beer bottles and trash into the basement while the two girls and I scrambled down the cellar stairs just as Bob's mother came into the house. Bob, mop in hand, was frozen with fear as his mother entered the house and began walking across the soggy carpet. Halfway across the carpet she became aware of the squishing sound and the cold water penetrating her thin shoes. She noticed Bob in the hall holding the mop and looking like a catatonic custodian. Both of them stared at each other for a minute unable to speak. "Oh my God, Bob, are you all right?" she finally blurted out. Bob came to his senses and said, "Mom, I am so sorry, I was starting a bath and the phone rang and I forgot about the tub." His mother was more concerned about Bob than the house and felt relieved that he was able to speak. As the two of them began cleaning up, the girls and I slipped out the basement door.

Over the next few weeks Bob's parents had most of the damage repaired, including the bed. It fell apart when they went to bed the evening of the incident, and they thought they had broken it. They never suspected that I'd been responsible for the damage and they treated me in a cool but civil manner. On the one hand they were disappointed that Bob was not going to college, but on the other, they seemed at least slightly pleased that Bob was happy and looking forward to his Air Force adventure. A few days before our departure for basic training, Bob and I were amazed to find out that his parents were planning a going-away party for us. Teenage parties in those days were always held in the basement of the parents' house for a variety of reasons. Although alcohol was not allowed in the house, kids would go out to their cars and have a few drinks, then return to the basement. Many of the kids were new, inexperienced drinkers and would get sick and vomit before they reached the outside. Needless to say, the cement basement floor was much easier to hose down than the carpeted living room.

We didn't see Bob's parents that much because they usually left for work in the morning before we woke up and they were usually asleep when we came back home at night. About two days before the party, Bob and I were creeping into the house about 2 AM when we noticed his parents in the living room. They asked us to come in, and we noticed that Bob's mother had Beth's underwear in her hand. We suddenly realized that we had forgotten to clean up all the wet clothes and beer bottles we had hastily dumped down the basement stairs a few weeks earlier. Bob's parents were really mad and made us feel guilty for having betrayed their trust and hospitality. We both felt bad because we had forgotten to get rid of the evidence of our bath party and had upset his parents. After having chewed us out for a half-hour they said they would still have the party because so many family members had been invited, but that we would have to spend the next two days cleaning and preparing the basement for the party. Our going-away party was typical of teenage parties in the late fifties. To the kids it was just one of many weekend blasts held on Saturday night. To the adults, though, it was a little more significant, almost like a graduation party. I think Bob's family was actually proud of him.

2

The AIR FORCE for DUMMIES

The day after the party, November 11, 1958, we were scheduled to be inducted at the Boston army base. A few carloads of friends drove us to the base around 7 PM and bade farewell. Bob and I stood in a long line and were given lots of forms to fill out. Next we were ordered into a room to be sworn in. A generic army officer stood before our group of about fifty and asked if anyone had been involved in any criminal activity not reported on our forms. I suddenly recalled an incident a year earlier that I had not reported. I felt a wave of fear go through my body. The officer then asked the question again and added that if anyone were caught failing to report any criminal convictions or had lied on his form, he would be dishonorably discharged. This really got my attention. I didn't have a clue what a dishonorable discharge was, but it sounded scary. My hand went up, and everyone in the room glared at me. Bob became ashen white again. The officer told me to go with the sergeant at the back of the room. As I left the room, Bob was taking his oath with the other men.

He looked panic-stricken and terrified as he was being inducted into the Air Force without me. I was taken to a room in the bowels of the army base in an area that looked and felt like a prison. Waves of anxiety and regret intensified as I waited a long time in what appeared to be an interrogation room. As I waited, I began to wonder if being in the military was like being in jail. The sergeant and officers were not as brutal as the Massachusetts state police, but they certainly weren't jolly. They were very much like the local police: impersonal but not hostile.

They were not at all interested in us as human beings. We were just a product or resource that they had to process. After I'd waited about an hour, a legal officer entered the room. He had the same air of detachment and impartiality, but with a touch of compassion. He asked me why I had not mentioned that I'd been charged with assault and battery on my application for a security clearance, nor discussed it in my various interviews with recruiters. I explained that I had been charged with assault and battery when I was seventeen and was told by the judge that if I stayed out of trouble until my eighteenth birthday, he would drop the charges from my record. This explanation must have evoked some curiosity on the part of the legal officer. He seemed genuinely interested and asked me to tell him what had happened. So I told him about an incident that had occurred a year earlier.

Four or five of my buddies and I were cruising around in my 1950 Dodge convertible, a unique model similar to what was called a "business coupe." Unlike most convertibles, it didn't have a back seat. Instead, the trunk was extra large and extended six or seven feet, all the way to the back of the front seat. So when I had more than three people in the car, two or three extra kids could stretch out in the trunk. I had cut a large hole in the forward part of the trunk so that the kids in the trunk could communicate with those of us in the front seat and also pass food or beer back and forth.

As we cruised along the main drag, one of my buddies, Duffy, noticed a guy we called "Elvis" walking along the street. He was the quintessential Elvis: tall, with Elvis-styled hair, black motorcycle jacket and big black boots. This Elvis was neither friend nor foe. He was from the neighboring town and none of us knew much about him. For some reason, however, Duffy decided he wanted to pick a fight with Elvis. I am not sure whether he had a grievance with Elvis or just felt like honing his fighting skills. Duffy was a nice guy, but he was also a fighter; his main interests were lifting weights and boxing. I pulled the car over, and Duffy jumped out and began challenging Elvis. We all climbed out of the car to watch the fight. Elvis must have thought we were all going to attack him, because he pulled off his big leather belt with a razor blade soldered to the buckle. Most of the kids who took shop classes created these belt weapons, which were a big fad at the time. Somehow Duffy neutralized Elvis's belt, and they began fighting while the rest of us watched. We were all on the sidewalk in front of someone's house when we heard someone yell, "Call the police—it's a gang fight!" It usually took ten to twenty minutes for the local police to arrive at the scene of disturbances, so we weren't in a big hurry. Unfortunately a state trooper was only a mile away and was dispatched to the scene. As soon as we saw the flashing lights, we all jumped in my car and sped off. We knew we couldn't outrun the state trooper, but we were hoping that he hadn't noticed us leaving the scene. From the rearview mirror it looked as if the trooper was stopping to talk with Elvis and other witnesses. After driving down North Main Street about a mile, we turned right at the first light with the hope that if the police were following us, they wouldn't be able to see us turn. As we continued down the road, I kept checking the rearview mirror but saw no cars behind us. About ten minutes later, however, just as we began to relax, I noticed a pair of headlights closing in on us from behind at high speed. Then the flashing blue lights came on and our hearts sank.

I pulled over to the side of the road, and before I could get out of the car, the door was yanked open. The next thing I knew, I was being slammed up against the side of the car by the state trooper. Next he ordered my two friends sitting in the front seat with me to come out with their hands up and lean against the car while he searched them. He knew there were five of us and demanded that we tell him where the other two had gone. We said we didn't know, but a few seconds later the trunk hatch opened a bit as my pals in the trunk tried to see what was going on. Even though I knew we were in serious trouble, I was delighted to see the look of surprise on the trooper's face when he saw the trunk lift open. He quickly regained his composure, though, and told my friends to come out with their hands up. He had never seen a trunk rigged like that and was mildly impressed. Of course he never drew his gun nor was he afraid. Life was more innocent in those days. Teenagers raised a lot of hell but rarely committed serious crimes or violence. The state police were probably the most uptight and unfriendly cops we encountered. The local town police, on the other hand, knew us by name and seemed to enjoy the cat-and-mouse game of trying to catch us in the act of many of our goofy pranks.

On balmy summer nights we would often hang out in a grassy parking area next to a small beach on the lake. By 1 AM one of the neighbors would become aggravated enough by the noise and call the police. As soon as we would see the cop car coming down the gravel road to the beach, we would all run in different directions to throw the cops off. On one particular night we had successfully evaded the police until we came to the main street, which we had to cross to get home. We waited until there was no traffic, then made a dash across the street into the graveyard. Just as we crossed, a car parked behind some trees and bushes put on its headlights: the cops. They had outsmarted us and were waiting. Now they jumped out of the car and began the chase. We scattered like jack rabbits and took off. These cops were not middle-aged doughnut-downing, coffee-drinking desk jockeys—they were only about ten years older than we were and could run pretty fast. While one officer started after Dick and Jim, the other ran after Pete and me through the graveyard. We were actually having a hard time losing him when he suddenly yelled out, "Hey, you guys come back. I lost my gun! Help me find it!" Apparently all the running and jumping over gravestones must have dislodged his gun from its holster. Without hesitation we ran back to where Bob the cop's voice was coming from. As we approached, he grinned and said, "I thought it was you guys. Now help me find my gun—it must have fallen out between the vehicle and here." We fanned out, groping and feeling along the ground. After about ten minutes Pete found the gun and yelled out. As Officer O'Connell approached, Pete pointed the gun at him and said, "Here you are, sir!" The officer took the gun back and admonished Pete never to point a gun at anyone. Then he told us to go home.

On the night of the "gang fight," however, the state trooper was in no mood to send us home. Instead he took us to the state police headquarters in a neighboring town and had us booked for assault and battery. Being formally charged with a crime was a shock to me. This was the last thing I had expected just a few hours before when we we'd been just cruising around. Because we were juveniles, we were not put in jail, but released to the custody of our parents, who had to come to the state police headquarters and pick us up. It was about 3 AM when my parents arrived. Needless to say, they were upset and angry. On the way home I explained that I had just been watching Duffy and Elvis in their pugilistic competition, and my parents believed my side of the story. A month later we were all summoned to appear before a judge at the courthouse. Apparently, because we were all under eighteen, there would be no formal trial, but rather a hearing in the judge's chamber. My mother wanted me to make a good impression on the judge and bought me a new sport jacket and some very formal black shoes, which for years hence were known to the family as my "court shoes."

On the appointed day we all appeared with our parents in the judge's chamber along with Elvis and his foster parents. Dressed in our best funeral suits, we adopted an appropriately somber mood. After we'd been seated around the room, with a big table in the middle, the judge announced that he had been talking with Elvis and his parents before we had arrived, and Elvis had recanted his story. Apparently when it had come to time to swear to tell the truth or risk perjury, he had opted for the truth. Although we were relieved that Elvis had changed his tune, we could tell we weren't completely off the hook by the tone of the judge's voice. He admonished us for our behavior and told us he would leave the charge of assault and battery open until our eighteenth birthdays and dismiss it if we stayed out of trouble.

As I finished telling my story to the army legal officer, he stood up and said he had to make some phone calls and would be back in a few minutes. I wasn't sure if my failure to report this incident on my form meant that I would not be able to join the Air Force. Poor Bob, I thought as I wondered if he might be on his way to basic training without me. The officer returned about thirty minutes later and said that everything had checked out, and that I would be able to take the oath with the next batch of recruits. After taking the oath, we were ordered onto a bus, taken to the airport and put on a civilian airliner bound for San Antonio, Texas. No one I spoke to knew anything about Bob. The sergeants in charge were not at all interested in answering my questions and behaved like prison guards.

San Antonio was much smaller in 1958 than it is today. I remember flying over ranch land and looking down at the longhorn cattle and prickly-pear cactus as the plane approached the airport. I was excited about traveling to a new place, but also tired from the all-night flight and puzzled by the treatment I had received from the sergeants and officers. It wasn't exactly what I had expected. The recruiter had been so friendly and good-natured, but these guys were grouchy. After landing in San Antonio, we were rounded up and taken to Lackland Air Force Base, just outside town. That's when things got *really* grouchy! As we stepped off the bus, a drill instructor wearing one of those pointy hats that you see in Marine movies screamed insults at each one of us. In the 1950s there were no realistic war movies like *Full Metal Jacket* or *Platoon*. Most kids my age had a romantic notion of military service, based on John Wayne movies and exaggerated stories of exotic ports and loose women told to us by our friends who had already joined the service. Needless to say, I was ill-prepared for the intense psychological training that turns undisciplined teenagers into fast-moving robots willing to obey the command of their superiors at the snap of a finger. A few hundred of us were lined up and told to start marching. We were a scruffy amalgam of inner-city tough guys, rural bumpkins and a select group of geeky intelligent guys who were destined to become the technicians most needed by the Air Force. In a matter of hours we were transformed into convincing-looking soldiers all wearing the same uniform and identical crew cuts. It was when we tried to march as commanded that we looked pretty green.

CONFESSIONS OF A CLOSET YOGI

When we arrived at our barracks, I finally saw Bob. We'd been assigned to the same unit and we would go through basic training together after all. We soon discovered that joining the Air Force on the buddy system didn't really mean what we'd thought it did. With all the drills, inspections and marching, there was virtually no time to spend hanging out with anyone, let alone your buddy. After a few days a routine was established: jumping out of bed at 5 AM, doing basic exercises, marching to the chow hall, going to classes and training with weapons. Every minute was controlled and had strict protocols. One of the rules was always to say "sir" when speaking to the drill sergeant. Whenever the sergeant would ask a question, the first word out of your mouth had to be "sir." For example, if he asked how much five plus five was, you would say, "Sir, five plus five is ten." My brain had a hard time with this. I kept forgetting to say "sir" first and kept saying it at the end of the sentence. Finally the drill sergeant lost his patience with me and screamed at me to go to his office. I knew I was in trouble but had no idea what the two sergeants were going to do. They yelled at me as if I were an evil enemy prisoner and ordered me to squat down and hold my arms out in front of me (a very uncomfortable position) and yell "sir" until I couldn't speak any longer. I guess they wanted to teach me a lesson and set an example for the rest of the troops.

After a few weeks we became more proficient in following orders quickly and precisely, and the drill instructors reduced their yelling and insults. They would grudgingly offer a smile or nod of approval once in a while. We now were also given a few minutes of free time every day. The "patio break" was the ultimate luxury. If we didn't foul up, we were usually allowed fifteen minutes a day at one of the many soda machines around the base, where we could have a soda and a cigarette. Near the end of the ten weeks, each of us would receive the assignment for the school he would be attending after completing basic training. These schools ranged from high-tech electronics training to cooking and truck driving. Your school assignment was based on a variety of aptitude tests and personal preference. As members of our unit began returning from their appointments with the assignment officer, they would be either happy to get into the school they wanted or disappointed and upset with some miserable assignment, like working in the sewer plant at a remote radar station in Greenland. One day two of the guys returned from the assignment office laughing as if they had just heard the greatest joke of their lives. Then they tucked their pants into their socks, put on helmet liners and pretended to direct traffic in the barracks. I thought this was pretty wild and crazy behavior. If the sergeant came in, they would be in big trouble. I walked over and started talking with them. They thought it was hilarious that they were being sent to air police school. These two weirdos were Rob and Wally, with whom I would share many of my adventures over the next ten years. They were both intelligent and more sophisticated than your average eighteen-year-old, and Wally had attended an Ivy League college before dropping out. Apparently the air police was where they sent the misfits and people who had no useful skills or technical abilities.

The next day Bob and I were scheduled for our school assignments. Bob had accounting skills and was planning to attend the administration school at an air base in west Texas. When Bob returned from his appointment, he was pretty happy. He'd gotten the school he wanted and was glad he hadn't been assigned to food service. I was next. The assignment center was a huge room with hundreds of desks where sergeants sat with new recruits, explaining their training options. My name was called, and the sergeant greeted me in a pleasant manner, much like the recruiter back home. He looked at my records and said, "Looks like you signed up for meteorology or aerial photography." I felt a glimmer of hope. "Unfortunately both those schools are filled," he said. "Let's take a look at your test scores and see what we can do." He checked my aptitude scores and said, "Well, son, we need mechanics and electronic techs, but your scores aren't high enough. We have three choices for you: medic, air police or food service." I remembered my mother's telling me that if I joined the service, I would be emptying bedpans. Both my parents had been against my joining the service and had wanted me to go to college, but I'd told them I wanted to have my "wild years" first. Bedpans didn't appeal to me, so I didn't want to become a medic, and food service was the most dreaded job in the Air Force. The only choice was air police. I remembered Wally and Rob directing traffic and thought, oh well, it's not as bad as emptying bed pans or peeling potatoes.

The air police (AP) training school was right there at Lackland Air Force Base, so I began to pay more attention to the AP trainees as they marched by. They often looked as if they had been crawling around in the mud. Their uniforms were beat-up and they marched around with combat boots, helmets and World War II carbines. This looked even worse than basic training, and I wondered what I was getting into. After finishing basic training, everyone in our unit shipped out to attend the various schools around the country—everyone, that is, except Rob, Wally, me and a few others who would be going to the AP school just a few blocks away. We felt left out but decided to make the best of it. While everyone else had a few weeks to visit family before attending school, we were given only a weekend pass to go into San Antonio. This would be our first time off the base since arriving three months before. Rob, Wally and I decided to rent a room in San Antonio and do up the town. We started hitting the bars as soon as we stepped off the bus. The weekend was a drunken blur. All I remember is men and women in uniform throwing up in the hotel hallways and one very disturbing incident:

Somehow I got separated from Rob and Wally and found myself in the bus station. Thirsty, I looked around for a water fountain. When I found it and was about to drink, I saw a big sign above the water fountain saying "COLORED ONLY!" Looking around, I saw a room full of black people staring at me. It's hard to describe how embarrassed, ashamed and shocked I felt. When I had grown up in New England in the 1950s, there was only one black kid in our high school and he'd been sort of a celebrity and very popular. I didn't know anything about civil rights or segregation. It was beyond my comprehension that anyone could treat another human this way. I quickly retreated from the bus station and returned to the base, where it took me a few days to shake off the shame and embarrassment.

While we were waiting for the next class session at AP school to start, we were assigned to the PATS (Personnel Awaiting Training Status) barracks. This was sort of a purgatory or limbo where they put people who had no official job or were not in a training program; it was one step removed from prison. Every morning at five o'clock the guards would come into the barracks and haul us off to a variety of work details that mostly consisted of kitchen police (KP). The person in charge of our barracks was a despicable punk named Peabody. He had no rank and, like us, was also waiting to attend the AP school, but somehow he had weaseled his way into this position of authority. He took an immediate dislike to Rob, Wally and me—probably because we were always goofing around. We soon realized that we were being given the worst work details on a permanent basis. KP was by far the most miserable job. Peeling potatoes and washing pots for fourteen hours at a stretch while at the mercy of embittered mess sergeants day after day was close enough to being in prison to make one think about escaping or getting even with Peabody, or both. One night I was awake about 3 AM and noticed someone tying knots in the towels draped on the foot of each person's bunk. Then at 5 AM the guards would come in and wake those whose towels were tied in knots and haul them off to KP. This was how Peabody assigned the KP details!

The next night the three of us waited until the towels were knotted, untied the ones on our beds and tied the ones on the bunks of the guys who, up till now, for no discernible reason, had escaped KP. At 5 AM the guards came in and hauled them off to KP. We made ourselves scarce whenever we saw Peabody, but after a week he was onto our game. He seethed with anger, but there was nothing he could do. It would have been very hard to prove that we had untied the knots, and if he'd gone to the higher authorities, they would have questioned him: why had we been given so much KP? We knew our game was up, however, when the guards came right to our beds even though our towels were untied—Peabody must have clued them in! After a few days back on KP we decided to hide in the latrines when the guards came in to take us away. We would go into a stall and stand on a seat, so that when the guard came in and saw no legs or feet, he would leave and arbitrarily grab the first person he saw. The guards had no personal vendetta against us; they were just doing their job, which was to deliver fifty warm bodies to KP every morning. At 5 AM it was dark in the barracks and outside so they didn't even know who we were.

Outsmarting Peabody and the guards was the highlight of our military career so far. Not only did we have the joy of aggravating Peabody, but instead of slaving in the kitchen from dawn till dark, we were free to roam about the huge air base and hang out in the snack bars listening to rock-and-roll music and eating food of our choice. There were thousands of nondescript troops in fatigues everywhere you looked, so we kept on the move and didn't hang out in one place too long. After almost a week of freedom we realized the guards might begin to suspect something, so we developed a new plan: We let them wake us at 5 AM, and while they were marching the fifty of us to the chow halls in the dark for KP, we would quickly step out of formation and roll into a ditch and hide until they were out of sight. None of the other troops marching with us said anything. They just kept marching along as though nothing had happened.

When AP school finally started, it was worse than I'd thought it would be: it was like another three months of basic training. Usually after finishing basic training, you would be sent to job training, and it would be pretty much like a normal job or school. You would attend classes five days a week and evenings and weekends would be free time. But AP school was hard to take after the illicit freedom of the PATS barracks. We had to jump out of bed at 5 AM; put on our helmets, boots and a bunch of equipment and march everywhere we went. Most of the day was spent outside doing various combat activities: crawling under barbed wire with machine guns firing over our heads; throwing dummy grenades; attacking with bayonets; and training with weaponry. Actually the weapons training was fun, except for the fact that we would be outside in the cold rain all day. We would be bused to a nearby army base to fire a variety of weapons. Everyone enjoyed the automatic weapons, which were World War II vintage. The favorite was the 50 caliber machine gun. We were constantly warned by the instructors to fire them in short bursts or they would get red hot and be destroyed. One day a fellow named Warner couldn't resist holding onto the trigger and wouldn't let go. Predictably, the gun turned red-hot, and the sergeant started screaming at him to stop. They practically had to pull him off the gun before he would let go. I will never forget the strange grin on his face while he was firing the gun. He later ended up in the same AP unit that I was in, and I got to know him a little better. He was intelligent and knew how to perform his duties, but he had the maturity of an eight-year-old. He spent all of his time in his room reading comic books and was not interested in partying or washing. Because he never goofed around and did exactly as he was told, he was promoted before the rest of us.

Rob and Wally were assigned to a different barracks than mine, so we weren't able to get together very often. They were in the same barracks as Peabody, however, which gave them an opportunity for revenge. Fortunately he was a very heavy sleeper. One night we snuck up to his bunk while he was asleep and very quietly tied him in by wrapping a long line of rope around the bed. Next we sprinkled lighter fluid all around his bed, lit it and started to yell, "Fire! Fire!" He woke up with flames licking around him and tried to jump out of bed. The look of horror on his face when he realized he couldn't get out of the bed was worth all the misery he had caused us.

Toward the end of our training we were given formal AP uniforms with leather straps and a holster for a club and a gun. These outfits looked a lot like the old-fashioned British Army uniforms with leather shoulder straps. We had to wear the straps all the time with our white hats and formal blue uniforms. They were very cumbersome, especially the big clubs attached to the belts; whenever you sat down, they would catch on the chair or table. Along with our new formal look we were given motivational talks by the commandant of the school, who was the spiffiest person I have ever seen in uniform. He wore a gleaming black helmet that must have taken hours of polishing to achieve the blinding brilliance it radiated. His uniform was starched and pressed so stiff that it was hard to imagine being able to sit or walk in it. He lectured us on the importance of the role of the air police. It was our responsibility to uphold the discipline of the Air Force. Even the slightest infraction of dress code was a symptom of a lack of discipline. Whenever we saw someone with his hat off, buttons undone, or dirty shoes, it was our duty to reprimand him or give him a citation for dress-code violation. The commandant also tried to instill in us an elite mentality. We had to set an example by wearing impeccable uniforms and always behaving in a manner that would inspire other troops to maintain a high level of morale. Most of us were unmoved by his lofty speeches. None of us had volunteered for the air police. We were mostly just a bunch of teenagers looking for a little adventure, and we weren't used to being on the enforcement side of the law.

Graduation from air police school was like finishing a prison sentence: there was no celebration. Instead we immediately went to the assignment office to find out where we would be sent. This was a moment of anticipation and dread for most of us. For some it didn't matter where they would be sent; Hawaii, Greenland and Saudi Arabia were all the same to them. They would do their job, eat military food, hang out on the base and never leave to see the outside world. For the rest of us it mattered a great deal. Traveling to foreign countries was one of the main reasons we'd joined the Air Force. With a last name beginning with *W*, I was near the end of the line for assignments. We would watch each guy as he got his assignment to see if he was happy, sad, horrified, or indifferent. The most-sought-after assignments were Europe, Asia (this was 1959 and the U.S. was not at war there) and tropical islands like Hawaii. The most-dreaded places were the cold, remote ones like Greenland and other locations above the Arctic Circle. The next-most-feared places were the Strategic Air Command (SAC) bases located in the northern parts of the U.S., like the Dakotas, Montana, Maine and upstate New York. SAC bases were some of the worst duty because they needed lots of guards for the B-52s and B-47s that were always parked on icy, windswept airfields. As Rob and Wally came out of the assignment office, they seemed a little subdued, which was unusual for them. They were both being sent to the same SAC base in Oklahoma. At least they could raise hell together there. I was assigned to Ellsworth Air Force Base in South Dakota. It could have been worse; at least it was near the scenic Black Hills.

The next day we all left for a week's leave to visit home. I said goodbye to Rob and Wally, and we promised to keep in touch. When I arrived home to visit my family in Ohio, I realized how much I had changed; civilian life now seemed so comfortable, soft, relaxed and free. I wondered if I had made a big mistake. On the one hand, life seemed so pleasant away from the military; and yet on the other, I was looking forward to the travel and adventure that were possible in the next few years. When my leave was up I was ready to be on my way to South Dakota. I'd enjoyed my visit with my folks, but I had grown weary of the decaying, polluted steel-mill town of Lorain and yearned for the natural beauty and old friends of Massachusetts. On my military salary of seventy dollars a month, the only travel option to South Dakota was by bus. The end of March is one of the more gruesome times to travel the Midwest. There were few interstates in those days, and the bus rattled on hour after hour over potholed two-lane roads through endless fields of dead cornstalks. Occasionally there would be old, grimy gray snowdrifts along the highway to add a touch of variety to the gray sky and brown land. Every few hours the bus would pull into a town and stop at the bus station long enough for us to grab a bite to eat, and to pick up new passengers. The stations were dreary has-beens filled with diesel exhaust and cigarette smoke. The food was exceptionally putrid: tired old charred red hot dogs and gray slabs of gristly hamburgers on petrified buns.

This went on for two days and nights. I had a lot of time to think and wonder what the hell I was doing sitting on a bus in this miserable, withered part of the country. This was certainly not what I had expected. I'd had visions of exciting and challenging work, traveling to exotic lands and lots of wine, women and song. I thought of my buddy, Bob, who'd been sent to France and was probably sitting in some café having drinks with some sexy French girls. As the bus finally entered South Dakota, I began to wonder if I was even capable of being an air policeman. I had been assigned to the Combat Defense Squadron, which I knew was basically guard duty, and I would not need any police skills. Still, I had never done anything like that and didn't know what to expect.

The air base was about ten miles east of Rapid City, at the foot of the Black Hills. The driver actually pulled off the main highway and drove me directly to the gate. As I stepped off the bus a brutal gust of icy wind almost knocked me down. My hat flew off my head, and I chased it across a muddy, slushy field, soiling my dress blue uniform in the process. When I approached the air policeman at the gate, I looked pretty sloppy. Remembering what the AP commandant had said about the importance of always being in proper uniform, I was afraid he would chew me out or write me up, but he just looked at my orders, not paying any attention to my appearance, and said, "Hey man, you're going to be a hawk fighter! Glad it's you and not me."

The shuttle bus dropped me off in front of a decrepit, old, wooden World War II barracks. There were deep snowdrifts blown up against the sides of the building, and the steps were barely visible in the hard-packed snow. I was assigned a bunk in a large, unkempt room with about ten other guys. I soon learned that this was the holding pen for new arrivals to the squadron and also for those awaiting discharge. As I started unpacking, two unsavory-looking characters came over to my bunk and started looking over my belongings. They weren't exactly

the Welcome Wagon; they acted more like criminals than air policemen. The situation felt like a gulag in Siberia. I walked across the street
and reported to the squadron headquarters. It was a bit of a relief to
find that the clerks and sergeants were actually friendly. They told me
I would be assigned to a flight in a few days and gave me a pass to the
chow hall. When I returned to the barracks, I noticed that about half
my belongings were missing. I went back to the HQ building and reported the theft. When I told them what barracks I was living in, they
had an "Oh, no, not them again!" look on their faces. It turned out the
two guys who'd taken my things actually were criminals and were in the
process of being kicked out of the Air Force.

After this uninspiring introduction to life in the real Air Force,
I decided to try my luck at the chow hall. The food was no worse or
better than the basic-training food: OK if you were really hungry or if
you'd enjoyed eating in the school cafeteria back home. As I filled my
tray and looked around for a place to sit, I noticed a group of rowdy,
sloppy-looking troops in one corner of the mess hall. They were bundled
up with heavy snowsuit-style pants and parkas and many were wearing
a mix of civilian scarves, sweatshirts and sweaters. I thought to myself,
These guys are in big trouble if the Air Police catch them out of uniform! Then
I noticed that they were carrying M1 carbines. That's funny, I thought,
what would mechanics be doing with rifles? Then I noticed the air police badges on their greasy parkas. I couldn't believe my eyes: here were
the upholders of discipline and dress code looking like a bunch of kids
in filthy snowsuits who had just come in from playing in the snow all
day. They even had the rosy cheeks that kids get when they have been
outside for a long time.

I walked over and sat down next to them. They knew right away
that I was a newcomer by my dress uniform and lack of foul weather
gear. When I told them I had been assigned to their squadron, they all
laughed. One of them said, "Enjoy being warm while you can, because
you will be out in the 'hawk' in a few days." One of the black guys said,
"Boy, you better get some warm threads before you freeze your butt

off." They seemed like a good natured group for having such a miserable job, and they were a lot nicer than the criminals back at my barracks. I returned to the barracks a little more encouraged than when I'd left. At least these guys seemed to be having fun working together. As I walked up the grimy stairs, I heard some familiar voices. When I got to my bunk on the second floor, I saw a couple of my friends from AP school. They had been there only a few hours and were complaining about some of their things being missing. It was a relief to have some friends living with me. Together we were able to keep the thugs at bay until they were officially kicked out of the Air Force.

The next day we all reported for duty and were assigned to a team called a "flight." When I arrived for duty, we had to stand at attention while the lieutenant and sergeant assigned the different posts and inspected the troops for neatness. The jobs were assigned according to rank. The worst jobs were standing outside for eight hours guarding B-52 bombers. It was cold, windy and deadly boring. These posts were given to the lowest-ranking men, the airmen third class. The next-highest rank was the airmen second class. These men were given slightly better jobs, like staffing gate shacks, which were sometimes heated. The airmen first class were given the best jobs: patrolling around in warm trucks. Naturally, being the low man on the totem pole in terms of rank and time on the job, I was given the worst job. My first night on duty was cold and very windy. We were transported out to the flight line in the back of a pickup truck. Riding in the back of a truck at thirty miles per hour in zero degree weather magnifies the cold twenty times, so that by the time you are dropped off in front of your airplane, you have already lost a lot of body heat. The B-52s were each loaded with two hydrogen bombs and ready to take off and obliterate some Soviet city. The crews stayed in an underground bunker a few hundred yards away and were ready to jump in a truck and arrive at the plane in a matter of minutes. My job was to protect the plane from unauthorized persons coming near or onto the plane.

The first few hours were sort of an adrenaline rush. I was all alone in the almost total darkness with this creaking and moaning monster of an airplane. The bomb bay doors were always open, so I decided to take a look at the two nuclear weapons. They resembled a couple of ordinary olive drab trash cans, only longer. Suddenly I heard a loud commotion at the back of the plane. The hair on the back of my neck stood on end, and visions of enemy storm troopers sneaking up on me filled my awareness. I readied my weapon and crept around to the back of the plane. The sound was terrifying. I crouched down and aimed my flashlight at the noise. Just then a gust of wind picked up a huge, shapeless, scratchy object and hurled it in my face. It took me a while to regain my composure and realize that the wind had blown a bunch of tumbleweeds into the wheel wells where they'd made a horrible scratching noise.

After the initial excitement had worn off, I looked at my watch and noticed I still had five hours to go before being relieved at midnight. As the hours went by, it became colder, and my ability to keep warm steadily diminished. My eyes adjusted to the darkness and I became more aware of the surrounding environment. It was completely inorganic: acres of asphalt and machines with no plant material whatsoever. The only incursions of the natural world were the patches of snow and ice on the tarmac. There was the constant roar of jets taking off and landing, spewing warm, toxic fumes over the flight line. My thoughts again turned to Bob enjoying the cafés and idyllic countryside of France. When they picked me up at midnight, I was as tired and cold as I had ever been. Most of the rest of the troops in the back of the truck had been doing this for a year or so and were goofing around and joking. They asked me how I was doing, and I said "Cold!" They laughed and said, "Wait till the hawk comes; then you'll have something to complain about."

After our eight hour shift from 4 PM to 12 AM, most of us went to "midnight chow," a greasy meal of runny eggs, rugged bacon, recycled toast and evil coffee. Some guys actually went into town to party, while the rest went back to the barracks to unwind for a while before going to sleep. Life in the barracks was a lot like a college dorm, with lots of loud music and unruly activity. The barracks, an old wooden World War II vintage structure, had been remodeled into rooms about twelve feet square, in which four men lived. I was in a room with a good old boy from Tennessee, a cool black dude from Toledo and a laid-back farm boy from southern Ohio. We had a lot of laughs, and no one seemed to mind the total lack of privacy.

As the weeks and months dragged on I became more comfortable with life on the flight line. Spring was approaching and the weather was becoming milder and more tolerable. But the job was still excruciatingly boring. There were very few breaks in the monotony. Reading and listening to transistor radios were forbidden. Occasionally someone on foot patrol would stop and talk for a few minutes, but even this was against the rules. The only real break in the eight-hour shift came when the sergeant stopped by in the truck to see how you were doing. He would let you sit in the truck and have a cup of hot coffee for fifteen to twenty minutes. The sergeants were older career military men, many of them World War II veterans who were well aware of the misery of our jobs; they'd always give us a break when they could.

The day shift was the least boring and most comfortable. Usually the crews would come out to the plane for maintenance. We were supposed to check their badges and make sure they knew the secret password of the day. Most of the time the flight crews tolerated this minor inconvenience. One day, however, the pilot, who happened to be a colonel, forgot the password. If I let him onto the aircraft without his knowing the password, I could be in big trouble. Suddenly it dawned on me that here I was, an eighteen-year-old kid with an unloaded carbine on my back (due to many accidental shootings in the past, we had to keep our bullet clip out of the gun and load it only in an emergency), telling this career colonel with a loaded 38 on his side that he was not allowed onto his airplane! I could tell he found the situation absurd and was losing his patience. Fortunately some other crew members arrived and they knew the password and vouched for him. This allowed both of us to save face, but I was still struck by the absurdity of the process: if the colonel had been a spy or evildoer, he could have simply shot me!. What a joke! It wasn't so bad for the crews to play this silly game; they could go back to their comfortable alert bunker, have a meal, read a book or go to sleep. But I had to stand out in the cold for eight hours with an unloaded weapon pretending to protect the plane and its H-bombs.

This event was a real eye-opener for me. I realized then why the older, more seasoned troops didn't take the job very seriously. They violated the rules regularly by sneaking books and reading them by flashlight at their post. Another violation was listening to radios. The transistor radio was newly invented, and we would hide them in our parkas and run a wire to the aircraft, which served as a massive antenna, allowing us to listen to stations from all over the country. The biggest violation, though, was sleeping on guard duty. In wartime it was punishable by death. Often a guard would climb up into the wheel well of the B-52 to escape the fierce wind and bitter cold. Sometimes he would fall asleep there. When the patrol truck would pull up to the plane and failed to be greeted by the guard, the first place the patrol would look would be the wheel well. The method for proving that a guard was asleep on duty was to get his gun. Usually when a guard found a comfortable place, he would set his gun down or lean it up against a wall. This made it easy to grab it before the fellow could wake up. The first time a guard was caught would usually result in his being relieved of duty and reprimanded by the sergeant. The next time meant jail or discharge.

Whenever I would find a place to get out of the wind, I would wrap the sling of my carbine around my arm in case I fell asleep. I was lucky and always woke up before the patrol truck arrived at my post. One night three of us were assigned foot patrol around some hangars and decided to find a warm room in one of them and take turns sleeping: one of us would stay awake while the other two slept. Unfortunately the third guy, who was supposed to keep alert, fell into a deep sleep. The next thing we knew, we were being kicked awake by the sergeant and his assistant. They had our guns and we were unceremoniously hauled off to headquarters. Fortunately the lieutenant was not on duty that night. The sergeant and his assistants acted like disappointed parents. After they'd made us feel sufficiently guilty, they gave us a warning and let us off the hook.

The officers and senior sergeants knew we had a miserable job and tried not to be too tough on us, attempting to strike a balance between maintaining strict discipline and giving first offenders a second chance. This worked fairly well until one night when a young guard, who today might be described as a "troubled youth," went berserk. He loaded his carbine and fired the entire clip of bullets at the two H-bombs hanging in the bomb bay. The bullets bounced off the bombs and put a few holes in the plane but fortunately didn't hit anything volatile. The young trooper was quickly sent to a hospital, and we never saw him after that.

This incident shook up the commander, who was ultimately responsible for anything his men did. The senior officers thought it would be a good idea if they had a better psychological profile on each person who worked in sensitive areas. Our lieutenant was a kind-hearted fellow who had been a psychology major in college, and he took it upon himself to psychologically evaluate each one of us. On his usual round of talking with the troops at their posts, he started quizzing us on our individual and family histories. Word quickly got around that he was checking everyone out to see if we were crazy. So, when he came to interview us, we each started making up sordid, pathetic and depraved life stories. This had a demoralizing effect on the poor chap; obviously, he'd had no idea that he had so many deviates under his command.

Life off duty, while not as grim as standing alone outside in the cold, also became routine. When we were not working, there were three choices: sleeping, hanging around the barracks, or going to town. Rapid City was, for the most part, a cowboy town with lots of country-and-western bars. The traditional activity of off-duty military men is to go to bars, drink and look for women. For us it was a sport similar to fishing. "Landing" a woman was the ultimate goal and the most popular pursuit on the base. Music was also a major part of off-duty life. In 1959 there was very little television available, but many troops had record players in their rooms. Although rock-and-roll was the dominant music, there were two major subcultures: jazz and country. The good old boys listened to country music and the black guys—plus a few of the older and more sophisticated white guys—preferred jazz. I liked hanging out with the older guys who preferred jazz. They were "short timers"—men with less than a year to go. Most of them had served overseas for three years and were finishing out their last year in the military. Their entire focus was on what they were going to do when they got out. They invariably had a calendar on their wall with the days marked off, like prisoners waiting to be released. Most were in their twenties and seemed old and wise to us teenagers. One of them, a black man named Delbert, invited me to move into his room when his roommate was discharged. This was a great opportunity for me. He was a jazz aficionado and his room was the main hangout for the black guys to get together and listen to music. Thus, in addition to being exposed to the great jazz musicians of the fifties, I learned a whole new lexicon of words that have become part of mainstream American language over the last fifty years.

As the summer began to wane, I realized how much I missed the ocean, the lakes and my old friends back in Massachusetts. I had accrued enough leave for a two-week vacation but did not have the money for transportation, so I decided to hitch a ride (called a "hop") on a military plane back east. (Most aircraft crews will give you a ride if they have room. The only catch is that you have to go wherever they take you.) On my first day of leave I went down to the control tower and checked to see if there were any flights out. The only one available was a small army four-seater headed for an air base in Colorado Springs, Colorado. I'd heard that a lot of airplanes stopped there on their way east or west, so I "hopped" on with a buddy who was also going on leave.

The two army officers were welcoming, even though the plane was very small. As they taxied out to the runway, it became apparent that the fellow in the pilot's seat did not know how to fly! He was just learning, and the other officer was trying to teach him. It didn't seem like a formal instructor/student relationship, but more like a friend trying to give his buddy a chance behind the wheel. It was the weirdest takeoff I have ever experienced—like riding in a washing machine and a roller coaster at the same time. The combination of strong, gusty winds and the evident total lack of experience of the person trying to fly the plane unhinged even the experienced pilot. He kept yelling instructions at the hapless guy behind the wheel, which served only to confuse him more. Finally we gained enough altitude to level off and head south for a gorgeous flight over the Rockies. Then it was time to "land." This was like a combination kamikaze dive and bungee jump. The student pilot put the plane in an extremely steep dive. His buddy, the real pilot, realizing that the ground was coming up much too fast, grabbed the controls and pulled the stick as hard as he could, causing the small plane to boing up like a bungee jumper. Once on the runway, the plane bounced like a tennis ball until finally jerking to a halt near the control tower. As we stumbled off the plane, the student pilot reminded us that he was headed for an army base in Kansas and that we were welcome to come along as soon as he'd refueled. We politely declined, however, and headed for the control tower building where my buddy ran into the restroom to change his underwear.

The next flight out was a C-54 cargo plane going to St. Louis, Missouri and on to Long Island, New York via North Carolina. This looked more promising: a larger plane, headed in the right direction. We asked the crew for a ride and they agreed. Soon we were on our way to St. Louis. The next morning we took off for Long Island. After stopping in North Carolina, we headed up the Atlantic coast for Mitchel Field. As we approached the New York metropolitan area, the plane sounded and acted funny, as though it were running out of gas. The pilot emerged from the cockpit, and in a matter-of-fact tone, informed us that one of the engines had burned out and we would have to make an emergency landing on the nearest piece of flat ground! We should have known that a free flight home was too good to be true; we should have taken a bus or hitchhiked on land instead. The plane commenced a steep descent in preparation for landing. Unfortunately there were no airports in sight. As we swooped in low over the treetops, there was nothing in sight but mile after mile of tract homes. It looked as if we were going to take the roofs off a couple of houses when a small landing strip appeared right in back of them. The pilot plopped the plane down on the tiny landing strip, coming to a halt just before we hit a small industrial building. Pretty fancy flying for a big old cargo plane! We had no idea where we were.

The pilot reemerged from the cockpit looking a little sheepish. He apologized for not having gotten us to Long Island and informed us that we had landed in New Jersey, at an old factory with a small landing strip. Unfortunately this was the end of the line, and we were now on our own. Once on the street we headed for the first intersection and began hitchhiking. Guido, my buddy, was going to Philadelphia to visit friends and family, and I was headed to Massachusetts, so we split up after a few rides put us on the New Jersey turnpike. We always wore our uniforms when hitchhiking, which insured quick results getting rides. The late fifties was a time well before the Vietnam War and close enough to World War II and the Korean War to evoke sympathy for servicemen who needed rides. It was a more innocent time, and people were not as fearful about picking up hitchhikers.

Returning to Massachusetts in the summer was delightful: old friends, parties almost every night and great weather. I stayed with my old friend Jim at his parents' house on the lake, where we had spent all our time hanging out for the last five years. Nothing had changed in the year I had been away. It felt very comfortable being back, yet at the same time static or stagnant. I realized that I had changed. My universe was larger now than when I had left, and I knew that as much as I loved being back, I could never return to the familiar life still enjoyed by my friends. Something was driving me to move toward new and different adventures. I didn't let this revelation stop me from enjoying the traditional activities of summer in New England, however.

A few days after I'd arrived, we decided to load up Jake's truck with beer and drive out to Provincetown. We left for Cape Cod quite late on Saturday night, and by the time we were halfway to P-town it was 1 AM and we were very drunk and sleepy. Jake pulled off the main highway at Brewster, a classic Cape Cod village with an idyllic harbor. We drove the truck almost into the water at the town beach and everyone crawled onto the sand and fell asleep except for Rick and me. It was a warm, full-moon night, and we sat at the water's edge enjoying the gentle sound of the ocean lapping at the beach while moonlight shimmered on the small waves of the harbor. As our eyes adjusted to the darkness, we noticed a small dinghy pulled up on the shore. We couldn't resist taking it out for a row in the harbor. Once out there we came upon a flotilla of small boats and decided to take a few of them out for test rides. We tied the dinghy to the mooring of a small skiff, started the skiff's motor and took off buzzing around the bay. Next we moved up to a bigger boat with a more powerful motor. After having tried out a few more boats, we noticed lights coming on in the houses along the shore. The noise of the outboard motors was waking everyone up, and we could see flashlights coming down to the water. Suddenly we were blinded by a huge spotlight as we sped along. Then came an ominous voice over a loudspeaker: "Come in and give yourselves up; we have arrested your friends."

Instinctively we took evasive action by putting the boat on a zig-zag course and heading for the far end of the harbor. As we approached the shore, we noticed what appeared to be a mooring ball close in. We tied the boat up there, jumped in the water and swam for shore. By now it was starting to get light, and we could see police and boat owners combing the shore in search of the criminals. It was slow going without shoes, but we hiked up away from the water and behind the houses along the shore. Every once in a while we would see someone looking for us and crouch in the bushes till the danger had passed. By the time we got back to the beach where Jake and the rest of the guys were, it was full daylight. From our vantage point in the bushes it appeared that the cops had arrested them and were waiting for us to be brought in. They probably had our IDs, and without clothes (and especially shoes) we realized it was time to give up. So we walked up behind the officer guarding our buddies and we said, "Hi!" His body jerked up off the ground as though he had received an electric shock. He appeared stunned for a moment, then went to the radio in his patrol car. After a brief discussion he returned to us and said, "The chief wants to have a little chat with you gentlemen; follow me down to the station."

The chief was an older, heavyset man who appeared to have seen it all and knew exactly what he was going to do. He was probably retired from some big-city police force, and running a small town law enforcement office was just enough activity to keep him from being bored. It was obvious that he had been at home in his comfortable bed when the calls had come in about the boats. He looked at us like a stern father and said, "Boys, I have a lot of angry citizens out there. So here's what I am going to do: First of all, you two who took the boats for a joy ride are going to put them all back on their proper moorings; then you're all going to leave town and never come back. Second: you're all underage and you have a truckload of beer. I am going to confiscate it, if you know what I mean!" This all sounded reasonable to us, so we drove back to the beach and returned each boat to its rightful mooring under the scornful gaze of the sleepless summer residents whose quiet Sunday morning had been so rudely disrupted. When we got to the last boat, we weren't sure where it belonged, so we tied it up to a mooring ball close to shore, hoping that the owner would see it and return it to its proper mooring. Despite the loss of our beer, we continued to Provincetown and had a splendid day on the beach.

A few days later, there was a note from Jim's mother on my bed: the Brewster police chief wanted me to call him right away. As I made the call, I had the sinking feeling in the pit of my stomach that I was in big trouble. It turned out that the mooring ball we'd used to secure the last boat was actually a buoy marking an underwater rock. When the tide had gone out, the boat had smashed against the rock and sustained considerable damage. The owner was charging us with malicious destruction of property, and there was nothing the chief could do about it. He suggested I call the boat owner and offer to pay for the damages. I did so and apologized profusely. He was very upset, however, and neither expressions of remorse nor offers of remuneration would placate him. I called the police chief and told him that I was in the service and had to return to my base. He called back later that day to tell me he had made arrangements with the judge to hear my case the next morning at 10 AM; he also promised he'd be there to "represent" me.

I got up early the next morning, put on my uniform to gain some sympathy from the judge, and hitchhiked to the courthouse on Cape Cod, some hundred miles away. When I arrived, I didn't see the chief anywhere, so I walked into the courtroom and sat through a trial in progress. The chief still hadn't appeared by the time an official called out, "The County of Barnstable versus Lawrence Wardwell." The judge looked at me and asked me whether I was pleading guilty or innocent. I said, "Guilty, I guess." Just then the chief came in, and the judge asked him to give a report on the incident. After hearing the chief's account, the judge gave me a suspended sentence and ordered me to pay restitution for the damaged boat. He also said that, because I didn't have any money, my military pay would be garnished; once the damages were paid, he would dismiss the charges so they would not be on my permanent record. The chief gave me a ride out to the main highway, wished me luck and reminded me that I was banished from his village forever.

When I returned to South Dakota, it was hard to get back into the routine of walking around on the tarmac for eight hours a day and living in the barracks. Summer was drawing to a close, and I was not looking forward to another brutal winter standing outside. One morning shortly after I'd returned, I was watching the sun begin to shed its light on the surrounding brown and treeless hills. I looked to the Black Hills about twenty miles west of the base, and for a fleeting moment the sun illuminated Mount Rushmore, and I could see the four presidential faces carved into the mountain. Something about that sight set off a wave of bliss inside me. Experiencing that magnificent sunrise and spectacular view of Mount Rushmore, I felt very small and insignificant in a beautiful universe. The realization came to me that knowledge was the only way to escape from this stultifying situation. Fortunately the Air Force provided many educational opportunities, so I signed up for college courses at the local university. The military supported anyone who wanted to become more educated by paying half the tuition and giving time off to attend classes. The classes helped get me through another long, cold and boring South Dakota winter.

One of the few other activities available to us at the base was the gym, with its indoor swimming pool. One afternoon I noticed that one of the windows in the locker room was ajar. I thought how nice it would be if I could get into the gym after our evening shift and go for a midnight swim in the heated pool. That night the weather was particularly vicious: fifty mile-an-hour winds, blowing snow and below-zero temperatures. We were all chilled to the bone, so I suggested we sneak into the gym and go for a nice warm swim. The first night only two went swimming, but then the word spread, and the next night we had more than ten participants in the illicit midnight swim. A few days later we were in town partying with a group of women and invited them out for a swim. This was even more exciting, because bringing women onto the base was illegal (in addition to the crime of breaking into the gym). As we approached the guard at the base entrance, he immediately noticed that a female was driving and there were several more in the car. He said, "Hey, you guys should know better: no women allowed." We explained that it was her car and she was going to drop us off at our barracks and come right back. He fell for it, and we were off to the pool!

One of us climbed in through our special window and opened the door for the rest of us. We all threw off our clothes and jumped in. We were having quite a frolic when someone saw the lights of a car pull up: the night watchman! It was dark in the building, and we could see his flashlight coming down the hall toward the pool. It was too late to run and hide, so we huddled against the sides of the pool with just the tops of our heads, from the nose up, above water. The watchman entered the pool area and started shining his light around the room. There were puddles of water and clothes strewn about the floor, and he immediately started shining the light into the pool. For some reason, however, he didn't shine his light along the edge of the pool and so missed the half dozen heads in the water. He must have thought the clothes had been left there by someone during the day and went on to the locker room without noticing our special window. Had we been caught, we would have been thrown in the brig and kicked out of the service.

Winter doesn't give up easily in the northern plains. Even when the thermometer starts creeping above the freezing mark, the wind never relinquishes its grip. Finally in May the sun gets strong enough to beat back the cold and bring some comfort to the ill-fated troops whose destiny is to spend their entire four-year Air Force career outside guarding airplanes. Two winters down and two to go, I thought as June came into full bloom. This must be how it feels to be in jail; counting the days to freedom.

Later that month we were sent to Minot, North Dakota, for sixty days--not exactly Hawaii but at least it was different from South Dakota: more remote, a place of endless flat fields with no hills or trees for relief. When we returned later that summer, we were offered another exciting travel opportunity: Alaska! It had a reputation for grand scenery: spectacular mountains, glaciers and wildlife. Most tourists in their right mind travel to Alaska in summer. We were given the opportunity to go to Fairbanks in winter—one of the coldest, darkest places inhabited by humans on the planet. Still, my adventurous spirit got the best of me, and I volunteered to go. By the end of October we finally received our orders to go to Alaska. The weather was still comfortable in South Dakota and even warmer in Kansas, which was our jumping-off point for Alaska. The flight to Fairbanks was a miserable fourteen-hour non-stop aboard a lumbering old rattletrap of an airplane called a "C-94." The C stood for "cargo," which meant the plane was just a big, empty shell with no seats, soundproofing, or heat to speak of. After we'd taken off the crew chief came back to the cargo area, where there were about fifty of us, and announced that the last person to throw up in the toilet had to clean it up before we arrived in Fairbanks.

When we arrived at Eielson Air Force Base, about twenty miles outside of Fairbanks, it was 2 or 3 AM, but the base was teeming with activity. Bombers, fighters, refueling tankers and U-2 spy planes were taking off and landing every few minutes. I learned later that because Alaska was so close to the Soviet Union, it was a great location for a base from which to launch an attack. The Soviets were also well aware of this and did their best to protect their airspace and to harass anyone flying too close. This resulted in constant engagements with Soviet aircraft and occasional shooting back and forth. The level of military activity on this air base was much more dynamic and real compared with the remote and abstract nature of the Cold War as experienced from the SAC bases in the lower forty-eight. When I stepped off the plane, I was smacked in the face with a blast of arctic air. It had been in the fifties when we left Kansas; here the temperature was around zero, and every-thing was frozen solid and covered with snow! There was a bus waiting to take us to our barracks, and as we boarded, the driver yelled, "Don't touch any metal with your bare hands. Your flesh will freeze instantly to the metal, and when you go to remove your hand, part of it will stay stuck to the metal!" The driver dropped us off in front of what looked like a set from the film *Stalag 17*. It was a low, one-story wooden bar-racks covered in icicles and with so much frost on the windows it looked like a meat freezer. Inside, it was the oldest, most rotten building I had seen in the military. It actually looked and felt like a POW camp. There was one big room filled with cots and, at the back end, a cement latrine that was covered in a strong-smelling white powder. The powder was all over the floor and toilet seats. When I asked someone in the latrine about the powder, he casually answered that it was DDT. Apparently there had been an outbreak of crabs and lice, and he warned me to be really careful when sitting on the toilet.

The next morning I woke up at 8:30, and it was still pitch black outside with the temperature below zero. I thought, *This not a good place for an outside job.* The days would be getting shorter and the temperature falling for the next few months. By December it would be fifty below zero at night and warm up only to twenty below during the day. The sun would creep up at about 10 AM, stumble along the tops of the distant mountains for a few hours of pathetic daylight, and then descend behind the mountains into a black abyss, leaving us in total darkness for another twenty hours! Later that day we reported to headquarters for orientation and our assignments. We were given piles of arctic gear and received warnings about frostbite and other hazards posed by the extreme temperatures. On one level it seemed like an exciting challenge, but on another level just the thought of standing outside at fifty below zero was enough to give you mental frostbite. Before reporting for duty the next day, we moved from the "stalag" to a huge, newer barracks that was much more comfortable and close enough to the chow hall that you could walk to it without spending half an hour getting dressed for the cold.

Our first shift began at 4 PM. We were loaded onto the back of a pickup truck for the coldest ride I had ever had in my life. Forty miles an hour at twenty below zero was almost enough to flash-freeze your whole body. As we pulled up to the guard shack on the flight line, I noticed a number of four foot high brown piles outside the shack. On closer inspection, these turned out to be a frozen blend of old coffee, urine and cigarette butts. At forty below zero, everything freezes almost instantly, and when the old coffee was emptied from the urn, it froze right where it had been emptied and never melted. We were dropped off in front of a line of B-47 bombers and relieved the guards who had been there for the last eight hours. They looked more miserable than anyone in South Dakota ever had, and they didn't joke or horse around the way the troops in warmer climes did.

After about an hour the cold began to penetrate all my special thermal clothing. It was not a damp chill but more of a weird burning pain. When the body's temperature drops below a certain level, it begins to shut down; after a while the sense of discomfort leaves, and you no longer care about freezing to death. This is why there were patrol trucks checking on us every couple of hours. The sergeants driving them knew how wretched it was just to stand there for such a long time and would drive from post to post and let us sit in the warm truck for twenty or thirty minutes to thaw out. Although this provided some temporary relief, it did more harm than good. After sitting in the truck for half an hour bundled in thermal gear, you would begin to sweat intensely before being turned out to the cold again. The rubber insulated boots were terrible because they did not breathe so that your feet would be soaked with sweat when you went back out to the fifty-below air. This caused your feet to start freezing at a faster rate than if you had stayed outside the whole time. After about four hours they would bring us a ridiculous sack lunch prepared exclusively for those of us working outside. It consisted of two baloney sandwiches on Wonder Bread, a small carton of milk and an orange. By the time we finished the sandwiches and milk, the oranges would be frozen so solid that we would throw them down on the tarmac just to watch them shatter like pieces of glass. The only relief from this misery was the northern lights. On most nights they were phantasmagoric—not just colorful rays waxing and waning in the sky, but intensely colored lightning bolts coming right at you, dancing up and down and all around as you stood half frozen and awestruck for what seemed like hours.

Not only was Alaska colder than South Dakota; it was also more monotonous. Going outside was a painful ordeal, so most of the time the troops hung out in the barracks playing cards, reading, or listening to music. This routine was slightly more pleasant than being in prison. Every once in a while a group of us would venture into Fairbanks. Everything in town was frozen, especially the river, which was a mass of crumpled blocks of ice. What little sunlight was left was obscured by the thick, foul ice fog. One night we were invited to a black nightclub by Leroy, who had been part of our small group in South Dakota. The club was a cavernous room that held five hundred to a thousand people.

It was like being transported to a jazz club in New York City—great live music and folks dancing all over the place. We were the only three white people in the place, and it felt good to be with Leroy who introduced us to his friends.

When my ninety days in Alaska were up and I was given the opportunity to stay another ninety days, I did not hesitate to decline. This was my third winter in the Air Force, and I was beginning to resign myself to four years of boredom and miserable guard duty. By the time summer came around, I realized I would be stuck in South Dakota for the rest of my time in the Air Force. The really good assignments were given only to those who had at least three years left, and I had just a year and a half to go. No one was ever sent to a desirable place unless he re-enlisted for another four years. Then one day a rumor began circulating that two assignments to Germany—one of the choicest locations—were being given to our squadron. About a week later I was flabbergasted to learn that I was one of the two people who'd been given the assignment, even though I had only eighteen months left. No one could explain why I'd been chosen. Maybe it was a mistake.

3

DREAMING in GERMAN

Europe in 1961 was much different from the Europe of today. Every-thing was different: the buildings, cars, clothes, food, restaurants and shops. It had been only fifteen years since the end of World War II, and the continent was still recovering. Most people could not afford cars and rode motorbikes or bicycles. Apartments often had a shared bathroom in the hall, and there were no shopping centers or supermarkets. All aspects of life seemed old compared to the U.S., yet at the same time much more charming and unique. After arriving in Frankfurt, I had to take a six-hour ride on a military bus to Bitburg Air Base, which was in a rural area near Luxembourg. There were no freeways, just narrow, winding roads between villages that were often too small for a bus. I felt as if I had been transported back in time about a hundred years. The German countryside was enchanting: dark evergreen forests, small farms that were well maintained, even an occasional castle. Every ten to twenty miles we would slowly negotiate our way through small villages with outdoor cafes filled with people of all ages enjoying food, beer, wine and the company of family and friends. I was enthralled by what I saw and couldn't wait to get out and explore this new world.

Within an hour of settling into our moderately comfortable bar-racks on the base, a couple of the new arrivals and I decided to explore Bitburg, a German version of an American GI town. During World War II, General George S. Patton came through the area and when the troops refused to surrender he had flattened the whole town. This had resulted in the entire town being rebuilt using modern construction techniques and design. Bitburg therefore was clean, neat, and pleasant, but did not have the old-world charm that characterized so many of the other towns in Europe.

After a short bus ride from Bitburg we arrived at Trier, where we would take the train to the city of Luxembourg. Trier was an ancient Roman city with the ruins of a large coliseum at the center. One of its major streets was named after Karl Marx, who'd been born in Trier. By the time we arrived at the train station, we were hungry; to our surprise we found a high-quality restaurant right there in the station. None of us could speak German, but the waiter was friendly and patient as we pointed to the menu and used sign language and primal sounds to convey what we wanted to eat. The table was covered with a white cloth, there were cloth napkins and the food was fresh and delicious. This was a far cry from the dingy bus stations and shriveled hot dogs served at lunch counters that we were used to back in the States.

Luxembourg was a very French oriented city: French language, cars, food and beer. The bar and nightclub section of town was our immediate goal upon arrival. We were all in our teens and used to the higher minimum age requirement for drinking in the U.S., so we were a little intimidated when entering our first bar. There were a lot of servicemen in the bar: Americans, French and British. They were much older than we were, but no one bothered us about IDs. It was a great feeling of liberation and maturity to walk casually into a bar, have a few drinks and talk with the women who either managed the bar or worked there. They seemed to genuinely like American GIs even though we were kids. By midnight we were all old pros at the bar scene and pretty drunk. At the stroke of midnight all the bars closed, and we found ourselves in the street looking for a place to sleep. There were many small, cute hotels in the district, but every one of them had also closed at midnight!

After having wandered the streets for another hour, we decided to go back to the train station and sleep on the benches. This worked for about an hour, but then the gendarmes came in and kicked us out into the street. We had no choice but to wander the streets again until we came upon a small car with U.S. military license plates. There was some-one behind the wheel, apparently sleeping, so we knocked on the win-dow and asked if we could join him. He mumbled something—a sound we interpreted as "OK"—and we climbed in. I instinctively hopped into the back seat and one of the guys climbed in front. He was just getting comfortable when the driver leaned over and threw up on him. The stench was overwhelming, but we were too tired and drunk to care. The next morning we jumped out of the car as soon as we woke up. My back was aching and stiff, but I was grateful not to be covered in vomit like the poor fellow who'd slept in the front seat. On the train ride back to Germany I reflected on how much I enjoyed my first twenty-four hours in Europe and was excited about living there for the next year and a half.

The air police squadron at Bitburg was very different from the one in South Dakota. It was much smaller, and the security and law enforcement operations were combined instead of being two separate units. The headquarters was like a small police station. There was also a much greater variety of jobs than at Ellsworth: guarding airplanes, of course, but also town patrol, highway patrol and a special unit assigned liaison duty with the German police in Trier. There were millions of foreign troops in Germany—mostly American, but thousands of French and British troops as well.

At the end of World War II, Germany had been divided into four sectors for the purpose of occupation. The Soviets were in the East, and the French, the British and the Americans each had their own sector in the West. In the fifteen years since the end of the war, the function of the occupation forces in the West morphed into defending freedom from the communist hordes lurking behind the Iron Curtain only a few hundred miles away. Even though Germany was no longer technically occupied, the Germans had no legal authority over American military personnel. This responsibility fell instead to the military police, who worked closely with the German police to maintain law and order among the millions of foreign soldiers on German soil. This situation provided some interesting job possibilities within the air police squadron. However, these off-base law enforcement jobs were usually given to the older, more experienced men. This meant that new arrivals like me would be assigned to guarding airplanes.

My first week of duty wasn't too bad; the planes were different, the scenery was new and the summer weather was cool. The planes were tiny F-104 fighters and larger, heavier F-105 fighter-bombers. The latter carried small tactical nuclear weapons for stopping the overwhelming number of Soviet tanks poised to overrun the outnumbered Western forces in Germany. Unfortunately they were difficult to fly at low speeds and would occasionally crash just short of the runway, cutting huge swaths in the forest around the air base. After a few weeks, however, even the crashes lost their excitement and the routine became boring.

That all changed one warm and sunny day! I was assigned to a gate shack at a remote corner of the base that guarded the entrance road to a nuclear weapons depot; only a few special vehicles a day came through the gate. It was a great place to read a book without being caught. I was pretty engrossed in my novel, when out of the corner of my eye I noticed some movement behind the trees about fifty yards from the gate. Suddenly a camouflaged figure darted out from behind a tree and leaped behind a rock. I rubbed my eyes in disbelief and looked again. Then two, four, six, twenty guys in weird uniforms with bushes on their helmets started sneaking up on me. I was paralyzed! I looked at my little carbine with its clip of six bullets and thought, *I am going to die at twenty years old!* Before I could think another thought, I picked up the phone, which was a direct line to headquarters, and blurted out that I was under attack! I could hear the sergeant at the other end yell out, "Wardwell is under attack at the back gate!" By now I could see about fifty of these commandos crawling and creeping toward me in the brush. I was too stunned to panic or run. Then I heard a demonic, sub-human howling sound that snapped me out of my stupor. After about thirty seconds I realized it was the desk sergeant on the phone laughing his brains out! I yelled back at him, "What's going on?" Every time he tried to say something, he would break out in his weird laugh again. In the meantime the enemy troops were closing in on me! Finally he stopped laughing long enough to tell me that the French army garrison located next to the base had notified headquarters that they would be conducting maneuvers—but headquarters had forgotten to tell me. I sheepishly slung my carbine back over my shoulder and tried to step out of the guard shack in a nonchalant fashion. By now the commandos were running along the outside of the fence, past my post and back into the woods. I waved at them, but they were too absorbed in their games to pay much attention to me. Needless to say, it took a long time for me to return to my book.

Despite the boring nature of my work, I was delighted to be in Germany. European culture fascinated me and fortunately there were many tours and events sponsored by the Air Base for military personnel and their dependents. I took advantage of these opportunities every chance I got. I also enrolled in the University of Maryland German language courses offered on the base, as well as noncredit courses in spoken German, and soon became fluent enough to enjoy long conversations with the many Germans I met in my travels. After I had been there for about two months, I was walking down the main street of the base when I saw a familiar figure walking toward me. It was Rob, my old buddy from basic training and air police school. I had lost track of Rob and Wally soon after they'd been sent to Oklahoma from Texas. Now Rob took one look at me and pretended to run away. I chased him down, and he told me that he and Wally had spent two and a half years in Oklahoma, until Wally had been sent to Okinawa and he'd been sent to Saudi Arabia. Just when he'd been thinking he was doomed to spend the rest of his time in the Air Force frying in the desert, isolated from civilization, the Saudis had kicked the Americans out, and Rob had been sent to Bitburg. He was now assigned to the same AP squadron as I was, so we were able to spend a lot of time together partying and traveling around Germany. He, too, was interested in education and was taking as many college courses as he could. Although we loved Europe, both of us couldn't wait to get out of the military. Like most noncareer people in the military (or inmates in prison), we often talked about what we were going to do when we got out. Both Rob and Wally planned to go to North Texas State University, near Dallas. Rob invited me to join them, and it sounded like fun.

Four months after I'd arrived, my life had developed into a routine of tedious guard duty, stimulating college classes and off-base excursions. Not bad compared with South Dakota. Then one day, while I was on guard duty, the patrol truck came out to my post, and the shift leader told me to report to the sergeant in charge of the unit after work. I spent the rest of the day trying to remember what I had done wrong lately to warrant a talk with the boss. As I walked into the sergeant's office, he was sitting at his desk; without looking up from his papers, he said in a markedly unenthusiastic manner, "Wardwell! You've been assigned to the highway patrol. Report to the highway patrol office at 0700 hours tomorrow." I didn't know what to say. I was numb, mystified that I'd been chosen for this, the most coveted job in the squadron. The men chosen for it were mostly older, more experienced career types or else outstanding airmen who'd been noticed by their superiors as sharp troops. I was neither. Besides, it usually took three or four years of waiting to be chosen, and I had been there only four months. Once again, as with my transfer to Germany, I thought, *This must be a mistake.*

The next morning I put on my dress uniform and headed for the highway patrol office in a state of disbelief. I felt as though I were pretending to be someone I was not. There were four or five men in the office when I walked in, and they greeted me with mild curiosity; they probably couldn't believe it, either. My appearance didn't help much. I was smaller than average and looked young for my age—more like a high school kid than a cop. Then the sergeant in charge came over to me and said, "Wardwell, I hear you speak pretty good German." *Aha,* I thought, *this is why I was picked for the job.* He continued: "You've been taking college-level English courses, too?" When I answered in the affirmative, his face lit up. He explained that most of their accident and investigation reports were sent back from headquarters because they were poorly written. It was driving him nuts and causing hours of extra work, and he sure could use my help. The men in the highway patrol were not stupid, he said, they had a lot of street smarts, experience in law enforcement and common sense, but writing was not their forte. Also, like most Americans, they couldn't speak more than a few words of German. This was a distinct handicap when interacting with the local people. I had never imagined that the courses I was taking for my own benefit would result in my appointment to one of the best jobs in the squadron! Out of two hundred guys, Rob and I were the only ones taking the University of Maryland courses, and the senior officers must have noticed. They were always being evaluated on the basis of the performance of the men under their command, and they were held responsible if one on their troops screwed up or even got a traffic ticket. On the other hand, if their men were improving themselves by continuing their education, they got credit for it.

Riding around the bucolic countryside was a lot more fun than standing out on the flight line and walking around the same old boring aircraft. It was fun chasing speeding American servicemen, investigating accidents and responding to weird incidents like one in which a husband threw his wife out of the car because she had attacked him. We often worked with the German police. Although they had no jurisdiction over U.S. military personnel, they could detain and hold Americans until we picked them up. Most of the German police were much older than we were and had been in either the Gestapo or in the military during World War II. They even looked like the Gestapo with their classic German military uniforms and jackboots. Although they appeared authoritarian and mean, they acted more like jolly old uncles and were always joking around with us and seemed fascinated by everything American. Every time we came to their office on business, they would offer us a glass of beer. It was a gesture of hospitality similar to offering a cup of coffee. After a few refills we would all be feeling quite festive, and they really appreciated the fact that I could speak German and translate the jokes

back and forth. I had never seen police who had such fun. I guess working with the Americans was a hell of a lot more fun than working for
Hitler.

The hardest part of the job was trying to stay awake on the midnight to 8 AM shift. Working the day shift was the most fun, because
we would travel around the countryside on patrol eating in cafes and
schmoozing with the Germans. The evening shift, from 4 PM to midnight, was the most active. It was when most Americans were out on
the highway speeding or getting into accidents. The midnight shift was
usually boring or gruesome. It seemed that the worst accidents happened after midnight, probably because the military people were more
drunk and sleepy by then. If there were no accidents, then we would
often set up a speed trap to catch drunks and speeders returning to the
base in the wee hours. There was considerable pressure to write a lot of
tickets. The quantity of tickets issued was an indicator to the senior officers that we were doing our jobs and not just goofing off. Also there
was a competition between the various highway patrol teams to see who
could write the most tickets.

My partner, Airman Kalso, was an older reenlistee. Like many
of the career enlisted men, he was from the rural South and saw the
military as a means to escape the dead-end poverty of life in a small
West Virginia coal mining town. He had little education and drank too
much, but he took his job very seriously and tried to do everything by
the book in the hope that he would be promoted to sergeant. Promotions were very hard to come by in the air police, however. In most other
military career paths—especially the technical jobs—men were usually
promoted to sergeant within four years. In the air police it took much
longer. Airman Kalso had been in the Air Force nine years and was still
dreaming about being promoted to sergeant.

As the senior member of our team, Kalso was in charge and took
our challenge to write a lot of tickets very seriously. Between midnight
and 6 AM there was very little traffic on the main road from Trier to
Bitburg. We spent hour after hour parked behind some trees waiting

for unsuspecting Americans speeding back to the base. The only way to distinguish between Americans and Germans was the special license plate displayed on the vehicles owned by U.S. military personnel. After an hour or so of sitting in the dark vehicle, I would fall asleep in a very upright position with my hat pulled down almost over my eyes, so that my partner couldn't tell if I was asleep. Kalso would sit there for hours with his eyes glued to the road, rattling his dentures hoping to catch a violator. Whenever he saw a suspect vehicle, he would yell over to me, "Did you catch the plates on that one?" This would wake me up, and I would automatically say, "Looks American," and we would take off in hot pursuit. Most of the time we would have to terminate the chase when we got close enough to see that the license plates were German. This was always disappointing to Kalso, but he never gave up, and we would go back and start the routine all over again without him suspecting that I was sleeping.

Promotions are very important to those planning a career in the military; they define who you are much more than in civilian life. Every four months the promotions would be handed out, preceded by weeks of rumors. Some guys didn't give a damn, whereas others relished the idea of more power and authority over their fellow airmen. I now had less than a year to go in the military, which meant it was very unlikely that I would be promoted. The idea of a pay increase and the ability to eat in the noncommissioned officer's dining hall was appealing, but I was more interested in educating myself than in wearing more stripes on my sleeve. So when I heard the rumor that I'd been selected for promotion, I thought it strange because so many guys had been there a lot longer than I had, and they were really sharp troopers and had worked hard to get promoted.

When the four promotions to airman first class came down, two were given to a couple of deserving guys who had reenlisted, and the other two were given to Rob and me. While I was not exactly an outstanding airman, Rob was a true hell-raiser who hated the Air Force and didn't care if he was kicked out. Neither of us could believe that we'd been chosen over so many better candidates. Then we realized that we were the only ones taking college courses; that must have been the reason. The man most responsible for this decision was the operations officer, Captain Reeves. We didn't have much interaction with him on duty, but Rob and I would see him quite often when we were taking our night classes. He, too, was taking some classes, and he would often come over to say hello and be genuinely interested in us. Education must have been very important to him, and perhaps that was why he'd promoted us. Although it felt good to be promoted, I felt bad for the guys who hadn't made it. Some of them were openly resentful; others tried to hide their disappointment. The hardest part for me was going to work at the highway patrol office and facing one of the men who had worked long and hard for the promotion, only to lose out to someone like me, who couldn't wait to get out of the Air Force.

The Trier liaison unit was by far the best duty in the squadron. Jerry and Bobby were older reenlistees who lived in a huge eight-room apartment on the top floor of a military housing complex that served as their living quarters and office. The complex was on top of a hill overlooking the city of Trier and the Moselle River. Not only did they enjoy the luxury of living off the base, but they were also given a generous allowance to buy their own food. Except for the telephone in their office, they were completely autonomous from the base. We would see them about once a week when they would drive up from Trier and file reports at the highway patrol office. Jerry's tour of duty in Germany was coming to a close in a few months, and rumors about who would replace him were circulating around the office. The position always went to a career person who could work well with the Germans and take on the law enforcement responsibilities for a large area. When I was chosen for the job, the other men in the highway patrol were not surprised, they were shocked: here I was, a kid who'd been on the highway patrol only a few months, being given this supreme assignment that they had been waiting and hoping for years to land.

Jerry and Bobby were less than thrilled about my joining them in

Trier. They had probably expected one of their good old boy senior airmen friends to get the job. I was assigned to work with them for Jerry's last month to learn the ropes before he went back to the States. When the three of us drove to Trier in their highway patrol truck, they wasted no time letting me know that I was the low man on the totem pole. During the three years they had been in Trier together, they had become good friends and had developed their own little fiefdom. They were like local sheriffs; much of their time was spent making the rounds of local police stations, bars and shops. They dragged me along on these trips and perfunctorily introduced me as Jerry's replacement. I was given a room in their huge apartment and briefed on how they divided the cooking and cleaning chores. It was obvious that to them I was an interloper who was cramping their style, but I didn't care. I was thrilled to be off the base and not only living on my own, but also working independently, even if the men I worked with resented me. They liked to order me around—which they had a right to do—but I was supposed to be training to be Bobby's *partner*, not his assistant. After a few weeks of this dismissive treatment, I was beginning to get fed up. Once a week we would go back to the air base at Bitburg to check in, file reports and run errands. On one of these trips I was in the mailroom picking up our mail when Bobby walked in, threw his laundry bag at me, and said, "Take this to the cleaners, and meet me at the truck in ten minutes!" I threw his laundry back at him and said, "I don't need this crap. I quit!" Bobby's jaw dropped and he stood there stupefied while I walked out.

I was so mad that I didn't care what the consequences were, and I walked right into the master sergeant's office and declared, "Sarge, I want off the Trier liaison!" The wise old master sergeant looked at me patiently for a moment, then asked, "Why?" I hadn't really thought he would ask me that question. I'd thought he would simply be happy to send me back to guarding airplanes and give my job to someone else. Even though I was furious with Jerry and Bobby, I couldn't tell the boss that they were giving me a hard time. So I just said. "I don't get along with them," which sounded kind of lame. The sergeant looked at me with a sarcastic grin and said, "Oh, so you guys don't get along. Well isn't that tough shit!" He then ordered Jerry and Bobby into his office. When they appeared a few minutes later, they looked a little sheepish. They had no idea what I'd told the boss, but they probably realized they had pushed me too far. The sergeant gave them his best don't-give-me-any-bullshit look and said, "Wardwell here says he doesn't get along with you two and wants to quit! What's going on?" They looked at each other with reddening faces, and Bobby said, "I guess we *have* been a little hard on him." The sergeant leaned back in his chair as if he'd known all along what was going on and said, "All three of you better get along or you're *all* going to be doing guard duty. Understand?" As we walked to the truck for the ride back to Trier, Jerry and Bobby acted as though nothing had happened. Over the next few days they seemed genuinely to warm up to the idea of my living and working with them. I was even invited to participate in some of their social activities. They were true 1960s playboy wannabes. Bobby had an Austin-Healy sports car, and they would drive around dressed up in sport jackets with a shirt and an ascot instead of a necktie. They also sported English golfing caps and looked rather continental—except for their military crew cuts and white socks.

The parties in our apartment were a great opportunity for me to meet their German friends and practice my German. By the time Jerry left for the States, I had developed friendships with a number of Germans and was going out on dates with young women I'd met at the parties. This was by far the most enjoyable time for me since I'd joined the Air Force—even more fun than my halcyon days of partying before I'd joined the service. I thrived on living in an entirely new culture: speaking and even dreaming in German. The physical beauty of Europe was a source of constant pleasure, and I would often go on hikes with my German friends. There were trails and ancient walking paths that meandered through forests and up steep hills, often ending at medieval castles with outdoor cafes. Sundays were very busy on the trails, with whole families dressed up in their best suits and spending the day walking between cafes and Gasthauses, where they would stop for a meal or a glass of beer or wine and socialize with the other patrons. There was nothing like this in the States, and I was smitten by the charm of the European lifestyle.

Even work was fun! In addition to patrolling the area and responding to accidents and incidents, it was our duty to maintain good relations with the German police. Though we had the legal right to perform police activities as a result of a treaty with Germany, we were still guests in a foreign country. The best way to ensure our welcome was to entertain the Germans, and our office/apartment was a perfect location for this activity. The main office was more like a large living room, with lots of comfortable chairs and a state-of-the-art 1960s stereo system. The German police loved to come by for visits and hang out for hours drinking beer, wine and American whiskey. We would also give them cartons of cigarettes, which cost us only about a dollar a carton.

One day, before the Germans arrived for their weekly visit, I created a huge, seven-foot-tall monster by filling an extra-large Air Force parka and flight pants with newspapers and adding a giant monster head that I had stolen from some festival. I attached the top of it to the ceiling in one of the spare rooms, so that when you entered the room, the first thing you would see would be a towering monster standing in the corner. Next I recorded some bloodcurdling monster sounds and left the first twenty minutes of the tape blank, so that I could be sitting in the living room enjoying beer and jokes with the Germans when the noises started. After about twenty minutes of lighthearted conversation, the hideous sounds started coming from one of the empty rooms down the hallway. I jumped up from my chair and yelped, "My God, what the hell is that?" and ran down the hall toward the sound. Helmut, one of the older and most corpulent of the German police, came running after me while the others sat in stunned silence. I threw open a few doors, pretending not to know which room the sounds were coming from. The monstrous roars were getting louder and more menacing as I opened the door to the monster's room. Helmut, who by now was sweating profusely and gasping for breath from the exertion of having run down the hall, took one look at the monster and dropped to his knees. I stood there paralyzed as Helmut turned a ghastly ashen color, made some weak gurgling sounds and fell over backward writhing like a beached sea mammal. The first thought that came to mind was that I had committed a terrible international faux pas. I could see the headlines in the German tabloids the following day: "American Air Policeman Kills Police Officer With Cruel And Dimwitted Prank!" Just then the other Germans came running into the room, took one look at poor Helmut, and started roaring with laughter. Then Helmut started laughing, too, and they all were rolling around on the floor unable to stop laughing. I never did figure out whether they were laughing at me or just enjoying the experience.

The worst part of the assignment was being awakened at 2 or 3 AM by a call from the German police urging us to come right away to help with an accident or some weird incident involving Americans. Most of the time Bobby and I would go together on the call. Bobby was a lot more experienced than I was and had supreme confidence in his ability to handle any situation. On nights when Bobby wasn't there, I dreaded the jarring calls in the middle of the night—especially when the German police would call and start screaming, "Come *schnell*! Come *schnell*! Big fight, big fight at the Schuhe!" The Schuhe was a cavernous, evil and dank nightclub where hundreds of Americans would go to get drunk and either find a woman to pick up or find a man to pick a fight with. Often they would participate in both activities, generating large brawls that would spread through the nightclub like wildfire.

These calls from the German police always created a wave of fear and anxiety in the pit of my stomach. It wasn't so much the fear of physical violence—I had received my share of black eyes and fat lips from fights and brawls—but the fear of walking into the maelstrom of flying fists and furniture and trying to bring it under control. We had the advantage of being equipped with clubs and guns, but we were under strict orders never to draw our weapons unless someone was trying to kill us, and never to hit anyone in the head or torso with our clubs. The club was to be used only in an emergency of the highest order. As a result no one ever used a club or a gun. Fortunately, by the time I would get dressed, hop in the truck and drive to the Schuhe, the Germans would have the situation under control. Also, just driving into the parking lot with the blue lights flashing on the air police vehicle had a notable quieting effect on the melee. When the truck pulled up, the drunken brawlers probably thought it contained a squad of club-wielding brutes. Little did they know it was a twenty-year-old inexperienced kid all by himself.

Despite the fact that we were strictly forbidden to draw our weapons, there were a surprising number of shootings. Most were self-inflicted by young troops fooling around while on duty. Practicing quick drawing was a fun way to alleviate the boredom of being alone for eight hours with nothing to do. Unfortunately even the quickest drawers would sometimes accidentally pull the trigger while yanking the gun out of the holster. This usually resulted in the gun's being discharged before it left the holster, leaving a rather large hole blown in the leg!

One night Paul, a fairly bright young airman, was assigned to guard a command center when his best friend walked in. In a playful gesture he pulled out his pistol and yelled, "Freeze!" The gun accidentally went off, and his friend was killed instantly. Most of us knew and liked both of them and were shaken by this tragedy so close to us. Captain Reeves was devastated. All the men in the squadron were his responsibility, and to see the lives of two good men destroyed was hard for him to take. It was his legal responsibility to conduct an inquest, and a group of us were chosen to sit in on the proceedings and issue our opinion in a manner similar to a jury. The inquest was not actually a court-martial, where the prosecution battled the defense, but many questions had to be asked and answered to make sure the shooting had been an accident. After two grueling days it was concluded that the shooting had been accidental and no murder charges were filed. Paul was kicked out of the service, and he chose to visit the parents of his buddy and tell them how sorry he was for killing their son. We all felt that was punishment enough for his act of stupidity.

A few weeks later, on Easter Sunday at about 6 AM, I was awakened by frantic knocking on our apartment door. As I stumbled down the hall toward the door, Bobby came out of his room and shuffled along with me. When we opened the door, our downstairs neighbor, Irene was standing there looking distraught and disheveled, with bloodstains on her clothes. She started sobbing and begged us to help her. "Ricky and I had an argument, and he threatened me; the next thing I knew I had stabbed him!" she blurted out. Bobby and I were still half asleep, so we invited her to tell her story over a cup of coffee. Bobby knew almost everyone in the housing complex and was good friends with Irene and her husband, Ricky. As we sat down in the kitchen and slowly emerged from sleep into waking, it became apparent to both of us that there was something missing from Irene's story. Bobby finally figured it out, "Ricky!" he yelled out to Irene, "What the hell happened to Ricky?" Irene looked at him as if he were distracting her from an important thought and said, "Oh, Ricky. An ambulance took him to the hospital." I couldn't believe that all this mayhem had taken place in the apartment just below us and we'd slept right through it! Irene seemed more concerned about her wrecked, bloodstained apartment and the fact that the kids would be waking up soon and looking for their Easter candy than about what happened to her husband. She pleaded with us to help clean up her apartment before the kids woke up. Bobby offered to help her and I went back to bed.

I couldn't have been asleep for more than an hour when frantic knocking on our apartment door again woke me up. This time it was Suzy from Arizona. She and her husband, Whitey, were real cowboys and always wore jeans, cowboy boots, shirts, belts and lots of turquoise jewelry. This kind of dress was extremely unusual in Europe in the early 1960s. I don't think I ever saw a German in Levi's nor did I see many Americans wearing them. Suzy was small framed and wiry and had kind of a no-nonsense, frontier woman way about her. I noticed that she had a .45 automatic pistol in her hand, so when she said, "Larry we've got to talk," I didn't hesitate to let her in. As we sat down for a cup of coffee, she deposited the gun on the table and proceeded to tell me that she'd almost shot Whitey the night before but had chickened out at the last minute. She asked me to keep the gun so that she wouldn't be tempted to kill her husband. I didn't know what to say except to discourage her from killing Whitey. She said she had more guns at home and that she would bring them by in the next few days. This seemed like a really good idea to me, so I offered to pick them up right away, but she said, "No, I will bring them by your office." Still half asleep, I agreed, and she left. As I climbed into bed again, I realized that something had been missing from my conversation with Suzy, but I was too groggy to figure it out. Finally it came to me in that gap between waking and sleeping: why did she want to kill Whitey?

A few days later I was working in the office when the doorbell rang. It was Whitey. Apparently Suzy had obtained a restraining order against him, and he was not allowed in the house. He had to get his belongings out, and the only way this could be done was to have an air policeman supervising him. Their apartment was in the building next door, so I walked over and met Whitey outside the apartment. Suzy came to the door, and knowing that Whitey was there to get his stuff, she let us in without saying much. The apartment was decorated like a Santa Fe gift shop with cow skulls on the walls and lots of Southwest art— plus a few gun racks. There was an awkward silence as I stood around watching Whitey carry his things out to his car. After a half-hour I was getting bored, so I offered to help Whitey carry his stuff. I took a few loads out to the car and was on my way back to the apartment when I heard angry voices coming from within. Suzy was screaming at Whitey. I ran to the window and saw Suzy aiming a semiautomatic shotgun at Whitey. Instinctively I burst through the door and surprised Suzy. She was angry but also eerily calm and seemed quite comfortable with the shotgun in her hands. I decided to test her by moving closer to her, but after a few surreptitious steps in her direction, she figured out what I was up to and pointed the gun at me and told me to back off. Whitey apparently knew she meant business and sat glued to his chair, his face bearing an expression of resignation and fear like a cornered deer. The most hysterical person in the house was the German maid. She was old enough to have seen the horrors of World War II and was cowering and sobbing in the corner.

I didn't have my weapon with me, which made the situation much less complicated. The last thing I wanted to do was to get into some kind of stupid gunfight that had the potential for serious injury or death. All I could think of was to try to talk Suzy out of killing Whitey. This, however, set her off screaming at Whitey again. She kept calling him an "evil pervert." Apparently he had molested their son, and she had caught him or had some kind of evidence. She kept referring to something incriminating in the children's bedroom closet, and she ordered the maid to go in and get it, but the hapless maid was totally panic-stricken and couldn't respond to Suzy's command, so Suzy ordered *me* into the bedroom to bring out whatever was on the closet shelf. I refused, figuring she wouldn't shoot me without some kind of discussion. Instead she ordered Whitey into the bedroom to get the evidence out of the closet. Whitey didn't argue, and as soon as he'd entered the bedroom out of range of Suzy's shotgun, I lunged for the weapon. When my hand hit the gun, she started firing off lethal volleys of buckshot all around the living room. Gaping holes were blasted in the stuffed furniture, dishes on shelves were blown to smithereens, windows exploded and chunks of plaster and dust showered down on us as we struggled for control of the gun. Finally, after what seemed an eternity but in reality was only a minute, I was able to wrest the gun from her amazingly tight grip. My ears were ringing from the sound of the gun going off so close to my head, and my eyes were burning from the gun smoke and falling plaster.

Once the shooting had stopped and the dust had begun to settle, the maid crawled out from behind the couch, Whitey peeked around the corner from the bedroom and all the neighbors started peering in through the blasted-out picture window. We were all in a state of mild shock, stunned by the destruction caused by the shotgun pellets and wondering how the events of the last five minutes could have happened. Slowly regaining my senses, I noticed there were more guns mounted on the wall, and I concluded that it would be smart to take Suzy outside and put handcuffs on her to prevent her from getting her hands on more weapons. It was embarrassing to put handcuffs on this small, now subdued woman in front of all her neighbors, but I didn't know what else to do. I then called headquarters, and they sent someone out to pick her up.

A few days later Suzy came by the office for a chat. Somehow neither one of us seemed angry or upset, even though we'd come close to killing each other. The military authorities had decided to ship her back to the States as soon as possible because she was subject to German law and might even be charged with attempted murder. This could prove an embarrassment for the Americans, so they thought the best way to deal with her was to get rid of her. I asked her about Whitey, and she said she was going to leave him but not divorce him; that way she would always know where he was, so she could eventually kill him. I didn't know what to say, nor did I want to probe her for details of whatever perverted things Whitey had done to their kid. As soon as she'd left the office, I called headquarters and reported what she'd said. They didn't seem very interested, however, because she would be leaving in a few days and would no longer be their problem.

As the cool German spring blossomed into the fullness of early summer, my life was coming to resemble the delightful routine of an expatriate enjoying the cafe culture of Europe, rather than the drudgery of military service. Most of my time was spent with my German girlfriend, Erica, and a group of mutual friends. We would all get together two or three times a week and go for walks in one of the many ancient villages along the Moselle River or else visit old castles, always ending up at an outdoor cafe enjoying great beer, wine, coffee and food. Even the most humble cafe had great food, and it was always served on plates with silverware and cloth napkins. I found this way of life so superior to the American culture of burgers, fries, milkshakes, TV dinners and television game shows that I began to look upon the American way of life with a snobbish disdain. A year earlier, on the frozen plains of South Dakota, I could never have imagined how great my life in Europe would be. I was enjoying everything a twenty-year-old guy could ask for: beautiful women, fun and adventure. Although I was getting out of the Air Force in five months, I really wasn't looking forward to going back to the States. It seemed so bland and boring there compared with the charm and sophistication of Europe. I looked into the possibility of staying in Europe after my discharge, but the jobs available were dead-end minimum wage positions, and I knew that I should finish college.

The fact that I would be leaving in a few months meant that someone would be joining Bobby and me to train as my replacement. The man chosen turned out to be Sergeant Harrington, who was much older than us, outranked us both and was therefore our boss. At the time he seemed really old—probably thirty-five or forty! Fortunately he was a great guy, fun to be with and to work with. Now that there were three of us, I would be able to take a month's leave and see more of Europe. The first two weeks were spent on Lake Constance in southern Germany, Austria and Switzerland with Erica and two other friends, Karl and Heidi. We traveled in Erica's car with German license plates, spoke only German and stayed in guesthouses. When people we met found out that I was American, they were surprised and mentioned how well-behaved I was. Traveling as a European through Austria and Switzerland was an exhilarating experience for me. I felt as if I never wanted to go back to the States. Hiking in the Alps and relaxing in outdoor cafes in spectacular mountain settings was an experience beyond my wildest fantasies when I first joined the Air Force a few years ago.

A few days after we'd returned from Switzerland, I set out for Greece with my buddy Rob. We had heard there were regular flights to Athens from the base and that all you had to do was check with the control tower and find out when the next C-130 cargo plane was due to arrive. The C-130s delivered supplies for all the airbases in Europe, and it was easy to catch a ride. Often they would land for only a few minutes, unload their cargo and take off again without ever shutting off their engines. We had to wait only an hour or so at the control tower before a C-130 landed. I asked the air traffic-controller if it was going to Greece, and he said the best thing to do was to run out to the aircraft and ask the crew where they were headed. The plane rolled to a stop and kept its engines roaring, and we dashed out to find a crew member. Over the scream of the engines, we yelled out, "Are you going to Athens?" and the man nodded in the affirmative. So we threw our bags on board, the cargo-bay door closed and the plane started down the runway for takeoff. After we'd been airborne for a few minutes, Rob asked the crew member when we would arrive in Athens. "Athens?" he replied with a bemused look in his eye. "I thought you said 'England'!" Rob and I looked at each other and almost simultaneously asked, "Where in England?" The crew member said we would be less than an hour's train ride from London and that every few days a plane left for Libya with a connection to Greece.

After a few days of fun and sightseeing in London, we arrived in Libya for a layover en route to Athens. The contrast between the cool green countryside of England and the scorching hundred-degree-plus blast furnace of the desert was overwhelming. Everything about the place seemed alien. We had no appreciation or understanding of the Arabs and their culture. The American and British military people were very isolated from the Libyans, with most of the families living on the air base and rarely venturing into Tripoli, the capital city. As soon as we arrived, we went to the noncommissioned officers' club on the base for a few drinks. It was like an outdoor version of Rick's Place from the movie *Casablanca*. There was a cabaret singer, a live band and palm trees next to every table. The next morning, as we were sleeping off the previous night's excesses, we could hear one of the Arab workers outside our window performing his morning prayers. Rob got agitated about this disturbance to his sleep and started yelling obscenities until the poor fellow stopped. This was dreadful behavior on our part, but it probably expressed the attitude of the average American serviceman to the Arabs at the time.

The U.S. air base in Libya was completely self-contained; the only contact with the local population was when Libyans entered the base to perform menial jobs. After having spent a day enjoying the amenities on the base including a beautiful ocean beach, we were becoming restless while awaiting our flight to Athens, so we decided to venture into town. Tripoli was a major third-world city with few motor vehicles and thousands of donkeys, horses and camels used for transportation. Americans were not very welcome, and large areas of the city were off limits to the U.S. military for safety reasons. After having toured the officially approved part of the city, which was quite sanitized and westernized, Rob and I found ourselves wandering into the off limits section with its huge bazaar. I walked into a tent where some interesting knives were displayed and Rob continued meandering through the maze of tents and tables offering everything from coffee to camel lips. The shopkeeper was having a discussion with a few colleagues and seemed to resent my intrusion into his tent. I picked up one of the knives and asked, "How much?" He growled, "You buy—five dollar!" I said, "Maybe," and put the knife back down on the table, thinking to myself that I really didn't like this guy, then I started to walk out of the tent. Immediately two of his buddies blocked the door and gave me a menacing look, which caught me by surprise. The shopkeeper picked up the knife and yelled at me, "You buy—five dollar!" I yelled back at him, "No!" He nodded to his pals, and they started moving a little closer to me. I was getting angry, not thinking about the possibility of serious danger, when Rob appeared outside the tent with a Libyan policeman. The policeman then proceeded to tell me how stupid I was to be in this area—let alone to go into a shop and argue with the local folks. After a brief talk with the merchant and his crew, the policeman escorted me out of the tent and back to the main part of town with the admonishment that I was lucky to be alive. The gang in the tent, he said, would have gladly slit my throat for five dollars.

The next morning we flew to Athens and were overwhelmed by the stunning beauty of the marble ruins, olive trees, brilliant blue skies and magnificent beaches filled with voluptuous women in bikinis. What a contrast with Libya! After a week of basking in the magical atmosphere of Athens in the 1960s, we returned to Libya for a day—no detours to the bazaar this time—and took off the next day for Germany in a C-130. The plane was filled with the usual cargo, crew and people like Rob and me catching a free ride. About two hours into the flight the cabin started filling up with the smell of burning electrical wires, and the crew chief came running to the back of the plane, where the cargo-bay door was located, with his parachute on. My first thought was that he was bailing out, but after he'd fiddled around with some wires for a few minutes, he announced that we were making an emergency landing in Naples, Italy. As the plane approached the airport we could see all the fire engines and emergency vehicles lined up along the runway. The crew knew that the fire had damaged some of the controls, but they weren't sure of the extent of the damage. Finally the plane touched down, and we taxied to a stop without a hitch. The maintenance crew came out and made some repairs, and we took off for Germany the following morning.

The more I grew attached to my new life in Germany, the more I became aware of how ephemeral my situation was. I had only a few months left and felt that Europe was my new home. Yet, as much as I was enjoying myself, I realized that my highest priority was my freedom, and that even though I could remain in Germany for two or three more years if I reenlisted, I had to get out. As the warmth and light of summer faded into the damp and dark of fall, my personal world also became dark and cold, reflecting the increase in hostility and tension between the U.S. and the Soviet Union. The Cuban Missile Crisis totally disrupted the life of those of us enjoying military service in Europe in the fall of 1962. The air base at Bitburg went on a permanent alert status, which meant that more troops were needed at the base; because there were three of us on a two-man assignment in Trier, one of us had to return to duty at the base. Unfortunately, because I was due to return to the States in two months anyway, I was chosen. This was horrible! My wonderful life as a European was destroyed, and it was like being captured and thrown back into prison. I was returned to duty on the flight line, driving patrols and guarding airplanes. Even worse, I had to live in a small room in the barracks with three other guys and eat the gruesome food in the mess hall. Because of the alert status, I rarely got any time off to go to Trier and see my girlfriend and socialize with all my German friends.

I was desperate and determined to do anything I could to spend my last six weeks back in Trier. Even though there was no possibility of getting my old job back, there were people who lived at the housing unit in Trier who had normal eight-to-five jobs at the base, commuted every weekday and had weekends off. If only I could get one of those jobs and ride back and forth with one of the commuters, I could live in Trier and enjoy my old lifestyle. The problem was that there were no day jobs available in the air police squadron, especially during the crisis with the Soviets. One day, however, I noticed a group of air policemen in old fatigues doing maintenance work around the headquarters office. This group was called the "flunky flight," due to the nature of the work they did. An airman was assigned to it as a form of punishment for screwing up. Others in the flunky flight were awaiting discharge for various reasons. The leader of the team was a rumpled old sergeant with the greasiest hat I had ever seen. He had planned to retire a month earlier and had been just about on the point of discharge when a review of his medical records had revealed that over his thirty-year career he had spent a total of twenty-seven days in the hospital receiving treatment for venereal diseases. The Air Force, considering this to have been unproductive time, had required him to work another twenty-seven days before he could retire.

The big advantage of joining this bunch of misfits was that they worked five days a week and had weekends off. If I could be a flunky with them, I'd be able to work eight to five and live in Trier instead of in the barracks. When I asked the sergeant if I could work for him, he laughed and said the only way to get a job on the flunky flight was to screw up and be assigned to it as punishment. Over the next day or so, I racked my brain trying to figure out a way to get assigned to the flunky flight. My back started to bother me again, now that I was sitting for long periods of time in trucks on patrol. Then, in a flash of brilliant creative intelligence, I realized that I could try to get assigned to the flunky flight for medical reasons! My rationale would be that sitting down for long periods of time stiffened up my back, whereas if I had a job that allowed me to get more exercise, my back would improve.

The next day I went to sick call and complained about my back. The medics, always skeptical about back complaints by potential malingerers, listened to my story warily. When I told them that I wasn't trying to get relieved from duty but actually wanted a menial job with a squad of miscreants and goofballs, they seemed relieved and agreed to write an order that required my superiors to reassign me to the flunky flight for medical reasons. When I took my medical orders to the wise old master sergeant, he gave me a disgusted look and grumbled, "OK, Wardwell, if that's what you want, you've got it." It was great! I had my life back. I surreptitiously moved out of the barracks (which was against regulations) and back to the air-police apartment in Trier (which was also illegal). Even though I had to hitch a ride every day to the base, at least I could spend evenings and weekends with Erica and my German friends.

My career with the flunky flight actually turned out to be quite interesting and fun. The air police squadron was moving into a new headquarters building that had previously been occupied by a missile squadron. The building was littered with bins of missile parts and electronic gizmos, and it was the job of the flunky flight to clean it all out and prepare it for the new air police headquarters. Most of the guys on this detail were not high achievers and goofed around more than they worked. As a result, the building was not quite cleaned out by the time the squadron commander and the other administrators moved in. Having all these bosses on-site made it harder to goof around, but we were determined to have some fun in our remaining few weeks in the Air Force. Our favorite room was the electronic supply room which was located right off the main lobby and perilously close to the commander's office. It was filled with fascinating small motors, electrical switches, gauges and dials. Out of the various miscellaneous components, we flunkies started constructing a table-sized machine with absolutely no useful purpose whatsoever. This project consumed our time and energy for days. We became so obsessed with it that we even worked on it during our lunch hour and after work. Why did we become so devoted to a worthless machine? It was more than just having fun; it engaged our creative potential to a level beyond anything else we had experienced in the military.

At first the sergeant in charge of the flunky flight seemed oblivious to our activities in the electronic supply room. As long as it looked as if we were working, he didn't care what we did. However, due to the room's proximity to the other offices in the lobby, he began to get nervous about the higher-ranking officers' noticing what we were doing as they walked by the supply room. Before long someone noticed just how convenient our room was to all the other offices and ordered a clerk to set up the sacred coffee urn in the room. This move dramatically raised our profile. Now everyone from the clerks to the commander visited the room three or four times a day. As the traffic began to increase in the room, we decided to act as if we knew what we were doing and ignore the people coming and going. Most were so absorbed in their own projects that they didn't even notice what we were up to. The fact that no one paid any attention to our project emboldened us to make the machine even bigger and seek parts from other sources. We knew that if we were to order parts from the base supply squadron, we would need a name for the machine. So, with the same creative spontaneity that had fostered the creation of the machine, we cognized the name: KB-97.

One day, while we were fine tuning some of the components, the inevitable happened: as the commander came into the room for his coffee, the machine caught his eye. We all froze up with fear. Looking at the machine with benign curiosity, he asked, in a tone that suggested he was trying to be interested in his men, "Well, what are you men working on?" We froze up again. Then, before I could think of anything else to say, I blurted out, "Sir, it's been taking us so long to do it by hand that we have decided to build a machine to do it." I could tell by the expression on the commander's face that he did not want to reveal his ignorance of exactly what his troops were doing by hand, so he turned around as he left the room and said, "Very good, men. Keep up the good work."

As tensions between the U.S. and the Soviet Union increased during the Cuban Missile Crisis, President Kennedy issued an order automatically extending by *one year* the length of service for anyone scheduled for discharge who was considered essential to military operations. This struck terror into the hearts of those of us who were about to be discharged. In truth we feared an automatic extension more than the threat of nuclear annihilation. Even though we were part of a nuclear strike force, Cold War geopolitics seemed remote and abstract to most of us, absorbed as we were with our own small world of work and play. Now the dreaded automatic extension began striking all around us like a virus. Men who had technical skills and knowledge were obvious targets, but then cooks, medics and even bus drivers were being extended in what appeared to be an arbitrary manner. Every day I met someone like me who had put in his four years, had only a few weeks left, and then was suddenly extended for another year. The final few weeks of my tour of duty were filled with a mix of emotions ranging from the dread of being extended to the elation of impending freedom, to the sadness of leaving Erica and my German life. Thankfully, after heart-wrenching farewells to everyone, I flew to McGuire Air Force Base in New Jersey for my discharge processing and freedom.

4

EXILED to CLEVELAND

Arriving at the dingy, fluorescent-lit, smoky, bus station in Lorain, Ohio, was a real comedown. As I stepped outside the station to wait for my mother to pick me up, I looked around. Nothing could be farther from the delightful outdoor cafes and flower-festooned sidewalks and plazas of Germany. Directly across the street stood a power plant surrounded by mountains of coal. It was belching a whitish-gray smoke that blended with the hideous orange sky filled with iron particles from the nearby steel mill. Behind the plant was pathetic Lake Erie with its greasy, dead-fish-laden waters slopping up against the rusted freighters and banged-up barges tied to its crumbling docks. The entire landscape was littered with the remnants of industrial decay and alien, inorganic odors. I felt as if my life had come full circle since I had departed Lorain on a bus four years earlier as a green recruit. I was wiser and older and I'd had a lot of great experiences in Europe, but I also felt as though I were starting all over again. It didn't take long for the euphoria of being a civilian to wear off. Middle America in the early 1960s, with its endless televised drivel, overcooked gruelish food and grotesque home furnishing was like being in a giant nursing home. It was comfortable in a mind-numbing way, but I was too young to be an inmate. I had to escape, but I had no money to go anywhere.

My first priority was to get a job. The most sought after jobs at the time were factory jobs, which offered very good pay, benefits and job security. In the 1950s and 60s a job at the plant was a ticket to the good life: home ownership, new car and a houseful of appliances. My father worked for Ford and tried to get me hired there, but when I showed up for my interview dressed in my European outfit, which included a suede sport jacket and pointy black shoes, I must have looked like a pimp or a drug dealer. Apparently what I did not look like was good assembly line worker material; I was never called back. The Cleveland newspaper's help wanted section had a lot of relatively interesting jobs advertised by personnel agencies, but many of these jobs required a college degree. I thought my military experience and college courses might at least serve to get me in the door for an interview. After a couple of weeks of interviews in my suede coat and pointy shoes, I was actually called back for a second interview at a book publishing company. The vice president who called me in was dressed in a very expensive suit with color-coordinated shirt, tie and socks. Perhaps he liked my unusual clothes, which made me stand out among the other applicants. During my second interview he seemed genuinely interested in my background and liked the idea that I wanted to continue my education. He recommended that I be hired.

The World Publishing Company had offices in New York City and Cleveland. The more exciting and perhaps glamorous editorial department was in New York; the more mundane work of producing the books was done in Cleveland. My job was to coordinate the production of the book covers with the books themselves. It was borderline boring, but a hell of a lot more fun than installing rearview mirrors on Fords as they rolled along the assembly line day after day. It was a perfect job for Middle America: nice, clean white-collar work with good pay and pleasant working conditions. The people in the office were nice middle class folks who talked about sports and installed things in their houses on weekends. For most of them this was the American dream come true: five days a week at the office with weekends and holidays free to take advantage of the sales at the local mall. I kept thinking there must be more to life than this.

After a few months I received a letter from Rob and Wally, my buddies from the Air Force. They were attending North Texas State

University in Denton and they invited me to join them. Even though the job allowed me to enjoy the fruits of a college education, I had a strong desire for more knowledge. At the end of August 1963, I quit my job, packed my belongings in my new car and headed for Texas. After two days of driving through the steamy heat of the Midwest, the parched heat of the plains of north Texas actually felt good. There was something about the air in Texas that was withering and dynamic at the same time, like the state itself, which contained both shriveled, deserted towns and vital, fast-paced cities like Dallas.

5

LOWER EDUCATION in TEXAS

Denton was a combination of all these qualities: a small, sleepy Southern college town in the process of morphing into a semibustling industrial and academic city that was being taken over by outsiders, yet maintaining a friendly innocence. When I arrived at Rob and Wally's apartment complex, it looked deserted. There were about twenty units surrounding a pool, but no signs of life anywhere. I thought for sure there would be someone swimming or lounging around the pool in the fierce heat, but there was just the eerie whine of air conditioners. Wally and Rob had mentioned that they lived in apartment 2, which I located across from the pool. Rather than knocking on the door, I decided to surprise them by crawling under the picture window at the front of the apartment and then jumping up and screaming and pounding on the window. As I sprang up and started screaming and pounding, I noticed an unfamiliar man and woman on the couch experiencing a very intimate and private moment. The shock of the screaming and pounding knocked them off the couch while I stood there dazed and embarrassed. Before I could figure out what to do next, the door opened, and a lanky Texan popped out, grinning sheepishly. "Hi, I'm Doug," he said. "You must be Larry!" I apologized for the interruption, and he said, "No problem; it was fun." I should have realized that anyone crazy enough to live with Rob and Wally would have enjoyed my prank. Doug invited me in and introduced me to his girlfriend, who was also very friendly but perhaps a bit traumatized by the incident.

The apartment was a basic two-bedroom, one-bath unit that

looked a little too normal for guys like Wally and Rob. Doug and Wally
lived in one room, so I moved into Rob's room and by the time I finished unloading my stuff, Wally and Rob had returned from their jobs
as waiters at the Pat Boone Restaurant. They claimed to be attending
summer classes, but there wasn't much evidence of academic pursuits
like textbooks, paper and pens! Their main concern was that they were
out of beer, because Denton was a "dry" town and the closest place
to buy beer was in Dallas forty miles away. So off we went to Dallas,
returning with a car full of the cheapest beer in Texas. By then it was
very late, so I assumed that Rob and Wally would have a few beers and
retire for the night—especially considering that they had final exams
the next day at 7 AM. Instead, we sat around the pool drinking beer and
reminiscing about our Air Force days in the warm Texas night air until
5 AM when Wally suggested we watch the sun come up from his special
viewing spot. By this time we were so drunk and tired that the reality
of final exams in just a couple of hours had completely eluded our consciousness. Rob mumbled incoherent, negative-sounding phrases about
a tower, but Wally became very excited about the magnificent sunrise
we were about to see. Finally Rob gave in to Wally's arm-twisting and
we agreed to go see the sunrise.

After staggering through the backyards of some of the single family houses surrounding our apartment complex, we came to the base of
a very tall ham radio tower. The tower was higher than the surrounding
hills for better reception, which also made it an excellent place from
which to view the rolling countryside. Wally jumped onto the tower
and, without hesitation, began climbing to the top. Rob's motor skills
were so impaired by alcohol that he could hardly walk—let alone climb
a sixty-foot tower. I helped him grab onto the tower, and we started
our ascent slowly. I had drunk too many beers to be undertaking this
climb, but not enough to erase my fear of heights. Rob, for his part, was
completely disoriented and kept slipping and stepping on my hands,
which caused strong-enough pain and anxiety signals in my intoxicated
brain for me to realize that this was not much fun! Suddenly it started

raining, and we could hear Wally howling with laughter from the top of the tower. As we looked up to see him, we became aware of a warm, salty rain showering down upon us. We cursed him and pleaded with him to stop, but he kept howling and urinating on us. Rob and I hastily retreated down the tower, while Wally continued his "rain" of terror. By the time we had returned to the pool to wash the urine off, the sun had come up, and there was barely enough time for Rob and Wally to grab a quick breakfast and rush off to their final exams. As they bolted out the door, I realized that this was not exactly the way I had pictured university life. I knew from our days in the Air Force that Rob and Wally were wild and crazy, but I had assumed they'd settled down to a more rigorous academic life. After all, we were no longer teenagers seeking excitement and adventure, but young men in our early twenties with the goal of graduating from college and starting a career.

Wally was a year or two older than Rob and me and had attended Colgate University before dropping out and joining the Air Force. He was quite literate and had both a sharp intellect and a wicked sense of humor. His spontaneous imitations of current newsmakers and actors would keep us rolling on the floor with laughter until we begged him to stop. For some reason he was majoring in business, which seemed dreadfully boring to Rob and me. His personality was much more of a free spirit, perhaps suited to a life in theater or literature. Rob, too, was intelligent, with a bizarre sense of humor. He was quite sophisticated and exuded a New Jersey sharpness that instantly dispelled any illusions that he was a Texan.

Both Rob and I had thought that a career in public relations would be more creative and interesting than accounting or management. So, while we'd been stationed in Germany, we had both decided to pursue a degree in PR. When Rob had arrived at college, however, the advisor had told him that to get a job in public relations required a degree in journalism. So we both became journalism majors. For some reason we just didn't consider other fields of study.

The early 1960s were more like the fifties than the late sixties. The three of us were apolitical. Although we liked President Kennedy, we found military life absurd and the rhetoric of the Cold War irrelevant. The icons of American culture that we identified with at the time were the cool, hip, swinging playboys like Frank Sinatra and his "rat pack." *Playboy* magazine was at the peak of its popularity and represented a bold and honest hedonistic lifestyle that appealed to young men of our generation. In addition to its focus on the anatomy of women, there was a token quasi-intellectual article in every issue that served to legitimize the magazine. Although we had a strong disdain for the American middle class routine of work, family, television and suburban house, we were not as alienated as the beatniks, with their berets and grungy lifestyle. While Elvis Presley and fifties rock-and-roll were fading out, Bob Dylan and the Beatles had not quite entered the national consciousness. Even though the civil rights movement was making headlines, it seemed far removed from our daily lives. The idea of public service or dedicating one's life to a cause greater than one's own gratification was never discussed among us. Our priority was to live life to the fullest, become educated, and get an interesting job along the way. So when Wally and Rob came skipping into the apartment that afternoon after finishing their finals and said, "Let's go to Mexico and celebrate for a few days before the fall semester starts," I immediately agreed, even though it meant not showing up at a meeting with an advisor to plan my college career. Within minutes we were on our way to Mexico.

Monterrey was not the typical border town we had experienced when we'd been stationed in San Antonio four years earlier. It was a large city about a hundred miles from the border with wide boulevards, parks and nice hotels—actually rather boring for guys like us looking for wild nightlife. Eventually we found the seedy part of town, with its bordellos and kinky bars. One night we were the only gringos in a nightclub that featured exotic dancers who would interact with the audience as part of their routine. One of the dancers, stunningly beautiful in her alluring costume, spotted us and came over to our table in the middle of her routine. After having dancing around us in a very suggestive manner for a few minutes, she sat down on Wally's lap and started writhing around and kissing him passionately. Wally was absolutely thrilled that she had chosen him as the object of her passion. As she started to take her clothes off, the rest of the audience started roaring and shouting in Spanish that was unintelligible to us. Just as she was about to remove her pants, she jumped up on the table, ripped her top off and pulled her wig off, revealing a hairy male chest and crew-cut hair. The audience howled with laughter at the three stupid gringos; Wally just sat there in stunned silence.

My first day of classes brought with it a bit of culture shock. Most of the professors were from other parts of the country or had been educated out of state, but the students were almost all from Texas. The girls all wore the same outfit: a skirt and blouse with a big gold sorority pin and white bobby socks and black suede loafers. The men also were dressed alike. They wore brightly colored, highly starched button-down shirts with fraternity pins attached and expensive dress pants with shiny black tassel loafers. These folks had taken conformity to a much higher level than the preppy outfits I had seen in New England, and although I found the dress code disturbing, it felt good to be taking classes on a full-time basis. I had come to realize that education was my highest priority, and now I was fulfilling that desire.

When I returned to the apartment complex after my first day at college, I received another shock: there was a complete big band jazz ensemble sitting around the swimming pool belting out some great Stan Kenton-style jazz. It turned out that almost every apartment in the complex was filled with jazz musicians. Apparently North Texas State University had an excellent jazz program that attracted musicians from all over the country. Barry, the manager of the complex, would rent apartments only to jazz musicians who played instruments that were needed to make the band complete or to wackos like us.

It was quite a contrast to be surrounded at home by a crowd of relatively grungy jazz musicians from New York and New Jersey after having spent my day among the uniformly dressed fraternity and sorority students. The dress of the musicians was a study in nonconformity. Many of them wore berets and had goatees or beards. They wore a lot of black or dark-colored shirts and pants with ankle high, black leather slip-on boots they called "hippie boots." Before the hippie movement started in the late sixties, the word hippie was used in jazz circles to describe someone who tried to look hip or cool. The musicians lived in their own subculture and made generous use of words like *groovy*, *dig* and *cool*. This unique environment was encouraged by Barry, the apartment manager, and his wife, Marla, who were graduate students in psychology. They were free-thinking "beatniks" who were fascinated by our antics and spent a lot of time hanging out with us.

Rob and Wally had full time waiter jobs at the Pat Boone Restaurant to pay their way through college. I applied for a job there, but nothing was available. I managed to get hired as a desk clerk, however, at the motel attached to the restaurant. Every evening after the restaurant closed, Rob; Wally; Martha, the restaurant hostess; and Jeff, the motel manager, would sit around the pool in the balmy Texas night air drinking beer, telling stories and cracking jokes. Even though I was still on duty at the motel, Jeff would invite me to join in the festivities. A graduate of Texas Christian University who always wore his class ring, Jeff was a fraternity member with crew-cut hair, and he always dressed in expensive suits with starched button-down shirts and Ivy League ties. Martha, the hostess, was a local Denton woman in her mid-fifties with two daughters in college. She became a combination surrogate mother and member of our "rat pack." We would often retire to our apartment poolside and continue the party when we got off duty at midnight. Doug, our Texan roommate, would sometimes join us, but he never drank or smoked. Although just as uninhibited as anyone else in the group, he felt no desire to drink. He was an art major and created strange symbolic paintings. His grandmother, who was supporting him while he was in college, lived in town and every once in a while she would show up at the apartment unannounced to make sure he was leading a good, Christian life. She would burst in the door like a member of the Woman's Christian Temperance Union, take a look at the ashtrays full of cigarette butts, the half-full beer cans covered with flies on the tables and the variety of underwear from both genders on the floor and start screaming at poor Doug about living with a bunch of Yankee degenerates who didn't eat greens. Doug was always obsequious to Granny, promising to eat more greens and introducing his live-in girlfriend as one of our sisters.

Even though his granny threatened to stop paying for his college expenses, Doug was enthusiastic when we came up with plans to convert our apartment into a nightclub. Our apartment was already becoming like a bar: the windows were covered with black velvet curtains, which kept it dark and murky inside and we had a state-of-the-art stereo system with a microphone and PA system that we used to make announcements outside at the pool. One blazing hot afternoon Rob and I noticed a couple of young women sitting around the pool sunning themselves, and we decided to lure them into the apartment with our civil defense alert routine. Rob was great at making civil defense siren sounds over the PA. After we'd caught their attention with the siren, I announced that this was a drill and that everyone should report to the shelter in apartment 2. As I was making the announcement, Rob appeared outside the door wearing a khaki uniform and a white pith helmet with a sign on it saying "Civil Defense." (This was at the height of the Cold War, and these types of alerts were common in public buildings). He frantically urged the women to quickly get in the shelter. At first they hesitated, but when Rob became agitated and panicky, and told them they had only ten seconds to get in the shelter, they jumped up and ran toward our apartment. As soon as they'd entered, I slid this huge wooden beam across the door and secured it in the heavy-duty wooden brackets on each side of the door. (Doug had built this apparatus to give the place a medieval ambiance). Our "guests" couldn't see a thing because it was pitch dark inside and they had just come in from the blazing sunshine. As I ushered them over to the couch, Rob slipped out of his civil defense uniform—including his underwear—and quickly sat in the darkest corner. He had mentioned to me earlier that he wanted to see their reaction to being trapped in a civil defense shelter with a naked man!

The women were more confused than wary, and were impressed that I was wearing a formal waiter's jacket, shirt and bow tie. I served them cocktails with cloth napkins and they relaxed and started chatting with us. As their eyes gradually adjusted to the dim light, however, they started staring at Rob in disbelief. Finally one of them said to him in a thick Texas drawl, "Wha, yer nekked!" Rob replied in a professional tone that he'd had a very busy day and just had to get out of his civil defense uniform. About this time they started looking around and figured out that they were not in a shelter, but instead locked in a weird, dank room with a couple of lunatics. Rob did not get the screaming reaction he had hoped for, so he stood up, announced that the alert was over, and escorted the women to the door naked, thanking them for their participation.

Probably the main reason our apartment evolved into a bar was the fact that Texas was a dry state. That meant that no liquor could be served in bars and restaurants; only beer was allowed. In Denton there were no alcoholic beverages sold anywhere in town—not even beer. Dallas, forty miles away, was the closest place to get alcohol.

We decided that opening our own bar would be much simpler and provide a public service to ourselves and our friends. Our apartment was already being used informally as a bar and we even had a name for it called the "Crow Bar." The name was derived from Old Crow bourbon, our favorite hard whiskey. Our jazz-musician neighbors and other friends were always stopping in for a drink or joining our frequent parties. Usually everyone would chip in to pay for the beer or liquor, but as word of our activities spread, the volume of liquor and money involved got out of control. Sometimes we would end up with a large pile of cash and other times all the beer would be gone and there would be no money. We had to set up something more systematic to compensate us for our time and resources spent.

Doug, who didn't drink, was probably the most excited about our new initiative. He spent many hours building a bar modeled after something he had seen in *Playboy*. He created a large black bar in the shape of a piano and upholstered the edges with stunning red leather. Barry, the apartment manager, was also very supportive and asked the building owner if we could have another refrigerator. We had met Mr. Arnold, the owner, a few times; he seemed very conservative and reserved, yet we suspected that he knew what we were up to and got a vicarious thrill from our activities. Our suspicions were confirmed a few days later when he appeared at our door with a large grin and a new refrigerator.

Another aspect of the bar was our "prop" closet. I can't remember how it all started, but within a few months we had amassed a huge rack of costumes including a gorgeous pope outfit, Roman gladiator costumes, colonial-era clothes, cowboy suits, lots of nun and priest outfits and tons of military uniforms including real rifles and pistols. Patrons at the bar loved to put on different costumes and act out different characters. We would often put on skits during breaks in the Sunday afternoon jazz concerts around the pool. One of the most popular was the "Papal Procession." Doug would suit up in the pope outfit, Wally would dress up like mother superior, while Rob and I would dress up as priests. Doug would lead the procession blessing the crowd in Latin, followed by Wally as the nun. Rob and I would bring up the rear swinging fake balls of incense on chains and chanting in Latin. At the head of the pool the pope would turn around and face the crowd and wave. All of this looked fairly realistic until the pope started fondling the nun. Soon they were lying on the ground in a passionate embrace, struggling to unbutton their cumbersome robes. This was pretty outrageous for the early 1960s and the crowd loved it.

Between our full time jobs and Crow Bar activities, there wasn't much time for the pursuit of academic excellence. Rob and I, being journalism majors, took some of the same classes. After a couple of months I began to get restless with some of the journalism courses. The headline writing workshop was particularly tedious: twice a week we would sit for hours in a creaky, musty, wooden floored basement classroom on miserable, unpadded chairs typing out headlines for stories given to us by the teacher, who seemed more like a fundamentalist preacher than a professor. There was very little room for creativity or whimsy in his class. Rob and I were constantly trying out weird headline ideas on him. He knew we were libertines and heathens, which made it difficult for him to tolerate us, so when one of us would walk up to the head of the classroom with our headlines typed out for his review, his extra-large ears would turn bright red, indicating he was out of his comfort zone even before he looked at what we'd written.

Studying journalism was more like learning a craft or skill, but I was more interested in gaining knowledge, particularly in the liberal arts. Most of the other journalism students were actually planning to become journalists and joined the journalist professional society called Sigma Delta Chi. There were also field trips to major newspapers like the *Dallas Morning News* to meet with real journalists. In early November the class was invited to a speech at the local press club to be given by President Kennedy. I was getting bored with the field trips, so I decided to skip this one. Later that morning I ran into one of my fellow journalism students who'd gone on the field trip, and she told me that the president had been shot. No one else on campus seemed to know about the shooting, or care, and people carried on with business as usual. When I returned to the apartment later that day, however, Wally and a group of friends were gathered around the TV watching the grizzly events unfold. I had never seen Wally so somber. He was the most irreverent person I had ever met, and even he was stunned by the assassination. The next few days were the darkest I had experienced in my life so far. Even the most alienated among us, who were always mocking Americans, were in a state of disbelief. No one was in the mood for parties or pranks.

After a few days of mourning, our creative juices began to flow again. Our civil defense routine was getting stale so we needed a new program to lure young women into the Crow Bar. Someone suggested that we offer "massage and therapeutic baths" for women. We discovered, to our surprise, that women were actually interested in being massaged and bathed by crackpots like us. Of course we knew absolutely nothing about massage, but we had a lot of laughs pretending! The "massage" sessions were more like a Marx Brothers routine. We acted like doctors and used all the technical jargon we could come up with as we fondled and groped our "clients." The hardest part was to try to keep from laughing while we were performing our services. The women must have known the whole madcap event was a joke, but they went along with it for the laughs. One afternoon Rob and I were in the bathtub bathing one of our "clients" when we realized we had put way too much laundry detergent and dish soap in the tub, resulting in the soapsuds' flowing out of the bathroom into the hallway. Suddenly we heard the front door to the apartment fly open as Barry, the apartment manager, came running into the hall. He came around the corner too fast to stop before he hit the suds and then more or less surfed down the hall in a wave of soap bubbles, until his ride was ended when he slammed into the toilet. Although Barry was a graduate student in psychology and had studied deviant behavior, he wasn't prepared for the sight of Rob, me and the young woman in a tub erupting with suds that were filling the bathroom. He sat there speechless for a long time until we introduced him, after which he mumbled, "Well. I got to go," and sloshed his way cautiously back down the hall.

Once the Kennedy assassination had finally faded from the front pages, attention turned to what seemed to be a lot of military coups d'état taking place around the world. There were constant reports of some disgruntled colonel in a "banana republic" taking over the radio and TV stations to gain control of the flow of information, which often led to the quick fall of the existing regime. Rob, Wally, Doug and I thought it would be a hoot to have our own coup in Denton, Texas. The first step was to check our supply of uniforms and weapons. There were enough fatigues for all four of us, plus I had a .45 semi automatic pistol, while Doug had an M-1 rifle. The plan was to charge into the Pat

Boone Restaurant, catch everyone off guard and announce the coup. To accomplish this, we needed some inside help. Luckily, even though Martha was in her mid-fifties, she loved to participate in our adventures. As the hostess of the restaurant, she would offer no resistance and control the phone to make sure no one would call the police for help.

To add to the drama of the event, we needed to take a prisoner. Frederick Forrest, an actor who years later would appear in many major films, had just returned from an engagement in New York City. He was a college buddy of Jeff, the motel manager, and was chilling out at the motel for a few weeks; he often joined us at the motel pool and the Crow Bar. Fred would make the perfect prisoner. He ate almost all his meals at the restaurant, and although we decided not to tell him in advance, we were confident that once he realized who the perpetrators of the coup were, he would turn on his professional acting skills, which would greatly improve the quality of the event. On the evening of the coup we put our old uniforms on and practiced our tactics while awaiting the call from Martha at the restaurant. At about 2100 hours Martha called and notified us that Fred was having a romantic candlelight dinner with his girlfriend.

Within minutes of the call we charged into the restaurant, our weapons drawn, and announced there was a military coup underway and we were taking over the local radio station. The patrons were dumbfounded; they looked at us in shock and disbelief rather than fear. We told everyone to remain calm, saying that we were not going to harm anyone and that as soon as we located our "suspect" we would leave. One of us spotted Fred at the corner table and we rushed over to him. He knew we were putting on some kind of hoax, but was really surprised when we accused him of treason and started to grab him. He started screaming hysterically and fighting back, but he was soon overpowered and outnumbered. His girlfriend didn't know what to think; everything seemed so real! We hauled Fred out to our camouflaged, weird-looking vehicle and sped off. In the meantime Martha announced to the restaurant customers that the whole thing had been a prank, and most of them laughed and relaxed. At the time we didn't consider the possibility that something could have gone terribly wrong with our little stunt.

The "Crow Car" was a wonderful example of a collaborative work of art. It started out as a mundane-looking 1954 Ford four-door sedan and within days was transformed into the strangest looking vehicle in Texas. Doug, the art major, focused on the outside paint job, covering the entire vehicle—including the windows (except for the front windshield and a small porthole in the back window)—in a garish green and black camouflage. On the trunk he painted a fantastic, shark-like demon face with huge jagged teeth. When the trunk was opened from the inside, it looked like a giant monster opening its mouth. In 1963 Texas nothing as weird as this was ever done to a car. While Doug painted the outside, Rob, Wally and I renovated the interior by tearing out everything except the steering wheel and other vital controls. This left a rather large space that now included the trunk. We replaced the seats with cushions and set up a small bar to make drinks. It was very dark inside because all the windows had been painted over, so we installed quite a few candles to create a more intimate environment. On our first test run we pulled alongside a young woman walking from campus and opened the trunk in a fierce growl. As she jumped back and screamed, Wally hopped out wearing a waiter jacket and bow tie and offered her a martini on a tray. Apparently these events unfolded too fast for her, and she ran away. But the Crow Car served us well for many months. It was fun picking up your date in this strange vehicle driven by a uniformed chauffeur, with a waiter to serve cocktails. Finally, however, the reverse gear broke down and the car wouldn't go backward. Rob and I took it to a used car lot and traded it in on a 1950 Dodge convertible. Our selling point was that the camouflage made it a great hunting rig. The dealer either forgot that we told him there was no reverse or didn't care. Anyway, he gave us $100 for it toward the purchase of the $150 convertible.

By the end of the school year the reputation of the Crow Bar had spread to some of the town officials and businessmen. They loved having a late night bar in their hometown without the hassle of driving forty miles to Dallas. One local entrepreneur, who owned a plastics factory in town, would reserve the whole Crow Bar for his wealthy clients, who would fly in on their own custom plane. We would set up a banquet table and they would be served by young women wearing just their underwear and tuxedo jackets. The busiest time at the Crow Bar was from 11 PM to 3 AM, which didn't leave much time for sleep. The jazz musicians, who often stayed up all night, introduced us to Dexedrine, a weight loss amphetamine called "beans." This allowed us to study after 3 AM when things had settle down and still be alert for our morning classes. The speed would wear off by noon leaving us feeling exhausted and disheveled. If we were lucky, we could grab a few hours of sleep before starting work at 4 PM. The businessmen who frequented the Crow Bar all knew us personally and admired our wild lifestyle and our hospitality skills. There was always something wacky going on, yet it was a great place to have a sophisticated conversation. One of these friends of the Crow Bar was Jim Saunders, a local entrepreneur and a member of the music faculty at the university. He loved opera, and he was pursuing his dream of building an exclusive club that was a replica of the Metropolitan Opera in New York City. He realized, however, that the word opera in the name of the club would not be the best way to market his club in Texas, so he decided instead to call it the "Greater Denton Athletic Club." This macho title was intended to attract wealthy Texans who, although relatively sophisticated, considered anything associated with the opera to be too homoerotic for their taste.

A few days before the grand opening, Jim took a large group of us on a tour of the new club at 3 AM. It was like stepping into another world. The entire club had an Italian Renaissance motif, with a magnificent, red-carpeted dining room and a small stage for a string quartet or jazz trio. There was also a "gentlemen's club" style bar with stuffed leather chairs and fine glassware for serving wine and cocktails. The athletic part of the club appeared to be an afterthought. It was nothing more than a small exercise room with a sauna: a little added incentive to sign up new members. After the tour Jim opened the bar up to us, and we all had drinks on the house. By now it was morning and we were getting hungry, so we drifted into the kitchen for something to eat. Usually in restaurant kitchens there is a ton of food on shelves, in the fridge and in the pantry. But here there was not a morsel of food in sight! Finally we discovered a hallway off the kitchen with a locked door and a large sign saying "Chef's Headquarters—Off Limits!" Jim explained that he had known the chef from his days as a marine pilot and had found out the man had recently retired, so he'd offered him the job. Jim didn't know anything about civilian food service or the complexities of restaurant management, but to those of us who had worked in restaurants for years, hiring an old military cook for an exclusive club seemed like a bad idea! Despite our misgivings about the chef, we all said yes when Jim asked us to work in the new club as waiters, waitresses and bartenders.

It was difficult quitting our old jobs at the restaurant and motel, but we were excited about working at the new club. Before we could enter the magnificent dining room to serve the higher echelon of Denton society, however, the chef gave us a military-style inspection. He checked our shoes, fingernails, shirt collars, haircuts and shaves and made sure our new red tuxedo jackets were spotless. This was quite a departure from the laid-back style at the Pat Boone Restaurant and the Forest Park Motel, but we were willing to put up with it for the opportunity to work in such an exciting place. We didn't realize what a martinet the chef was, though, until it came time to eat. In most restaurants the staff can eat almost anything they want, except for the most expensive and rare menu items. But this chef had other plans for our meals. Instead of being offered a choice of different items served at the club, we were told to line up and were dished out a grizzly chili made by his assistant especially for the staff. We were fed this slop every day, until one day Wally found a large bovine kneecap in his bowl of chili.

Wally had unique methods for dealing with unpleasant experiences like this. He had a very strong sense of justice and felt that he deserved to eat as well as the customers he was serving. The most expensive item on the menu was a chateaubriand steak. This meal was the specialty of the club, and we were trained to serve it by placing a cart next to the customer's table with a small grill on it. The grill was fueled by a napalm-like gel that was easy to light and highly flammable. The idea was to grill the steak exactly the way the customer wanted it. If done correctly, the procedure was quite dramatic and romantic. The dining room was intimate, with soft candlelight and a live jazz trio playing standard love songs. The flames of the small grill and the smell of burning cow flesh added to the primal ambiance in the dim, cavern-style room. As soon as the steak has been cooked to the customer's specifications, the waiter would extinguish the flames by quickly plopping a large cloth napkin down on the grill with a flourish. One day Rob overdid it with the panache and threw his napkin a little too forcefully onto the burning gel in the grill. The force of the cloth napkin hitting the flaming gel splashed it up onto the diners' table and started a series of small fires on their food and other parts of the table. Fortunately two other waiters and I spotted the flaming table immediately and rushed over and started beating the flames out with our napkins. Regrettably there was significant collateral damage. To put the flames out, we had to whack at them quite vigorously, which caused chunks of flaming food to fly all over the place, including onto the clothes of the customers. We all hovered around the hysterical couple, wiping them off and apologizing profusely. They were too stunned to get up and leave, so we promised to start all over with a brand-new meal and a new waiter.

As one of the waiters wheeled the cart full of charred and half-eaten food back into the kitchen, Wally lunged at it, found the remains of the steak, ran into a corner with it and started devouring it like a ravenous and dangerous dog. The rest of us pounced on Wally, trying to pry the steak from his clenched fist. Just then we heard the chef come out of his office, and we fled back to the dining room, leaving Wally lying on the floor with a half-eaten steak in his hand. He quickly jammed the steak into his pocket and pretended to have fallen. The chef mumbled something derogatory at him and returned to his office. But now that Wally had tasted the nearly raw flesh of expensive steak, he was like a wild predator, willing to do anything to get his jaws on the succulent meat. His favorite tactic was to keep an eye on the young, romantic couples who were most likely to get up and dance in the middle of their meal. When he noticed a couple lingering over their meal, he would whisper to the jazz trio to play an irresistible dance tune and encourage the couple to get up and dance. As soon as they started dancing, he would clear their table—including the unfinished steak—and whisk the food into the kitchen. Often the rest of us would intercept him as he entered the kitchen and try to grab the steak from his tray before he could get to it. After the dance number was over, the couple would return to an empty table and call Wally over to ask him what had happened to their very expensive meal. Wally would explain to them in a very apologetic manner that he'd naturally assumed they had finished eating when they'd gotten up to dance, then he'd ask them if they would like some after-dinner drinks. Most of the couples would be too embarrassed to complain and would order drinks while the rest of us gathered in the kitchen to eat their dinner.

After the club had been open about a month, I was having breakfast before going to class one morning when Wally burst into the apartment and announced that the club had burned down. I thought he was playing a trick on me, so I dismissed him with an "Oh, sure" and continued reading my book. "Come on, man," he insisted, "I'll show you!" So we jumped on our motor scooter and sped off to the club. The entire building was charred, crumpled, melted and smoldering. The only part that remained recognizable was the bar. The roof was burned off and the blackened bar and singed stools were standing in the sunlight covered with ash and assorted debris. Jim was standing in the corner grieving as much as an ex-marine who had seen much worse could. We poked around in the rubble and found a few bottles of charcoal covered beer with the labels burned off and joined Jim in a "toast" to the new club, which he vowed to start rebuilding in a few weeks. While we were enjoying our burnt beer, Wally and I both had the same idea; we'd ask Jim if we could have the burned booze, bar stools and anything else we could salvage for the Crow Bar. He readily agreed and we spent the morning carrying loads of liquor, glasses and bar stools to the Crow Bar.

Despite all these new furnishings, the Crow Bar began to lose its charm. The all-night parties were becoming a little tedious, and opening up the bar at 2 or 3 AM to a bunch of drunks was not fun anymore. By the end of the spring semester, Wally had a steady girlfriend and by the middle of the summer session Doug, Rob and I were also involved in serious relationships. This dramatically changed the whole dynamic at the Crow Bar. Because the bar was such a popular phenomenon, there was a constant flow of friends and supporters in our apartment. At first this had been exciting, but now that we all had girlfriends, privacy was becaming a precious commodity. Wally and Doug shared one bedroom, and Rob and I shared the other, which made it difficult to have intimate time with our girlfriends. Even when we could manage some private time in the bedroom, the constant noise of people having a wild time in the bar seriously degraded the romantic potential of the evening. When Wally's girlfriend Julia moved into an apartment above the Crow Bar, Wally began spending most of his time at her place. Because he had been to college before the Air Force, he had enough credits to graduate at the end of the summer term. Julia was also going to graduate at the end of the summer and they planned to get married. At first this was quite a shock, but Wally was older than the rest of us, and we were all becoming more appreciative of the joys of a committed relationship after such an intense year of thrill-seeking stunts and abnormal festivities.

By the middle of summer I was spending most of my time at the apartment of my girlfriend, Susan, to get away from the madness of the Crow Bar. Sometimes we even had a quiet evening of eating dinner and watching idiotic television shows—something I thought I would never do. Perhaps we were all maturing or else just burned out from all the extreme and surreal activities. I was also thinking a lot more about what I wanted to do with my life. Political science, history and philosophy now seemed much more stimulating to me than my journalism classes, so I changed my major to international studies. When I had started college in the fall, I had thought I wanted to have a career in public relations, but the more I learned about it, the less I liked it. Rob and I had both read Vance Packard's books on advertising and PR and we had come to the conclusion that PR people were "corporate stooges." Even though Rob, Wally and I reviled the corporate life as withering, conformist and destructive to the human soul, both Rob and Wally were planning to get regular jobs in business after graduating. Business held absolutely no appeal for me. Instead, the idea of a career in public service started to become more appealing. I still wanted to go overseas, so I decided to take the Foreign Service exam. On my first attempt I came close to passing but was weak in American history, so I decided to take more history courses and try again.

By the time the summer session ended, our attention was definitely on our girlfriends instead of the Crow Bar. Ironically Doug, who didn't drink or smoke, was the only one interested in keeping the bar open. Wally had moved in with Julia. Rob and I decided that even if we closed the bar, people would still be knocking on our door all the time, so we moved into another apartment while Doug found another partner and opened a new bar across the pool from the Crow Bar. With the athletic club destroyed, Rob and I needed to get jobs. Rob started work as a waiter at the local Holiday Inn, and I became a maintenance man at our friend's plastic factory. The other maintenance worker was a young black man named Judson, who actually grew up in Denton. At that time the blacks literally lived on the other side of the tracks from the whites. Judson had just returned from California where he had been living for some time and apparently exploring the potential that cannabis had for enhancing one's perception. He and I talked for hours in the warehouse about the nature of human consciousness—its potential and limitations. Until this time I had always thought of marijuana as just another way to get high. It would come up occasionally in conversations, but alcohol and amphetamines were still the drugs of choice among my friends. Alcohol was for recreation and speed was for staying awake and studying. Expansion of consciousness was a whole new aspect of taking drugs that aroused my curiosity. I asked Judson to get some marijuana for me, and he said he could get some the next time he went to Dallas.

Rob and I enjoyed setting up our new apartment in relatively normal fashion. We each had our own bedroom, which made it easier to spend private time with our girlfriends. The women who were interested in us were definitely not typical students at North Texas State; they were drama majors and independent thinkers who apparently found us interesting and offbeat. As the fall semester progressed, my activities developed into a welcome routine. I found myself spending occasional weekends and holidays at Susan's parents' house in suburban Dallas. They were normal middle class folks and I'm sure I was not what they expected their daughter would bring home for approval. I didn't look or act the part of a football-playing fraternity brother who was majoring in business. Instead I was this oddball from Massachusetts who was not interested in sports and was—judging from my repertoire of adult jokes—perhaps a little too worldly to be spending a lot of time alone with their daughter. It didn't take long for them to warm up to me, though, perhaps due in part to the inherently friendly nature of Texans.

It took Jim only a little over two months to rebuild his beloved athletic club. We were all invited to the grand reopening and looked forward to working there again. As Rob, Wally and I entered the club for the gala celebration, we saw Jim in the lobby proudly giving a tour to a group of wealthy opera lovers (his favorite type of potential members). Seeing us out of the corner of his eye, he quickly excused himself to usher us into the bar to avoid any mortification which might result from an encounter between us and the potential new club members he was trying so desperately to impress. Jim was thrilled with the response to the opening night and kept busy showing off the club to all the new members. Meanwhile we kept ourselves busy in the bar enjoying the free drinks and food. After a few hours, it appeared that Rob had had too much to drink; he was sitting in his chair in an apparent catatonic state, unable to respond to any verbal stimuli. Wally had the brilliant idea that a sauna might help to revive him, so we quickly lugged Rob down the hall to the fitness room (to avoid any embarrassment for Jim), took his clothes off, dragged his body into the sauna and laid him out on one of the benches. There wasn't much more we could do for him, so we returned to the bar.

After about an hour we noticed Jim greeting another group of dignitaries at the front door of the club. We both realized that it would take Jim about ten minutes to reach the fitness room with his tour, so we ran down the hall to the sauna and tried to wake Rob up and get him dressed before Jim proudly opened the sauna door for his guests. Rob just wouldn't wake up. We shook him and yelled at him to no avail. Finally Wally decided that spraying Rob with the fire extinguisher mounted on the wall just might do the trick. He ran into the sauna like a professional firefighter and started extinguishing Rob! At first Rob didn't even move as his naked body was sprayed with the white powder. Then he bolted upright and started screaming and moaning in rage. He looked at Wally and lunged for him, but he was half blinded by the fire extinguisher chemicals in his eyes. Wally dropped the extinguisher and we both started to run, knowing that Rob could be very violent when he was drunk and angry. Now he was in the worst rage we had ever seen, plus he was almost blind and emitting frightening, gorilla-like screeches that made the hair on the back of your neck stand up.

As we ran out of the fitness room and into the lobby, Jim and his entourage of dignitaries were rounding the corner on their way to the room we had just left. Wally and I ran past them as though we were fleeing a natural catastrophe. The guests looked a bit befuddled, but Jim knew instantly from the fear in our eyes and the white fire-extinguisher powder on our clothes that disaster was imminent. There was nothing we could say or do as we ran past the elegantly dressed socialites. Just as we passed them, the door of the fitness room burst open with terrifying force and crashed into the wall. Then Rob appeared in the doorway looking like a creature in a B-grade horror-porno flick: his entire body was covered in white powder except for his red, swollen eyes and his genitals. At first Jim and his guests stood there in stunned silence. Then Rob launched into his horrific screaming and charged the guests like a wounded werewolf. The situation was too much for the genteel group, and they panicked and fled as fast as they could in their long dresses and high heels. Jim, the fearless ex-marine, suddenly turned pale and sickly-looking and retreated with his clients into the dining room, where they could lock the door. As Rob headed for the unsuspecting patrons in the bar, Wally and I both knew that if Rob started tearing up the bar, the situation could get really ugly. Fortunately the bar was fairly dark and Rob—who still couldn't see very well—became disoriented. Wally and I grabbed him from behind and hauled him outside and around the back of the club. The cold evening air seemed to subdue Rob and we were able to get him in the shower and wash him off.

By this time Jim had his guests secured in the dining room with a platoon of waiters guarding the doors and serving them anything they wanted to drink or eat. As we were scrubbing Rob down, we heard the door to the fitness room open and slow, deliberate footsteps coming our way. It was Jim! The look in his eyes combined unbounded hostility and a tinge of sadness, as though he wanted to cry. He looked around at his ruined fitness center, then turned to us and said with defiant hatred, "You will pay for this!" The next morning we received a call from Jim's secretary with the message that if we did not repair the damage to the club that morning, he was going to sue us. It only took us a few hours of scrubbing and replacing the fire extinguisher to satisfy Jim, who by now was in a more forgiving mood. He still refused to hire us back, claiming that it would be better for his nerves not to have us around.

So it was back to the grungy warehouse for me and the Holiday Inn for Rob. Although our jobs were depressing and boring compared to the Greater Denton Athletic Club, we were enjoying our newfound privacy with our girlfriends at our apartment. We didn't miss the hilarious maelstrom of the Crow Bar, but instead relished the generic, tranquil joys of monogamy and routine. When the semester ended and it was time for Christmas break, I spent the holidays in Dallas with Susan at her parents' house, actually watched some football games and even went to church.

The settled routine enabled me to devote more time to my studies. I was now in the last semester of my junior year, enjoying the upper-level courses in political science and history. The idea of a career in government became increasingly appealing to me as I became more aware of the multitude of problems facing the U.S. in the mid-sixties. Working on foreign policy issues captured my imagination, and I had the somewhat naïve notion that the government needed more young "liberal-minded" people like me to offer new ideas. Although I was basically a liberal by temperament, left wing ideology as well as right wing ideology seemed to me of little help in making progress toward ending the Cold War. In early 1965 the war against the communists in Indochina was still in its early stages, and there were no protests or even discussions about it at North Texas State. Most of the students were content with the status quo and ready to take their places in middle class America as soon as they finished school. The only exceptions were some of the theater majors, some of the psychology students and oddballs like Rob, Wally and me. And even Rob and Wally, who considered themselves devoutly anti-establishment, were willing to get jobs in corporate America.

About a month into the spring semester, Susan and I had a silly argument one Saturday morning and she stomped out of the apartment and drove away. I thought she would return in a few hours, but she didn't. A week later she finally appeared at the door; I thought she was ready to talk, but she just wanted to get her belongings and move out. That was the last I would see of her for more than a month. We were both stubborn and refused to call each other. A few weeks later Rob and his girlfriend split up. Now we were just a couple of lonely, overage undergraduates. No more Crow Bar fantasyland with lots of friends and wild parties. The Crow Bar had been a great place to meet women; now with it closed, we were out of circulation and it felt as if someone had pulled the rug out from under us. We'd been at the center of a rollicking, unbounded universe of unpredictable and bizarre social activities, and now we hardly ever saw anyone we knew. It was depressing.

It didn't take Rob very long to begin recycling some of his old girlfriends. He often brought one of them, Lucy, to the apartment to spend a few days. She was a cocktail waitress and dance-hall girl whom he and Wally had met in Dallas. Lucy had loved the Crow Bar and participated enthusiastically in our most unconventional escapades. Her life's ambition was to go to Chicago and become a Playboy Bunny. Sometimes she would spend one night with Rob and the next night with me. It was fun, but not fulfilling. The urge to do something meaningful with my life grew stronger every day. I began to realize that with Rob and Wally graduating in June, there was no reason for me to stay in Texas. Instead I could finish up my last year of college at Cleveland State University while living at home with my parents, which would allow me to be more one-pointed in my studies with far fewer distractions.

Near the end of the semester in early June, Susan and I decided to go out to dinner and talk about our relationship. I wanted to try to get back together, but Susan was not interested. She was graduating and wanted to move on and go to graduate school. I realized then that it was time for me to move on as well and leave Texas. Rob and I decided to take the train together back east. Lucy had called from Chicago, saying that she was working at the Playboy Club and wanted us to visit her, so we decided to stop and see her. Rob and I were excited about going to the original Playboy Club, but when we arrived at the location Lucy had given us, we realized that there was something wrong: this was the "Bunny Club," a dreadful cheapo imitation of the real Playboy Club. Rob and I hoped there was some mistake, but when we asked for Lucy, she came right over to us and gave us both a big hug. She was happy and excited to see us, so we swallowed our disappointment and didn't say anything to her about it. The sleazy, phony dance hall was the perfect catalyst to bring me to the realization that this was not the life I wanted to lead. I was now more than ready for something new and different.

6

AUSPICIOUS ENCOUNTER at the COLUMBUS AIRPORT

Returning to Lorain, Ohio was not exactly an auspicious start to a "new and different" life; nevertheless I was looking forward to getting a job for the summer and attending a new college in the fall. Early summer is the best time to arrive in northern, industrial Ohio; the green leaves on the trees hide a lot of the environmental degradation and spruce up the bleak landscape. As usual, my parents were supportive of my plans and even had a friend arrange a job interview for me at one of the major industrial plants near Cleveland. I was looking for a summer job, but somehow the family friend thought I was looking for a career position. When I arrived at the plant's personnel office, I was given what appeared to be preferential treatment and ushered upstairs to the corporate offices, where three young executives were waiting for me. They must have heard good things about me from my parents' friend because they were all exceedingly cordial. After about twenty minutes of discussing sports, TV shows and various summer-related activities like fishing and mowing, they revealed that they were looking for someone to join their management team. When I mentioned that I wanted to finish college, they suggested that I could attend nights. At first I was mildly interested because they were being so nice to me, but I knew in my heart that I just couldn't live the Middle American dream, so I told them I was interested only in a summer job. They seemed a bit befuddled that I was passing up what appeared to them to be a wonderful opportunity, but they wished me luck, and I left feeling a little guilty that my parents' friend had taken the time to set up the interview.

After a few days of scanning the help wanted pages, I found an ad for a bartender at McGuffey's, one of the leading restaurants in the area. I decided to bluff my way into the job by claiming that I had been the head bartender at the Crow Bar in Texas. It worked! The manager asked me to start that Friday night. Weekends at McGuffey's were extremely busy in the summer, and they were desperate for another bartender to deal with the hordes of people at the bar. The restaurant was located in the town of Vermilion and built on the waterfront, where the Vermilion River opened into Lake Erie. The big attraction in the summer was that customers could arrive by boat for dinner and drinks. In the 1920s and 30s the town had actually been a vacation spot with an amusement park, sandy beach and summer cottages. Now it was a besieged enclave surrounded by manufacturing plants and industrial parks. The water in the river was a murky brew of industrial and agricultural chemicals that flowed slowly into the terminally ill Lake Erie. Having spent my summers on relatively pristine lakes and ocean beaches in New England, I was not very impressed by Lake Erie and its stinking waterfront, but for the folks of northern Ohio, I suppose that was as good as it got.

Walt, the head bartender, was a salty old retired sailor with raunchy tattoos on his arms and an especially obscene one around his belly button that he revealed to selected customers on special occasions. He seemed glad to have my help and he put me to work between Marty and Jerry, two other seasoned bartenders who also welcomed me. About an hour into the evening, the restaurant was overflowing with customers and the bar was packed with people five deep who were clamoring for drinks. I was definitely in over my head; I knew how to make only about half the drinks that people were demanding from me, and I was getting farther and farther behind while Marty and Jerry were just hitting their stride. Marty soon noticed the logjam of thirsty customers building up in front of my section of the bar. He went over to Walt and had an animated discussion with him that I couldn't hear over the roar of the crowd, but that I assumed was about me. I saw Marty nod his head in compliance with Walt's instruction and then head back toward me. He didn't look very happy, and I resigned myself to being thrown out on my rear end. Marty looked at the mess I had made of my bar area and at the crowd of impatient customers and said, "Hey, kid, you need some bartender training. Watch me, and do as I say. We will get this straightened out pretty quick."

Over the next few hours I observed Marty's lightening-fast hand throw together mixed drinks almost as fast as I could see. When things slowed down a little, he let me take over to see if I had learned anything. I remembered enough of his techniques to earn some favorable comments from him and to begin to enjoy the art of high speed drink mixing. The next night there was an even bigger crowd, but I held my own and was almost as fast as Marty and Walt. After the third night the owner came over to me, complimented me on my good work, gave me a raise and offered me the job as the main bartender during the day in addition to working nights on weekends with Walt and Marty. By the following weekend, I was thriving on the crowds and the pressure. I was having so much fun whipping up drinks that the owner assigned me to the service bar—a separate bar that filled drink orders from the waitresses to take to their customers at the tables. It was even more high-pressure than the public bar. Often there were a dozen waitresses lined up to order drinks for their customers. The greater the pressure, the more I enjoyed it, and the faster I made the drinks for the grateful waitresses, the more tips they shared with me. After work most of the employees hung around the kitchen and had something to eat and a few drinks. Often the party would continue at someone's house and I wouldn't get home with the family car until just before my father needed it to drive to work in the morning. My parents were great; they never said anything about my being out all night and were always generous and supportive of my plans and lifestyle.

Now that I had a fun and lucrative summer job, my next step was to figure out where to go to college. Cleveland State didn't have a program in international relations so I decided to try Ohio State University. Its catalog was massive with a multitude of classes and programs in my chosen field, so I decided to drive down to Columbus to talk with the people in admissions. I looked up the daughter of a friend of my mother's, who was living in Columbus and attending Ohio State. We stayed up so late talking and drinking that I had just a few hours before my appointment at the admissions office, so I drove over to the campus and found a parking spot in front of the office. It was too hot and uncomfortable to sleep in the car, so I opened the door, staggered outside and passed out on the lawn. The sound of an approaching commercial-size riding lawn mower is not a bad method of being roused from the stupor of alcohol-induced sleep. The mower's whine gets gradually louder as the machine gets closer, until the sleep state gently yields its grip on your consciousness and you're back on planet earth with a soft landing. This method is preferable to the shrill, annoying buzz of an alarm clock, which can jolt you and leave you disoriented and grumpy. The man on the mower seemed lost in his own thoughts as he ignored me sitting on the grass as he roared past me. I looked at my watch and realized I had only a few minutes before my appointment. My rumpled clothes were covered with grass stains and clippings that I tried to brush off as I entered the admissions office.

The admissions officer was very pleasant and patient for an apparatchik. She spent more than an hour with me planning what courses to take in order to graduate the following June. (She also tried hard to ignore the grass clippings in my hair and on my clothes.) In addition to courses in my major, Ohio State required a broader range of liberal arts classes than North Texas Sate, including music, philosophy, art and more English. By taking a full load each quarter, I would be able to finish in one year. The only catch was physical education. At North Texas State, I had received my required three hours of PE credit for my four years in the military. But Ohio State would not automatically grant PE credit for military service. If I did not get PE credit, then I would have to attend another full quarter just to get the needed three credits to graduate. The admissions officer suggested that I talk to the head coach to see if there might be something in my Air Force record that would be worth the three credits. So I made an appointment with the coach and walked into his office with my military papers. Apparently he had dealt with people in my position many times and knew exactly what to do. I think he enjoyed outwitting the bureaucracy, and he wasted no time looking at my records to see if some training I'd had in the military would qualify for the three crucial credits. He asked if I had EMT training or lifesaving, or been on any sports teams, marching teams, color guards, honor guards and so on. I couldn't truthfully say yes to any of these and I could see that he was temporarily stymied. He sat silently for a minute with a defeated look in his eyes, and I started to get worried. Just then he leaped out of his chair in a powerful explosion of determination to win this game and yelled out, "First aid!" For a minute I didn't know what the hell he was talking about. I could see that he was starting to get agitated and impatient with me. Then he looked me straight in the eyes with an almost menacing glare and said, "Four years in the air police? You must have given someone first aid." I couldn't really remember, but I knew that I had no choice but to say "Yes, of course." "Great," he said with a twinkle of victory in his eyes as he signed my PE-credit documents, shook my hand and wished me luck.

About a month later, I returned to Columbus to start the fall semester. After a summer of bartending and late nights, I was ready for a more Spartan lifestyle than I'd had in Texas. I didn't have any friends or a car, so I started looking for a cheap room near the campus. The first place I looked at was a well worn, three story Victorian house that appeared to just barely meet the minimum sanitary standards required by the city. Every square inch of floor was covered with hideous twenty-year-old linoleum. The only room available was a dingy attic with two beds, two desks and one small window. The house was managed by Bessie with the help of Eldred, her erstwhile assistant and husband. Bessie was a huge woman in her fifties with long gray hair tied up in a 1930s bun and dressed in an old-fashioned long skirt. Eldred was a small, scrawny fellow who, despite the fact that he looked exactly like Hitler, was a mild-mannered country preacher who always jumped when Bessie ordered him around. They were both simple country folk from the hills of West Virginia and were dedicated Christians. There were no women or alcohol allowed in the rooms. The rest of the renters were either reclusive graduate students totally devoid of social skills or older exchange students from India and Africa. After a brief interview, during which Bessie tried to determine if I was a deviate by cocking her head to one side and giving me a fierce alpha-dog stare, she agreed to rent me the room.

There was a whole new world to discover at Ohio State. The university was gargantuan compared to North Texas State: sixty thousand students and its own bus service and airport. Although most of the students were from Ohio, their sheer number ensured a much greater diversity and a more cosmopolitan atmosphere than at my previous school. There was also a greater variety of clothes worn by both students and faculty. In the fall of 1965, alienation on campus from mainstream American culture and the war in Vietnam was in its nascent stages. This was reflected in the intentionally shabby dress of a small but growing number of students. The graduate students in liberal arts were the most politically aware and the most critical of the values and policies of the government. They organized antiwar "teach-ins" and a variety of student protest groups. Their clothes were also the seediest and their hair the greasiest and longest—a sharp contrast to the business-suit-clad graduate students at North Texas State.

My senior level courses in international studies were usually small seminars on topics like Southeast Asian politics and communist insurgency. The more I studied foreign affairs, the more I leaned toward a career with the government, despite the fact that I didn't agree with its heavy-handed approach to communist revolutions in Asia. I decided to take the Foreign Service test again, even though I had not taken any more American history courses. This time I did better than the last time, but I still was weak in American history. The next test would not be available until after I would graduate, so I decided to look into other job possibilities when the recruiters came to the campus to talk to graduating seniors in the spring.

My social life was a sharp contrast to the whirlwind of laughter, friends and crazy stunts of the previous two years in Texas. I had no friends. Most of the graduate students living in Eldred and Bessie's rooming house were pathologically antisocial. They were probably the sixties equivalent to the nerds of today who stay in their room for days glued to the computer screen and eating junk food. The Indian graduate students were older and much more sociable. Although they were devout Hindus, I was able to take them out to topless bars and persuade them to drink whiskey, smoke cigarettes and eat hamburgers. Quite a diplomatic and cross-cultural accomplishment for a nonprofessional! There were dozens of bars along the main street bordering the campus, ranging from scruffy, left wing intellectual hangouts to adolescent beer halls. Some nights when I had nothing else to do, I would have a beer or two at various bars to sample the unique atmosphere at each one. Sitting at the bar in one of the more lightweight establishments one night I got into a conversation with a guy named Les, who seemed older than the typical nineteen and twenty year olds in the bar. It turned out he was also an Air Force veteran, and he was struggling to complete his degree in math with just a few more difficult courses to go. When he mentioned that he was having difficulty studying in his noisy apartment, I told him that Bessie's rooming house was as close as you could get to a monastery near the campus.

A week later, Les squeaked by Bessie's interrogation and moved in with me. He had a part-time job delivering pizza and would often return to the house late in the evening with leftover pizza to share with Bessie and Eldred. They would discover the pizza on the kitchen counter in the morning and devour all of it without even warming it up. One morning I was in the oversized kitchen having breakfast when I heard Bessie coming down the hall to check for pizza. I instinctively ducked down behind the counter and waited for her to begin eating the pizza. Just as she was about to stuff a huge slice in her mouth, I sprang up from behind the counter and let out a demonic howl! She lost her grip on the pizza and fell back on the table, clutching her chest in a classic cardiac arrest motion. When she realized it was me and not Lucifer, the color came back into her face, and her shock and embarrassment first turned into a smile and then a weak but pleasurable laugh.

Bessie was a warm-hearted person, but she and Eldred took the Bible a little too seriously. There were no jokes or even funny parts in the Bible and they both needed to lighten up and have a few laughs. The next morning, as I was pouring milk on my cereal, I heard an unusual whooshing sound coming from behind me. I turned around and a giant, gray-haired woman in a gray dress erupted from behind the counter and emitted a shrill coyote-like scream. The hair on the back of my neck stood on end and I broke out in a cold sweat as the milk carton dropped from my hand and smashed on the floor. Bessie got me! She stood there in the kitchen, her huge body heaving up and down with uncontrollable laughter for at least five minutes. From then until the time I moved out Bessie and I would hide from each other in the kitchen every chance we got and scare each other silly.

The time to move out of Bessie's house arrived sooner than I had planned. Les turned out to be more of a party animal than I had thought. Often he would return to the house around midnight and talk me into going out to some of the clandestine, illegal bars and nightclubs that the black folks had set up in various houses and apartments around Columbus. Les found out about these establishments through his pizza-delivery job and soon gained the trust and acceptance of the owners and patrons. There were no official closing hours at these places and often there would be all-night card games and jam sessions. Les would introduce me to just about everyone in the bar and we would spend hours drinking and joking with his buddies. Then we would go back to Bessie's with a couple of six-packs and stay up for another hour or so before passing out for the night. We were afraid that Bessie would see all the empty beer cans if we just dumped them in the trash, so we threw them in a small crawl space that connected our room to the attic. After a few months the pile of cans in the crawl space became quite large. Bessie must have become suspicious of our nefarious activities, because she inspected our room one day and found all the beer cans. She was devastated! Although she really liked us, our crime was too heinous for her to consider any redemption or repentance on our part. We were lost to the devil and had to get out right away! The next day at work I mentioned to Pete, one of the waiters where I worked, that I was thrown out of Bessie's and needed a place to live right away. As it happened, someone had just moved out of one of the units in Pete's apartment building so it was available. The apartment was in a small, dingy building with only six units. Each unit was only one room with a beat-up kitchenette against one wall and a moldy bathroom. Still, the price was right and we only needed it for a few months, so Les and I moved right in.

The year 1966 was a watershed for many young people. The alienation of a relatively small group of "beatniks" and musicians like Bob Dylan metastasized into a mass movement of hundreds of thousands of young adults as the tragic effects of the Vietnam War began to impact their individual lives. Not only were the left wing, liberal arts graduate students questioning the war, but now the infection had spread to many students who were on track for a life in the corporate suburbs. There was a dramatic increase in organized opposition to the war, including almost daily teach-ins, sit-ins and demonstrations. It was easy for me to identify with the counterculture; however, I was not a true believer in the counterculture revolution. I became a member of S.L.A. (Students for Liberal Action), a group dedicated to organizing teach-ins and demonstrations rather than the overthrow of the U.S. government. I believed that the Vietnam war was wrong because it was not in the national security interest of the United States, not because it was being conducted by evil imperialists who controlled the government. The other main feature of the counterculture was the use of consciousness-expanding drugs. I was definitely interested in the expansion of consciousness and began looking around for the opportunity to try marijuana and LSD.

Les was planning to go back to New Jersey for the spring break to be best man in his brother's wedding and he asked me if I would like to come along for kicks. I had nothing else planned, so we bought a couple of half-price student tickets and headed for the Columbus airport. When we got there, the airport was mobbed with students trying to get out of town for spring break. Many flights were delayed or canceled due to a massive snowstorm in the Midwest. Our flight was delayed and there were so many students flying standby that we were given a number and had to get in line with a hundred other students. During the hour or so that we were standing in line, Les and I struck up a conversation with a cute blonde named Linnea who was in line right behind us. She had a great sense of humor and seemed to enjoy my weird stories and jokes, which turned a potentially boring wait into an hour of laughter and merriment.

When our flight to New York arrived, they announced that standby passengers with numbers 28 through 47 could get on the plane and the rest would have to wait four hours for an 8 PM flight. We looked at our numbers and saw that I was number 47, Les was 48 and Linnea was 49. I said goodbye to Linnea and Les and was just about to board the plane when I realized that Les had to be at the rehearsal for his brother's wedding that night and if he took the later flight he would miss an important part of the wedding! Without another thought, I bolted off the jetway and ran back into the terminal looking for Les. He was sitting in the lounge area talking to Linnea as I ran up and said, "Quick! Take my number and get on the plane—you have to be at the rehearsal tonight!" Les grabbed my standby ticket and bounded onto the plane just before they shut the door. (In 1966 airports were much more casual than they are today.)

Now what?! Here I was with this really attractive woman who was fun and interesting and we had four hours to kill. It then dawned on me that it was my birthday, so I invited Linnea to have dinner with me in the world-famous Columbus airport restaurant and lounge. As we talked and laughed over dinner and drinks, I realized there was something irresistible about her and I felt that it was my lucky day that I had bolted off the plane at the last minute. The next four hours went by even faster than the first hour of waiting in line. Linnea was fascinated with my bizarre stories of the Crow Bar and we sat in the restaurant almost the whole time while I regaled her with tales of my oddball activities of the past few years.

Our plane left about an hour late and we had a stop in Pittsburgh, where we sat in the lounge drinking beer and comfortably telling each other our life stories for another hour. Linnea was a junior at Denison, a small traditional college about twenty-five miles from Columbus. She was majoring in geology and was planning to teach or do geological field work when she graduated. After three years at Denison she was pretty dissatisfied with the sorority-fraternity lifestyle and felt estranged from the mainstream values of the students. She hadn't met anyone like me at Denison and really appreciated my irreverent and out-of-the-loop perspective on life in America. It was a rare and wonderful event to connect with someone who was so enchanting and also shared so many insights about culture, politics and the natural world. It was 2 AM when the flight arrived in New York. Linnea and I exchanged phone numbers and agreed to get together again in Ohio. She was going to Rye, in the New York suburbs, to visit her family and I was going to the New Jersey suburbs to join Les—or was I??

After being with Linnea for almost ten hours, I was so overshadowed by our fortuitous encounter that I had completely forgotten about Les and the wedding. As I was walking through the terminal, the reality hit me that I had no idea where Les lived in New Jersey. When we switched at the last minute, it didn't occur to either one of us to make sure that I had a phone number for him. He even had my luggage, which I had checked on his flight. So there I was: 2 AM at Kennedy Airport and no way to get in touch with Les. As the effects of my romantic encounter wore off, I began to get really sleepy. There was no chance of finding Les if I didn't even know where the hell he was! All I wanted to do was to lie down and go to sleep, but where? I sat down to try and figure out what to do. Remembering that I was in New York,

I tried to think of someone else I could visit. It came to me in a flash: Rob and Wally! They were both living in upstate New York, a few miles from each other. Wally was able to get a transfer with his company to his hometown near Ithaca. Rob became disillusioned with his job at a modeling agency in New York City and had found another job managing a department store in a town near Wally.

The two most appropriate words that describe the New York City Port Authority Bus Terminal in 1966 are evil and nasty, especially at 3 A.M. As soon as I got there I called Rob and told him I was coming to visit him. He mumbled a few obscenities and hung up. My bus didn't leave until 6 AM, but I was afraid to sleep for fear of being bludgeoned to death, or worse. The stench of urine and cigarette smoke in the terminal was sickening, but at least it was fairly well-lit and warm. I figured that if I stayed awake and vigilant I had a good chance of surviving the rest of the night until my bus left.

The bus ride was long and tortuous. Auburn was only about two hundred miles from New York City, but it took almost ten hours to get there. It was great to see Rob and Wally again; we reminisced about the Crow Bar and our adventures in the Air Force until the wee hours of the morning. They really enjoyed living close to each other, even though they led very different lives. Rob was living a modified Crow Bar lifestyle with a variety of women coming and going from his austere and incoherently decorated bachelor pad. He shared the apartment with a perfectly normal-appearing colleague from work, who had a very nice middle class girlfriend. I couldn't understand why they put up with Rob's noisy late night activities, but they never seemed aggravated or complained. Wally, on the other hand, had been transformed from a wild beast to a house-trained and domesticated family man. He, Julia and their two kids lived in a pleasant ranch house overlooking a lake. Wally had a garage full of lawn care products and landscaping tools, which he gleefully demonstrated for me. His favorite piece of equipment was a flame-thrower that he enthusiastically deployed against any insurgent flora he suspected of being a weed. This aggressive weed control policy resulted in a decimated lawn pock-marked with hundreds of charred craters. Compared to his neighbor's lush, verdant pastures, Wally's lawn looked like a bombing range in the Mojave Desert.

When I returned to Columbus for my final spring session before graduating, the bulletin boards on campus were plastered with posters recruiting engineers, accountants and other graduating seniors with business skills for jobs with major corporations such as General Motors, Proctor & Gamble and General Electric. I was looking forward to graduating and getting a job, but I wasn't qualified for or interested in any of the jobs offered. After scouring the halls of the placement office, I found a bulletin board with postings for government jobs. Both the CIA and the DIA (Defense Intelligence Agency) needed intelligence analysts and were looking for graduates with degrees in political science and other liberal arts subjects. This wasn't exactly what I was interested in, but I thought working in Washington for the government might open the doors for an eventual position overseas. So I signed up for interviews with both the CIA and the DIA.

Before going in for my CIA interview I had to sign a document stating that I would not tell anyone about the interview. The CIA interviewer greeted me with the perfunctory egalitarianism of a man who was more comfortable with a military hierarchy than civilian informality. After looking over my military records and college transcript, he asked me if I liked guns. It seemed like a weird question, so I asked him, "Why?" He then explained to me that my mediocre grades and my military experience made me a much better candidate for a position as an overseas operative in Asia than an analyst in Washington! This evoked an image in my mind of uncomfortable jungles and para-military misdeeds, so I told him that I wasn't interested. He tried to hide his disappointment, kind of like the sadness of a car salesman who had just lost a sale and wasn't going to meet his quota for the week. Even though he had discouraged me from the analyst job, I told him that I was much more interested in that type of work. He said, "Well, you will have to take a day-long test to see if you qualify." He signed me up for the test,

which was secretly given in a creepy abandoned warehouse. The exam
was a series of psychological tests to screen out the mentally, culturally
and politically unfit; I never heard from them again.

A few days later I was scheduled for my interview with the DIA.
I walked into the interview room expecting to encounter another ar-
rogant hack looking for warm bodies. Instead I was greeted by a lighthearted, down-to-earth recruiter who didn't require me to sign any secrecy agreements. With the aid of charts and diagrams, he proceeded
to brief me on everything they did at the DIA. It was a fascinating
overview of the entire intelligence community and the variety of jobs
available. I was impressed with his openness and willingness to answer
all my questions. Although the CIA collected and analyzed political and
economic intelligence, which interested me more than the military intelligence produced by the DIA, I got the impression from the recruiters
that the DIA was not as uptight to work for as the CIA so I decided to
apply for the DIA job. All I had to do was fill out a lengthy application
form and wait to hear from them—no day-long psycho tests or preten-
tious secrecy nonsense.

About a week after the semester started, I received a letter from
Linnea. In those days very few students had their own phones. I had
thought about her often, but never got around to writing her, so I was
very happy to hear from her. I was a little worried that in a lucid moment she had realized I was a nut log and didn't want to see me again.
She mentioned in her letter that she had never met anyone like me and
would like to see me again. I borrowed a friend's beat-up old car and
drove out to Denison to spend a wonderful spring day with her, walking
in the woods and talking for hours. Later that day we went to a local
pub for a few beers and some food. I enjoyed basking in the warm radiance of her presence and found it very difficult to go back to Columbus,
so I asked when I could see her again. We made a date for the next week
and I drove back to Ohio State, engulfed in the pleasurable glow of im-
ages of a beautiful, blue-eyed blonde holding my hand as we strolled in
the verdant spring countryside.

The next morning I was jolted out of sleep by the deafening clat-
ter of tank treads approaching my apartment building. Half asleep, I
stumbled over to the window and found a massive steel ball staring me
in the face. Next I heard a loud commotion in the hallway outside my
apartment. It was the other tenants screaming and cursing. I caught up
with one of them as she was running down the stairs and asked her what
was going on. "They're going to tear down the building!" she yelled
back as she ran out the door. I followed her outside and nearly collided
with a huge wrecking crane as it came to a rumbling halt right in front
of the entrance to our humble little apartment building. The owner of
the building lived in a well-maintained single family house next to the
apartment building and a group of tenants were pounding on his door
so I decided to join them. He opened the door sheepishly and let us
in. When we demanded to know what was going on, he immediately
confessed that he had sold the building to the university and that it was
going to be demolished to enlarge the adjoining parking lot. He didn't
realize they were going to tear it down so soon and assured us that he
would have them delay the demolition for a few more weeks until we
finished classes. As we walked back to the apartment building we realized that he had kept the destruction a secret to insure that the building was occupied with renters until the last possible moment! When I
returned from class later that day, I noticed that each apartment had a
gaping hole just below its window where the heating unit used to be.
We were spared the wrecking ball, but not the dismantlers.

Graduation was only a few weeks away and I hadn't really thought
much about what I was going to do after school. The only thing I knew
for sure was that I didn't want to stay in Ohio. Every once in a while I
would think about returning to Massachusetts and getting a job. I did
think a lot about Linnea, though. My visits with her were the highlights
of my life. Most of our time together was spent outside, walking and
enjoying nature. Her sense of wonder and curiosity about the natural
world kindled a whole new appreciation of nature that I had never experienced before. Being with her generated a superfluid bliss that I had

not felt with any other woman and I was becoming quite attached to her. However, I knew that we might never see each other again. She was going on a field expedition to Montana to study geology and I wasn't sure where I was going.

About two weeks before I was to graduate, I received an official-looking letter from Washington, D.C. It was from the Defense Intelligence Agency offering me a job as an intelligence analyst, subject to being awarded my degree. I was to report to a facility near Washington only a few days after graduation. At first I was shocked. I never expected a job offer so soon. Then I got excited about going to Washington. Even if the job didn't work out, I would be in a good position to look for something else. When Les found out about my job he offered me his beat up old VW bug so I would have something to drive when I got there. My parents were happy that I was graduating and had a job. In order to receive my diploma, which I needed for my job, it was mandatory for every graduate to attend the graduation ceremony, so I invited my parents. The night before graduation, I was up all night at various graduation parties and finally got to sleep about two hours before the ceremony was to begin. The next thing I knew, Les was shaking me and yelling that I was missing graduation. I looked at my watch; it was 8:30, time for the ceremony to begin. I leapt out of bed, threw on some clothes and sped off for the stadium.

Just as I arrived, the Ohio State president or dean of something was finishing his boiler-plate speech and the graduates were getting in line to receive their diplomas. As I ran over to the line of graduates standing on the football field in front of thousands of family members and friends someone handed me a cap and gown, which I threw over my clothes as I found my spot near the end of the line. Ohio State was a huge, impersonal institution and I only knew a handful of the thousand or so students graduating. For those of us with last names at the end of the alphabet, the wait was interminable. I was feeling weak and hung over from the night before and from jumping out of bed so fast, so I lit up a cigarette for a little jolt of nicotine. I took a couple of drags on the cigarette and noticed some of the officials giving me a dirty look, so I took the butt out of my mouth and held it in my hand. Suddenly the stench of burning garment registered in my half-asleep brain. The cigarette in my hand was covered by the gown and was burning a large hole in it, generating a plume of smoke that was rising up from the line of students like a smoke signal. The only thing I could think of was to tear the gown off, throw it on the ground and stomp out the fire. The folks around me started laughing while the parents and relatives in the stadium gasped. It must have looked like a protest of some kind to them, so I quickly put the gown back on before the police could haul me away. When it came time for me to step up and receive my degree, I reached for it with my charred sleeve. When the dean noticed it, he instinctively recoiled in horror and pulled back his hand containing my diploma. From a distance it must have looked as though he was refusing to give me the diploma. It took him a few seconds to regain his composure before handing it to me. Now that I actually had possession of the document I was ready and excited to begin my new adventure in Washington, D.C. with the federal government.

7

INTELLIGENCE SCHOOL: CLASSIFIED CLOWNS

After a few days of rest and relaxation with my family, I packed up my shiny European suits and set out for Washington, D.C. in Les's woefully maintained VW bug. The closer I got to Washington, the hotter and more humid it became. In 1966 Washington was a somnolent southern town compared to the intense power center it is today. As I chugged into the city in my diseased old Volkswagen, the magnolias, oppressive heat and more black people than I had ever seen in my life left me feeling like I was in Alabama or Mississippi. My first priority was to find a place to sleep. I didn't have enough money to stay in a nice hotel, so I looked for some student housing near George Washington University. I found a dumpy rooming house with cheap rooms and lugged my meager belongings up to my third floor, un-air-conditioned cell. The heat was so unbearable that I made the mistake of opening the window as soon as I entered the room. It was like opening the door to a blast furnace. The black tarred roof of an adjoining building was almost level with the window. The heat generated by the sun shining on the black surface must have been 130 degrees. I ran out of the room and vowed not to return until very late at night, with the hope that it would then be cool enough for human habitation.

The only way I could think of to escape the heat was to find a bar and drink some cold beer. I found a section of town where there were a lot of bars and clubs and I wandered in and out of them drinking beer until most of them closed at 1 AM. It was still hot, but there was no place else to go except to my stultifying room. As I walked up to the rooming house, I realized that I didn't have my key to the front door. I pounded on the door for a few minutes, but to no avail. Everyone was either asleep or too lazy to come to the door. I thought about sleeping in the car, but I would have to leave all the windows open to keep from suffocating in the unrelenting heat and that wouldn't be a good idea on a city street. Then the thought of the roof just below the window of my room flashed into my mind. If I could find a way onto the roof, I could climb in my window.

The buildings next to the rooming house were adjoining townhouses almost identical to the one in which I was staying. If I could get into the adjoining building and climb out a third story back window, I could drop onto the roof that was connected to my building, walk over to my window and climb in. The building on the right had some Greek letters over the door, which indicated it was a fraternity. All the lights were out and I couldn't see a thing. I was desperately tired and had to report to my new job in a few hours, so I decided to try the front door. It was open! As soon as I opened the door, I knew it was a fraternity. The foul air inside had the familiar aroma of stinky socks, sweat-stained underwear, cigarette butts and stale beer. The layout of the building seemed very similar to the one where I was staying, so I felt my way up to the third floor and located a room that hopefully had a window opening onto the same roof as the one below my window. I could hear someone snoring inside, so I slowly opened the door and peeked in. The floor was littered with beer cans and there appeared to be two or three guys passed out on their beds. Then I noticed the window. Unfortunately there was a bed right in front of it, which meant that I would have to crawl over the guy in the bed, take off the screen and jump out onto the presumed roof just below. I didn't have any other options, so I tiptoed carefully across the room to avoid stepping on the beer cans and approached the snoring victim in the bed. I had to lean over him while I pushed up the screen, which was stuck and hard to move. The squeaking sound of the soot covered screen sliding open didn't seem to bother him, so I stepped on the side of his bed and straddled his face as I maneuvered myself out the window. I was impressed with my mind/body coordination after drinking so much beer. Fortunately the roof was right where I had hoped it would be and I easily slipped over to my window and crawled in.

Although I was overjoyed to fall into my bed, it was still too hot to sleep. As I lay there exhausted in a pool of sweat, I realized that I had to get out of the room. I flipped the lumpy, ancient mattress out the window and onto the roof, grabbed the musty pillow and flopped down on the makeshift bed. It wasn't much cooler than the room, but at least there was some air moving around to alleviate my misery. I must have been asleep for only an hour when I was awakened by a strange tickling sensation. It was too dark to see very well, but I quickly became aware of something crawling all over my body. For a moment I thought I was having a nightmare. The welts that covered my torso and limbs were no dream. I scrambled back into the room, switched on the light and saw dozens of daddy long legs spiders crawling all over my welt-covered body. I ran down the hall and jumped into a cold shower to wash them off and to soothe the red, itchy welts from the spider bites. By the time I dragged the mattress back into the room, it was dawn and the city was coming to life. I had to report to my new job in two hours. I just couldn't stay awake and collapsed on the mattress. I woke about fifteen minutes before I was due at work. There was no way that I could get dressed and find my way over to Northern Virginia in fifteen minutes. I looked in the mirror and frightened myself. My face was covered with red blotches and I looked like I hadn't slept in days.

When I arrived at the security gate to Arlington Hall Station I was an hour late. My instructions were to report to building 34B. I asked the guard where it was and he pointed to a windowless building a few blocks away. The entire facility had the austere atmosphere of a military base and the design of a college campus. I learned later that it had been a women's college that had been taken over by the military during World War II. Building 34B turned out to be a movie theater. Instead of a ticket window, there was a guard sitting at a table with a list of those authorized to enter. I showed him my orders and he motioned me in. There were about eighty young people listening to a presentation by a dandruffy, pasty bureaucrat with a large number of security badges strung around his neck. Most of the people were sitting in the front rows of the theater, but I noticed one chap sitting toward the back. I sat down next to him and asked him what was going on. "Orientation meeting. Hi, I'm Howie," he said as he offered his hand. "Have I missed anything important?" I asked. "Nah—look at all these great chicks," he replied as he surveyed the audience. I looked and over half the people in the audience were good-looking young women. "What do we do after the meeting?" I asked. "We have the afternoon and weekend off, then on Monday we go to some kind of spy school," he explained. My ears perked up, and then he said, "See those two over there? Let's ask them out for tonight." "Sure," I said, and asked him if he knew where the school was. He paused for a second and then answered, "No problem—I have a map in the packet they handed out to us. Hey, let's see if they want to go to Georgetown; there are some really cool bars there." At the end of the meeting we walked over to the girls and introduced ourselves. We quickly learned that Sally and Maryanne were from the Deep South and, although they were suspicious of a couple of Yankees from Massachusetts, their curiosity got the better of them and they agreed to go out with us.

Georgetown was the most charming section of Washington I had seen so far. The narrow cobblestone streets and nineteenth-century buildings with their small, well-landscaped courtyards were a sharp contrast to the generic high rise apartment buildings that littered the landscape of northern Virginia. We all had a lot of laughs and drank a lot of beer, going from one club to another until closing time, when the reality hit me: they were all going back to their air-conditioned apartments while I was returning to my miserable, stifling cell. I woke up the next morning with a determination that only deep suffering can inspire. I grabbed my stuff and fled the moldy, suffocating room, vowing to find a place suitable for human habitation by sundown. There were hundreds of pleasant, non-descript apartments with pools and other amenities available in the D.C. area that seemed suitable, but I was strongly attracted to Georgetown with its unique townhouses and qua-si-European atmosphere. Apparently a lot of other people felt the same way; the rents in Georgetown were astronomical. I was about to call up some more affordable apartments when I noticed an ad for a roommate needed to share a house with other professionals in Georgetown. After talking to one of the housemates for a few minutes on the phone, I had a feeling that it was a house full of young Republicans. It was obvious that they were looking for a clean-cut Caucasian who would add to the dignity and decorum of their house. He asked me where I worked and when I told him the DIA, he seemed impressed and invited me over for an interview.

I found my way to a narrow townhouse on P Street, a typical, quiet Georgetown side street with huge trees and old-style brick sidewalks. I hadn't experienced such a sense of connection and pleasure with a physical location since I'd left Europe. The inside of the house was matronly and furnished with oriental rugs and lower-end antiques that created a no-nonsense atmosphere. Mark, the self-appointed chief administrator of the house, greeted me at the door and offered me a cold beer while we discussed my qualifications and the protocols of the house. The rules and regulations seemed reasonable and the cost of sharing the rent on a furnished house in Georgetown was affordable. I was quickly approved by Mark and I moved in immediately. Although I had to share a room with someone else, the benefits of living in an already furnished house in the choicest part of town were worth the lack of privacy. Over the next few days I met the other housemates. Mark was an ex-Air Force officer working on his MBA, and the rest of the crew were either government employees or older, business-oriented graduate students. I had never lived with a straighter bunch of guys in my life, until I met Gerry.

I ran into Gerry while looking for the washing machine in the basement. It was a typical hundred-year-old stone basement with as-bestos-covered pipes, an old converted coal furnace and a cement floor.

A dim light was shining at one end of the cellar. As I walked toward it, Gerry popped out from behind a stack of books and introduced himself. He invited me into his "room." Although there was only a tiny window that allowed a small sliver of daylight into his abode, the space was attractively decorated with expensive Persian rugs and high quality furniture. Gerry was very different from the rest of the guys in the house. He was older, more sophisticated and politically progressive. Also, he did not own a car. Instead he rode an expensive, state-of-the-art ten-speed bicycle around town. Although I thought it a bit strange that he didn't drink or smoke and that he was an active member of the Christian Science Church, I appreciated his iconoclastic lifestyle and we soon became good friends.

The Defense Intelligence School was located on a moribund naval base next to the Anacostia River in southeast Washington. The fresh paint on the old World War II buildings, bright green lawns and immaculate streets and sidewalks could not hide the fact that the base was a has-been. The lack of traffic going through the security gate and the abundance of half-empty parking lots were clear indicators that it had seen more dynamic days. As I drove to my assigned building I noticed there were no people walking around, in sharp contrast to Arlington Hall and other installations I had seen. Upon entering the building I felt a strong wave of *déjà vu*. The obsessively over-waxed linoleum floor tiles, gray metal furniture and immaculate hallways induced a flood of memories of the hierarchical monoculture of the military life I had escaped four years earlier.

The marine guard asked me for my papers and directed me down the hall to room 325. Most of the people I passed in the hallway were military, and I began to wonder what I was doing there. As I approached room 325, I noticed a group of familiar faces standing outside the door. They were my fellow classmates, hanging around joking and having a good time. The sight of Howie, Sally and Maryanne alleviated the sense of discomfort caused by the military atmosphere. I walked up to them and asked them what was going on. Howie replied that there was a top secret briefing going on in the room and as soon as it was over, our group was going in to have a meeting. I asked him how he knew it was a top secret briefing. He pointed to an electric sign above the large double doors to the room, blinking the words "Top Secret" in bright red letters. A few minutes later a marine guard opened the door and about fifty middle-aged civilians and military officers emerged from what appeared to be a rather posh-looking theater.

After we were seated in the luxury seats, I noticed the stage was filled with state-of-the-art audio-visual equipment and elegant oak furniture. An avuncular Army colonel in his fifties stepped up to the expensive-looking oak podium, pressed a few buttons to electronically adjust the height of the podium and flipped a switch, which caused a half-dozen signs around the room to start flashing "Confidential." (This is one of the lower levels of classified information; the next highest is "Secret," then "Top Secret." After "Top Secret" there are higher categories of secret with bizarre-sounding names.) The colonel introduced himself, gave us a warm welcome and expressed his appreciation to us for joining the DIA. After four years in the Air Force it was hard to believe that this kind of cordial treatment was being directed at us from a high-ranking officer but, as he continued with his pleasant remarks, I realized that he was actually sincere. He went on to explain that for the next few months we would be learning everything there was to know about the intelligence "business."

After about two hours of describing the various aspects of the collection, analysis and production of intelligence, he adjourned the meeting for a two-hour lunch break. As we started to leave he mentioned that, as intelligence analysts, we could eat at any officer's club in the area. The closest one was at neighboring Andrews Air Force Base, so most of us piled in our cars and drag-raced down an abandoned runway to the club. The food was great (if you weren't concerned with nutrition) and the beer was plentiful and cheap. We all sat around two or three large tables, drank a lot of beer and introduced ourselves. Everyone seemed to be feeling light and lively, telling jokes and not taking their new jobs too seriously. Most of the people in our class were recent graduates with degrees in history or political science. There were also science majors and a few English majors. Quite a few had master's degrees or were working on other advanced degrees. The one thing we all seemed to have in common was that none of us had thought much about a career in intelligence. We were all recruited on college campuses and decided to give it a try. After meeting quite a few of my classmates I began to realize that this could be a fun summer at the Defense Intelligence School!

After lunch we returned to the school in various states of intoxication. Fortunately we didn't have to attend a lecture, which would have required a significant degree of mental alertness. Instead we were divided into groups of ten or twelve and assigned "homerooms." Each of us was given our own desk and a safe, which we shared with one other person. The safe was for storing our classified documents and books. The DIA was very serious about keeping classified information secure and we spent the afternoon learning the protocol for taking our books out of the safe and returning them. My safe-mate was a country boy from Indiana named Mort. He looked as though he would rather be riding a tractor than sitting there in a bureaucratic suit with a tie around his neck, which cut off the circulation to his brain. Mort also used a lot of folksy country-bumpkin language to make you think he wasn't very smart. For some reason, he wore the most revolting ties I had ever seen. It was hard to imagine that he actually took the time and energy to find such ridiculous ties. Perhaps someone back in Indiana gave them to him as a cruel hoax, or actually sincerely thought they would look great on Mort in his new government job.

The next few days at the school were a pleasant combination of lectures, hands-on workshops and research in the classified documents from our safes. Although learning about the intelligence community was fairly interesting, it was not intellectually challenging. In many ways it was like any other business that took a raw material, processed it into a product, then marketed it and sold it. In the intelligence business, the raw material was the information gathered from the agents in the field. The next step was the development of the intelligence product from the raw intelligence. This was often like assembling a puzzle with half the pieces missing. The marketing phase of the business was the briefing or presentation. The briefing was crucial to the success of the business. Even the most brilliant and thorough analysis or "product" could not be sold unless it was presented in the form of a briefing that "customers" (senior officers and government officials) found appealing. As a result we spent a lot of time learning briefing techniques. The most successful briefings incorporated lots of audio-visual aids. We soon found out that the generals and decision-makers in the executive branch loved lots of charts and slides, so we were given access to a state-of-the-art audio-visual department, which supplied us with anything we desired.

By the end of the first week we had settled into a non-demanding routine of morning classes, long lunch hours of cold beer drinking, sleepy afternoon research projects and then parties or dates in the evenings. Because our school work was secret, there were no assignments to take home. This freed up the evenings for recreation which, after four years of college homework and rigorous exams, were heartily welcomed by all. One afternoon, about a week after school had started, George, one of the students in our homeroom, didn't return from lunch hour. We were wondering what happened to him when we heard a shopping cart coming down the hall. As I got up to see what was going on, a Navy seaman pushed the cart into our room, proceeded to George's safe and began removing his books. We asked him what happened to George. He said he didn't know and was just following instructions to retrieve the books. George was never seen again, so we began to speculate that he had had a problem with his security clearance. He seemed a little effeminate and in those days gay people were considered a security risk because they could be blackmailed. Every time after that, whenever we would hear the shopping cart coming down the hall, we would start laughing and taking bets on who would be next! This added a new dimension of excitement to our otherwise uneventful routine.

The faculty at the school was predominantly good-natured senior military officers and older, almost-retired civilian intelligence analysts and operatives. They must have realized that we were a restless and rambunctious crowd after observing our irreverent horseplay and symptoms of group attention deficit disorder during some of the more soporific lectures. As a result, our weekly schedule suddenly began to include lots of field trips. Most of the trips were to other intelligence agencies in the Washington area and, although they were dignified and high level briefings and tours, it didn't stop us from having fun. One day, while we were in the middle of a tour of the intelligence operations at the State Department, someone passed around a jumbo pack of chewing gum, which most of us started chewing during a sensitive presentation by a very refined gentleman. At first he seemed slightly distracted by so many people vigorously chewing gum. Then his face turned beet red and he started losing his ability to speak coherently as he noticed that many of us were depositing our gum in the hair of the person sitting in front of us. This demonstration of lack of decorum and disturbing behavior by supposedly intelligent and highly-qualified analysts with top level security clearances must have blown the poor fellow's mind. He abruptly ended the lecture and walked out of the room. This meant that we had to wait for our bus in the lobby of the State Department. The sight of such a large group of people with gobs of gum in their hair was difficult for many of the officious, well-dressed and well-educated State Department officers to process as they hurried past. Most of them avoided eye contact and clutched their briefcases as they went by.

The gum incident was a watershed event in terms of our group's increasing boldness and irreverence toward the intelligence school. The day after the event, we were worried the State Department had notified the directors of the school about our aberrant behavior. However, the faculty acted like nothing had happened. I wasn't sure if they didn't care about our increasingly wild behavior or didn't quite know how to respond to us. Most of the class members had never been in the military and weren't trained to treat high-ranking officers with deference. On the other hand, our military instructors were probably reminded that we were civilians and therefore they had no authority over us. Even though many of us goofed around during class and drank too much beer at lunch time, we took our studies and work assignments seriously and produced high quality papers and briefings until one day, when we were given the whole day to complete a ridiculous assignment.

The project started with the viewing of an old scratchy movie starring Richard Conte, a well-known movie star of the 1940s and 1950s. The movie was only about fifteen minutes long. It included a scene in which Conte entered a building and ran up a flight of stairs. In the next scene we heard a woman's desperate screams, saw Conte dashing back down the stairs and the landlady running out into the hall to see what the screaming was all about. Conte bumped into her, shoved her aside and ran out the door. In the final scene, we saw a woman lying on her stomach on the couch in her apartment. She was either passed out or dead.

Our assignment was to figure out what really happened based on the few scenes we had observed, then present a detailed briefing on our interpretation of the evidence. Most of us were howling with laughter at the stupidity of the movie. When we were given all day to break up into teams of five to determine what happened, we laughed even harder. The whole exercise was a no-brainer and required only a room-temperature IQ to figure out that Conte did something to the woman on the couch that she did not appreciate. Our team decided it would be more fun to go out to a nearby tavern, drink some cold beer, have a few laughs and make up a bizarre story about what Richard Conte really did to the woman on the couch. After dismissing all the obvious scenarios like murder, a lover's quarrel, robbery and an overly aggressive door–to-door sales presentation, we concluded that, due to the position of the woman on the couch, Conte and the woman were in some kind of relationship. It was obvious that her scream was not one of intimate pleasure, but of intense discomfort. The key to finding out what he did to her lay in figuring out what kind of relationship they were having.

Based on the lack of evidence provided in the movie, we had only our imaginations to rely on.

After a few more pitchers of beer and heated debate, we finally came up with a story we could agree on. Conte and the young woman were both members of the local chapter of the Mensa Society, an exclusive club for very intelligent people with astronomically high IQs. It turned out that she was a former nun who wanted to become an exotic dancer. She had a perfect body for exotic dancing, except for one unfortunate blemish: a large wart on her rear end. Conte was a dermatologist, whose license was under suspension for a series of medical mistakes involving the mis-administration of anesthetics. After they had known each other for a few weeks he invited her to the annual Mensa bowling tournament, where they shared their life stories over a bottle of wine at the snack bar. When she found out he was a dermatologist and he found out about her wart, they grabbed each other in a passionate embrace and dashed off to her apartment for a romantic wartectomy. Apparently he fouled up the anesthesia again and as he penetrated her derrière with his scalpel, she shrieked in pain and passed out on the couch.

After coming to a consensus based on the limited information presented in the movie, our next step was to prepare our briefing. By now we had learned that visual aids were the key to a successful briefing. The more pictures, slides, charts and graphs used in a briefing, the more favorably it would be received by the official requesting the information. In 1966, there was no such thing as a personal computer for developing graphics. However, we did have at our disposal a very talented group of Navy specialists who could turn out some fabulous visuals. Instead of charts and graphs for our briefing, we had a series of stunning slides of the botched wartectomy showing various angles and degrees of magnification. The graphic artists were delighted to have the opportunity to let their creativity flourish after years of creating boring charts.

By 3 PM we had our briefing prepared. We entered the secret auditorium along with the other teams who would also be presenting. The instructor in charge of the exercise, Major Benson, was an easily exasperated, hapless individual who looked like he had been passed over for promotion too many times. As each team got up on the stage and gave their predictable briefings, Major Benson sat off to one side of the stage taking notes for his post-briefing critique of their efforts. After four or five briefings he was beginning to exhibit symptoms of post-lunch-hour fatigue. His head started nodding and his notepad slipped out of his hand a few times. By the time we started our briefing he was pretty groggy and didn't pay much attention to the chuckles coming from the audience during our explanation of the relationship between Conte and the woman. When the lights dimmed and the picture of the woman's rear end flashed on the big screen, the audience began to howl. Major Benson bolted upright in his chair as though he'd had an overdose of electroshock therapy. I thought, *Uh-oh, he's going to be mad*, but he just sat there and stared at the screen. When our briefing concluded, the audience applauded, but Major Benson continued to sit there staring at the blank screen.

Toward the end of the summer I started becoming restless and dissatisfied, even though I had a "good job." While the work was not very challenging, it was a public service job and had the potential to lead to more rewarding possibilities. My social life was great; there were lots of attractive, fun loving and intelligent women at the school, and I lived in the most interesting and charming part of Washington. I even had a new 1966 Volvo that a desperate dealer sold to me for only $2,600 when I was looking for a replacement for my broken-down VW bug. What more could a young bachelor ask for? Yet I could not see myself living a comfortable middle class life in the suburbs and working nine to five in an office every day. Then I realized what I was missing: it was Linnea! I had thought about her often. I missed the glowing delight, loving warmth and sense of connection I felt being with her. I hadn't heard from her since I left Columbus. She was planning to go on a geological field expedition in Montana for the summer and I had no way to contact her. I wondered whether she thought about me or had forgotten about our few days together in Ohio and had moved on with her life. Even though I might be making a fool of myself, I had to write her a letter and tell her how much I loved her and the reasons why. After I wrote the letter and sent it to her home address in New York, I felt great. It was like an epiphany. Even if I never heard from her again, I at least wanted her to know how I felt about her.

During the final weeks of the intelligence school, the pace of field trips and high level briefings dramatically increased. There was little class work or research assignments, just bus tours and presentations by senior intelligence officers. It was during these lectures that Mort developed his technique of rolling up his weird ties while listening to long-winded speeches. He would take at least twenty minutes to meticulously roll his tie very tightly and precisely up toward his chin. When it was rolled up as tightly as possible, he would tuck it under his chin and hold it taut with his chin against his chest and give a goofy grin. Sometimes he would just hold it there waiting for more people to notice it and sometimes he would snap his head back and release the tie with a flourish of self-satisfaction. The tie would unravel down his chest and he would sit there beaming with pride at the accomplishment of his bizarre feat.

Our last briefing before graduation was a combination keynote speech and commencement address by Bromley Smith, the National Security advisor to President Johnson. This was the highest ranking official to speak to us. The secret auditorium was packed with faculty members and other officials, along with us students. Somehow Mort and I ended up sitting next to each other in the front row, directly in front of Mr. Smith. He started his talk with a few anecdotes of working with LBJ, then went on to describe the importance of giving a good briefing. As one of the top "briefers" in the country, he described how he would tailor the style of his briefing to suit the preferences of the President. The use of high-quality graphics was very important, along with concise main points. The President was a very busy person and didn't have time for long, detailed reports.

As Mr. Smith continued to elaborate on these points, I noticed that Mort was getting a little bored. I thought to myself, *I hope he doesn't start rolling up his tie while we are so close to Smith.* Then he started! I couldn't believe he was going to do it right in Smith's face. It would be impossible for Smith not to notice! For the first ten minutes of the roll-up he didn't seem to notice, but as Mort was about to tuck the rolled-up tie under his chin, Mr. Smith looked down at him and stopped speaking. I began to get embarrassed. Usually I would get a kick out of this kind of stunt, but Bromley Smith was a nice, refined gentleman who was offering us important and useful advice. I felt like jabbing Mort in the ribs or kicking him, but Smith was looking right at us. After what seemed like an eternity of mortifying silence, Smith regained his composure and continued. Just then, Mort tucked the tie under his chin and started his idiotic grin. Smith couldn't help but see him and became distracted. I thought to myself, *What must he be thinking?* Here is a guy who spends his days consulting with the president and attending cabinet meetings. He is taking time out from his busy schedule to share his wisdom and experience with a group of future intelligence analysts who have supposedly been investigated for deviant behavior, and now he sees a lunatic with his tie rolled up under his chin staring at him from the front row! Suddenly, Mort snapped up his chin and the tie unraveled. Smith stared at him in disbelief, shook his head back and forth violently as though he was trying to wake up from a nightmare, and attempted to continue his presentation. He was too stunned to regain the coherence and lucidity he had exhibited before Mort did his tie trick, but he made a valiant attempt to pass on the lessons he had learned as one of the President's chief advisors. I was sure we were in big trouble but, because Mort was in the front row, hardly anyone else in the audience had seen him. And because Bromley Smith probably thought he was hallucinating, we never heard a word from anyone in authority.

    The final week of intelligence school was the most fun. Instead of turning in papers and taking exams, we were given a choice of a four-day field trip to the Jackson Naval Air Station in Jacksonville, Florida, or the Norfolk Naval Base in Virginia. About thirty of us chose to go to Florida. We hopped on a small commercial flight with the hapless Major Benson as our "chaperone." Benson was definitely in over his head as he tried to keep us under control. For most of us the trip to Florida was another spring break at the beach. We started drinking as soon as we got on the plane and every time the plane stopped to pick up more passengers we ran into the airport bar for a quick drink. After some of us almost missed getting back on the plane, Major B, who was responsible for us arriving at our destination, stood up in the aisle. He had inadvertently left a large dinner napkin hanging from the belt of his uniform, and it looked like a miniature loincloth. In front of all the other passengers he ordered us to stay on the plane at the next stop, which we completely ignored. This mutinous disregard for his command evoked a dramatic increase in his blood pressure, causing the veins in his head and neck to become dangerously swollen. As he ran off the plane trying to round us up, with his paper loincloth flapping in the wind and his head looking like it was going to explode, the rest of the passengers on the plane stopped talking to each other and looked after him with various expressions of anxiety and sorrow.

When we arrived at the Naval Air Station we were treated like visiting officials from Washington. They gave us some nice rooms in the officer's quarters and passes to the officer's club, where we resumed our drinking and mild hell-raising. By the time the club closed at midnight, most of us were exhausted and drunk and returned to our rooms to collapse on our beds. My roommate, Tony, had spent the evening visiting with an old college buddy who was now a naval aviator stationed at the base. When the club closed I noticed he hadn't returned to the room and assumed that he went somewhere to continue his visit with his friend. About 4 AM I was jolted awake by the door smashing against the wall as Tony staggered over to his bed and passed out without taking his clothes or shoes off. The next morning we were scheduled for an important briefing with the commander of the intelligence unit at 0800 hours, so I decided to wake up at 0700 to make sure I had time to take a shower and have breakfast before the meeting. The previous evening

Major Benson, who was still recovering from the episode on the plane, explained to us that the naval intelligence group had gone to a lot of trouble to make our visit worthwhile and enjoyable. He begged us to be on time for the briefing at 0800 hours. Most of us felt that we had caused Major B enough pain and suffering, so we all agreed to help each other get up in time for the briefing.

When the alarm woke me up the next morning, I opened one eye and saw the corpse lying on the bed next to me. It was Tony, looking like an embalmed cadaver. It took about ten minutes to get him into the shower, which seemed to bring him back to life. He was suffering the typical symptoms of a hangover: headache, nausea and thirst. I remembered that the standard treatment was a Bloody Mary (tomato juice and vodka). There was no vodka available so I ran down to the dining room and got a large glass of tomato juice with ice, which I assumed was the next best thing to a Bloody Mary. Tony gulped down the juice as we ran over to the briefing room. We had to run a gauntlet of security checks from Marine guards who were much more serious than the ones in the intelligence school. We were the last ones in the room. As I looked around for a couple of empty seats, I caught Major Benson breathing a sigh of relief as he saw us sit down. I looked up at the clock: it was fifteen seconds before 0800 hours.

At exactly 0800 hours the Marine guard opened the door and snapped to attention. A middle-aged naval captain entered and walked up to the podium. He had the body language and weathered face of a man who probably had spent the last twenty years at sea and couldn't wait to get out of the confines of an office job and back on a ship. As he began his presentation, I glanced over at Tony and noticed he was even more pale and clammy-looking than when he first woke up. The Captain proceeded to give us a genuinely warm welcome in spite of his tough, grizzled appearance. He acted as though we were VIPs from Washington; apparently he didn't realize that we were just a bunch of low-level analysts-in-training. As he continued extolling how important we were to the national security of the country, I felt someone grab my arm. It was Tony. He leaned on me so hard he almost knocked me out of my chair. As he clutched on to me he whispered in a desperate tone that he was going to throw up! I whispered back, "Tony! You've got to hang on until the briefing is over, then you can go down the hall to the restroom." He put his head between his legs and mumbled that he didn't think he could make it. By now we were causing a commotion and Major B was frowning at me. I was starting to realize how horrible it would be if Tony threw up during this Top Secret briefing in front of the captain who thought so highly of us.

As the captain began revealing some of the more fascinating and ingenious methods of spying on the Soviet Navy, I felt a whoosh of air on my face and turned to Tony. He was no longer in his chair. I turned around to see him bolting for the door. It happened so fast that he caught the Marine off-guard as he burst through the door, which set off a deafening and bone-rattling alarm that caused everyone in the room to put their hands over their ears and jump out of their seats. Just as the two Marines grabbed him, Tony vomited bright red tomato juice onto their starched green fatigues. The Marines hauled him away and sent in fresh troops to secure the doors and turn off the alarm, which was giving everyone an excruciating headache. As we began to return to our seats and settle down I looked over at Major B, who was staring straight ahead in a state of catatonic disbelief. I looked up at the captain on the stage. He was shaking his head and chuckling. When the room quieted down the captain smiled and said, "I hope that young fellow had enough fun last night to make it worth puking on my Marines."

That afternoon there was nothing scheduled so most of us headed for the beach where I caught up with Tony, who was feeling pretty chipper. He said the Marines had been very nice to him. They took him into the bathroom to clean up, then gave him some Alka-Seltzer for his hangover. After a great time at the beach most of our group retired to the officers club to continue our merriment. Toward the end of the evening I found myself having a conversation with Joe Nelson, who was even more dissatisfied with the prospects of a career with the DIA than I was. He had an advanced degree in Chinese studies from a prestigious New Jersey university, spoke fluent Chinese and was quite bitter about the probability that he wouldn't be using any of his specialized skills and education as a DIA analyst. As we glanced around the room at our fellow classmates enjoying themselves, we both came to the realization that we were very different from the rest of the group. Most of them seemed content to have a good job with decent advancement possibilities and would probably make a career out of working for the government. Joe and I, on the other hand, were restless and looking for something more challenging and fulfilling.

The hub of all the DIA activity at Arlington Hall Station was the largest and ugliest building on the former college campus. It was a typical World War II temporary wooden structure with creaking wooden floors covered with generic linoleum tiles that were actually worn through in spots. Compared to the Navy buildings of the same era, it was a seedy dump. I entered the main door and showed my security badge to the guard and asked him where the Soviet station was and he pointed to a grimy, narrow hall. About halfway down the hall, I found the Soviet office and looked in the open door. The large, pale green room was divided into a half-dozen cubicles with gray metal desks, completely bare except for multiple coffee cup stains. Even though the room was well scrubbed, it reeked of coffee and cigarette smoke. The only person in the room was a lone secretary typing at her desk. As I entered, she greeted me with a perky smile and said, "You must be either Larry Wardwell or Brad Reilly." Just then Brad entered the room. The secretary gave us a warm welcome and explained that we would be taking over Dr. Hoffman's job and he would be down shortly to brief us. Brad and I were assigned to the Soviet section but had no idea what our exact jobs would be. We were intrigued that we would be doing something requiring a PhD, and at the same time we wondered why two of us would be required to do the job of one person.

Hoffman was a middle-aged, mild-mannered fellow who looked

like an over-educated high school history teacher: intelligent, competent and friendly. He was carrying a huge stack of documents and three-ring notebooks that he plunked down on the desk in front of us. He proceeded to tell us that he was leaving because he'd just completed his doctorate in Soviet studies and the Army War College had offered him a great teaching job he couldn't refuse. He went on to explain that he had been the Order of Battle analyst for the Soviet Navy and Air Force. The position would be divided into two separate jobs; Brad was assigned to be the Soviet Air Force analyst and I was assigned to the Soviet Navy. The work would require extra-high-level security clearances beyond Top Secret, which would take a few weeks to arrange. In the meantime we would be working in this room until we were cleared to enter the inner sanctum of the Soviet branch on the second floor. He gave us each a stack of manuals and documents to study and said that he would check with us every few days to give us more material and see how we were doing.

When he left the room Brad and I looked at each other, shrugged, and opened our books. My first book was a thick manual describing the responsibilities of the Order of Battle analyst. The goal was to find out how many and what kinds of ships the Soviets had and where they were. This was one of the oldest intelligence methods in the history of warfare! My next book described every Soviet ship and its capabilities. About halfway through the book I couldn't keep my eyes open any longer and decided to get up and walk around. I looked over at Brad. His face was buried in his book and he was snoring lightly. At first I was alarmed that his apparent lack of enthusiasm for the first day on the job would be noticed by our boss, but then I realized there was no one in the room except the secretary, who was totally oblivious to us. I gave Brad a discreet shake and he partially opened his glazed eyes. Brad, who had a master's degree in international relations from American University, looked up at me and said, "I don't think this Soviet airplane thing is going to work out. I didn't spend six years in college to count MiG-21s."

After eating a hospital-style lunch of slimy mashed potatoes, shriveled canned peas and weather-beaten meat loaf in the industrial-style cafeteria, we returned to our vacant room. The secretary never returned from her lunch break and we had the whole room to ourselves. After reading our manuals for another hour or so, the combination of the greasy lunch in my stomach and the stultifying literature in front of my eyes was making it very difficult to maintain the waking state of consciousness. The hot, stuffy room became more diffuse and distant as I began drifting into the sleep state. Then something shiny and colorful coming through the doorway caught my eye and snapped me back awake. It was a high-ranking naval officer, whose full dress uniform was plastered with gleaming medals and colorful ribbons. I instinctively jumped to my feet before I was fully awake and felt like the room was revolving in orbit around me. For a moment I thought the grinning captain approaching me was Henry Fonda. He extended his hand and said, "Welcome aboard, Larry." After spending four years in the lower levels of the military hierarchy I was taken aback by this informal and earnest gesture of friendliness from such a high-ranking officer. For the next twenty minutes Captain Gresham expressed his appreciation to Brad and me. He explained that as soon as our security clearances came through we would be joining his team upstairs. He offered to help us in any way he could and treated us like we were colleagues rather than low-level newcomers. Our spirits were lifted as we looked forward to joining the rest of the analysts upstairs.

Finding the letter from Linnea mixed in with the bills and junk mail made my spirits soar even higher. I hadn't heard from her for months and wondered if she ever got my letter. She was back at college after a great summer studying geology in Montana. She had missed me and was hoping she could visit me in Washington. I was thrilled to find out that she was still interested in me and I called her right away to plan a visit. When I met her at the airport a few weeks later she looked even more gorgeous that I had remembered. Her radiant golden hair, blue eyes and luscious figure made it hard to resist a passionate moment right there in the airport, but I wasn't sure how she felt about me. So we had a slightly more serious hug than just buddies and walked out to my car. It only took a few minutes to reestablish the sublime, blissful glow I had felt in her presence last spring. Linnea had never been to Washington so we spent the weekend touring the sights by day and walking around the streets of Georgetown during the warm early fall evenings.

Washington is not considered a romantic city with its grand but sterile monuments and bureaucratic population, but the combination of warm evening sunlight on the marble monuments and falling in love with the woman of my dreams created the most romantic weekend of my life. It was wonderful to spend so much time with someone who also felt out of sync with mainstream American society. We both realized there was more to life than the quest for middle class affluence. The hippie movement was constantly in the media and there were many aspects of the back-to-the-land and non-hierarchical lifestyle that appealed to us. Even though the glow of that weekend lasted for weeks after Linnea returned to college, I found myself even more dissatisfied and out of place working for the government.

Brad and I were going stir-crazy in our stuffy office. The manuals and spy reports we were given every couple of days took only a few hours to read. We spent most of our time talking, reading magazines and staring through the nicotine-stained windows at the inviting green lawn and the gold, yellow and red foliage of early fall. Finally one brilliant day I couldn't take it any longer and said to Brad, "To hell with it! Let's get out of here!" He gave me a bewildered look and said, "Where?" "I dunno," I replied, "Let's just walk around the campus and get some fresh air." The contrast between the stale, drab office and the fresh air, sunshine and delightful autumn foliage outside made us feel like we'd been released from prison. After wandering aimlessly along the well-landscaped walkways between the buildings for about an hour, Brad started to get a little nervous. He said, "What if they come into the office and find us missing?" "Okay," I said, "let's head back." As we came around the corner of one of the buildings we saw Captain Gresham walking very purposefully, directly toward us, about a hundred feet away. Brad panicked and gasped, "Oh shit! He sees us! What will we tell him if he asks us why we aren't in the office working?" I looked at Captain Gresham rapidly closing in on us and before I could think, my lower brainstem kicked in. I turned around and started running around the corner of the building with Brad right behind me. As we crouched down behind some bushes, Brad was furious! "What the hell did you do that for?" he demanded. I was dumbfounded! I had no explanation! Brad continued fuming: "I am sure he saw us run away from him. He's going to think we are morons or nuts and take our security clearances away or fire us."

We returned to our office expecting to find the angry captain waiting for us, but everything seemed normal so we picked up our documents and tried to read them as though nothing had happened. We were both so anxious that we couldn't sleep. I kept looking up at the generic government clock every few minutes in anticipation of someone storming into the room to fire or reprimand us, but nothing happened for the rest of the afternoon. After a few days we started to relax. Then one morning, shortly after we arrived at the office, an unfamiliar naval officer entered the room accompanied by a security guard and asked us to come with him. He took us down the hall, through a maze of security check points, into a small, windowless office and asked us to sit down. He gave us each a folder full of papers and asked us to read them and initial each page to indicate that we understood the material. After a couple of pages of dense government jargon, I realized we were being given our new super-secret security clearances. Brad and I looked at each other in stunned silence! We couldn't believe it.

With renewed optimism Brad and I happily followed our escort to our respective departments. I was met at the entrance to the naval intelligence unit by lieutenant commander Charlie Hauser, who welcomed me "aboard" and introduced me to everyone in the department. After meeting everyone Charlie said, "Let's go see Captain Gresham. I'm sure he would like to have a few words with you!" His words were like a punch in the stomach; in the excitement of getting my security clearance and actually starting my new job, I had forgotten all about the incident with Captain Gresham. Now was the day of reckoning; it was time to face the music! Captain Gresham got up from his desk, walked over to me, shook my hand and told me how glad he was to have me aboard. He acted as though he had never seen me run away from him. I was completely mystified; I was sure he saw me. Maybe he was too embarrassed to say anything, or maybe he just didn't care.

My new office was another large well-worn room, much like the one that Brad and I had used for the last few weeks. This one was about twice as big and filled with people, desks, file cabinets and cigarette smoke. Charlie ushered me over to my desk, which was pushed up against the wall on one side, while the front of the desk was up against Charlie's desk so that we faced each other. The few windows in the room were sealed shut with the glass painted light green (of course); apparently to keep spies from looking in. There were about ten other people in the room—eight analysts and two secretaries, who seemed to be constantly hammering away on their typewriters at full speed. This was 1966 and there were no computers or fax machines. All written communication was composed in longhand and given to the secretary to be typed.

Most of the men in the office were naval officers ranging in rank from lieutenant junior grade to commander. The only civilians in the room besides me were the secretaries Mary and Sally, Ed the submarine analyst, and Arnold, who had a Ph.D. in Soviet studies. Despite the fact that the boss was a naval commander and almost everyone was in the military, the atmosphere was very casual, with everyone on a first-name basis. My job was to help Charlie keep track of all the surface ships in the Soviet navy. He was overwhelmed with spy reports and other intelligence on the Soviet ships, and needed help in analyzing all the information to get the best picture of what they were up to. Charlie dumped a stack of reports on my desk. He handed me a copy of a huge computer printout that listed every known Soviet warship and where it was last seen. Most of the reports contained photos of ships taken by agents in various ports visited by the Soviet navy. Whenever I could identify a particular ship, I would update the date and location in the huge book.

After a few weeks of counting ships I started to get bored. At first the clandestine photos of the ships, crews and various ports inside the Iron Curtain were fascinating, but after awhile I noticed that a lot of the photos from different spies were exactly the same. I mentioned this to Charlie. He explained that one spy might be working for two or three different agencies, but the identity of spies was a closely held secret that was never shared between agencies. This meant that one agent could be working for the CIA, the DIA and Naval Intelligence, sending the same report to all three agencies and getting paid by all three for the same information.

The only break in my routine came about once a week, when I had to go to the Pentagon or the CIA headquarters in Langley, Virginia. The CIA building was unlike any government building I had ever seen. The entrance was like a modern airport terminal: bright, colorful and teeming with briefcase-carrying bureaucrats bustling down various color-coded corridors. It was quite a contrast to the dingy and shabby DIA facility. The only other interesting break in my routine was when I went to the corner of our office where the submarine analysts worked. Every few days there were hair-raising incidents involving U.S. or Soviet submarines. Whenever there was new information about Soviet ships from the subs I was invited to the secret alcove, where the sub analyst would whisper the latest tales of submarine close calls.

While the work was boring, the folks in the office were cordial and fun-loving. Every Friday after work the entire office, including Commander Burton (the section chief) and the secretaries, would go the officer's club for drinks and laughter. Except for Lt. Peyson and me, everyone in the office was in their 30s or 40s and married. They were good solid folks who had decided to make a career out of the Navy or DIA. Most of the naval officers had recently been in Vietnam. They called this "getting their ticket punched," which meant they had completed a tour of duty in combat, insuring an automatic promotion.

In 1966 the Vietnam War was considered by most of the career military men in the office to be a minor skirmish in the overall global struggle against Soviet and Chinese communism. Working at the DIA was just another three- or four-year assignment for them. Most of them seemed to like it except for Commander Burton, who was a true sailor and couldn't wait to go to sea again as a ship's captain. As nice as they were to me, I realized I didn't have anything in common with them and yearned for more stimulating, philosophical and reflective discussions.

The guys who lived in my townhouse in Georgetown were also very pleasant and easy to get along with. The topics of their conversations were mainly sports and business, which didn't do much for me, so I would often go down to the cellar and visit with Gerry. He was also alienated from the 1960s societal matrix and interested in the counterculture that was spreading around the country. We were both fascinated by the alternative hippie lifestyle of dropping out of the rat race and pursuing a less materialistic philosophy. Gerry's well-appointed cellar was filled with left-wing magazines and anti-establishment books. He was much more sophisticated than the other guys in the house. He wore expensive clothes, spoke French and had a strikingly beautiful and intelligent girlfriend. We talked about moving into a house of our own for more privacy and, especially for Gerry, a bedroom that was not next to the coal bin in the basement. A few weeks after our conversation, I received a call from Pete, my friend at Ohio State. He was tired of school and Columbus, and invited himself to visit me in Washington. The only place for him to stay was in the cellar with Gerry, who didn't seem to mind. After a couple of weeks in Washington, Pete decided not to go back to school. The three of us moved into our own townhouse a block away. It was a narrow, three-story hundred-year-old house and we each had our own private bedroom.

The new house, while more expensive, provided us with a substantial improvement in our quality of life: no more measuring of orange juice shares, counting eggs allotted to each person and using only authorized bathrooms. A few days after we moved in we threw a huge party, with each of us inviting all of our friends. The house was packed with revelers until the wee hours of the morning, something never allowed in the previous, highly regulated residence.

Life was good but not complete without Linnea. Her visit earlier in the fall was so wonderful that nothing compared to being with her. Finally, a week before Christmas, she came for another visit. This time we didn't do much; we hung around the house and went for walks. Just being together was so wonderful we had no need for entertainment or sightseeing. After our weekend of warm romance, laughter and conversations about our common interests, it was very difficult to say goodbye. When we woke up on Monday morning to go to the airport, I looked out the window and discovered that Washington had been paralyzed by two feet of snow, which granted us another 24 hours together. We were both overjoyed. We spent the day frolicking in the snowdrifts that rendered the streets of the nation's capital useless. After she left the next morning I was in such a state of euphoria that I didn't even mind counting ships at work. When I arrived home later that day the house felt cold and empty without her. I didn't know when I would see her again. She had gone to New York for the holidays with her family while I resumed my bachelor life with Gerry and Pete. There were lots of parties and holiday festivities to keep us busy, but nothing could take the place of being with Linnea.

After visiting with my family in Ohio for Christmas I returned to Washington. The New Year's holiday was coming up with more parties and events. Gerry and Pete were busy planning a big bash at the house. They were excited about all the other New Year's events going on around town, but all I could think of was Linnea. After spending only a few days with her my fun-and-games lifestyle seemed hollow and pointless. One gloomy, cold night I was having an exceptionally unsavory dinner alone in our sparsely furnished dining room when the phone rang. It was Linnea; she said she missed me and wanted to know if I would like to spend the New Year's holiday with her in New York! Needless to say, I was overjoyed.

When I pulled into the driveway of her parents' house I felt a twinge of apprehension. The house was an elegant, contemporary home in an exclusive area of Westchester. Her father was a successful, high-powered businessman. I began to wonder what they thought of their daughter getting mixed up with an oddball like me! The walkway to the house was bordered on both sides by reflecting pools. The front door was huge and hand-carved out of some exotic wood. I felt like I was entering a museum. I started to think that maybe I had made a mistake. These folks might be formal and stuffy; not a good mix for someone as off-the-wall as me.

Linnea opened the door and my heart swelled. The joy of seeing her again melted away my apprehensions. As long as I was with her I didn't care where I was! Her parents turned out to be down-to-earth, fun-loving folks. We had a lot of spirited conversations together over meals. Sometimes Linnea and I would just sit by the fire in the living room, basking in the amorous warmth of our attraction to each other. The rest of our time together was spent in the city, strolling in the East Village, absorbing the energy of the nascent counterculture that would soon propagate across the country. Even though we had a fabulous time going to plays, delightful restaurants and New Year's Eve in Times Square, the carefree, hippie lifestyle of the people in the Village seemed the most authentic and alluring aspect of the city.

8

TOP SECRET ACID HEADS

As I became more and more dissatisfied with my job at the DIA I began to look for other job possibilities. Most of the jobs in the classified ads were in business or in boring bureaucracies. I eventually found an opening for a publisher's representative to work with university professors on their new books. After a pleasant lunch with the recruiter he looked over my application and noticed that I had belonged to the Students for Liberal Action (SLA). He became very concerned and started grilling me about my involvement in the organization. The interview didn't actually turn ugly, but he never called me back. A few days later I was expressing my frustration about not finding a meaningful job to my housemate Gerry, when he suggested that I join the Georgetown Junior Chamber of Commerce (JC's). I was surprised, almost shocked, to learn that he had been a member for a few years. The organization consisted of young professionals who got together every few weeks at a restaurant, had guest speakers and did a lot of networking and community service. The fact that my liberal, anti-establishment friend was a member of the JC's shattered my image of the organization as a group of corpulent businessmen with swollen fingers adorned with fancy rings. I was also surprised to learn that most of the members were not businessmen but lawyers, architects and government workers, who were looking for connections and a chance to serve the community. One of the projects we did as a group was to take young black kids from the inner city to Georgetown University basketball games. The kids appreciated getting out of the grimy housing projects, even for a night, and loved the games.

Most of the guest speakers at the JC meetings gave rather dry presentations on the subject of business or government. One night, however, the guest was J. D. Kuch, the foremost advocate of LSD in the Washington, D.C. area. She gave a lecture on the expansion of consciousness and the ability of LSD to open one's awareness to levels of perception not experienced by most people. Her descriptions of "acid trips" that she had taken sounded like many of the mystical experiences I had read about in religion and philosophy classes. The audience was enthralled by her accounts of divine oneness with all of creation, enhanced sensory perception beyond description, sublime tranquility and waves of love for all of humanity. LSD was not a recreational chemical for her, but a tool for spiritual growth. These experiences were so far removed from the everyday routine of the average person that it was difficult for the audience to identify with what she was trying to put into words. For me, however, her tales of higher consciousness created a strong desire to have the mystical or transcendental experience she described. My increasing dissatisfaction with conventional living gave rise to a yearning for a more meaningful life. Her description of a "higher" state of consciousness seemed to offer some insights into a deeper reality.

The next day Lieutenant Bill Peyson and I had lunch together. Other than being the only young bachelors in the office, we didn't seem to have much in common. He was a typical clean-cut military officer and seemed quiet and reserved at the office. As we were walking over to the officer's club for lunch I decided to share my encounter with the LSD lady the night before, just to see what his reaction would be. After I finished telling him how excited I was about the possibilities of LSD he looked over his shoulder and said, in a matter-of-fact tone, that he and his friend Lieutenant Commander Walt Solinger were good friends with Timothy Leary. They went to his ashram/commune in Millbrook, New York every few weeks to take LSD trips. Timothy Leary was the world's leading proponent of LSD. He began experimenting with the drug as a psychology professor at Harvard in the early 1960s and was eventually fired for actively promoting the use of LSD. He inspired thousands of young people with his slogan, "turn on, tune in, drop out." Naturally, this activity was not compatible with being a professor at one of the leading educational establishments in the country and he was dismissed.

When Bill finished telling me his story my body became numb, as though I was given a massive shot of Novocaine . I felt my jaw slacken and thought to myself, *How could this be?* Here was a straight-arrow military officer in the middle of top secret activities "dropping acid" every other weekend with his former aircraft commander. Bill went on to explain that he and Walt had become interested in Eastern philosophy while stationed in Asia and that their LSD experiences were similar to those described in the Bhagavad Gita and other Vedic and Buddhist texts. He then asked me if I was interested in going to Millbrook with them for an LSD trip. Without hesitation I said yes. He arranged a meeting with Walt to discuss bringing me along on their next trip to Millbrook.

Walt's apartment was not what you would expect for a naval aviator. It was more like a Buddhist temple, sparsely decorated with oriental furniture and wall hangings. In the center of the living room was a small altar covered in bright cloth on which there were numerous natural objects like sea shells and stones. Like Bill, Walt was tall and lean, but not as quiet and reserved. He was about ten years older than Bill and me and, although he had been a pilot for over ten years, the Navy had sent him to numerous post-graduate programs at a variety of universities. Walt was also very articulate and sophisticated. He could just as easily discuss airplanes with hardcore pilots as he could Eastern philosophy with Timothy Leary and Allen Ginsberg.

After we discussed the reasons why they thought LSD was a useful tool for individual spiritual growth, Walt asked me if I had read the Bhagavad Gita. I had read parts of it in college religion courses, but hadn't remembered much about it. He pointed out that the central message of the text is that underlying all the diversity, conflict and incoherence in the world is a transcendental field of consciousness. The experience of this can be transformational and give one a completely new perspective on life. This state of bliss, or *samadhi*, has been written about and experienced by mystics for centuries. Taking LSD can give one a momentary glimpse of this state. Walt, Bill, Tim Leary and many others felt that by taking LSD one could be "turned on" to a higher, more enlightened and enjoyable state of life, one that was "tuned in" to the unity of all life and love of all mankind. When someone had this experience of a more profound reality they could "drop out" of the material rat-race of mainstream society and find true bliss living an alternative lifestyle more in harmony with nature.

As we pulled into the entrance to the estate in Millbrook it looked like most rural properties of the wealthy. There was a gated entrance opening onto a long driveway up to the main house. The grounds seemed mildly neglected and the grass was longer than you would expect, but everything else seemed normal. When we approached the predictably large, white, Victorian manor house I realized this was no ordinary estate! Almost the entire front of the building was painted with a huge face of Buddha. We drove around to the back of the house and entered the large, commercial-sized kitchen. Walt and Bill introduced me to three women in their twenties and thirties who greeted them like old friends. We wandered in and out of various rooms in the house, saying hi to several people who knew Bill and Walt. Everyone we met had taken LSD and was in various stages of processing the experience. Although the LSD "trip" was primarily an inward journey, they all seemed genuinely humbled by the experience. It was as if they had been to a very far away and magical place for a long time and were adjusting to the everyday mundane reality of daily life on planet Earth. This was easier for some people than for others. The atmosphere of the house was relaxed and casual, even when we walked into someone's living space. Most of the rooms were decorated with Asian art and psychedelic posters. In some ways the house seemed like a typical pad rented by a bunch of college kids, however it had a pleasant, minimal orderliness and cleanliness that reflected a more mature group of people.

After touring the house we walked over to a small magical stone building which had originally served as a private bowling alley for the owners of the estate. It was now converted to a sort of shrine for taking LSD. After years of experimenting with it, Tim and his colleagues had discovered that a beautiful physical environment enhanced the LSD experience. The hardwood floors of the building were covered with exquisite oriental rugs and lots of comfortable pillows for lounging around. The overall atmosphere was serene and meditative.

Bill and I made ourselves comfortable on the cushions while Walt went over to the main house to get the LSD. Although I was not excited or anxious about embarking on this new adventure, I was definitely looking forward to experiencing something that could not be adequately described by those who had had the experience. A few minutes later, Walt came waltzing into the room with a tray full of snacks, fruit juice and the LSD. He looked as if he had just been visited by Santa Claus! We each took a small tablet and grinned at each other while waiting for the acid to take effect. After about fifteen minutes I didn't feel any different so I looked over at Walt and Bill, who were both sitting in the lotus position with their eyes closed and quietly chuckling to themselves. I wondered what was so funny. Suddenly I knew, and I broke into a fifty-year laugh! This was what it was all about! The entire universe was one big cosmic joke! Bubbling, humorous bliss was the essence of creation. This joyful, divine, silent chuckle was the underlying reality beyond all worries, anxiety, fear, pain, ego and intellect. What an overwhelming relief to be completely free of all the ridiculous, petty concerns of human life. It all seemed so laughable! Every permutation that arose from this infinite sea of holy humor was a burst of brilliant color.

After a century of sublime, colorful and hilarious rapture, I began to hear the most extraordinary music I had ever heard. It was ancient sitar music from India; every note sprang up from this underlying field of pure, unbounded divinity in a tingling sparkle of luminous color. The music continued like this year after year, until I got the urge to open my eyes. On the floor in front of me was a tray of marvelous food: perfectly ripe fruit that created an ecstatic explosion of unbelievable flavor with every bite and homemade hot bread slathered with heavenly honey and pure, fresh butter. The three of us just sat there eating and quietly laughing for eternity. After we finished our repast, Bill suggested we go for a walk. When he opened the door I could hardly believe my eyes; the slightly seedy estate had been transformed into a magnificent paradise with every living object radiating a glorious celestial glow. The colors and light were almost too much to bear. Every step brought new waves of delight as we walked around the grounds. When we went back into the house and engaged the other folks in conversation, I felt humbled and honored to talk to another human; just being alive was such a gift that nothing else was necessary for complete fulfillment.

The next morning was a "return-to-Earth" experience. I lay there in my sleeping bag on the floor of the converted bowling alley where we had started our LSD voyage and spent a few hours reflecting on the overwhelming experience of the previous day. I knew I had gone somewhere else and was now back in the real world. Or was the other place the real world? Although I had returned from the celestial realm, I felt transformed by going there. While my environment was no longer sparkling in celestial light, I still felt a humble joy in just being alive and a profound sense of reverence for the natural world around me. The ineffable experience of the mystics that I had been reading about now seemed comprehensible and attainable. A few hours' tour of this plane of reality was enough to whet my appetite to explore it further.

Tim Leary lived on the second floor of the main house in a suite of rooms that included a large hall filled with colorful pillows and cushions instead of furniture. He was in his combination academic and psychedelic office, unpacking from his trip to New York, when we dropped in to say hello. He greeted Bill and Walt with a big hug and was delighted to hear that I had just taken my first LSD trip. This was an important rite of passage to Tim, who felt it was his mission to turn the world on to "acid" in order to spread love and harmony to all mankind and to rid the world of war and hatred. Tim was lighthearted and whimsical with a twinkle in his eye, yet he was very serious about his goal of establishing a "higher level of consciousness" on this planet. We spent most of the morning visiting with him in the large hall filled with colorful pillows. He was very excited about the many guests from around the world who had come to Millbrook to learn more about this new lifestyle and its potential for changing the world. That evening he was having a large group of Indian dancers perform in the hall while everyone was high on LSD. These events were more than just an opportunity to get stoned and have a good time. The harmony, rapture and universal love enjoyed by the group was considered a spiritual experience and LSD was a religious sacrament.

Before leaving that afternoon, the three of us wandered around the estate, visiting with most of the people who were living there. There was a surprising variety of personalities and different approaches to spiritual development. Next to the main house there was an ashram with about twenty people living together. We met the leader of the group who seemed like a regular guy, but for some reason he had a certain spiritual authority that inspired the others in the house to follow him. They had a much more regimented and monastic lifestyle than the folks living in the main house, who were more casual and spontaneous. In front of the main house, in the middle of a meadow, was a small one-room house made of stone. Tim's ex-wife lived there alone and was on a more individual quest. She was fasting and spending most of her time in solitary contemplation, and, although she was happy to see us, she was obviously in a silent mode so we left after fifteen minutes and decided it was time to drive back to Washington.

When I arrived at work the next morning Bill was at his desk, discussing the latest sports events of the weekend with a couple of other folks in the office. I thought, *Here was a guy who has spent the last year taking LSD with Tim Leary, discussing philosophy with Allen Ginsberg and hanging out at the most famous hippie commune in the country. Now he was perfectly comfortable talking sports with his fellow naval officers in an environment that must be considered the antithesis of "turning on, tuning in and dropping out."* Returning to the lame, green, stuffy, smoke-filled room and my coffee-stained desk stacked with tedious reports and photos of pathetic Soviet ships and sailors wasn't so easy for me. I longed to be back at the bucolic commune in Millbrook. As I sat at my desk looking around the room at all the inorganic metal file cabinets, banged-up desks and creaky old chairs, I kept asking myself, *What am I doing here?* Something had to change! While the job was not intolerable, and I didn't feel like quitting and becoming a hippie, I was definitely more discontented with my job after my powerful experience over the weekend.

Later that evening I had a chance to tell Gerry about my LSD experience. He seemed genuinely awed by the spiritual nature of the experience but, since he didn't drink, smoke or take drugs, he decided it was not for him. However, he had just met some great people who were VISTA volunteers, a government program similar to the Peace Corps serving inner-city, disadvantaged youth. They were very enthusiastic about LSD and were trying to get him to take it. After hearing my glowing report on taking LSD at Millbrook, he thought it would be a good idea to invite the VISTA volunteers to dinner. Nan and Mel certainly didn't look like government employees. They had a distinctively disheveled and scruffy appearance about them: not quite far out hippies, but close to it. Over a simple dinner of pasta and cheap wine they explained that psychedelic drugs had opened their minds to the wonders of the natural world and to the unity and interdependence of all humanity. Mel had a master's degree in psychology and Nan had a bachelor's degree, but they didn't want to be part of mainstream society. Rather than drop out and become hippies, they decided to use their talents helping out black kids from the housing projects in Washington. It was delightful to share experiences and mutual alienation with Mel and Nan. When the dinner was over, they invited me to visit them and help out with some of their projects.

Mel lived in an old neglected house in a rough part of town near Capitol Hill with two other VISTA volunteers, Harry and Bernie, while

Nan lived a few blocks away in a decent townhouse with a couple of other women who had regular jobs. The inside of Mel's house was even more neglected than the outside. The interior decorating reflected an above-average use of mind-altering drugs with colorful posters, banners and psychedelic prints lit up by black lights on the walls. In lieu of conventional furniture there were lots of well-used mattresses scattered around the living room. The kitchen reflected a diet heavily fortified with recreational foods and beverages. Mel, Harry and Bernie were well educated, cosmopolitan and more interested in humanitarian activities and self-discovery than careers and material comforts. VISTA volunteers were given a subsistence stipend to keep them from starving, so the three of them pooled their meager resources to rent the house and buy food to eat. They had an old beater car left over from college that was used only when they could afford gas. One of their projects was to take young seven- to ten-year-old kids on field trips to parks and sporting events. Nan and Mel asked me if I would like to help by taking groups of kids to the park.

Although I had driven through some of the roughest parts of Washington I had never ventured out of my car and I was always glad to find my way back to the more genteel neighborhoods of the city. Mel had given me directions to an apartment building in the middle of one of the most run-down housing projects. The plan was for each of us with a vehicle to pick up a bunch of kids and take them to a group picnic at a nice park. I was not prepared for the level of decay and sadness that greeted me when I entered the housing complex. It was incomprehensible that people could be living in these appalling conditions in the capital of the wealthiest country in the world. I didn't sense any danger as I wandered around trying to find the apartment where the kids had gathered to be picked up. Maybe I was clueless, or it was before the drug epidemic had started. Also, the place seemed abandoned and I didn't see too many people to be afraid of. The smell of old urine in the halls was the most difficult part. It was unrelenting; every derelict stairwell and beat-up hallway emitted such a strong stench that I felt like running outside and gasping for fresh air.

I felt a little awkward when I knocked on what I hoped was the right door. It was opened by a pleasant but worn-out looking mom and I realized I was in the right place. She was happy to see me and the kids were raring to go. They weren't shy at all. They were ready to goof around, which was my forté. The best part was driving to the park and letting the kids help me drive as I pretended to be lost. We drove around in circles in a parking lot until we were all dizzy and howling with side-splitting laughter. I was delighted to be of service to these kids from broken families who rarely got this much undivided attention.

My LSD trip with Bill and Walt and meeting Nan and Mel opened up a new world that I had been longing for but had not found since I had been in Washington. We were all seeking spiritual growth and exploring new frontiers of the mind with LSD and marijuana. In one sense we were part of the counterculture, but we all still had jobs and felt a sense of responsibility to help change the values of society without completely dropping out. When not working, I would meet new friends, either through Bill and Walt or Nan and Mel, who shared my frame of reference and disaffection with conventional culture. It was new, exciting and fulfilling except for one thing: Linnea wasn't with me. I hadn't seen her for months and wasn't sure how she felt about me. She was going to graduate in a month and had not decided what she was going to do. She was either going to study geology in Norway or work at the Smithsonian Museum. If she went to Norway I probably wouldn't see her again, but if she came to Washington it would be a dream come true.

It is difficult to have a government job during April and May in Washington. The parks and monuments are exploding with blossoming trees, shrubs, flowers and weeds. The seductive fragrances and dazzling colors of so many gorgeous plants seem to create a primal magnetic field that repels one from the gray, lifeless office buildings of the U.S. government. Even the weather conspires to keep people outside. The bitter cold of the winter is gone and the muggy heat of the summer is still a month away. On one of these glorious days designed to turn even the most ardent bureaucrat into a truant, I had just forced myself into the musty-smelling DIA building and was commiserating with one of my classmates from the intelligence school about how hard it was to come to work on such a beautiful day, when she told me about another job opportunity. There were a few job openings in the Department of Intelligence Collections at the Pentagon. She was also bored with her job and had been looking for something more interesting. Rather than analyzing intelligence information, the collections department was responsible for "collecting" intelligence. This involved everything from developing an overall strategy for spying on a particular country to creating a plan to gather specific information.

The collections department wasn't actually in the Pentagon, but was in a small, four story office building next to it. As I walked up the austere cement stairwell to the second floor for my interview I kept thinking that, even though I am in another crummy old building, the job couldn't possibly be as boring as my present position as official ship counter for the Navy. I was greeted by Rhonda and Dave, a couple of classmates from the intelligence school, who took me around and introduced me to everyone. The department was set up similarly to my office at the DIA. There was one large room with about ten individual desks where most of the people worked, and a warren of smaller rooms occupied by senior members of the group.

Rhonda and Dave occupied a couple of desks in a small alcove off the main hallway; they asked me to sit down at one of the desks for a discussion about the available position. I had been expecting an interview with a supervisor, but apparently there was no one officially in charge. They explained that the folks in the large room were working on overall collection efforts and the men in the private rooms were involved in individual projects. It was their job, and mine, if I wanted it, to assist them in a variety of projects concerning overall policy and planning. The men in the private offices were old hands in the intelligence business and had been promoted over the years to colonel or the equivalent civilian rank. Rhonda and Dave liked working for these guys but there

wasn't a lot of work to do, so they spent a lot of time reading old documents and either filing them or throwing them away. Sometimes, when
there were no documents to read, they read books and magazines to
while away the time.

I looked at some of the documents they were reading. The material seemed more interesting than counting ships. The boredom from
having nothing to do seemed more appealing than the boredom from
looking at the same old reports and photos of ships. To get the job, all I
had to do was to fill out some forms, have my boss sign them and I was
on my way. There was one section of the form where I had to explain
why I wanted to transfer to the new job. I wrote that my old job was tedious and I wanted to do something more interesting. When I took the
form into Captain Gresham's office to have him sign it, he read the part
where I said the job was tedious and boring and he looked genuinely
crestfallen. He apologized to me for not realizing I was unhappy with
my job, then asked me if I would consider rewriting that section of the
form because it would make him look bad in his next evaluation. I felt
so sorry for him that I didn't hesitate; I changed my reason for leaving
to a burning interest in intelligence collection policy.

Colonel Beech had been in the Air Force for over twenty-five years.
During World War II he had worked with the French underground on
various missions against the Nazi occupation. For some reason he felt
comfortable telling me about some of the more harrowing and suicidal
missions on which he'd had to send his men, knowing they would never
survive. He didn't seem to mind being assigned to an uneventful desk
job in an obscure cubicle at the Pentagon. Perhaps he even felt he deserved a soft assignment in his final days before retiring. After I had
been hanging around the office for about a week without much to do he
called me into his office again. Although I enjoyed listening to his stories, I was hoping that this time he would have something a little more
challenging for me to do. As I entered his office he asked me to close the
door behind me. *Aha,* I thought to myself, *he has something confidential*

and exciting for me to do! He asked me to sit down, another clue to the
gravity of the mission. "Larry," he said in a slightly uncomfortable tone,
"I don't know exactly how to say this, but I need a lot of photocopying
done. I don't mind doing it myself, but it just wouldn't look right for a
colonel to be standing at the copy machine for extended periods of time
making lots of copies." I felt a little deflated and disappointed when he
asked me to do his copying, but I understood his dilemma and was more
than willing to help him out.

My next assignment came from Bob Watson, another old spy-war-
rior who was also close to retirement. He was more gruff and tough than
Colonel Beech and constantly reminded me that to be a good spy you
had to like playing cops and robbers. For some inexplicable reason it was
his job to articulate the rationale for the United States' intelligence efforts against communist China (the "Chi-Coms"). The project involved
writing a large tome describing the recent history of the communist
takeover in China and the nature of the threat this posed to American
interests. It was one of the documents the Defense Department used
to justify its various intelligence activities against China when asking
Congress for funding. Every year the funding request had to be rewrit-
ten and updated before being presented to Congress. Bob was busy with
another project and asked me to rewrite the paper. This sounded like a
good opportunity to utilize my political science education and would be
a welcome break from my photocopying assignment. When I started
reading the document on China I couldn't contain my laughter! I read
it to Rhonda and Dave and we all cracked up. It was hard to believe that
something as simplistic and deficient in intellectual rigor could be the
policy of the United States. Over the next few days I edited out all the
diatribes and inflammatory rhetoric about the communist menace and
tried to present what I thought was a more cogent and realistic assess-
ment of the goals of the Chinese regime.

When I finished, the paper read more like a college level research
project than a junior high school history lesson. I proudly presented the
new draft to Bob with the hope that he would have some more lame

documents for me to rewrite. About two hours later he called me into his office, where he was sitting with a baffled expression on his face. "You changed the whole thing around!" he exclaimed. "This not how China should be characterized; this is not what people want to read!" I argued that my version was more accurate and the old paper was full of outdated propaganda. He looked at me and said, "That's not the point—we have a serious enemy. We need money for our intelligence programs and this paper serves to convince the budget people to give us the funds." Even though he wasn't mad I figured it was futile to argue with him, so I left his office with my hopes dashed for any more writing and analysis jobs.

Later that evening, while I was recounting to Gerry how I had come to another dead end in my career at the DIA, the phone rang. It was Linnea. She had decided to take the job at the Smithsonian for the summer! I could hardly believe it. After a year of seeing each other for only a few days at a time, we could be together for the whole summer. When she arrived a few weeks later she moved into a small apartment a couple of blocks away. Having her so close was like being in paradise. Even though we were both working full time we were able to spend a lot of time together in the evenings, on weekends and during long, romantic picnics on our lunch hours. Spending so much time together seemed to strengthen our relationship. Every moment was pure delight. As the summer wore on we also grew closer to our new circle of counterculture friends: Gerry, Nan, Mel, Bill and Walt. While we were all urban dwellers, most of our weekends were spent at the ocean or hiking in the countryside. All of us came to the realization that working for the government in Washington was not the way to change the world or find personal fulfillment. Even Mel and Nan, who as VISTA volunteers were having a direct, immediate and positive influence on the lives of inner-city kids, were having doubts about what they were doing and talked about "dropping out" and moving to California. Walt and Bill were both planning on leaving the Navy and dropping out. Walt, who was actually being transferred by the Navy to U.C. Berkeley to finish his

Ph.D. in political science, planned to join Tim Leary in California.

Working for the government by day and living the life of an anti-establishment hippie by night was like living in two separate worlds. Occasionally the two worlds would overlap when I would bring some left wing or "acid-head psychedelic" magazines to the office to read during times when there was nothing else to do, which were becoming more frequent. One day I brought a copy of *Ramparts*, an extremely radical and at times obscene magazine, to the office to share with my friends. We were howling over the lead story, which accused President Johnson of molesting President Kennedy's body during the plane ride from Dallas. The story, complete with illustrations, was so sick and outrageously offensive to President Johnson that we couldn't contain our merriment. It was one of those moments of such uncontrollable laughter that I was just about to roll around on the floor when Colonel Beech came out of his office to see what the commotion was all about. He didn't seem annoyed, just curious as to what was so funny so, with a twinge of embarrassment, I showed him the article. I didn't really expect him to go into a state of uncontrollable guffaws, so when a distinct look of revulsion came over his face I wasn't too surprised. He handed the magazine back to me, shook his head like a disappointed parent and retired to his office without saying a word.

In some ways this event was a metaphor for the gap between the generations and cultures that were separating from each other with increasing velocity. On one side was an established, unquestioning society compliant with the demands of the traditional institutions of religion, employment, education and the assumptions that the latest appliances, clothes and cars were mandatory necessities for happiness. On the other side was a young, irreverent, impatient, self-righteous mass movement unwilling to accept the dogma promulgated by the older generation. The Vietnam War was the catalyst for this intense shredding of the fabric of American values. For those living in the alternative universe of the counterculture, Lyndon Johnson, Robert McNamara and the military hierarchy were demons who were sowing death and destruction on the innocent peasants of Vietnam, while the older members of the World War II generation saw American ideals threatened and trampled upon by an unruly, drug addled mob of ungrateful misfits.

Obviously neither one of these world views was entirely accurate. This became very apparent to me as the war and the protests began to escalate in 1967. Even deep within the bowels of the Pentagon there was spirited debate about the threat posed by the Vietnamese to the national security of the United States. Although most younger people like me who worked for the DIA thought the war was a mistake, and probably most of the older generation who had witnessed World War II believed in the domino theory, there was always a mutual respect for those who disagreed with each other. One of the high-level supervisors in our department was an active supporter of Bobby Kennedy (who was running for president) and was constantly involved in good-natured, humorous debates with the tough old colonels. Even though the atmosphere was cordial and I could express my alternative views freely, I knew my days at the DIA were numbered. My "other life" of carefree cavorting in the world of natural beauty with my wonderful woman Linnea and our like-minded friends was so much more charming and fulfilling that I just had to find the right time to quit.

9

IT HAPPENED ONE NIGHT!

Linnea and I spent most of our time together outside. As soon as I got home from work I would shed my suit and tie, slip into an old pair of Levi's and sandals, join Linnea and head for a park or spend the warm summer evenings exploring the streets of Georgetown. The simple pleasure of walking and talking with her was a powerful and enlivening antidote to the deadening eight hours spent every day in the office. It didn't take long for me to realize that this was the woman I wanted to marry. Everything about her was great. Spending the summer with her was beyond my wildest fantasies. Near the end of the summer we took a trip to Cape Cod; after that week I realized how complete my life had become with her as my partner. Her job would be ending in a few weeks and she wasn't sure what she wanted to do after that. We were having such a wonderful time together that I didn't want to disrupt our lighthearted and joyful lifestyle by pressuring her to stay in Washington. I certainly didn't want to spoil anything by asking her to marry me. Then one warm candle-lit night it just happened! We were sitting in my apartment after dinner. We just looked at each other and said, "Let's get married!" I felt like the luckiest dog on the planet. I was overwhelmed that this luscious, attractive woman who was so warm-hearted and intelligent would actually consider marrying a crackpot like me. We decided to get married the next month, in the back yard of the townhouse I shared with Gerry and Pete. Having rejected all the trappings of conventional weddings, it was remarkably easy and simple to arrange the wedding. Just a few friends and immediate family were invited. We didn't even buy wedding rings or rent costumes. We had to accept only one traditional aspect of the wedding—the outdated law that weddings in D.C. had to be performed by a licensed clergy member. We found a sympathetic minister in Georgetown who agreed to marry us in the back yard.

After the wedding we spent a week camping by a lake in the Adirondacks. When we returned to our small basement apartment on Capitol Hill we both realized that city life was not for us. The deep silence and fresh air of the forest offered us a serenity and sublime pleasure that could not be matched by living in Washington, so we decided to quit our jobs in the spring and take off on a camping trip across the country. Linnea was now working at the U.S. Geological Survey. It was a boring office job, but we still managed to meet every day for a picnic lunch at one of monuments.

Shortly after I returned to work from our camping trip Rhonda, Dave and I received notice that our jobs were being terminated. This was not much of a surprise given the fact that there had been hardly anything for us to do. This meant we could shop around in the DIA for another job. I soon found out about an opening in a joint CIA-DIA operation that involved examining captured or stolen Soviet weapons and military-related equipment. The top prize was a MiG-21 jet fighter, for which a huge pile of money had been offered to a defector. In addition to big-ticket items like planes and tanks, practically anything produced by the Soviet bloc countries and the Chinese, including consumer goods, provided valuable information. It seemed like the most interesting job available so I decided to give it a shot. The project was located in a new office building in Rosslyn, a rapidly growing section of Arlington, Virginia, just across Key Bridge from Georgetown. (Somehow the CIA always managed to have newer and more comfortable facilities than the DIA.) There were just a couple of DIA people assigned to the project and they needed one more to take the place of someone who had left. The senior DIA analyst was a pleasant young guy named George. Rod, the other analyst, was a recent college graduate like me who had only been there a year. I was able to ask Rod confidentially how he liked working there and he said he was pretty happy. He had just returned from an operation overseas that was a lot of fun, although most of the time the job was boring. Both George and Rod liked me, so I took the job.

Barry was a tall, gaunt and severe-looking man in his 40s. As a disciple of Swami Premananda of the Church of the Lotus Blossom in Washington, he would often give one of the Sunday morning lectures based on the teachings of Swami Paramahansa Yogananda, his guru. Swami Yogananda was the author of the amazing book, *Autobiography of a Yogi*, and the founder of the Self Realization Fellowship. Yogananda had come to the West to teach Kriya yoga during the 1940s and 1950s and he had become very popular with people who were seeking the spiritual knowledge and experiences not available from the established religious institutions of the day. Walt and Bill had been attending services for a while and invited Linnea and me to go with them one Sunday.

The church was surprisingly western-looking for a Hindu shrine. It looked like a generic Christian church from the outside except for a large lotus blossom on the front entrance. The inside was set up like a basic American church with rows of pews and a small podium at the front for the speaker. Even the attendees looked like the average Sunday morning congregation; the women wore dresses and high heels and the men wore suits and ties. The similarities ended when Barry started his lecture. He described his search for enlightenment at the feet of Swami Premananda. After years of practice and study he had become dissatisfied with his progress toward enlightenment or self-realization. When he heard about the "altered states of consciousness" experienced by people who had taken LSD, he was struck by the similarities between their experiences and the mystical experiences reported in the ancient yogic scriptures. He went on to explain that the goal of yoga was to live in this state of oneness and tranquility at all times and that this required years of practice and study. The overwhelming joy and instant connection with a source of eternal peace of mind that he and many others had experienced with LSD seemed like a shortcut to attaining the state of nirvana sought after by the practitioners of yoga. Barry's experiences with LSD were so profound that he felt obliged to tell the congregation at the Church of the Lotus Blossom about them and encouraged them all to try LSD. This didn't sit too well with the Swami. He was skeptical that a few wonderful drug experiences could bring about the transformation required to create a permanent state of enlightenment and declared that the use of drugs was incompatible with the practice of yoga. Eventually Barry could not accept this and decided to leave the church, quit his government job and travel to California with his partner Maria in their new Volkswagen camper.

Although Walt, Bill, Linnea and I had liked the atmosphere in the church and the teachings offered by the Swami, we thought he was a little too "uptight" for not allowing Barry to turn the whole congregation on to acid. Being ignorant of the process of meditation and other yogic practices designed to permanently establish a more enlightened state of consciousness, we couldn't understand why the Swami was against the use of psychedelic drugs as a tool for gaining enlightenment. By the late '60s a significant number of people who used these drugs were having profound mystical experiences. This phenomenon led to a unique confluence of events when these relatively young seekers came into contact with various well-established yoga movements. While a number of these groups had been around since the late 1800s, most of them had not expanded into the mainstream of Western culture.

The Theosophical Society, which started in England around the 1890s, consisted mostly of intellectuals and free thinkers of the leisure class who were fascinated with Eastern mysticism and philosophy. While their interests were very eclectic and wide-ranging, groups like the Self Realization Fellowship followed the specific teachings of Yogananda and accepted him as their master or teacher. These devotees and seekers of enlightenment were not alienated bohemians or flaky wannabes living on the fringes of society. They were bankers, lawyers and businessmen who led normal lives except for the fact that they were pursuing a path of spiritual development not available to them from the established churches of that time. One look at the photos in Yogananda's book would clearly demonstrate that his followers were definitely not hippies! There is even one photo of Yogananda with President Herbert Hoover at the White House.

The nexus between these established spiritual organizations of the older generation and the impetuous, flourishing, anarchic mass of disaffected youth searching for a new world view was the experience of psychedelic drugs. For many, LSD and other powerful psychedelics ripped away all the conventional boundaries of time, space and social structures. The traditional dogma of the prevailing religious and social institutions provided an inadequate frame of reference for these experiences. This missing paradigm led Richard Alpert, a Harvard psychology professor and LSD colleague of Tim Leary's, to look for answers in the ancient spiritual systems of the East. These philosophies offered a world view that was much more compatible with the altered states of consciousness induced by LSD than the paradigm offered by conventional academic research and theories of the mind. Alpert left Harvard and journeyed to India with the hope of finding a teacher who would reveal to him the ancient knowledge of the ultimate reality of life that he had glimpsed during his experiments with LSD. When Alpert found his teacher in a remote part of India he was stunned to find out the guru knew intimate details of his life. As a result he decided to stay in India, change his name to Baba Ram Dass and study at the feet of his master. When he eventually returned to the U.S. he wrote the bestselling book, *Be Here Now*, which became a spiritual guidebook for thousands of seekers.

Maharishi Mahesh Yogi had been traveling the world teaching Transcendental Meditation since 1958. By the mid-1960s he had set up numerous centers of the Spiritual Regeneration Movement in major cities across Europe. Most of his followers in the U.S. were in southern California, where he was hosted by Helena "Mother" Olson, one of his most enthusiastic devotees. The Olson's house became the center of meditation activities in southern California and home to Maharishi. Mother Olson's delightful book, *Maharishi at 433*, recounts with warm humor what it was like living in the Los Angeles suburbs with a yogi in the house. By the late 1960s the seemingly disparate streams of culture represented by the older, established spiritual movement formed by the followers of Maharishi and the brash, younger generation of truth seekers collided on college campuses across the country. Thousands of students started learning Transcendental Meditation (TM) and Maharishi became an international celebrity, appearing on television shows and at large public gatherings. When the Beatles discovered him in 1967 it generated a huge wave of publicity, and Maharishi was on the cover of magazines such as *Time* and *Life*.

Even Barry, who after many years of meditation, had decided that LSD was the most effective way to gain enlightenment, was intrigued by what Maharishi had to say. He invited us all to his apartment one night to see Maharishi on TV. What struck me most about Maharishi was his quick wit and sense of humor. He didn't seem to take himself seriously and his message evoked a celebratory approach to life, even though he was a monk who had spent many years meditating in seclusion in the Himalayas. Barry, however, was not very impressed with Maharishi and thought he was too jocular and not particularly serious about the very important work of becoming enlightened. At one point he even suggested that Maharishi was a spy for the CIA who was discouraging young people from taking drugs.

10

POLISH SAUSAGE and HUNGARIAN LIGHT BULBS

The first day at my new job with the CIA was much like the first day at my other jobs with the DIA: reading manuals and reports. At least the office was new and had large glass windows overlooking the Potomac River and Georgetown. I even had my own cubicle, which consisted of a desk at the entrance of two six-foot-high rows of file cabinets with about eight feet of floor space between them. All the files were weird little library-style 3 x 5 cards with pictures of Russian and Eastern European manufactured goods on them, including Russian rifles, Polish sausages, Hungarian light bulbs and Bulgarian bombs. The CIA was responsible for economic as well as political intelligence, so they had spies take photos of anything they could get their hands on. There were certain techniques that enabled intelligence analysts to determine the industrial capacity of a country by examining manufactured items. The task of trying to figure out what the Soviets were capable of producing by looking at pictures of the stuff they produced was mildly interesting.

The most exciting part of this project was to travel to different parts of the world and actually examine weapons, electronics and other military-related equipment that had been stolen or captured from the Russians. Most of the people in the office were old CIA hands. They liked to tell hilarious stories about how they were able to surreptitiously get their hands on classified Soviet hardware, including a satellite. The CIA folks were all about twenty years older than Rod, Gary and me. They were serious professionals who, although very pleasant and helpful to us younger, more hip guys, weren't inclined to goof around as much as we preferred. Whenever life among the moldy files of crappy Soviet consumer goods became unbearably tedious, we would take a break and play tricks on each other, or just leave the building to have a cup of coffee or a cold beer. Gary, our team leader, was a few years older than Rod and me, had worked at DIA for a number of years, and was planning to make a career of it. Rod, on the other hand, was more like me. He had recently graduated from college in Massachusetts with a master's degree in history, taught school for a year and was looking for something more interesting. He didn't take his job too seriously, but he had to complete four more years as an officer in the Army National Guard to avoid being drafted and sent to Vietnam.

As the war in Vietnam captured the nation's consciousness, it became the most common topic of discussion in the office. One day I mentioned to Rod that I was going to participate in the huge anti-war rally and march on the Pentagon the following weekend. He looked at me with an embarrassed grin and said, "See you at the Pentagon! My unit has been called up for riot control duty and I am in charge of a platoon of troops who are assigned to defend the building." For the next few days Rod came to work in his shiny new Army uniform ready to begin training his troops. Every evening after work he had to practice riot control techniques in anticipation of the hundreds of thousands of demonstrators who would be marching on the Pentagon. Neither one of us had any animosity toward the other; it was as though we were both on different teams in a friendly softball game.

The smell of patchouli oil was overwhelming at times as Linnea and I wriggled our way through the teeming mass of humanity crammed into every square inch of the National Mall between the Capitol and the Lincoln Memorial. Most of the people who made up this herd of a quarter of a million determined souls had spent days traveling in cars and busses without many opportunities to wash up. So, while the patchouli oil aroma was annoying, it served to mask the body odor generated by a half-million sweaty armpits. The experience of being swallowed up by this undulating sea of people was both thrilling and terrifying at the same time. The power of such a mass demonstration was something that could not be ignored by President Lyndon Johnson and the entire country. Along with the exhilarating sensation of the strength of the collective will of hundreds of thousands of demonstrators, Linnea and I also felt the fear that one of us might be swept away by a rogue wave of people surging from behind us.

We held on to each other with all our strength as we rode the wave of festive and good-natured humanity toward the Lincoln Memorial for the speeches and entertainment. When the music and speeches were over the crowd started to spread out and move toward the Pentagon a few miles away. We were near the tail end of the crowd marching toward the Pentagon. After about an hour the entire march slowed down and came to a halt. Word came back to us that the front lines had reached the Pentagon and were being confronted by troops and other law enforcement agencies. We weren't really interested in violent confrontation so we broke away from the crowd and meandered back to our little basement apartment on Capitol Hill with the satisfaction that we had participated in an historic moment in our nation's history.

Two months later Linnea and I found ourselves caught up in another tumultuous moment in American history. Shortly after the assassination of Reverend Martin Luther King, Jr., riots began to erupt in Washington, D.C. Our apartment on Capitol Hill was in a transition area between the gentrified townhouses of young urban professionals and the poorer black neighborhoods. We enjoyed living there, had fun with the kids on the street and never felt threatened. The area didn't have the charm of Georgetown, but it had a soulful funkiness that included a huge old-fashioned farmer's market within walking distance. Our apartment was only a few blocks from our good friends Nan and Mel, who we often saw for dinner and weekend trips to the country. The day the rioting and looting started our neighborhood seemed quiet and unaffected by the chaos that was occurring in other parts of the city, so we went to work as usual. That afternoon Linnea had a dental appointment near downtown. We had to drive through a few looted and burned areas that were under the control of the National Guard. It was disturbing to see armed soldiers patrolling the streets and so much destruction..

The dentist's office was on the sixth floor of a modern building with a 360 degree view of the entire city. As I was reading a magazine in the reception room while waiting for Linnea, I occasionally glanced out the window at the panorama of the Washington skyline. I noticed a small plume of smoke rising a few miles away. About twenty minutes later I looked out the window again and saw multiple huge plumes of black smoke billowing up from many different areas. It looked as if the city was being bombed! I just sat there mesmerized as though watching a movie, until the receptionist came in the room and announced that the rioting was out of control and the police and military had blocked off large areas of D.C. Already there were massive traffic jams on the main arteries leaving the city. The reality of being trapped in a burning city finally dawned on me. I felt a unique surge of a fear I had never experienced before. There didn't seem to be much of a choice except to jump in the car, head for the expressway out of town, and just hope that we wouldn't get stuck in a traffic jam, pulled out of the car and attacked by an angry crowd.

Linnea emerged from the dentist's chair groggy from the painkillers and came over to the window to view the burning city. We noticed that most of the smoke was coming from the direction of Capitol Hill and realized it would be foolish to go home. It was a shock to be turned into refugees in one afternoon, but we had to think fast and figure out how to get out of town. The radio reported that all the major streets and expressways leaving the city were clogged with traffic. On the way to our car we remembered that Gerry, my old housemate from Georgetown, had moved to Maryland just over the border from Georgetown and there was a way to get there by taking a series of smaller side streets.

As we drove away from the dentist's office we could see the chaos on all the major streets so we began wending our way over to Georgetown, where it seemed much calmer. From there to Gerry's house it seemed almost like a normal Friday afternoon. Gerry, as usual, lived in the basement of a pleasant single-family house in a nice woodsy area just a block from the old C&O canal, which ran from Georgetown to West Virginia. It had been turned into a national park and had a delightful hiking trail beside the canal. It was such a relief to escape from the smoke and destruction of the city and savor the relative solitude of Gerry's house in the suburbs. For the rest of the weekend we hung out there, listening to the radio for news about the riots and enjoying hikes along the canal. By Sunday afternoon the police had suppressed the riots and had placed the city under curfew. We decided to call Mel and Nan, who lived a few blocks from us, to find out what the damage was to our neighborhood and to see if it was safe to return. They had spent the weekend holed up in their second floor apartment, unable to go out on the street. They hadn't been able to check out the damage on our street, but offered to let us stay with them if our apartment was damaged or destroyed.

Driving into our neighborhood was like entering a war-torn city in a foreign country rather than returning home. Many of the stores were gutted and looted, and even though the private homes were intact, the entire area looked battered and ravaged. The streets were strewn with glass and debris and were devoid of life. It was as though the soul of the neighborhood had been ripped out and only an empty carcass was left. The street in front of our house was deserted: no cars, no people, just lots of glass and trash and the stench of the burned-out Safeway supermarket down the street. We parked the car in its usual spot and furtively dashed across the street to our apartment which, unfortunately, was at street level in the basement of a typical Capitol Hill townhouse. Even though there was no damage to our apartment we felt vulnerable being so close to the street in a part of the city that was under curfew and still experiencing sporadic looting and gunfire.

When darkness fell and the curfew took effect we kept hearing people running down the street and through the small backyards of the houses next to us. We turned off almost all the lights and kept nervously peering out the window every time we heard a suspicious noise. We were beginning to think we had made a big mistake by coming home so soon when we heard what sounded like gunshots in the street. Looking out the window, I saw someone dash behind the house across the street and heard more gunfire. I looked at Linnea and said, "Let's get out of here!" She replied, "Sounds great to me, but how? There's a curfew and they will arrest us if we are driving or walking around. Besides, it's a no-man's land out there and we could be attacked by some looters!" I thought for a moment and said, "Let's go over to Nan and Mel's and spend the night with them in their second floor apartment. It's much more secure two stories above the street and the main door to the building is locked."

After Nan and Mel reassured us their apartment was secure and above the chaos on the streets we decided that we could run the three-block gauntlet to their house without being shot or arrested. As we started out the door someone zipped past us and we heard what sounded like firecrackers or gunshots. We immediately did an about-face and practically fell over each other as we retreated back into our apartment and double-latched the door. Now what? We were too spooked to stay in the apartment, which could easily be broken into, and making a mad dash down the street to Nan and Mel's seemed like a foolish risk. I then had one of my rare brainstorms. We would call the police, tell them that we were threatened and ask them to drive us just a few blocks to our friends' house. Communicating this plan to the police was not as easy as I thought it would be. The dispatcher kept me on hold forever and when I tried to explain our situation to him, he didn't seem to be listening to me. He just took down the address and said someone would be there soon.

After an hour of anxiously watching out the window of our darkened apartment for the police car to arrive, I decided to call the police again. As I turned away from the window I saw a mail truck pull up in front of the house. I began to wonder why they would be delivering mail on a Sunday night in the middle of a curfew. Suddenly a SWAT team of five heavily armed men in full riot gear charged toward the front door. Before I could get to the door to open it, they started pounding on it and yelling, "Open up!" "Whoa! Take it easy!" I yelled back. This seemed to agitate them even more so I opened the door as fast as I could. Four of them tried to get through the door at once, as though they were in a Keystone Cops movie. Before I could speak, my eyes were burning and I could hardly see. One of the idiots had sprayed me with mace. By the time I got them calmed down enough to explain that we were all right and just wanted a safe ride to our friends' house the mace was wearing off enough so I could see. They had received a call from the dispatcher, they explained, about trouble at this address and decided to arrive "undercover" in the mail truck. Unfortunately they were not allowed to give us a ride in the SWAT team truck. I pleaded with them that it was only a few blocks and again they said it was against regulations. "How about driving along beside us as we walk over to our friends' house?" I asked. "Okay, but make it quick," they retorted. Even though we were escorted by an armed mail truck, it was the creepiest three-block walk we had ever taken. Compared to our place on the street level, Nan and Mel's second story apartment was like a guarded fortress, and the comfort of being with dear friends transformed our night of fear into a celebration of being alive and safe.

The riots and looting served to strengthen our resolve to save our money, quit our jobs in June and head for California, which had become the epicenter of the counterculture. Many of our friends had also decided to quit their jobs and move to California and we planned to reunite with them sometime in the summer. In the meantime we spent as much time as we could out in the countryside. Walt and Bill had met a fascinating guy named Martin who lived on a farm out in the Blue Ridge Mountains, and invited Linnea and me to join them for a weekend visit at his farm. Martin lived in a minimally remodeled farmhouse next to an idyllic rushing stream with a steady flow of pure cold water from the surrounding mountains.

Spring in the Blue Ridge Mountains is truly celestial; nearly every tree is blossoming with pink or white flowers. Beneath the trees and in the fields, wildflowers offer up a glorious botanical garden of yellows, reds and blues. Needless to say, the drive from the worn-out and grimy city to Martin's bucolic valley hidden in the mountains seemed like discovering Shangri-La. As we walked up to the house Elizabeth, Martin's wife, was sitting on the front porch smoking a cigarette and peeling apples. She appeared to be in her mid-forties and had a solid, no-nonsense air about her; sort of a cross between a nurse and a prison matron. She greeted Bill and Walt with a weary, perfunctory hello. She didn't seem too thrilled to meet Linnea and me, standing there with our bags ready to move in for the night. Bill asked her where Martin was and she sort of sighed and retorted, "How the hell do I know? I can't keep track of him!" Then she said in a more benign tone that he should be back from a hike in time for lunch. As soon as we were alone with Bill I asked him if it was really all right with Elizabeth if we stayed there for the night. He chuckled and said, "She is always like that. Martin is constantly dragging people home with him from all over the world and some of them are pretty whacked-out. If you offer to help her with the meals and washing the dishes she will warm up to you. She is really a softie with a tough exterior."

Martin looked like a character out of a Mark Twain novel. He was about forty-five and wore a worn-out pair of baggy pants with an old rope for a belt and a weather-beaten shirt shredded at the elbows. He exuded a calm, soft-spoken, southern quality, belying the fact that he was a retired army sergeant. Apparently he grew up in the hills of Virginia and joined the army when he was sixteen. He retired when he was in his late thirties and had earned a degree in psychology while in the army, which sparked his interest in the nature of the mind. He devoted most of his time to traveling around the world, meeting and studying with every teacher or guru he could find. His library was filled with books on religion, philosophy and psychology, ranging from Tibetan Buddhism to Freudian psychology. Nutrition and natural healing were also of great interest to him and he had tried every diet and nutritional product on the market. After years of study and experimentation, he had developed a simple natural diet and a philosophy that seemed to work for him. He was always willing to try anything new that came across his path as long as it did not require him to become a true believer.

After a simple lunch made mostly of vegetables and fruits that Elizabeth had grown on the farm, Linnea and I helped her with the dishes and clean-up. This simple act of courtesy went a long way toward breaking the ice with Elizabeth, who now seemed to actually enjoy our company. Martin invited us all into the library where we sat on the floor and discussed our life goals and dreams. Bill, Walt, Barry, Maria, Linnea and I had similar goals of living a more sharing and sustainable life in a community of like-minded people. We all planned to leave our current mainstream jobs and seek a path of developing a higher state of consciousness or self-actualization. Martin, who had been doing this for years before the counterculture, communes and dropping out had become popular, had some very specific ideas of his own. He was fascinated with the idea of communal living as an alternative to the nine to five rat race of working fifty weeks a year just to earn enough money to buy a house and pay the bills. Over the last ten or fifteen years he had purchased a number of old, run-down farms and worn-out fields for very low prices. This was before people from the Washington area became interested in buying country property for vacation and retirement homes. Some of the properties had rustic cottages that he rented out for income. On a couple of properties there were old farmhouses where groups of hippies lived communally. Martin's dream was to create a community of people who shared their resources and devoted some of their time to working on income-producing projects for the benefit of all the members. This system would provide more free time to enjoy life and pursue paths of personal growth. Martin's idea of personal growth was based more in psychology than spiritual development. He had attended many "encounter-groups" and felt they were a useful tool for discovering one's "hang-ups" and attachment to the "ego." However, his goal of becoming a "selfless" individual dedicated to serving others was similar to the goals of yoga and other Eastern philosophical systems.

After our discussion Martin took us on a walking tour of his properties, which were nestled in the valley surrounding his main farmhouse. The cabins and old houses were occupied by young people who had left the city and were trying to live off the land with varying degrees of success. Some had bountiful gardens while others had pathetic patches of withered, insect-infested beans and squash. None of the houses had running water or indoor plumbing, but some of them were neat, clean and in good repair, indicating a more coherent group consciousness; other houses were filthy crash pads. Martin's relationship with each of these groups was not so much a leader or teacher, but more of a facilitator. His main function was to meet with each group on a regular basis to help the participants find themselves through group therapy. Some had strong personalities and had a fairly clear vision of creating an alternative lifestyle based on living simply and communally with other like-minded people. Others were more confused, even disoriented. They shared a common alienation from the culture of work and acquiring wealth, power and material well-being, but they weren't sure what the best alternative for them should be. Martin spent many hours offering suggestions and guidance, but he never tried to push anyone in a particular direction.

The weekend at Martin's gave Linnea and me an intimate glimpse of life on a hippie commune. We enjoyed the camaraderie with compatible folks, the relaxed atmosphere and the sharing of meals with good friends. But long meetings and group living didn't appeal to our independent spirits. Despite these drawbacks we were smitten with the natural beauty of the area and relished the opportunity to spend more time with our friends. Over the next couple of months we spent almost every weekend at Martin's farm, hiking, sharing meals and helping Elizabeth. We loved the deep silence of the mountains and the soothing sound at night of water flowing over the ancient Appalachian rocks in the stream next to our bedroom. This was the lifestyle we wanted: enjoying simple pleasures, living close to nature and seeking greater spiritual development. It was time to retire from our government jobs, which had become increasingly irrelevant to our goals in life. The folks at the office weren't too surprised when I announced I was leaving. I already had a reputation for being a "hippie" and a health food nut, for which I received my share of good-natured ribbing. When they found out I was headed for California on a cross-country camping trip it was obvious that I was "dropping out" and joining the counterculture. Everyone in the office presented me with a nice going-away present and signed a creative, hand-drawn card depicting me as a longhaired weirdo with beads around my neck.

11

The SEARCH BEGINS

After Linnea and I quit our jobs and moved out of our apartment we both experienced an overwhelming sense of euphoric freedom. It wasn't so much that our jobs were unbearable, but that we were starting out on a completely new adventure, both physically and spiritually. After a year of reading spiritual books, experimenting with drugs and discussions with numerous friends and acquaintances about higher states of consciousness, we realized that lasting happiness and fulfillment were not based on material success but on the development of one's state of consciousness. The glimpses of an unbounded unity with all life and the taste of a blissful awareness that transcended the emotions and the intellect had motivated us to begin a journey in search of this greater reality. There was nothing to restrict us from doing anything or going anywhere we wanted. It was a dream come true, only better! I was blessed with this wonderful woman of my dreams to share this adventure with. After spending a few restful days at Martin's farm, where he gave us a long list of people and places to visit ranging from health spas and yoga retreats in Mexico to a commune on California's Mendocino coast, we packed up our camping gear in our two-door 1966 Volvo and headed west.

Our first stop was Beechwold Clinic in Columbus, Ohio. Natural health spas and healing centers were few and far between in the late 1960s, especially in the Midwest. We had heard about Beechwold from Linnea's family who were health food enthusiasts and we decided to check it out. It was definitely not a fancy spa, but rather a humble house with mildly threadbare furnishings in a generic residential area.

The house had been converted to a non-hierarchical natural medicine facility where four or five doctors practiced their specialties. The director of the clinic was Dr. Resnick, who had a peaceful, mystical air about him. He took our blood samples to check for nutrient deficiencies and toxins like mercury and lead, made dietary suggestions and prescribed bottles of wild-looking potions for us to take. Another practitioner was Roger Breski who was a massage therapist, yoga instructor and student of Eastern religions. While he was massaging us we would have long conversations about spiritual development through yoga postures (asanas) and meditation. He mentioned that he was going to see Maharishi, who was coming to Columbus with the Beach Boys, and invited us to join him. Maharishi had been in the media so much in the past few months and so many celebrities had learned Transcendental Meditation (TM) that we were very curious to learn more about it, so we accepted his invitation. About two hours before the Beach Boys concert was to begin Roger called us and said that the event had been canceled. Apparently Maharishi had been opening the show with a half-hour lecture on developing one's full potential through meditation, using a lot of abstract analogies and concepts that were not appreciated by rambunctious rock concert audiences. They would often yell at him to get off the stage which, to his credit, he found amusing, but it freaked out the tour managers. By the time the tour got to Columbus, the attendance was so low they had no choice but to cancel.

After a few days of rest and holistic treatments we were hooked up to Dr. Keaton's fiendish-looking electronic machine. The vitality of our livers and other organs was determined by hooking up electrodes to our bodies, which were connected to a large machine about the size of a refrigerator. The machine had all the qualities of a 1930s horror movie. It was made of a sinister-looking dark wood with several large analogue meters and dials that he fiddled with constantly. The only thing lacking to complete the horror film effect was the arcing of electrical sparks and the zapping sound of thousands of volts produced by the machine. This was holistic medicine a la 1968! During our final evaluation with Dr.

Resnick he invited us to have dinner with him that evening, and then join him on a trip to a town a few hours away, where he was scheduled to deliver a talk on natural medicine.

As we drove along he revealed to us that for quite some time he had been hoping someone would come along who could manage the clinic, especially after he retired. He had an intuition that we were the people who were intended to run the clinic for him, so he offered us the job. It sounded like something we would enjoy very much and find fulfilling, but Linnea and I both knew our destiny was to continue on to California. Dr. Resnick was disappointed, but understood that it wasn't the right time for us to stop our quest and settle down.

Taos was still hanging on to its authenticity when we arrived in June of 1968. The atmosphere in town emanated a pre-tourism peacefulness unique to small New Mexico villages. After weeks of traveling and camping around the state it seemed like a perfect place to stop and spend some time. Linnea's parents had recommended that we stay at a hacienda built and operated by a young couple from Chicago. Bob and Joan had built a classic adobe building with multiple units in the foothills of the Wheeler Peak Wilderness area. Everything about the place was so enchanting that we decided to rent one of the units for a week and enjoy the luxury of a classic New Mexico house, complete with our own adobe fireplace. Our days were spent basking in the high-altitude sunshine, hiking in the radiantly green and white aspen forests and visiting with Joan and Bob. They were about our age and shared a lot of ideas about living a simple, quiet life away from the stress and intensity of the city. It only took a few days to become good friends with them and as our week came to an end, Bob invited us to stay for another week, free of charge, to keep Joan company while he was away on National Guard duty.

After going on a few moderate hikes to habituate to the higher altitude, we decided to take a hike in the Wheeler Peak Wilderness, which was about 12,000 feet. After years of living at sea level back East we

weren't sure how the high altitude would affect us, but we couldn't resist the lure of the majestic peaks that beckoned us. The higher we went
into the mountains the more we could feel the power of the deep silence
permeating the ancient rock. There is something captivating about being so high and so far away from the maelstrom of human activity down
below. The silence begins to seep into your bones and create a transcendent bond between you and the surrounding environment, making it
difficult to think about returning to the valley below. As we continued
on up the mountain we started to feel the effects of the high altitude.
Instead of the severe headaches that many people experience, Linnea
and I both started to feel lightheaded and giddy. Finally we couldn't go
any higher and just sat on the trail soaking up the overwhelming stillness and grandeur of the mountain.

As we reluctantly descended the mountain we could feel the air
become thicker and less rarified. It was now easy to understand why the
yogis in India spend years meditating in caves high in the Himalayas and
described their descent into the cities as going down into the "mud." On
the drive back to the hacienda I absentmindedly turned on the car radio.
Instead of the usual local DJ playing pop music there were distressing,
confused sounds of people shouting and pushing each other in a large
public place. After a few minutes of this live broadcast of pandemonium
the announcer started describing Robert Kennedy lying on the floor of
a hotel kitchen with a fatal bullet wound in the head. Listening to this
madness coming into our car over the radio was like being pulled back
down into hell after being in heaven. We returned to the hacienda and
sat with Joan, listening to the radio in a state of disbelief, unable to talk
about it for the rest of the evening. While this second assassination in
two months was astoundingly monstrous, it didn't have the impact on
us that the King assassination did. The riots following King's murder
directly affected our personal lives. Now we were in a remote area of
New Mexico where, physically and emotionally, we were insulated from
events in the rest of the world. When we left Washington we had pretty
much given up on trying to be of useful service to humanity by work-

ing within the system. These terrible events and the increasingly insane war in Vietnam seemed to be expressions of a deeper disorder in the collective consciousness of society that required a transformation of human awareness on a more profound level than political or social activism could accomplish.

Robert Kennedy's assassination and the turmoil surrounding it made us realize how lucky we were to be on our sabbatical from a society from which we were becoming increasingly detached. The combination of total freedom from any responsibilities and the ability to travel wherever and whenever we desired was a rare opportunity that we appreciated every day. The Southwest in the 1960s was still quite untamed and unspoiled. We were able to hike down into the Grand Canyon before the rim was turned into a shopping mall, the air was stained with brown pollution and the silence was shattered by the constant clack and whump of tour helicopters. Even Phoenix was a quiet, sleepy city with no traffic jams or packed freeways roaring in every direction. After being scared out of our wits when a mountain lion growled outside our tent in the Superstition Mountains, we threw our camping gear in the car, drove into Phoenix in the middle of the night and stayed in a small mom-and-pop motel on one of the main streets. Downtown Phoenix was so peaceful that we spent a few days hanging out around the pool and recovering from our encounter with the cougar.

Mexicali was one of those grimy, dusty border towns one instinctively tries to get through as quickly as possible before anything bad happens. Linnea and I breathed a collective sigh of relief when we reached the searing desert on the outskirts of town. As we headed west toward Tecate the landscape became more mountainous and barren. Martin had told us about a wonderful natural resort in Tecate called Rancho la Puerta. Apparently the resort offered excellent nutritious meals, swimming pools, mountain hikes and lectures by the founder, a well-known author with an unusual Hungarian name. He was supposed to have developed his own cosmic philosophy based on science, psychology and Eastern religion and we looked forward to learning more about him and spending some time at his spa. As we continued on into the brutally hot, life-less desert of broiled rock and gravel we began to wonder if Martin was playing a cruel hoax on us. Finally, after hours of driving through what seemed like a giant oven in our black Volvo sedan with no air condition-ing, a few patches of green desert plants began to appear here and there. As we continued, the cactus and chaparral became more abundant and the jagged mountains of bare rock gave way to gentle hills covered in grassy vegetation. There was even a hint of the Pacific Ocean in the air as we drove into the pleasant village of Tecate. Rancho la Puerta was like the Garden of Eden compared to the desiccated landscape we had just driven through. There were flowers everywhere, inviting swimming pools and well-designed but unostentatious Spanish-style buildings well integrated into the landscape.

When we inquired at the office about the cost for staying at the resort for a few days we were shocked at the price. It was so far beyond anything we had imagined that we asked the clerk if there was any place to camp in the area. She said there was a campground right across the street. We set up camp that night and the next day we walked across the street and enjoyed the resort with the rest of the high-end clientele. The staff didn't seem to mind, even allowing us to sign up for meals. Quite a few of the clients were there for weight loss and purification through fasting on fresh juice and raw food diets. In the late mornings there were lectures by the Hungarian doctor about nutrition, wellness and spiri-tual development based on his arcane system of beliefs about universal truths common to all religions. Linnea and I appreciated his unique in-sights into the underlying unity of all life but they seemed unnecessarily convoluted and complicated for our taste, so we spent the next few days hiking, swimming and talking with the many interesting Californians who were staying there. This was our first taste of the West Coast ethos, which seemed much more health conscious, casual and forward think-ing than the tradition-bound and rather formal values of the East Coast. Everyone we met was interested in some aspect of personal growth and didn't care where we were from or what we did for a living. We were becoming enamored of the West Coast lifestyle: laid back, avant-garde and always outside in the sun!

Indra Devi's ashram was another place in Tecate recommended by Martin, so we found our way out to the ashram on the outskirts of town. The focal point of the ashram was a small temple used for meditation. Indra Devi was not there but her disciples gave us permission to enter the temple. As we slipped off our shoes in the foyer we could feel the silence of the atmosphere pulling us down to a meditative state. The inside of the temple was filled with the fragrance of fresh flowers and incense. There were a few chairs facing an altar with statues of various Hindu gods, but most of the floor space was taken up with devotees meditating on colorful cushions. We felt a little bit like intruders but we couldn't resist lingering there for a while and soaking up the peaceful atmosphere. As we walked out, I whispered to Linnea that I wish I knew how to meditate. She replied that she also yearned to experience that inner peace generated by all those people meditating in the temple.

After almost two months of traveling we were ready to settle down for a while in the San Francisco Bay Area and explore the opportunities available for spiritual growth. However, before that, we still wanted to see more of Baja and reach the Pacific Ocean, which I had never seen. The paved road ended at Ensenada, a small seaport about a hundred miles south of San Diego. Heading south along the Pacific, the road quickly dissolved into a sandy lane ending in a series of tracks along the dunes. There were no signs, no houses, not even any of the trash that now litters many of the roads in Mexico. These were the days before plastic bags and bottles were available in large quantities to the people of poorer countries. Occasionally we would see a vehicle barreling toward us at breakneck speed. Fortunately they were always on another track! Eventually, after three or four hours, the main tracks split off into a half-dozen smaller, less traveled trails leading to the ocean. We reached the top of the dunes with our tent just as the sun was setting over the Pacific. The view was overwhelmingly magnificent. The glowing red-hot sun was extinguishing itself as it sank into the cold blue ocean. As far as the eye could see there was just the ocean and miles of uninhabited pristine beaches and dunes. We felt like we were the first explorers to discover this spectacular part of the planet.

After a few blissful days of swimming and strolling on the beach of what seemed like an undiscovered island paradise, it was time to head north to visit our friend Mel from Washington, D.C. who was now living in Costa Mesa, on the southern edge of L.A. Mel was working in his family's retail business to earn some money to bring Nan out from the East Coast. By the time Linnea and I arrived in Orange County to visit Mel, it was the Fourth of July weekend. He invited us to spend the day at the beach with him on the Fourth but had no extra room in his crash pad-style apartment, so we decided to find a campground nearby.

The closest one was a county park near Camp Pendleton, the huge Marine base. There were so many Marines celebrating the Fourth of July in the park that Linnea and I felt like we were camping on a Marine base! After we had pitched our tent and were cooking our dinner, a group of rowdy Marines in the campsite next to us started calling us dirty hippies and other obnoxious and threatening epithets. I looked over at their camp and, from the dozens of beer cans lying around on the ground, concluded that it would be a good idea to move to another site. Unfortunately the campground was filled up, so there was no possibility of moving. I decided to go over and have a rational chat with them. I really didn't understand why they were calling us hippies. My hair wasn't very long; longer than a Marine's crew-cut, but not down to my shoulders like the stereotypical hippie. After months in the sun Linnea's hair was platinum blonde and down to her shoulders, but neither one of us wore outlandish clothes, beads or Indian headbands with feathers. The only reason I could think of for all their anger was that we probably looked like students and that, in their minds, all students were against the war and hated the military. I thought if I went over and explained to them that I wasn't a student, I didn't hate the military and I had worked in the Pentagon just a few months before, they would calm down and we could enjoy some peace and quiet.

As I approached their campsite they looked at me in disbelief. They must have thought I was coming over to pick a fight with them! For some reason I really wasn't afraid. It seemed unlikely that all four of them would jump me and beat me up without out any provocation. I said hi to them and they just glared at me, so I tried to explain that I wasn't really a hippie, but a former intelligence analyst with the DIA and if they didn't believe it, they could look at the Washington, D.C. license plates and the special permits on the car that gave me access to military facilities. They didn't want to hear anything I had to say. Just the way I looked was enough to stir up all their pent-up anger and bitterness about the demonstrations against the war in which many of their buddies had been killed or mangled. It was nothing personal against me, I just happened to be the lightning rod for all their frustration and grief. I returned to our campsite deflated, defeated and feeling very sorry for these brave young men who were being slaughtered and maimed as a result of a misguided belief in a goofy domino theory by the otherwise brilliant leaders of the Pentagon.

Visiting Mel was an eye-opening introduction to the southern California drop-out lifestyle. We met him at the apartment he shared with an unknown number of acquaintances who were researching the effects of various psychoactive drugs on their brain cells. The beach was just a short walk away and it seemed that swimming, surfing and getting high were the main focus of their activities. Jobs and careers were obsolete options that were discarded from their daily lives. All they needed was a part-time job to buy food and dope and to pay the rent.

The scene at the beach was very primal; there were swarms of dogs and longhaired humans running around on the beach chasing hundreds of flying Frisbees. The behavior of the humans and the dogs was a remarkable display of their common genetic code, which was expressed in the instinct to run after and catch prey. Sharing the beach with all these happy, carefree folks was a pleasant relief from our camping experience the night before with all the angry Marines. It seemed like there were two separate universes, depending upon an individual's state of consciousness. Linnea and I naturally gravitated toward the alternative universe of living close to nature and enjoying the simple pleasures of life, but we also felt comfortable in the mainstream universe and were not inclined to completely drop out and live on the streets and beaches of southern California.

Later that evening Mel, Linnea and I got together with Bernie, our old friend from Washington, who had also quit his job with VISTA and returned to California with Mel. Bernie was a much more adventurous and dedicated user of drugs than the rest of us. Also, he looked like a classic hippie of the 1960s with shoulder-length hair, a full beard, lots of beads, and wild and colorful clothes. After a pleasant dinner Bernie invited us to a party in a section of Los Angeles where a lot of unusual folks lived. There were around a hundred really strange people crammed into a fashionable three story Spanish-style house with a large open roof offering spectacular views of L.A. The smoke from opium, hashish and marijuana was so thick in the dimly lit rooms that it was difficult to walk without stepping on someone lying on the floor. Naturally there was loud acid rock music playing, which made it impossible to talk to those few people who weren't completely stoned. Each person wore a unique costume. Some of them were stunningly creative while others were incoherent and just plain weird. Linnea and I looked and felt out of place. The atmosphere, while friendly and peaceful, seemed a little contrived and superficial. It was almost like an East Coast cocktail party where people felt the need to be accepted and impress the other guests. This was not our idea of a spiritual community so we left for San Francisco the next morning.

The farther we drove from L.A. the more we liked it. By the time we got to Big Sur we were in the California of our dreams: vast expanses of the Pacific slapped up against mile after mile of steep, sun-baked hills and long lonely beaches. The first night we camped on the headlands above a driftwood-littered beach embraced by huge sea stacks on both ends. As we ambled along the beach in the glow of spectacular sunset colors and sounds of the waves extinguishing themselves on the massive rocks, we saw the smoke and flames of a large fire. As we approached the fire we noticed it was inside a huge driftwood structure and there were sounds of singing and drumming coming from within. The people inside must have seen us walking toward them because all ten of them greeted us at once as we walked up. They had been living there for months and were quite proud of their makeshift home, and even offered some of their meager food rations to us. Their days were spent gathering wood and enjoying the captivating atmosphere of Big Sur. Living close to nature was their religion and philosophy which, they claimed, had helped them find meaning in their lives that was not available to them in the structured world of the various universities out of which they had dropped. It was delightful to sit in their driftwood sanctuary on the beach and talk about higher states of consciousness and human development as the flaming red sun slid silently beneath the waves, relinquishing the cloudless sky to billions of brilliant stars.

12

HOMECOMING

The streets around the campus of U.C. Berkeley were teeming with estranged students, nonspecific revolutionaries, angry Black Panthers, flower children drenched in patchouli oil, anti-war protesters dressed up like Uncle Sam, skinny health food fanatics and saffron-robed Hari Krishnas singing and selling books. There were dozens of alternative restaurants and world-class bookstores to choose from including Shambala, a great source for books on mysticism and Eastern religions. Posters announcing concerts, mass protests and lectures on subjects like meditation, religious communes, astrology, psychedelic drugs and courses at the Free University were plastered on every lamp post, shop window, stairwell and outside wall. For seekers like Linnea and me this was home at last. Everyone we met was involved with changing society in one way or another, either through radical political activities, pursuit of spiritual development or joining a group of likeminded people and forming an experimental community.

After settling into a small efficiency apartment near campus we spent our days and nights attending lectures and meetings offered by various organizations, all of them promising some form of spiritual growth. Most of them had a rigid belief system that seemed to have some elements of truth but required a commitment to their philosophy that turned us off. Perhaps the weirdest one offered us membership in a family of "chosen souls" who were destined to become enlightened. We had to attend six lectures, each one revealing a little bit more about the divine plan of their spiritual leader, whose name they promised to reveal at the last lecture in the series. Finally, at the sixth meeting, they revealed that the leader was Reverend Sun Myung Moon and we could become members of his sacred family, thereby assuring our salvation.

Our next attempt at gaining enlightenment was to attend a meditation session offered at noon every day on campus at the student union building. The meditation was led by a soft-spoken Indian swami in western dress and attended by hundreds of students eager to experience the deep inner peace described in so many of the books that were popular with the counterculture. The swami didn't really offer any instruction in meditation. He just asked everyone to close their eyes and begin. We assumed that everyone knew how to meditate so Linnea and I would just sit there for thirty minutes and try to quiet our minds. After a week of just sitting there we gave up and continued our search.

From our perspective, Berkeley was the most exciting place on the planet, even more exciting than San Francisco, where thousands of hippies had established their own nation in the Haight-Ashbury district. While many intelligent and idealistic people were willing to experiment with communal social and economic lifestyles, Haight-Ashbury was also a magnet for dysfunctional and opportunistic individuals who degraded the atmosphere until it eventually devolved into a drug-infested, seedy tourist trap. Although drugs and hippies were also abundant in Berkeley, it didn't attract as many seriously drug addicted, confused teenagers who lacked the skills needed to navigate the complexities of living on the street. Berkeley was seething with revolutionary zeal, yet there was a more mature and creative aspect to the local movement. The establishment of People's Park by members of the alternative community on a large vacant lot owned by the university was a direct assault against the authority of the university and the Berkeley police. This required a level of organization, creativity and clear-headedness not demonstrated by the rapidly degrading hippie community of Haight-Ashbury.

Most of the street vendors and peddlers around the U.C. campus in Berkeley were homeless transients or terminal drug addicts trying to scrape up some dope money to get through the day. They were a pretty bedraggled lot and stood out even among the thousands of scruffy hippies and students milling about the area. The most common item offered for sale from these sweat-stained, grizzly dropouts was the *Berkley Barb*, a radical alternative newspaper. There were vendors on every street corner desperately trying to unload their stacks of papers so they could earn a few dollars for food and drugs.

After a few weeks in Berkeley we became used to these ubiquitous entrepreneurs and hardly noticed them until one of them looked vaguely familiar. It was Barry, our old friend from Washington, Swami Premananda's protégé from the Church of the Lotus Blossom. The last time we had seen him was at his going away party when he and Maria left Washington in their new VW camper for sunny California. Barry didn't look very sunny. He looked old and haggard, as if he had been living on the streets. We were shocked to see him in such disrepair as we walked over to greet him. Barry wasn't that glad to see us even though we were really excited to run into him. He was probably embarrassed by his disheveled looks and obvious drug dependence. Apparently he had split up with Maria and seemed to be on a downward spiral. We invited him to come to our apartment for dinner and he perfunctorily agreed but we never saw him again. It was difficult for us to see someone whom we had regarded as a highly developed spiritual seeker looking so degraded and sickly.

While spending our days exploring the Bay Area and attending lectures and concerts at night was a pure delight, we soon realized that we had to find some way to make money. The help wanted ads were depressing. After months of freedom and living close to nature it was difficult to think about returning to some stuffy office. The outdoor jobs available were low-paying field labor or required specialized skills. One day, while skimming the classifieds, I happened to glance at the real estate ads and noticed a house for sale in the Oakland Hills for $8,500. For some inexplicable reason I blurted out to Linnea, "Let's go look at this cheap house." She gave me that odd look she had whenever I suggested we do something wacky and replied, "Why do you want to look at a house in Oakland? I thought we wanted to live in the country?" "I don't know," I said, "Let's just take a look." Within an hour we were in the hands of a real estate agent who was either a career criminal on probation or a pathological liar. He must have known we were clueless about real estate so he proceeded to describe this magnificent home in the most glowing terms he could think of.

When we arrived at the address where the house was supposed to be, we couldn't see it. The lot sloped downhill away from the street and was an overgrown jungle of bamboo, huge aloe vera plants, scraggly fruit trees and assorted bushes. I had to give the real estate agent credit for keeping a straight face. He must have known we were horrified, but he just continued in an upbeat tone. "Well, let's take a look!" *A look at what?!* I thought to myself. *There is nothing here but a bunch of weeds and half-dead trees.* As we got out of the car I noticed what looked like a narrow driveway leading into a tunnel in the brush. Upon closer examination there was a structure built inside the vines and high bushes that could be loosely described as a carport. Unless you got out of the car and walked into the tunnel of bushes you would just drive by, assuming there was no house.

Once we were inside the carport/tunnel things started to get interesting. On one side there was a mysterious-looking green wooden gate that beckoned us to open it and see what was on the other side. The gate opened onto a rickety old deck attached to a small structure overlooking a series of terraced gardens that had been neglected for years. On both sides of the lot there was a fence and very thick bushes, which created an atmosphere of secrecy and solitude that we found appealing. The realtor, noticing we were warming up to the place, was quick to point out the double-sized lot. He showed us a gate at the back of the property that opened up to another garden area of neglected fruit trees. Walking back up the path, we were able to see what the house looked like. It was a small 1940s-style bungalow apparently built from used and scavenged materials. The entire building was no more than twenty-four feet wide by thirty feet long and was covered with the light green asbestos shingles that were popular in the 1950s. As we opened the door to the living room Linnea and I noticed the hideous Chinese red carpet bordered by an oak floor that was painted dark green. Some of the green paint was actually on the edge of the carpet, which led me to believe the owner must have painted the floor while the carpet was on it, so I picked up the carpet. I found a beautifully varnished oak floor in excellent condition. We then noticed two huge industrial-style metal windows that must have come from an abandoned factory. After recovering from the insane interior decorating in the living room I looked out the big factory windows and was stunned to see a spectacular, sweeping view of the entire bay with the city of San Francisco gleaming in the distance.

The rest of the house wasn't too bad: a small bathroom, one bedroom and a storage room that opened onto the carport/tunnel. I noticed the window in the bathroom was also painted dark green, not just the trim but the entire window, including the glass. My first reaction was that they probably did it for privacy. Then I noticed several other windows were also painted completely green, which indicated deficient decorating skills on the part of the owners or perhaps some disorder associated with green paint. In spite of all the weird green paint and general shabbiness of the place Linnea and I agreed that it would be a fun place to fix up and sell for a profit, which would provide a place for us to live and a way to make some money. We had no experience in real estate so we made a low offer of $7,000, expecting they would refuse and come back with a counter offer, which would give us more time to consider our new venture. The very next day the realtor called back and said the owners had accepted our offer. At first we were shocked, and then we realized it was such a good deal that we couldn't go wrong! In less than two weeks we were living in our new home.

Although we didn't have any serious construction skills, Linnea and I spent most of our days painting and removing the old green paint from the floor and windows. After living in a tent for two months and working in offices for two years we were having a blast remodeling our funny little house. Most of our evenings were spent in Berkeley, which we found a lot more interesting than Oakland. One night we ran into Walt the naval officer who, along with Bill, had taken me to Millbrook for my LSD trip. He was now attending U.C. Berkeley and working on his Ph.D. in political science, courtesy of the U.S. Navy! We had a great reunion dinner with him the next evening and got caught up on the latest news about Bill, who was now out of the Navy and spending most of his time at Martin's farm in Virginia. Walt was still in the Navy but planned to resign after finishing his Ph.D. He was active with Tim Leary's group in Southern California and very excited about living on a commune in Mendocino County. He invited us to visit and consider living there. Our goal was to live in the country in a community of like-minded people, so we accepted and drove up to Mendocino the next weekend.

The rolling golden hills of Sonoma and Mendocino counties, sprinkled with deep green oak trees, began to morph into magnificent fern-floored redwood groves as we headed away from Highway 101 toward the coast. Soon we were driving through cool, dark forests of nothing but redwoods. A few miles before reaching the ocean we took a right onto a dirt road toward Fern Creek Ranch, where we were supposed to find the commune. At the end of a dusty potholed road we came upon two huge redwood stumps, one on each side of the road, with a small faded hand-painted sign that read "Fern Creek Ranch." We passed through a few overgrown fenced pastures and arrived at the main compound in a clearing surrounded by giant redwoods. In the middle of the clearing was a white farmhouse surrounded by the type of vehicles that one would expect to see on a commune: beat-up VW buses, rundown pick-up trucks and flamboyantly painted old cars. We noticed Walt's car parked off to one side of the house, but we didn't see him or any other people around the compound. As we walked up to the farmhouse we heard what sounded like a meeting in progress in the living room. From the window we could see about twenty people sitting around in a circle engaged in an animated discussion. The door was wide open so we walked in; Walt noticed us right away and came over to us with a warm greeting. He explained that the meeting would be over in about fifteen minutes, suggested that we find a place to pitch our tent, and invited us to come back for dinner.

We located a secluded redwood grove, set up our tent in the soft needles under the trees, and wandered along a trail in the redwoods, occasionally coming across a small cabin or campsite inhabited by members of the commune. Eventually we found our way back to the main house to meet Walt. As we approached the house we could smell marijuana drifting out of the windows as the meeting droned on. It reminded me of the "encounter group" sessions that Martin often held at his farm in Virginia. Linnea and I found that, while this kind of group therapy was helpful, it was not the path to enlightenment that interested us. We admired the ideals and the motives of those who were willing to give up the comforts of private homes and good paying jobs for the opportunity to experiment with communal living. Working and sharing meals and housing with twenty-five other people was not the easiest thing in the world, but they were determined to find a better way to raise their families and create a community based on cooperation rather than competition.

During the dinner after the meeting Walt introduced us to many of the commune members. Most of the people were highly educated; they had left successful careers to live in teepees, experiment with psychedelic drugs and grow vegetables. Some had taken their kids out of school and moved their entire families into a small house with two or three other families. Living like this seemed harder on the adults than on the children, who adapted to their new world quickly and spent most of their time playing in the woods. Although it took a lot of time and energy for the adults to develop a system for living together, there was also a lot of free time to enjoy the simple pleasures of relaxing in the golden California sun and splashing in the ocean.

Both Linnea and I had experienced years of living communally while in college and in the military. We felt so fortunate that we had found each other. Our life together was so blissful that we had no desire to invest the time and energy required to live on a commune. Also, the constant use of drugs by so many people began to turn us off. Our initial exposure to LSD and marijuana back East was in a more spiritual context of experiencing a higher state of consciousness which, hopefully, resulted in a more enlightened state of mind. The social and recreational use of drugs began to seem to us no different than the use of alcohol. Both substances had their limitations in terms of spiritual growth, with negative side effects on the physiology. The more disillusioned we became with the drug scene, the more determined we were to find an effective path to enlightenment.

On one of our evening walks through the Berkeley campus we noticed a poster announcing a lecture on Transcendental Meditation at a local movie theater. The poster said that someone named Jerry Jarvis would be speaking. We didn't know who Jerry Jarvis was, but we had been curious about TM since we left Washington and so we decided to attend. It seemed a little strange to go to a movie theater for a lecture on meditation. The stage had an overstuffed chair and some flowers on a table next to it, which evoked a casual comfort that was more appropriate for an event in Berkeley. Before Jerry came on stage we noticed three or four assistants in suits and ties fussing around with the lights and sound system. It seemed really strange to see people dressed so formally in Berkeley. *They must be Young Republicans*, I thought. Who else would dress like that in such a radical anti-establishment environment as Berkeley?

Jerry Jarvis came out on stage with a bright shining face and wearing a casual sport jacket and tie. He had a very relaxed air about him. I noticed that he was wearing Hush Puppy shoes. These were the soft suede shoes with crepe soles usually worn by retired math teachers and guys who dressed in leisure suits. Jerry was too young to be retired so he must have chosen the Hush Puppies purely for comfort, not for his image. Before becoming the director of the Students International Meditation Society he had been a journalist in Washington, D.C. He was so impressed with the technique of Transcendental Meditation and the philosophy associated with it that he joined Maharishi in teaching the technique around the world. His lecture was surprisingly non-mystical. After reading so many books about yogis and other mystics we had expected him to talk about spiritual development and yoga. Instead his talk focused on developing the full potential of the mind and its practical benefits. He claimed the average person used about 15% of their mental potential and that accumulated stress blocked us from developing the full potential of the mind. TM was supposed to eliminate or reduce stress and thereby allow us to use more of our mental potential.

Jerry went on to emphasize that the goal of TM was not to have a mystical experience during every meditation but rather to experience the results of meditation in daily life. Meditation cleared and calmed the mind which resulted in more coherent activity; for example, we would make fewer mistakes, have fewer emotional upsets, less stressful reactions to the vagaries of daily life and more enjoyment. These positive benefits were due to the physiological changes that took place when the mind settled down during meditation, creating a unique state of consciousness called "restful alertness." During this deep rest the body has a chance to release deep-rooted stress and rejuvenate itself quite naturally.

While this straightforward, almost clinical explanation of Transcendental Meditation lowered our expectations of experiencing instant samadhi (or oneness with creation) during meditation, we were intrigued by the emphasis on results in daily life and decided to attend another lecture by Jerry the following evening. There was also something about his inner calm and lightheartedness that suggested there was some truth in what he was saying.

During the second lecture Jerry described how TM was different from meditation techniques involving concentrating the mind, like staring at a candle or trying to empty the mind of thoughts, so that one could experience the inner silence of pure consciousness. He claimed that transcending during TM was effortless because the mind was naturally drawn to something more charming and the charm of the transcendent was irresistible to the mind. Jerry compared TM to diving. He said in diving we just take the correct angle with our body and let go for an effortless dive deep into the water. The key to TM was very similar: take the correct angle with the mind and it will automatically dive to deeper, more charming levels of awareness. As a matter of fact, effort would actually interfere with the process, just like trying to fall asleep interferes with our ability to sleep. This approach was the opposite of any of the techniques we had tried and many of the books we had read on meditation, which emphasized trying to rid the mind of thoughts that interfered with experiencing inner peace.

Apparently many others in the audience thought the same thing and peppered him with skeptical questions about being able to transcend thought effortlessly. Jerry explained that, by using a Sanskrit word called a mantra, the mind naturally settles down to finer and finer levels of thought, until even the most subtle level of the mantra dissolves and the mind experiences pure consciousness. This state of pure consciousness has been called Samadhi, Nirvana, or Being, as Maharishi calls it. It is the universal state of total self-sufficiency and unity with all of creation described by mystics in just about every religious tradition. Many of us in the audience had experienced glimpses of this state of bliss consciousness either through psychedelic drugs, other meditation methods or just spontaneously. The one thing we all had in common was that once we had a taste of true freedom, or liberation, we all wanted more of it.

Jerry pointed to a picture on the table next to him. It portrayed a swami with piercing eyes, dressed in robes. He explained this was Guru Dev, Maharishi's teacher. Maharishi gave all credit for the knowledge of TM to Guru Dev and the tradition that he embodied. To express gratitude and to create the optimal conditions of deep silence conducive to learning meditation, the teacher performs a brief ceremony called a "puja" during the instruction of the technique. The requirements for learning meditation were to bring a few pieces of fruit, some flowers and a white handkerchief. These "ingredients" were used as offerings in the ceremony. Also there was a donation of $35 for students and $75 for those with full time jobs. The Students International Meditation Society (SIMS) was a non-profit educational organization and the funds were used to maintain the centers and ongoing programs.

All of this sounded reasonable to Linnea and me so we decided to learn the technique. We liked the fact that it didn't require us to accept any belief system or even believe anything Jerry said; all we had to do was give it a try. After attending so many lectures and presentations on techniques and organizations offering everything from enlightenment to joining the chosen family of god, it was refreshing to find something that didn't require us to become believers! At the end of Jerry's lecture those of us who decided to learn TM stayed behind for a brief interview with one of the "initiators" who would be teaching meditation that weekend.

Linnea and I were assigned to a young Englishman named Charles Harris. Dressed in a tweed jacket and wool tie, with short hair, he looked like a stuffy British civil servant. It was hard to believe he had quit his professional job and run off to the banks of the Ganges River in India to study with Maharishi alongside the Beatles and a variety of other celebrities. Charles had been an engineer in England and, after meditating for a few years, had concluded that teaching meditation was more inspiring than sitting in a stifling office all week. He exuded a blithe calmness that seemed to be a result of his years of meditation. The focus of the interview was a one page questionnaire in which we were asked questions about our mental health and prescription and recreational drug use. Apparently psychoactive drugs like marijuana overexcite the nervous system and this interferes with the process of transcending to a state of deep silence in meditation. If someone had used these drugs during the last two weeks they were asked to stay drug free for two weeks and then learn TM to get the best results.

When we arrived at the TM center near the Berkeley campus the next morning with our fruit and flowers for our initiation into meditation, we found a line of about a hundred people extending out the front door and up the sidewalk. An hour later I was standing outside one of the initiation rooms, with my fruit and flowers arranged in a basket by one of the volunteers at the center. After a few minutes Charles opened the door and a delightful aroma of flowers and incense enveloped me as I entered the room. He offered me a seat in a comfortable chair facing an altar covered with a white cloth and a portrait of Guru Dev, Maharishi's teacher. As soon as I sat down I felt like I could hardly keep my eyes open. The atmosphere of deep silence in the room was so palpable that I could feel myself slipping into a meditative state before even learning how to meditate. Charles quietly explained that he was going to per-form a brief ceremony of gratitude and asked me to stand next to him in front of the altar. At first I was curious about the fruit, flowers, burning candle and incense arranged on the altar, but when he began singing Sanskrit words in a hushed whisper, every fiber in my body seemed to turn into Jell-O as my consciousness started to transcend the small room filled with flowers and the wonderful aroma of sandalwood.

The next thing I was aware of was the gentle voice of Charles whis-pering a comfortable-sounding Sanskrit word that I instinctively knew was my mantra. As I began thinking the mantra, it seemed to bring me deeper and deeper into a state of pure consciousness with hardly any other mental activity except for the faintest impulse of the mantra, which eventually faded away. When I heard Charles saying something barely audible I knew I had been somewhere else for quite some time. As my awareness became more localized I realized he was asking me to open my eyes. The room was even more beautiful than when I first came in. All my senses were enlivened as though I had smoked marijuana, but I also experienced a powerful inner silence that I had not experienced before. The drug experience was more of a euphoric high, while medita-tion was more of a detached inner calm or peace.

On our way home after our initiation Linnea and I both remarked that, while our experience of meditation had been deliciously relaxing and silent, we both felt energized rather than the foggy feeling associ-ated with waking up from a deep sleep. We spent the rest of the day working on our funny little house and meditated for a half-hour right before dinner, as instructed by Charles. The experience was restful and relaxing, but not quite as powerful as our meditation at the TM center earlier in the day. There seemed to be more thoughts during the meditation and a few more distractions, but we did notice more energy that evening and continued working on the house. Charles had told us to meditate twice a day, once in the morning before breakfast and once in the evening before dinner. He claimed that meditation was a preparation for activity and would result in more clarity of mind and greater energy if we meditated first thing in the morning. He also said that it was best to meditate before meals because when we are digesting food it raises our metabolism. This interferes with the process of transcending, which lowers the metabolism.

The next day we meditated in the morning and evening, then attended a meeting at the Berkeley campus with Charles and a group of thirty other people who had also just learned TM. Charles asked the group if anyone noticed any results in daily life since starting meditation. Some people said they felt much more relaxed, others felt tired and kept falling asleep during meditation, a few people didn't notice any changes; most of us noticed perhaps more energy and clarity of mind. Charles explained that the folks who were under the most stress would have the most dramatic results in the beginning because the contrast from high stress levels to more relaxation and inner calm was the greatest. He also suggested that if anyone felt tired or sleepy during meditation, it was an indicator of a lot of fatigue in their system and they should not try to stay awake during meditation. "During meditation the body gets what it needs and if it needs sleep, then don't resist!" he explained. "Just let yourself fall asleep. Then, when you wake up, continue meditating and you will feel much more alert and energized."

As the meeting continued some of the people complained about too many thoughts during meditation and difficulty settling down. Charles explained thoughts were a normal part of meditation and that we shouldn't try to force them out. He said, "TM is effortless. Any effort on our part will interfere with the process of transcending. To-morrow night, after we have meditated for another day, we will discuss the role of thoughts in meditation." After answering questions for half an hour, Charles had us all close our eyes and meditate together. This group meditation seemed to create a pervasive influence of silence in the room. When he asked us to slowly open our eyes at the end of the meditation everyone, including those who complained about too many thoughts, appeared to have had a profound experience of what Charles called "restful alertness," a state of consciousness in which the body is in a state of deep rest and yet the mind is alert. With everyone sitting there engulfed in the group silence, Charles ended the meeting.

After another day of meditating morning and afternoon we met with Charles again in the evening to discuss our meditation with the group. With two days of meditation under our belts a few people were experiencing dramatic results in their daily lives: much more energy and an improved ability to handle stress. Others felt like Linnea and me; nothing dramatic but definitely some increase in mental clarity and en-ergy. For those who were still feeling more tired than before they started TM, Charles assured them they would feel better after a few more days of meditating. After answering some questions, Charles suggested we have a group meditation. Everyone seemed to really enjoy these sessions and most of us felt the group meditations were more powerful than when we meditated at home. Charles explained that a group of people meditat-ing created a collective influence on the environment very conducive to transcending. He went on to remind us that, even though meditation is a very pleasant and at times blissful experience, the purpose of TM was not to achieve a "good" or "successful" meditation, but to experi-ence the results of meditation in our daily activity. Thoughts were no barrier to proper meditation, but rather the byproduct of some physical activity in the body. This activity was actually the body "normalizing" due to the deep rest it received during meditation. Rest, he claimed, was fundamental to our well-being; during the sleep and dream states of consciousness the body normalizes by throwing off the accumulated stress and fatigue of the day. A similar thing happens during TM, only the body gets an even deeper rest than sleep and releases deep-rooted stresses that interfere with optimal functioning of the nervous system. The goal of TM is to develop the full potential of the nervous system, which is a physiological correlate to the state of enlightenment.

On the third evening meeting with Charles he spent most of the time discussing what we could expect from continued meditation. He used a simple analogy to explain this gradual transformation. He compared the process of gaining enlightenment with that of dying a cloth in India. "First they dip the cloth in yellow dye, and then dry it in the sun. As it dries, it fades and is dipped in the dye again and dried again. Each time it fades less until, eventually, the color is bright yellow and does not fade." It's like that with meditation, he went on. Every time we meditate we become a little more established in pure consciousness or inner calm, until eventually that state of inner silence is stabilized in our awareness. This has practical as well as spiritual implications. The more we are grounded in that silence the fewer mistakes we make and the more successful we will be in accomplishing our goals. Someone in the audience didn't quite understand how maintaining inner calm in the midst of our daily activity resulted in fewer mistakes. Charles explained that when we are tired and cranky we all know we make more mistakes, and when we are fresh and well-rested we perform better. If we meditate and get adequate rest we simply function more effectively. This sounded good to Linnea and me so we decided to incorporate meditating morning and evening into our daily routine and see what the long term effects would be.

After a few months of enjoyable work on our house we had transformed it from a neglected shack to a delightful cottage. It didn't take long for us to realize that our remodeling project was being done under the watchful eye of our next-door neighbors. We had repaired the deck overlooking their backyard and painted a large red, yellow and orange mandala on the side of the house, just above the deck. From the neighbor's vantage point all he could see of our house was the brown wall with the colorfully painted mandala. Every once in a while we would see him working in his backyard and wave to him. The day after we put the mandala on the side of the house his curiosity got the best of him and he came over and introduced himself.

Bobby was from North Carolina and had a wonderful southern accent. He spoke as though California was just another county in North Carolina. "Ah thought y'all was hippas when I saw y'all movin' in. Then when y'all started paintin' them weird designs on the house I said to my wife, 'That's it. They's definitely hippas.'" We invited him in to look around. He seemed visibly relieved that it was not a crash pad with old mattresses on the floor and stoned hippies lying all over the place. After realizing that, except for the mandala on the side of the house, we were pretty normal, Bobby revealed that it wasn't so much the "hippas" that made him angry, it was the Black Panthers. "Them Panther fellers are the real troublemakers," he went on. "They're fixin' to start a war and take our property away. They gotta git that 'Stokey' Carmichael and shoot him or throw him in jail." (Stokely Carmichael was one of the leaders of the Black Panthers who felt that non-violence, as advocated by Martin Luther King, was not successful in bringing about civil rights for blacks and that blacks should defend themselves against violence with violence.)

We had to tell Bobby that we didn't agree with him but we liked having him as a neighbor. He said he was happy to meet us, and he was in the construction business so if we ever needed anything to let him know. Then he invited us to come over to his house with him and meet his wife and eight-year-old son. In contrast to our mandala-decorated and garage sale-furnished tiny bungalow, Bobby's was a fairly new generic ranch-style house with avocado green shag carpet, a huge console-type T.V., hideously obese chairs and a sofa covered in mustard-colored vinyl. Both Bobby's wife Lindsey and his son Billy also spoke as though they were still in North Carolina. They had lived in California for five years and were remarkably immune to even the slightest influence of West Coast culture. Bobby's pride and joy was the new in-ground swim-

ming pool he was installing. He had about a week's more work to do
on it and invited us to an inaugural pool party the following weekend.
Bobby and his wife were so friendly and fun to be with that we accepted
the invitation without hesitation.

As we walked out the door of our cottage to attend Bobby's pool
party I could hear his familiar rant about "Stokey Carmichael" and the
Black Panthers coming from his backyard. This time he was holding
nothing back; it seemed like every other word was the "N" word. I
started to have second thoughts about going to a party with a bunch of
racist rednecks. When I looked over the fence to see what was going on,
my jaw dropped! There was Bobby, standing over the grill poking at a
pile of charred bovine flesh with what looked like a small crowbar in one
hand and a beer in the other hand. He was holding forth to a group of
six black guys who were laughing and making fun of him. As I looked
around, I saw there were another dozen or so adults and kids splashing
and swimming in the pool. There wasn't a white person in sight! Linnea
was flabbergasted! How could this be? Here was this obviously racist
good ole boy from North Carolina with twenty black people swimming
in his brand new pool! Bobby greeted us like we were old friends, took
us around as though we were token white folks and introduced us to his
friends. They all worked in construction with him, seemed to genuinely
like him, and didn't seem to take his racist ranting seriously. Lindsey
and their son Billy were equally comfortable with their guests and were
having a great time. The irony of this situation did not escape me. Here
was this apparent racist with a backyard full of black buddies, and probably somewhere in the Bay Area there was an elitist liberal event going
on and the only blacks in attendance were the waiters.

As the remodeling of our house neared completion we started
thinking about selling it and finding some property in Mendocino
County, about three hours north of San Francisco. Then we discovered
that the house only two doors down was for sale. It was a larger and
more substantial house than ours and the price was only $10,000. The
paint was peeling on the outside and the inside was half remodeled and

half neglected. It looked like the owner suddenly had to leave without completing his project. The house was on a double lot that sloped downhill toward San Francisco Bay. Instead of being situated near the street with a large backyard like our house, this house was built at the back of the lot with a long driveway sloping down to it. Between the house and the street there was a long-overgrown yard with mangy bushes and gnarly weeds, which gave the property an abandoned look. In back of the house, however, there was a deck with a spectacular sweeping view of the Bay, which was much more dramatic than our view. The ground floor of the building was a half-finished basement with the potential for two bedrooms and a bathroom. The top floor included the kitchen, living room and another bedroom. The main entrance was also on the second floor, with a walkway leading from the driveway up to a porch and the front door.

Within a few weeks we were busy remodeling the house and were getting ready to put it on the market when Mel and Nan arrived in the Bay Area. They were looking for a place to stay, so we offered them the house to stay in while we were working on it. It was great to have our old friends, who had lived near us on Capitol Hill in D.C., living just a few doors down from us. Mel had seriously long hair and Nan looked and dressed like Janis Joplin. We often had meals together on our deck overlooking Bobby's place and more than once we heard him lamenting that the "hippas" were taking over the neighborhood. To allay his fears we invited him and Lindsey to go out to dinner and a movie with us in the Haight-Ashbury district of San Francisco. We thought if they had a firsthand experience of hippie life they might find it less threatening.

The Good Karma Café was one of our favorite hippie restaurants. They served traditional 1960s hippie cuisine with lots of gooey brown rice, steamed veggies that looked like they were chopped with a chainsaw and text book-sized chunks of slimy tofu. We thought this would be a nice healthy change of pace for Bobby and Lindsey, who ate the standard greasy, fried American diet. The décor in the restaurant was classic hippie with battered, mismatched chairs and tables and tie-dyed cloths and psychedelic posters covering every square inch of wall space. By the time we arrived at the restaurant we were running late and didn't have much time to eat before the movie started. Fortunately there was hardly anyone in the place so we assumed we could get served fairly quickly. Bobby and Lindsey seemed a little bewildered and uncomfortable with the weird décor and acidhead music, but they were also eager to try something new. After we had been seated for about five minutes I noticed the waiter was hanging around in the back near the kitchen and apparently hadn't noticed us come in. I walked over and greeted him, then asked if we could get served soon so we could get to the movie on time. He gave me a huge mellow grin and said, "Whoa, this acid is stupendous, man. I am sooo stoned, I don't think I can handle this, man." I replied that it would be great if we could just have something fast and simple so we could make it to the movie. "Hey man, what movie are you going to see?" he asked. When I mentioned that it was *2001: A Space Odyssey* I thought he was going to pass out. He rolled his eyes and kept repeating, "It will blow your mind, man. Blow your mind."

I was beginning to realize that the evening was not going as planned. We had hoped to impress Bobby and Lindsey with the mental health of the folks in the counterculture and expose them to some delicious and nutritious cuisine, plus see a cutting-edge new age film that would be more thought-provoking than the T.V. shows they watched all the time. Finally the waiter realized he was working in a restaurant and there were some customers who needed to eat. As he stumbled up to our table he suddenly stopped, looked at the four of us in amazement, and muttered, "Incredible, man. Incredible." It was a miracle that he served us some decent food. Bobby and Lindsey actually liked the chewy brown rice and the fish. It was a relief to see them enjoying the food and becoming comfortable with the strange surroundings.

None of us had seen *2001* and we were all truly awestruck during the entire movie. I kept looking over at Bobby to see what his reaction was. Every time I looked over he was sitting there with his jaw dropped open and his eyes bugging out. Later, as we walked out of the theater,

I asked him what he thought of the film. He replied, "This hippa stuff is right smart; real good eatin' and movies. I am gonna try some of that pot next."

Over the next few weeks we noticed some changes taking place at Bobby's place. The music emitting from the house changed from country and western to the Grateful Dead, Jefferson Airplane, the Beatles and Bob Dylan. Bobby's hair grew longer and longer and his clothes became more colorful. On warm summer nights the sweetish aroma of marijuana smoke, blended with the sounds of acid rock, would waft over our little cottage from Bobby's candlelit pad. Bobby no longer worried about "Stokey" Carmichael and the Black Panthers. His main enemy now was the federal government. By the end of the summer he had placed a for sale sign on his house and was making plans to move back to North Carolina, buy a farm and raise marijuana.

Linnea and I were thoroughly enchanted by our new life in the California sun. The drudgery of our gray, musty government jobs was becoming a distant memory as we happily settled into our new lifestyle of morning and evening meditation, remodeling our houses and taking off for the spectacular California coast and mountains whenever the spirit moved us. Most evenings were spent visiting friends or going over to Berkeley to enjoy the many counterculture events taking place nightly in and around the U.C. Berkeley campus.

Jiddu Krishnamurti was one of the more famous teachers of Indian philosophy. We had read his books so we decided to attend his lecture in one of the large auditoriums on campus. He spoke for a long time about the value of non-attachment and the necessity of gaining enlightenment, but he didn't offer much of a method for achieving these qualities of self realization. Apparently he was born with a highly evolved level of consciousness and didn't need techniques like the rest of us. Someone in the audience asked him what he thought of Transcendental Meditation. He sort of smirked and said we could get the same results from repeating the words "Coca Cola" over and over again!

Our next encounter with a guru came when we received a postcard from the TM center in Berkeley inviting us to an advanced lecture to celebrate "Guru Purnima," to honor Guru Dev, Maharishi's teacher. We arrived at the meeting a little late and, as we opened the door to the pitch black lecture hall, hundreds of people were sitting in the dark "ooohing" and "aahhing" at a small movie screen in the front of the room. On the screen was a scratchy, flickering old home movie of Guru Dev in the 1940s. It was taken at night in some rural village in India. The only lights were torches and the light from the handheld movie camera, which produced an eerie and haunting quality to the film. Apparently there was a large crowd of people performing a puja ceremony for Guru Dev. Whenever the camera was aimed at him, I noticed that his eyes were the most piercing I had ever seen. These amazingly penetrating eyes would start the crowd "ooohing" and "aahhing" again. When the movie finally ended about fifteen minutes later everyone just sat there mesmerized, as though they had had some sort of transformational religious experience. Linnea and I looked at each other with mutual discomfort. Neither one of us got it. The whole thing seemed a little weird to us, so we decided to leave before the refreshments were served.

Tim Leary had been living in Southern California for about a year and was traveling the country spreading his message of "turn on, tune in and drop out" to enthusiastic audiences. Tim felt that the country was undergoing a cultural revolution that couldn't be stopped. Soon everyone would be turned on, the military-industrial structure of the society would collapse, and a new paradigm of love and peace would emerge out of the ashes of the old corrupt system. Living in the Berkeley area in the late 1960s made this vision easy to believe. It seemed as though the entire Bay Area was caught up in this wonderful utopian transformation to a non-structured, non-competitive, lighthearted and sharing social network. So when Tim came to Berkeley to speak, he was greeted as a hero by the throngs who came to his lecture.

As he walked out to begin his talk a young woman jumped up on the stage, tore her clothes off, and started rubbing herself all over

Tim. If this was back at Harvard the security guards would have hauled her off. But this was Berkeley, the center of the revolution, and no one, including Tim, wanted to appear uptight or intolerant, so he began his talk with this naked woman hanging onto him. He presented his vision of a new society, one in which many people would experience some form of expanded consciousness either through psychedelic drugs, meditation and other forms of yoga, mystical revelations, or even psychotic episodes. He felt that millions of people would soon realize there was a much more profound and peaceful level of reality within their own consciousness that would transform the whole society from a dysfunctional mess into a loving, joyful utopia.

Every once in a while the young woman would release herself from Tim and dance around the stage in a primal combination of Tai Chi and strip tease. This distracted the audience from Tim's highly abstract discourse on what he termed "the yoga of LSD." Tim, however, was more delighted than distracted, and he continued with his talk. He explained that, when he started experimenting with LSD at Harvard in the early 1960s, he had no frame of reference for the sublime and ecstatic spiritual nature of the experiences that he and others were having during their LSD sessions. There were no theories or models to describe the psychedelic experience and the only available texts which dealt with altered states of consciousness were the ancient books of the East. So he had gone to India, where he combined his LSD sessions with studying the *Tibetan Book of the Dead* and the *Tao Te Ch'ing*.

According to Tim, the *Tibetan Book of the Dead* was an incredibly specific psychedelic manual describing the sequence and nature of experiences encountered in the ecstatic state of consciousness. The *Tao Te Ch'ing*, on the other hand, offered valuable insights into the field of pure energy, which is at the source of life and manifests into the innumerable forms we experience in our daily lives. He considered both these books useful manuals for conducting LSD sessions. For Tim, LSD, if used properly, was a life-transforming tool and sacrament with the potential to bring about profound changes in the way we lived our daily lives. A few years later, as a result of his very public endorsement of psychedelic drugs, Tim was convicted of using illegal substances and sentenced to prison. That didn't appeal to him so he fled the country.

After a few months of remodeling and landscaping, we had transformed our second house from a neglected dump on an overgrown lot to an attractive home on a well landscaped lot with a deck overlooking San Francisco. Within a few weeks we had a good offer to buy it from a nice young couple who needed a place to live right away. They asked us if they could rent the house until their loan was approved. This arrangement seemed okay to us, so they moved in and started paying rent. There was, however, one contingency: because they were applying for an FHA loan, the house had to be inspected by the City of Oakland's building department. Totally ignorant of building codes, we assumed that the house was in good shape, so we made an appointment with the city building inspector.

As the building inspector walked up the stairs I greeted him with an innocent hello and a friendly handshake, as though he was one of the neighbors. He didn't reciprocate, but instead acted like a homicide detective investigating a crime scene. I was proud of the remodeling job and thought he would also like what we had done to fix up the house. This was my first experience with a building inspector and I had no idea how officious and unpleasant they could be. As soon as he walked into the house he started rattling off code violations and complaints about the quality of the remodeling. By the time he finished he had written up two full pages of violations that had to be fixed before he could certify the house. Some things were understandable, like termite damage and foundation problems needing to be fixed. But when he said we had to repaint the outside of the house again because he didn't like the type of paint we used, I was really aggravated.

The termite damage and foundation work were beyond my skill level so I hired Bobby and his crew to make the repairs. The rest of the work, including scraping and repainting the house, took me about two weeks to complete. As soon as I was done I called the city for another inspection. By now the buyers were getting anxious about the occupancy certificate and I was glad that we had completed all the repairs required by the building inspector. As soon as he stepped out of his car he looked at the porch light, shook his head and declared that it was a hazard. Then he whipped out his violation book and started writing up new violations! I knew there was nothing I could say or do to change the mind of this sadistic bureaucrat, so I kept my mouth shut and agreed to fix the violations on the new list.

The buyers, who had been living in the house for a month by now, were not too happy about the new list of repairs. Although they both worked during the day when I did most of the work, the house was still torn up from all the construction activities. They had to keep their vicious dog locked in the downstairs bedroom all day to keep him from attacking me while I worked on the house. This time I worked extra–fast, completed the repairs in less than a week and called for another inspection. I kept my fingers crossed as the malevolent inspector got out of his car. Just as I was about to escort him up the stairs to the front porch, some sort of divine inspiration caused me to turn around and suggest we start with the downstairs bedrooms. As we entered the hallway the silence was shattered by the most ferocious, blood-curdling growl I had ever heard. A split second later the owners' vicious dog exploded out of the bedroom, lunged at the inspector and started gnawing at his leg. Now there were bloodcurdling screams coming from both the inspector and the dog. I quickly grabbed a broom and started whacking the dog, which caused him to let go of the terrified inspector. With the aid of the broom I forced the dog back into the bedroom and slammed the door. The inspector just stood there, shaking and speechless. He didn't seem too chewed up; just a few rips in his pants and some teeth marks on his leg, so I suggested we continue the inspection. He gave me a defeated look as though he had soiled his pants and said, "No, no, that's okay. I have to get going." He quickly signed the inspection papers and roared out of the driveway.

13

RETREAT to the MOUNTAINS

We were already two hours behind schedule when we pulled out of the RV sales lot towing our newly purchased travel trailer. It was a typical winter day in the Bay Area: mostly cloudy and mild with the ever-present potential for rain. Our plan was to leave by noon so that we would be able to drive into the mountains just east of Willits, about a hundred miles north of San Francisco, and park the trailer on our forty acre ridge-top home site before it got dark. The dirt road was tricky enough to navigate during the day in the winter due to washouts and landslides, but towing a trailer in the dark was treacherous and unwise. We were so excited about spending our first night at our remote mountaintop homestead that we decided to give it a try. By the time we got to Willits it was not only dark, but raining heavily. As we slowly snaked our way through the maze of gravel roads that gradually led up to the ridge-top property, the condition of the road steadily deteriorated. The potholes and landslides weren't so bad, but the surface of the road turned from gravel to an extremely slimy and slick mud. This caused us to continually lose traction, which resulted in the trailer fish-tailing all over the road. It was too late to turn around and go back so we continued to press on as the road became slicker and steeper, making it more and more difficult to get traction. Finally, the inevitable happened. As we rounded a steep bend in the road, the truck lost all traction, slowed to a stop, and lurched backward as though a giant hand had grabbed it and thrown it off the road.

The rain and fog were so thick that I could hardly see out the window to assess the damage. As I got out of the truck my feet went out from under me and I landed on my back in the mud, which was not soft and squishy, but more like hard-packed clay that was as slick as ice. I struggled to my feet and cautiously shuffled to the middle of the road to figure out what had happened to the trailer. Apparently it had slid off the road first and, because it was bigger and heavier than the truck, had pulled the truck with it into the ditch. There was no serious damage, but there was no way to pull both the truck and the trailer out of the ditch without a very large tow truck. The town of Willits was about ten miles away and it was 10 PM on a Saturday night.

Just as we were deciding to spend the night in the listing trailer, Linnea remembered seeing a mobile home with lights on about a mile back in the canyon. As we approached the house, Linnea and I looked at each other. We were soaked to the bone and covered with mud, and by now it was almost midnight. We didn't want to scare anyone by knocking on their door so late at night in such a remote place, but we didn't want to walk back to the trailer either, so I knocked gently. We waited nervously for a few minutes, but nothing happened. We thought someone was awake because we could hear music and there were lights on, so this time I knocked on the door with more urgency and aggression. The door swung open and a petite, professional looking woman in her early forties appeared. She was well dressed and looked like she belonged in one of the affluent suburbs of San Francisco, except for the fact that she had a .45 caliber automatic pistol strapped to her leg. "Hi, I'm Ruth. Can I help you?" she said in a friendly and matter-of-fact manner, as though strangers came to her door regularly on dark and stormy nights. I tried not to stare at the large pistol on her side as we introduced ourselves and explained our predicament to her.

She invited us in, offered her phone to call a wrecker, and gave us some hot tea. While I was trying to contact a wrecking service her two children came into the kitchen and introduced themselves. The girl was about fifteen and the boy was maybe twelve. The whole family seemed bright and refined; I wondered what they were doing living in a trailer so far from civilization. When Ruth found out we were planning to move onto our property she was delighted that we would be her closest neighbors, even though our property was almost two miles away. I asked her why they were living in the trailer in the middle of the forest. She explained that they had fallen in love with the property and were planning to retire there in a few years, Her husband had retired early from the Air Force and was now flying with Japan Airlines. She and the kids were staying on their property while they were figuring out whether to live in the States or in Japan.

The tow truck couldn't come out until the next morning so Ruth kindly drove us back to our listing trailer. We were grateful to be inside and out of the rain, even though being in the trailer felt like being on a sinking ship. The bunk was tilted to one side so severely that we kept rolling onto the floor. Finally we piled up some cushions on the side of the bed to keep from falling out and slept until we were awakened by a loud pounding on the door. I peered out the window and saw a large, heavy-duty tow truck parked next to the trailer. The driver didn't seem too happy when I explained to him that, not only did we need a tow out of the ditch, but we also needed to tow the trailer another mile up the mountain, to the top of our forty acre homestead. He looked at the muddy road, shook his head and said, "I can't guarantee we'll make it around the next corner towing that heavy trailer, and if it gets stuck I am just going to leave it there and drive home!" Linnea and I had a little conference and decided that we didn't have much choice but to try to tow it up the mountain. If we left it there in the road it could be over a month before the road would be dry enough to haul it up the mountain and in that time it probably would be stolen or vandalized. The first half-mile wasn't too bad, but when we started up the steep, winding driveway to the top of our property, the huge wrecker started losing traction and sliding all over the road, spewing mud from its monster tires and gouging giant ruts in the soft clay.

I thought to myself, *Well this is it; he is going to dump the trailer in the mud by the side of the road and go home.* The situation in the cab of the truck

was getting tense and the driver's language became decidedly less genteel. But I noticed a look of fierce determination in his eyes, as though
he was enjoying the challenge and not about to give up. Linnea and I
sat there not saying a word to him for fear of breaking his concentration,
as the engine of the giant truck screamed while the back tires kicked
up a steady spray of slimy muck that plastered the wildly fish-tailing
trailer. The situation was getting more and more out of control as the
truck ground its way up the mountain, obliterating our driveway and
turning the trailer into a thirty-foot glob of mud. Just before it felt like
the engine was going to blow up and we were going to slam into a large
redwood on the side of the road, we roared to the top of the property,
where the road leveled off. All three of us let out a loud "Yahoo!" as the
tow truck stopped at the spot we had picked out for the trailer.

As the wrecker slithered back down what was left of our driveway,
Linnea and I looked at our mud covered trailer and broke into hysterical laughter as we tried to locate the door under all the mud. It was so
crusty with mud that we decided to wait until the mud was washed off
by the rain before going inside. We walked over to a clearing where we
were going to build our house overlooking the verdant valley below and
the snowcapped mountains in the distance. We found a comfortable
spot, sat down and meditated. All the anxiety and discomfort of the
past twenty-four hours melted away as we settled down into the deep
silence of the mountaintop. It was easy to understand why the yogis of
the Himalaya Mountains spend their lives in caves, meditating without
venturing down into the cities. We felt blessed to be able to meditate
and transcend the stressful events in daily life and to enjoy the inspiring
natural beauty of northern California. The property was on the western
edge of the Coast Range of mountains that featured redwood, Douglas
fir and pine trees, with occasional small meadows that offered stunning
views of the vineyards in the valley below us and the mountains to the
east. For some reason we were driven to live in a remote, wild place far
from the city. We couldn't wait until we returned in the spring to create
our homestead far from electricity and phone services.

Within a few weeks the mild, short, California winter quickly
transformed into a sunny, dry spring. We started making arrangements
to sell our other house in Oakland and begin working on our new homestead in Willits. Because the house that we remodeled sold so quickly,
we thought the little house that we were living in would also sell fast.
However, it was too small and weird for most people, so we rented it
to a nice hippie couple who loved it. The small twenty-five-foot travel
trailer that was now our new home had no running water or electricity,
but that didn't bother us because we spent most of our time living outside. At night we would read by the gas lights and cook on the propane
stove. Hauling water from the old well next to a collapsed log cabin a
few hundred yards away was the biggest inconvenience, so we decided
our first project would be to get a well pump and storage tank for the
water.

With the help of a local plumber we hooked up a gas-powered
pump to the well and ran a water line to our five hundred gallon redwood tank. As soon as everything was hooked up we fired up the small
engine and waited for the tank to be filled with precious water from our
well. After about five minutes we heard an ominous sucking sound from
the pump, which meant there wasn't any more water being pumped
from the well. I shut the pump off immediately to keep it from burning
up and ran over to the tank, which we had situated on the highest part
of the property to give us a good gravity flow. There were only a few
inches of water in the bottom of the tank; thirty gallons at most, We
had assumed there would be plenty of water in the well and, after talking with the plumber, decided that the only way to find out what was
wrong with the well was to climb down in and check it out. As I lowered
myself into the well I felt myself being overcome by the darkness and an
unpleasant odor of something dead. It was so dark at the bottom that I
couldn't see anything as I lowered my body into the black water. To my
surprise my feet touched the bottom much sooner than I thought and
I realized I was standing in only two feet of water. I felt something soft
floating in the water and now that my hands were free, I quickly untied

the flashlight from the rope and flipped it on. Not good!! We had been drinking and washing with water that had lots of deceased and decayed mice floating in it. The abandoned well probably hadn't been used in years and the mice must have fallen in and drowned .

As he stepped out of his house in Willits Bob looked more like an old cowboy with a rocket launcher than a water dowser. He moseyed out to our jeep, hopped in and deposited his mysterious four-foot-long metal tube on the back seat. It was about four inches in diameter and sealed at both ends. Most dowsers use forked willow sticks or two copper wires that spread apart when they walk over a water source, but Bob had his own unique style of dowsing. He pulled a sword-like brass rod out of the case and stuck it out the window as we drove up the mountain to our land. As soon as we entered the gate to our property he said, "Slow way down." As we crept up the hill toward the building site, every once in a while Bob's brass fencing sword would whip around in a circle, sometimes violently and at other times more gently. He explained that when he was over a water vein the rod would react by waving around in a circle. When there was a strong water vein it would react more violently.

As we slowly drove along our ridge-top road old Bob captivated us with amazing tales of how he had located water for hundreds of people in Northern California. Not only could he locate the water, but he could also determine how deep it was and how many gallons a minute it flowed. It was hard to believe he could determine all that information with his brass rod, but we figured we had nothing to lose. Most well drillers just drilled where it was convenient and took a chance on finding water wherever they drilled. Not satisfied with his search for water from the vehicle, Bob decided to walk all over the property. After a few hours he found some spots that caused the brass rod to whip around mildly, but nothing very exciting. Finally we walked over by the old well. As he walked past the well to the edge of the steep ridge, the rod started to swing around rather vigorously. Bob stopped and turned the rod around, holding it by its tip. This time the rod flipped up and down instead of going around in a circle, and Bob seemed to be counting each stroke. When it stopped he turned the rod around again and it started going up and down again. Linnea and I were both astonished at Bob's performance. It looked so genuine that it was hard to believe he was faking it.

After a few minutes of what seemed like a meditative trance Bob drove a stake into the ground where he had found the water, walked over to us and said, "Pretty good flow—about five gallons a minute at about 125 feet deep. Let's go back to my place and have a cold beer!" It was a typical hot, dry summer afternoon and the taste of a cold beer sounded good, but since we had started meditating about six months ago, we had both lost our taste for alcohol and drugs. We didn't want to hurt Bob's feelings, so we accepted his offer and started sipping our refreshing beverage. After drinking about half a bottle I started feeling really foggy and detached; it was almost like a bad acid trip. I wanted it to be over and be back to normal. Bob offered us another beer but we declined, thanked him profusely and headed home. On the way home Linnea remarked that she also felt weird from the alcohol. We realized that meditating must have refined our senses gradually and as a result the dulling effect of the alcohol was more noticeable. It was sort of like growing; we really hadn't noticed it on a day-to-day basis, but after a few months something would happen to make us aware of the gradual transformation we were undergoing.

As the sound of the enormous well-drilling rig lumbering up our road got louder and louder we realized that the moment of truth for Bob's water-finding skills was near. The rig, followed by another truck with pipes and auxiliary equipment, pulled into our building site. A dapper middle-aged man in expensive-looking western clothes and a spotless white cowboy hat stepped out of the truck, sauntered over to us and introduced himself as Len Williams. One look at us confirmed his suspicion that we were definitely not ranchers or loggers. Most of the people in this part of Northern California were involved in ranching or the timber industry. There were very few hippies or new-age people in the area in the late '60s. The local folks were not quite sure what to make of newcomers like us who just wanted to live in the country without raising cattle or chopping down the forest to make a living. We could tell he didn't think much of our rural living skills so he looked at our house site, pointed to a spot about thirty feet away and said that was the best place to drill the well. When I told him we had another place in mind he seemed mildly annoyed and shook his head. "Well, let's take a look," he said sarcastically. He took one look at Bob's stake marking the spot to drill and gave me a disgusted look. "You had this dowsed, didn't you?" he said. He grudgingly backed the drilling rig up as close to the stake as he could without going over the cliff. By the end of the day we had a well about 125 feet deep that produced five gallons a minute, just as Bobby had predicted!

Now that our water system was installed we turned our attention to building our house. Every few weeks we would drive to the Bay Area to look for used building materials, but didn't have a clue about what kind of house to build. Then one day, while driving down one of the main streets of Berkeley, we noticed a small cedar model home for sale on the lot of the Lindal Cedar Home company. Apparently they were going out of business and the little chalet had to be moved off the lot. The price for the whole house was only $2,700, the salesman claimed that it could be easily dismantled and rebuilt, and the carpenter who assembled the house was available to take it apart and rebuild it. The salesman said they knew the house was eventually going to be removed, so they had "just tacked it together for easy dismantling."

Lieb, the German carpenter, was just the man we needed to help us take the house apart and rebuild it. He was in his late forties, had been a carpenter all his life and had the strength of an ox. After we ripped the asphalt shingles off the roof we noticed that the house was not "just tacked together," but nailed together with hundreds of huge spikes. Some were so hard to pull out that once the powerful Lieb actually snapped his heavy-duty crowbar in two. As Lieb wrenched the house apart Linnea and I numbered the boards and stacked them in piles according to what section of the house they belonged to. Reassembling the house was much easier than ripping it apart and within a few weeks the house was finished enough to move into. Every room was paneled in natural cedar and the living room had a large window overlooking the distant mountains and the valley below. There was no electricity but we were perfectly comfortable with a gas refrigerator, gas stove and gas lights. Over the next few months we finished the roof, added another room and a deck, and began our homestead planting of fruit trees and gardens.,

Every couple of weeks we would take a break from the building and planting and travel to the Bay Area or to the Mendocino coast for a few days. Our only communication with friends and family was through the mail or the pay phone in town. We loved our remote homestead on the mountain, but we also missed our friends and the dynamic counterculture of Berkeley. One day we received an invitation from our old LSD friend Walt. He had finished his Ph.D. at U.C. Berkeley and was now living on the Mendocino coast. After living at the Fern Creek commune for a few months he had moved into a spectacular house with his new girlfriend. The drive to Mendocino was always a welcome relief from the dusty heat of Willits in the summer. As we approached the coast the temperature gradually dropped from a hundred degrees to around seventy-five. With the majestic expanse of the cool blue Pacific in the background, Walt stepped out of his stunning ocean-front home, gave Linnea and me a big hug and invited us in to meet Jan. She had also just finished her Ph.D. and they were both writing for serious new-age journals and magazines. It was enlivening to be with old friends who were committed to using their intellectual prowess to help transform the American culture to a more humane and light-hearted society.

After an invigorating walk along the headlands above the powerful Pacific crashing on the beach below, we returned to the house for a tasty lunch. Then Walt offered us a "special" fruit drink that didn't taste very special to me, but I didn't want to seem unappreciative so

I remarked that it was delicious. A few minutes later I felt strangely detached from our lively discussion, which dissolved into giggles and laughter. We had been sitting in a small circle on the floor when Walt and Jan sort of keeled over, lying on their backs and chuckling. Then it dawned on me that they had put LSD in the fruit drink. I didn't really want to take another acid trip after a bad trip that Linnea and I had experienced a few months before in Oakland. We weren't sure if it had been bad acid or just a bad trip that happens occasionally. It was as though we had been trapped in a dark place and couldn't wait for the LSD to wear off, which had seemed like a thousand years. Regaining our normal state of consciousness had never felt so good!

While Walt and Jan were busy lying on the floor giggling Linnea and I got up and walked outside. I asked her how she felt and she said, "They put acid in the drink, didn't they?" We weren't very happy about the situation but we realized there was nothing we could do about it, so we decided to take a walk along the ocean. After meditating for almost a year and experiencing the progressive growth of inner silence during meditation and activity, we now both experienced a foggy detachment from our inner being. This experience wasn't as uncomfortable as the bad trip back in Oakland, but nevertheless we couldn't wait for it to be over. We couldn't really get mad at them for putting LSD in the drinks. It was as though they were sharing their best wine with good friends; they assumed we would really appreciate and enjoy the acid. They meant well, but we couldn't wait to get "unstoned!"

Walt and Jan were ecstatically preparing a sumptuous feast for dinner when we returned to the house. Just as we were finishing the delightful meal Walt got a phone call from the manager of the Grateful Dead, who needed a plane ride to Mendocino from Marin County. He asked me if I would like to go along for the ride to keep him company and before I could think about it, I said sure. On the way out to the airport I had the realization that we were both high on LSD and that the plane ride might be more interesting than I bargained for. As we buzzed our way against the gravitational pull of the earth and into the heavens, the flaming, brilliant sun was diving into the cool blue of the ocean, creating such a glorious view from our little flying machine that we were both speechless for most of the flight. After a half-hour Walt landed the plane flawlessly and in less than five minutes we were back in the air with our passenger and his aromatic baggage. The whole trip took less than ninety minutes and when we returned to the house Linnea and Jan were just finishing the dinner dishes.

On the drive back to Willits Linnea mentioned that the LSD experience had made her realize that we were getting more results from meditation than we had perhaps realized. The wonderful enlivenment of the senses and inner self-contentment usually experienced with psychedelic drugs had been gradually and naturally developing in our awareness as our physiology changed over the months since we had started meditating. Drugs did not create the quantum leap in perception they once did and actually felt toxic and unwelcome to our nervous systems. She said that one of the newsletters we received from the TM center was an invitation to a weeklong meditation retreat at Asilomar, on the coast near Monterey, and that we should look into going. Even though we were blasted with LSD, the joy of seeing old friends made us realize how isolated we were on our ridge-top homestead. We loved every minute of our simple, secluded life in our little cedar chalet, with its beautiful views of the California mountains and vineyards in the valley below, but now that we had achieved our dream we wanted more. We were becoming more disillusioned with the counterculture as a way to transform society or at least create an alternative to the values of mainstream America.

Over the next few weeks, all of the alternative radio stations and newspapers in the Bay Area began featuring plans for a huge gathering of hippies at Altamont Park in the mountains east of Berkeley. It was billed as Woodstock West and over 500,000 people were expected to attend. The Rolling Stones and other well-known groups were going to play and admission was free. The more we listened to the promotions for the concert on our battery-operated radio the more we got excited about joining thousands of like-minded folks in a demonstration of how peaceful and fun-loving life should be. This could be the event that would show the rest of the uptight, un-turned-on, brainwashed and ignorant population that a new culture of kindness and tolerance was emerging from the younger generation.

The mountains east of Berkeley were almost treeless, golden, grass-covered mounds that divided the coastal areas from the hot and arid central valley of California. Even though they were not that far from the busy cities of Oakland, Berkeley and San Jose, the area seemed remote and barren. There were no vineyards like the area north of San Francisco, nor were there any fruit and vegetable farms like those covering the valley south of the city. On the map Altamont was only fifty miles from the freeways of the Bay Area, but it took hours of grueling driving on the winding two-lane highway, up and down mountain after mountain, to get to the park. As we drove within a few miles of the concert we started seeing cars parked along the road. The closer we got the more densely the cars were packed. Finally, about two miles from the park, we were stopped by a roadblock and had to pull off the road. As soon as we stepped out of the car we were greeted by a volunteer traffic director, who suggested it would be better to leave our vehicle and follow the signs to the park on foot.

As we walked closer to the site along the top of a ridge we noticed groups of people gathering on the hillsides that surrounded a natural amphitheater. The approach to the edge of the bowl started to get more and more congested with people dressed in multi-colored costumes ranging from medieval to 1960s classic hippie. Everyone was in a festive mood and didn't seem to mind the crowding and endless lines at the porta-potties. When we got close enough to the edge of the bowl to see down into it, we were stunned! From our distant vantage point the sight of nearly half a million people packed on the hillside surrounding what looked like a miniscule stage was both spine-tingling and frightening at the same time. The thought of hiking down into the swarm of raucous humans was terrifying so we decided to stay up on the top of the hill, far from the madness below. We were so far away that we couldn't recognize the group playing on stage. The only way we knew it was the Jefferson Airplane or Santana was by the sound of their music blasting over the huge loudspeakers attached to tall towers that were set up beside the stage.

Most of the folks around us were sitting on picnic blankets, drinking beer and wine or smoking dope. They were having a relaxed time playing Frisbee and soaking up the mellow, omnipresent California sun, without paying much attention to the stage show far below. Occasionally someone drunk or stoned would stagger around naked in a half-hearted demonstration of their liberation from the mores of the old culture that was now being superseded by the new age of love and sharing. As I looked around at the thousands of people sitting around us it was hard for me to imagine that this event was ushering in a new age. It seemed more like a bunch of drunks watching a baseball game. There was no sense of spiritual upliftment or group consciousness. I even felt strangely out of place, as though I had been invited to a bowling tournament in the Midwest.

Suddenly the music stopped and everyone looked down the hill toward the distant stage. It appeared some sort of melee was taking place. We could see objects flying through the air and the crowd nearest the stage began moving about in an agitated and violent manner. Then we heard the sirens of police cars and ambulances coming closer as a shock wave of rumors undulated through the crowd up the hill toward us. Apparently someone had had a run-in with the Hell's Angels, who were providing security for the performers. A large fight ensued, resulting in the stabbing death of the person who challenged the Hell's Angels. I looked at Linnea and said, "We drove all day for this! Let's get out of here." Unfortunately, about a half a million people had the same idea. The mob down below us started swarming in all directions like a disturbed ant colony.

Luckily our car was parked high on the hill surrounding the park and not in the park itself. After a two-mile sprint we left most of the horde behind us, jumped in our car and headed down the relatively uncongested highway back to the Bay Area. A few minutes later and we would have been caught in a massive traffic jam for hours. Although we were relieved to escape the mass confusion behind us, we were saddened that this highly touted event, which was supposed to showcase the glories of the alternative lifestyle, had not only failed to live up to expectations but had turned into a murderous disaster. It was depressing to realize that all these people who had dropped out of the mainstream, abandoned their careers and middle-class comforts and grew their hair long were not much different from the people they had rejected. It was a wake-up call for us and it took us a few days to process this realization and how it would affect our future plans.

California no longer seemed like the epicenter of transformation to a more enlightened society. We had been in contact with Martin and our friends in Virginia and were intrigued by the loose community they were developing near his farm in the Blue Ridge Mountains. It had been over a year since we had left the East Coast and, now that our homestead was ready for the winter, it seemed like a good idea to visit Martin and our old friends in the fall. As we drove into the mountains around Martin's farm in late October the gold, red and yellow autumnal colors were in their full glory. The spectacular colors made Martin's farm appear even more magical as we drove across the rushing river next to his house. Elizabeth welcomed us with a big hug and offered us one of their cabins to stay in. Over the next week we visited with Martin and some of our old friends who were living in his different houses or had purchased their own properties. We both liked the idea of living in a community of compatible people rather than in a structured commune. Having so many friends nearby to visit and share meals and work projects with for a whole week was a sheer delight. When it came time to return to California we didn't want to leave, even though we had a beautiful place to go back to. We realized that what was missing from our idyllic life on the mountain in Willits was living in a community of friends who shared the same values of spiritual growth, rural living and a healthy lifestyle.

Just before we left, Martin asked us if we wanted to look at a near-by place that was for sale. The property had fifty-seven acres, a stream running into a pond and a stunning view of Old Rag Mountain. There were a couple of two hundred-year-old chestnut log houses twenty-five feet apart from each other on a hillside overlooking the pond and the mountain. Having a stream and a pond for swimming was something we had missed at our California homestead, which was dry and dusty about half the year. One of the log houses had been partially restored, but there was no running water or septic system. We weren't sure if we wanted to take on a major construction project so soon after finishing our house in California, but the idea of living so close to our friends and having our own private space was very appealing. I called up the owner and told him that we would like to buy it but that we had to sell our home in Willits first. He said he would let us know if he received an offer before then, in case we wanted to bid on it at that time. We realized our house in California wouldn't sell until the spring so we decided to hope for the best and returned to California for the winter.

A few weeks before Christmas we received a mailing announcing a week-long TM meditation retreat over the holidays. Our friend Bernie had attended a few of these retreats and highly recommended them. I figured that if Bernie, the ultimate hippie who had tried just about every drug and spiritual development program available in California, thought it was a great experience, it must be good. He claimed that it was a great opportunity to go deeper into meditation and the knowledge associated with it. We both liked meditation and thought we were having some results in our daily life so we decided to attend. When I started filling out the application I came across a recommendation that we bring some more formal clothes, like jackets, ties and dresses. This brought me up short! I looked at Linnea and said, "Do we really want to go to this thing for a whole week if we have to dress up? What kind of people are they, anyway?" Then we remembered that Bernie, who had his hair down to his shoulders and looked like a member of the Grateful

Dead, didn't have a problem with it, so we sent in our application.

The Asilomar Conference Center on the coast near Monterey was a cluster of attractive, modern, natural wood and glass buildings separated from the ocean only by a series of sand dunes. The insides of the buildings were more Spartan than luxurious, but definitely not drab and institutional like most government facilities. Not having participated in anything like this before, we were a little apprehensive as we approached the registration table. The young volunteers manning the table were reassuringly scruffy-looking and very welcoming so we felt at home right away and looked forward to the orientation meeting in the evening. We were surprised at the hundreds of people in the dining room as we looked around for a place to sit. We found a couple of seats and sat down with our trays of delicious natural food. The folks at the table were engaged in an arcane discussion about higher states of consciousness and as soon as we sat down they stopped their discussion and introduced themselves. Almost everyone had been to a "residence course" before, and two of them had just returned from India where they had been studying to become meditation teachers. They just happened to be there when the Beatles, Mia Farrow, Donovan and other celebrities were there. For the next hour, the rest of us at the table peppered them with questions about Maharishi, the teacher training course and the Beatles. We were all so spellbound by their stories of saints and celebrities at the ashram in Rishikesh that we were ready to get on the next plane for India. The two new meditation teachers expressed a deep level of knowledge about the nature of human consciousness and ancient Vedic philosophy that whetted our appetites for more understanding of the Vedas and meditation.

Jerry Jarvis, the director of the Students International Meditation Society, came on stage with an infectious grin to welcome the three hundred meditators to the retreat. Even though he was dressed in a jacket and tie, he neutralized his formal and authoritarian image by wearing his trademark dorky-looking Hush Puppies shoes. He started his presentation with a list of rules given to him by the management of

Asilomar. Apparently at the last retreat, there were some unpleasant incidents involving drugs, nudity and furniture being thrown out the windows. He apologetically explained that the management had not been happy with the behavior of the meditators on the last retreat and if we didn't behave this time we would not be allowed to come back. Linnea and I looked around at the audience and noticed some people who looked pretty wild and crazy even by the standards of 1969 California. It was hard to understand why people on a meditation retreat would want to rip their clothes off and smash furniture—we were soon to find out. After he finished dealing with the facility policies, Jerry began describing the purpose of the course and the schedule of activities or non-activities. He started with the analogy of comparing meditation to shooting a bow and arrow. The farther you pull the arrow back on the bow, the farther it will go. Meditation was like pulling the arrow back on the bow. The deep rest gained during meditation prepared the mind and body for much more dynamic activity than regular sleep. Therefore the deeper the rest, the farther you can go in terms of successful activity. He then went on to explain that, just as daily meditation is a preparation for daily activity, meditating for a whole week will be so restful and rejuvenating that there would be an exponential development in mental clarity and energy.

Then someone in the audience asked, "What does this have to do with becoming enlightened?" "Everything!" Jerry replied. "Let's look at the opposite of enlightenment first. We have all probably experienced being tired, exhausted, cranky, stressed, freaked out, angry, frightened or intoxicated. That's when we are most likely to make mistakes, say things we don't mean, have accidents, fights and failure. In an ideal sense, enlightenment is when we have the utmost clarity of mind so that we don't make mistakes and all our actions are in accordance with the 'laws of nature.' This means that our thoughts and actions are 'life supporting' rather than negative or destructive. Nature is evolving and progressing and the more we are in tune with that process, the faster we will evolve toward a state of enlightenment or cosmic consciousness," he went on. "Meditation helps us grow toward enlightenment by removing deep-rooted stress that clouds our awareness and restricts us from using our full potential." Jerry then presented the program for the week by explaining the process of "rounding," which consisted of meditating for a half hour followed by fifteen minutes of performing yoga asanas or postures. This was considered one "round." The plan was to do one round after waking up and then, after a light breakfast, continue rounding until lunch time. After lunch there was a meeting with Jerry and then back to rounding for another three or four hours until dinner. The number of rounds we did was dependent on what time we got up. Some people might do five or six rounds while others might do as many as twelve. The goal was not how many rounds we did, but to sink progressively deeper into the meditative state during the week. By meditating all day the metabolic rate slows way down and the body gets a very deep and profound rest, which results in the release of deep-rooted stress. This is an effortless and natural process similar to what happens during sleep. The difference is that the level of rest is much deeper during meditation, allowing for much deeper stress to be dissolved.

"The release of stress can be experienced in many ways," Jerry continued. "Often it is a physical sensation during meditation like a twitch or jerking of the muscles or an intense thought accompanying some physical sensation. This usually lasts only a few minutes and then we feel some release. Sometimes when a really big stress is dissolved, we can experience an overwhelming thought or sensation or both. Maybe we feel like screaming or throwing the furniture out the window." Jerry continued, "This is just stress coming out and we don't want to act on these thoughts. The best thing to do is just sit there or lie down until the sensation subsides. Even though it might be uncomfortable, it will go away and we will feel lighter and freer as a result of a big 'block' of stress being released." When Jerry finished describing the mechanics of stress release, Linnea looked at me and said, "That's why some of these folks have done weird things here like throwing stuff around." Just then, as though Jerry had heard our conversation, he said, "If you ever get a strong urge to do anything in meditation, whether it's calling your mother or flying to Cuba, remember it is stress being released. Wait until the urge subsides, then continue meditating. If the discomfort persists, see one of the teachers right away and we can help you out."

The next morning we started our rounding. With each successive round of meditation and asanas we sank deeper into a silent, detached, meditative state. We could feel our metabolic rates slowing down as though we were in a deep state of rest, even when we were not actually meditating. All the distractions, concerns and desires of daily living seemed to melt away as we began to settle into a level of silence we had never experienced before. This experience of being grounded in an eternal oneness with all creation was something usually experienced only occasionally in meditation. Now we were beginning to experience that deep silence in our activity.

After lunch we had another meeting with Jerry, where he asked participants to describe their experiences. A number of people noticed that they were also experiencing a profound settling down of their body and mind and that it was a very pleasant state of separation from their usual thoughts and activities. Jerry then asked everyone who was having similar experiences to raise their hands; most of the audience did. He sat for a moment with his infectious grin and said, "This is what we call 'witnessing.' It is an indication that our awareness is shifting from being completely absorbed or overshadowed by our own individual ego to a more expanded and universal consciousness. Most people are completely identified with their 'small' self and have no awareness of their 'big' self, which is our true identity. The big self is our unbounded eternal nature that is beyond the boundaries of our limited egocentric world view. When we begin to witness everything from this unlimited silent level, we are growing toward a state of consciousness called 'cosmic consciousness', or CC for short. This state of CC becomes permanent when we are no longer overshadowed by our activity and we are grounded in that inner silence. This is not only a very blissful state but also a very practical state of consciousness because our minds are not clouded by the stress and negative emotions that result in mistakes and failure."

Someone then asked how long it takes to gain cosmic conscious-ness. Jerry responded that it depended on the individual. If we have a lot of stress and are in a very stressful situation, naturally it will take longer than if a person is in good physical and mental health and leads a healthy lifestyle. Then he asked if anyone experienced any discomfort or had any overwhelming thoughts that they just had to act on right away. A middle-aged woman said that she was having a lot of physical sensations in her neck and back, causing her to twitch and jerk during meditation. He responded by explaining that stress was being released and these intense physical and mental events during meditation were just as valuable as the most transcendent and silent experiences we have during TM. "Whatever happens during meditation happens for good," he continued. "We don't much pay attention to what happens during meditation; if we are meditating correctly what we look for is results in activity. Whether we are releasing a lot of stress during TM or re-ally enjoying the experience, we are transforming the nervous system to maintain more of that eternal silence in our daily life and that is a good thing."

After the meeting we returned to our room to continue our round-ing until dinner. With each successive round of meditation and yoga asanas, I felt myself sinking deeper and deeper into a state of silent sepa-ration from the buzz of activity that I could see around me. Although I felt separated from my environment, I was not alienated, but rather enchanted. As everyone finished their afternoon rounding and started drifting into the dining hall, the atmosphere at Asilomar had become so still that many people lost the urge to talk and sat at their tables eating in contented silence.

Jerry started the evening meeting with more questions about ex-periences during rounding. The variety of experiences included sleeping all day, extreme restlessness, visions of Christian and Hindu saints and an overwhelming sense of oneness with the entire universe. He remind-ed everyone again that our experiences would always change and that we were not to pay too much attention to them. The important thing was that we were accelerating our growth toward enlightenment by purifying and refining our nervous systems, allowing us to experience a higher level of consciousness.

So far, Linnea and I were enjoying everything about the retreat: the longer meditations, meeting lots of folks like us who were searching for enlightenment and alternative life styles, and the meetings with Jerry. It was a great combination of knowledge and experience.

As the week progressed our level of deep rest and blissful experiences increased almost daily and we both became convinced that this was what we had been searching for over the last couple of years. On the last night of the residence course, New Year's Eve 1969, Jerry and his wife Debbie decided to invite all the new TM teachers, or initiators, to come up on the stage to perform a group puja to bring in the new decade. The only other time we had experienced this ceremony was when we were instructed in meditation. Before the ceremony, Jerry explained that the purpose of the ceremony was to create an atmosphere of deep silence that served to enhance the transcendental experience during meditation.

On the stage was a large picture of Guru Dev, Maharishi's teacher, and at the base of the picture was a shiny brass tray where offerings of fruit and flowers were placed. Apparently this was an old Vedic ritual, performed during meditation instruction and special occasions. Jerry said that one way to look at it was not as a religious ceremony but as a formula or recipe for purifying the atmosphere. When the ceremony began, all the new teachers began singing the puja and the atmosphere in the auditorium became infused with grateful stillness that increased as the puja continued. When it was over no one could speak. People either sat and meditated or retired to their rooms in delightful silence.

The course ended the next day with a group meditation and a final meeting with Jerry. He said that with this week of intense purification we should notice an increased coherence in our activity and that, because we have been in such a deep state of rest, we should not plunge into activity right away, as it could be jarring to the system. The quality of our activity is directly related to the quality of rest we get, he continued. By the next day we should be normalized from all the meditation. "See if you notice an increase in 'support of nature' in your life," he said. Then he quoted Maharishi; "When you are in harmony with the laws of nature as a result of more clarity of mind, your action is considered 'right action' and your activity is life-supporting rather than life-damaging."

It wasn't until I hit the freeway heading north that I noticed I was definitely in a different state of consciousness than before the retreat. The hustle and bustle of the traffic rushing to get somewhere seemed almost absurd. *Why don't all these people settle down?* I thought to myself. Then I realized that it was me, not them. It was as though I had been in suspended animation for the last week and now, being out in the world again, I felt a pleasant, delicate detachment. The next day both Linnea and I felt more integrated and less detached. After reflecting back on the retreat, we agreed that the combination of meditation, knowledge, and meeting so many people who shared the same goal of spiritual growth had resulted in the most powerful transformation we had ever experienced. When Jerry announced there was going to be a one-month teacher training course with Maharishi in the summer of 1970, we hadn't paid much attention. At first it had sounded like too much of a commitment to make to something we were just trying out, but after our great experience at the retreat we began to seriously consider attending. Fortunately the course was going to be held at Humboldt State University in Arcata, California, not far from where we lived. Our one week course was so delightful and inspiring, the thought of a whole month with Maharishi began to sound like an offer we couldn't refuse.

As soon as we had a contract on our house in Willits, I called the owner of the place in Virginia and said we were interested. We offered to buy it for a few thousand dollars less than the price we were selling our house for. He agreed on the price over the phone and all we needed to do was to complete the sale of our house and move across the country. After a few weeks discussing the pros and cons of the one-month course with Maharishi, we concluded that we had nothing to lose and a lot to gain by attending. Not only would it be a great personal experience, but the possibility of become teachers of TM began to appeal to both Linnea and me. At the very least, teaching meditation could help people reduce stress and become more relaxed. If everything Jerry Jarvis claimed about meditation was true, then the effects of many people meditating in a society could actually create an influence of peace and harmony and reduce negativity. After becoming disillusioned with the counterculture as a model for transforming society, we wondered how we could be of service to mankind. Perhaps teaching meditation could be a way to change society for the better.

14

A MONTH WITH MAHARISHI

The drive north from the ninety-degree heat of Willits to the cool, sea-coast town of Arcata was magical. The enormous redwood trees dwarfed even the large tractor trailer trucks that roared under and around them. These trees radiated an ancient dignity that made our busy little human activity of driving amongst them seem so insignificant. The Humboldt State campus was nestled on a hillside between a redwood forest and the ocean. Most of the buildings were 1950s and 1960s utilitarian-style architecture common in many of the state and municipal institutions of California. While the campus lacked the grandeur of U.C. Berkeley, the surrounding area was untouched by the hectic rat race of the Bay Area and had a peaceful, pristine atmosphere. The school was practically deserted for the summer so the TM organization had the use of the whole campus for the course with Maharishi. Although we had been to a couple of residence courses, and were now familiar with the program of longer meditation and the philosophy associated with TM, Linnea and I were anxious to see what Maharishi was like in person. We had seen him on television and had enjoyed his light-hearted style of presenting the knowledge he had gained from years of study with his master in the Himalayas.

As we filed into the college field house for the first meeting with Maharishi, there were about fifty devotees crammed around the stage entrance waiting for Maharishi to show up. Every one of them had a few flowers in their hands and as he stepped out of his car, they lined up on each side and offered flowers to him as he made his way toward the field house entrance. He graciously and patiently accepted the flowers from every last person. It took at least fifteen minutes to walk about fifty feet, but he seemed in no hurry, even though over a thousand people had been waiting for an hour inside the field house. By the time he entered the building he was carrying so many flowers it was hard to see his diminutive frame behind the giant floral bouquet. When he stepped onto the stage, everyone in the audience rose to their feet, put their hands together and bowed their heads in a sign of respect. This overt display of reverence made me a little uncomfortable, but Maharishi seemed like such a humble and kind person that I joined the audience in their silent welcome and rose to my feet and clasped my hands. Actually, I liked the fact that there was no applause or cheering. Maharishi delicately placed his pile of beautiful flowers on the coffee table in front of a living room-style couch, sat down, clasped his hands together and bowed to the audience. In addition to the huge pile of flowers in front of him, there were large floral displays on each side of his couch and a large picture of Guru Dev with a garland of marigolds draped over it. The last time I had seen so many flowers was at a recent funeral.

After everyone sat down, Maharishi smiled and said, "Jai Guru Dev." Most of the audience answered, "Jai Guru Dev" in return. Linnea and I didn't know what this meant so I asked the person next to me. She said that Guru Dev was Maharishi's master and this was his way of honoring his teacher by praising him. He then welcomed everyone and asked if we were comfortable in our rooms and satisfied with the campus location for the course. Judging from the smiles in the audience most people seemed delighted to be there. About 75% of those sitting with us in the field house looked like college students and the rest ranged from age thirty to sixty. Naturally, the younger folks had longish hair and wore the scruffy attire of the era while some members of the older generation were actually dressed in ties and jackets. Maharishi sat silently and serenely for a few minutes while the atmosphere in the field house became very still. He then started telling a story of how the TM movement started over ten years ago in India. After his master died, he continued his life as a monk in the Himalaya Mountains, until one day he suddenly got the impulse to leave the secluded mountain ashram and go to the city in the valley far below. His fellow monks thought he was nuts and asked, "Why do you want to go down into the 'mud' when there is such silence and bliss here in the mountains?" He didn't really have an answer; he just knew he had to go.

When he got to the city he just started wandering around, which was not uncommon for monks in India. After a while a man came up to him and asked, "Do you speak?" Maharishi replied, "Yes," assuming that the man wanted to know whether or not he was a monk who had taken a vow of silence. Then the man said, "I mean do you speak to groups?" Maharishi wasn't sure how to answer. The man then asked him to speak to a group of people the next night. He agreed, and the next evening he was speaking before a large group in a local auditorium. The audience loved his simple message of meditating regularly to contact the inner field of pure "being" or consciousness, and then living more of that deep eternal silence in daily life. His ability to distill ancient Vedic wisdom into a simple format and relate it to the daily lives of ordinary people struck a chord with his audience. The following night the hall was overflowing.

It didn't take long for Maharishi's message and technique of meditation to spread to other cities in India and he soon found it necessary to form an organization to support his activities. After a few years he was invited to teach in Europe and Asia, and eventually in the U.S. Wherever he went, people always offered him a place to live and teach. By the early 1960s he was living at the home of one of his devotees in southern California and maintaining a busy schedule of teaching TM. At first his audiences were mostly those interested in Indian philosophy and meditation, then college students, academics and eventually people from all walks of life became interested. When he finished his story for our audience, Maharishi shrugged his shoulders and smiled. "What to do?" he asked the audience. "So many people want to meditate and I can't be everywhere at once so I will have to multiply myself," he exclaimed with a broad grin. "That is why I am so grateful that so many of you want to be TM teachers. To accomplish our goal of world peace, we need thousands of teachers to spread this beautiful knowledge around the world." When he said world peace, I looked at Linnea, rolled my eyes and whispered, "Meditation is great, but claiming to be able to stop war is going too far." Apparently other people in the audience were thinking the same thing, because as soon as he made that statement hands started going up. Someone stood up and asked him how he was going to enlighten the whole world. Maharishi sat and chuckled in delight for a few seconds and then explained how it could happen by using a simple analogy. "If the room is dark, you don't have to get rid of all the darkness; all you have to do is turn on one light and the darkness goes away. It is like that with meditation," he continued, "just a few people meditating can change a whole atmosphere of negativity."

This exchange started an avalanche of questions ranging from the absurd to the brilliant. Maharishi answered all of them with the same patient deference to every questioner. The worst questions were about diet. Maharishi must have known that there were many diet fads in the U.S., so when someone insisted that we all eat a macrobiotic diet, he laughed and said. "Just eat what your mother feeds you!" Many of the questions were about mystical considerations. When someone asked what he thought about reincarnation, Maharishi replied that he was against it. The questioner was bewildered by the answer and retorted, "What do you mean you're against reincarnation?" Maharishi's face lit up and he replied, "Why would you want to be reincarnated? Why not become enlightened in this lifetime and gain liberation from suffering? Then you won't have to come back again and make the same stupid mistakes!" A few people caught on right away and started to laugh, and then most of the audience picked up on his answer and started laughing, too. When the meeting finally ended I realized that not only did Maharishi have a lot of wisdom to offer, but his cheerful and humorous style kept us all riveted to our seats for three hours without getting bored or restless.

As with previous residence courses we began rounding and within a couple of days the atmosphere on the campus settled down to a profound silence as the fifteen hundred participants sank deeper into the meditative state. Often in the evening the fog would slink in over the campus from the Pacific and linger until the brilliant California sun overpowered it in late morning and chased it away. This added another level of stillness to the environment that enhanced the sense of being on a remote ashram away from the distractions of the world. The difference between this course and the other, shorter retreats was that this was also a teacher training course. We weren't sure what to expect in terms of academic rigor or demanding schedules, but after a few days of long periods of meditation, Maharishi announced that we would break up into smaller groups for meetings with a TM teacher. Morris, like many of the TM teachers that we met, looked like he wasn't really comfortable in his shirt and tie and fairly short hair. Apparently the TM teachers were required to wear this seemingly archaic attire to lend an aura of dignity and responsibility to their activities, especially in public. This was intended to mitigate any fear that meditation was just another weird fad associated with the counterculture. Morris seemed as though the last thing he wanted to look like was an insurance salesman, so he wore brown corduroy Levi's with a sport shirt and mismatched tie. He also had a bushy mustache and a big head of curly hair just so he wouldn't lose touch with his inner hippie. It was his job to lead us in a discussion of the main points of Maharishi's lectures, and to teach us how to lecture on TM in public.

Our group of ten was an interesting mix of Hollywood professionals, college students, drop-outs like Linnea and me, and a Christian Scientist schoolteacher accompanying her retired mother. Every day someone in the group was chosen to present the main points of the previous lecture and then we would discuss them in the group. The atmosphere was so relaxed that we spent most of the time joking around and getting to know each other. Practicing our TM lecture skills was another matter. About half of us, including Linnea and me, had very little expe-

rience in public speaking and felt unqualified to give a presentation on
TM. Memorizing the prepared script, then presenting it to the rest of
the group, was a little tedious, but Morris, our team leader, was sympathetic to our lack of enthusiasm and didn't insist that we memorize
the whole script. Fortunately our meetings were held outside, where
we soaked up the agreeable California sun and the fresh breezes off the
nearby Pacific.

The evening meetings with Maharishi were the best part of the day.
Every night was different. Often Maharishi would invite scientists to sit
up on the stage with him and discuss meditation in terms of physics,
physiology and psychology. Although he was a monk who represented
an ancient Vedic tradition based on subjective experience, he felt it was
important to objectively investigate the phenomenon of meditation in
the light of science. When he had decided to leave home at a young age
and become a monk, his teacher, Swami Brahmananda Saraswati, told
him to go to college and get a degree; then he could join the monastery.
Maharishi earned his degree in physics and joined Guru Dev as soon as
he graduated. By the late 1960s there were a number of scientists and
philosophers interested in the connection between Eastern philosophy
and quantum mechanics. When TM became popular on college campuses, students began inviting their professors to learn meditation and
to meet Maharishi. Often when he would meet with the scientists he
would compare Vedic concepts of the unmanifest and manifest aspects
of creation to the ground state of physics and its expression at various
levels of creation, starting with sub-atomic particles, then atoms and
molecules.

No matter how arcane the conversation with the scientists became,
Maharishi would always bring it around to the nature of consciousness.
He would often compare human consciousness to the layers of matter
described by science. Just as there are gross and subtle levels of creation,
for example, sub-atomic particles, atoms, molecules and actual physical
objects like a chair, there are levels of consciousness that range from subtle to gross. During meditation we may experience transcending from

the gross state of thinking to progressively more subtle and finer levels of thought until we transcend thought altogether and experience pure consciousness with no thoughts. This is often called samadhi or bliss consciousness and is the source of all thought. He explained that, just as in physics, when we function on the sub-atomic levels there is more power and energy; similarly, when we function on the more subtle level of thought, there is also more power and energy. Maharishi claimed that everyone is endowed with an innate "creative intelligence;" it is just a matter of contacting it and using it in daily life.

This statement of Maharishi's evoked a flood of questions from the audience. One person came to the audience microphone. He asked if Maharishi meant that the ability to function on these finer levels of creation was how the yogis were able to achieve special powers like levitation and becoming invisible. Maharishi replied that mastery of certain laws of nature on the subtle levels of creation was how some yogis were able to perform these "tricks." "But in TM we don't bother with these minor attractions," he continued. "We like to 'capture the fort.' For example, if we go to an area and find a gold mine, silver mine and a diamond mine, it is better to capture the fort that controls the whole territory. Then we have control of all of the mines instead of trying to capture one mine at a time." He went on, "Once we capture the fort of pure consciousness and maintain that awareness permanently we can have access to a variety of special abilities. The goal of meditation is to maintain pure consciousness in all our activity."

While I found these special abilities, described in many of the books that dealt with the mystical aspects of both Eastern and Western religions, fascinating, I hadn't actually considered gaining mastery of them myself. I related more to the pragmatic aspects of becoming more enlightened and less ignorant. Considering my present state of ignorance I was grateful for any increase in my ability to perform right action and reduce mistakes. For both Linnea and me, growth toward a more enlightened state was more of a necessity than a luxury. A higher state of consciousness not only offered the potential to function more in accordance with the laws of nature, but it could also liberate one from destructive negative emotions like fear, anger and anxiety. Since we had been meditating for almost a year we both noticed enough positive results that we began discussing the possibility of attending the upcoming teacher training course with Maharishi. A year earlier we never would have dreamed of spending four months meditating and studying with Maharishi. However, as the weeks went by at Humboldt, we could imagine nothing more sublime or enlivening than spending our days in blissful meditation, interrupted only by wonderful meals, discussions with many new friends and strolling around the delightful coastal campus in the celestial morning fog and afternoon sun.

Maharishi was planning to hold the second half of the teacher training program in Estes Park, Colorado, just a few weeks after the Humboldt course finished. This was too soon for us, so we decided to attend the next course, which was to begin in January in Majorca, Spain. Like many of our friends who had decided to attend the teacher training course, it was hard to imagine ourselves traveling around the country giving lectures on TM and teaching meditation, but we sure liked the idea of spending another four months with Maharishi. Also, while the idea of changing the world through meditation seemed a bit of a stretch, helping individuals relieve the stresses in their daily lives seemed like a worthy cause.

As we left the cocoon of bliss and light that had been our home for a month and headed south along Highway 101 toward Willits, we realized that the effects of meditating for a whole month were definitely more powerful than the one-week course at Asilomar a few months before. We both seemed even more grounded in the inner silence of pure consciousness and at the same time more integrated with our environment and not nearly as spaced out or separated from the maelstrom of activity around us. It was as if a veil had been lifted and we were seeing the true splendor of the world around us for the first time. Our mountaintop homestead was so inviting and comfortable when we arrived, it was hard to think about packing up and leaving it for a couple of two hundred-year-old cabins with no running water three thousand miles away, but we knew in our hearts that our future was not on this isolated mountaintop and that it was time to move on.

Some fifty miles west of Amarillo, Texas, our fairly new Jeepster Commando just up and died. There was nothing but fields as far as the eye could see in all directions. In those days there were no cell phones to call AAA so we stuck out our thumbs. It didn't take long for a trucker to pick us up and drive us around Amarillo looking for an open garage. It was after 5 PM on the Friday before the Labor Day weekend and just about every garage was closed. Finally, after an hour of cruising around in our new-found buddy's big rig, we found a shop that was open. The best they could do was to tow our Jeepster, with its little trailer containing all our belongings, into their garage and leave it until Tuesday after the Labor Day weekend, when the mechanic would be back on duty. There was no one in the entire city of Amarillo who could work on it over the holiday, so we had no choice. Spending Labor Day weekend in Amarillo wasn't exactly our idea of a fun holiday. As I was thinking of alternatives I remembered that Barry and Marla, the managers of the apartment building in Denton, Texas, where I lived while going to North Texas State, were living in Oklahoma City, just a few hundred miles farther down the interstate. Luckily, they were home when we called and invited us to spend the weekend with them. The tow truck driver kindly drove us to the airport, where we rented a car and headed for Oklahoma City.

Barry and Marla lived in a lovely neighborhood in what appeared from the outside to be a surprisingly normal upper-middle class house. They had been on the radical fringe of society when they were graduate students and I expected them to be living in a funky apartment in a rougher part of town. When Barry opened the door to greet us, a plume of sweet smelling smoke came pouring out of the house, which suggested they hadn't exactly joined the middle class. As we stepped inside, it was as if we had entered a time warp and had gone back to the halcyon days of the hippie movement of 1967 in Haight-Ashbury!

The Jefferson Airplane was blasting from huge speakers throughout the house, which was decorated like an East Village head shop. Barry
was now sporting shoulder-length hair and multicolored beads around
his neck. He proudly gave us a tour of the darkened house that seemed
to be mainly illuminated with black lights shining on psychedelic posters of the 1960s. The crowning glory of their special decorating skills
was a large dentist's chair set up in the middle of the living room.

Barry explained that the counterculture had just now reached
Oklahoma City and that he was so enthusiastic about it he had quit his
regular job and opened a "head shop" to support the movement. Marla
was working as a social worker and looked more normal than Barry, but
she was just as excited about the possibilities of the hippie revolution.
They even talked of buying land in the country and starting a commune. After dinner they offered us a joint, which didn't appeal to us,
especially after a month of meditation, so we explained to them that we
were now into TM and drugs weren't compatible with it. When we sort
of gave them an introductory lecture they seemed mildly interested.

The next day we all hung around and relaxed while some of Barry
and Marla's associates came and went with various packages. In the
afternoon Barry took us on a tour of his head shop, which was doing a
booming business. The posters and drug paraphernalia made me realize
how much we had moved on from the drug culture to what seemed to us
to be a more powerful path of transformation. We complimented Barry
on his wonderful shop, but declined his gracious offer of a complimen-
tary water pipe. We were a little concerned that he and Marla would be
offended by our refusal to accept their generous offers of psychoactive
materials, but they were perfectly understanding about our commitment to meditation. The holiday weekend turned into a wonderful visit
with a couple of generous and compassionate old friends.

Mid-September was still hot and humid in Virginia as we turned
off the dirt road to our new fifty-seven-acre homestead in the Blue Ridge
Mountains. From the top of the entrance road we could see the drive

looping down the small valley, crossing over a dam at one end of a pond and then curving up the other side of the valley to the houses. To our left was Old Rag Mountain, which had an unusual rocky, or ragged, summit. We had forgotten how beautiful the place was since we first saw it a year before. The two houses were two hundred-year-old log cabins that had been modernized many times over the past two centuries. The first remodeling job had been to paint over the gorgeous hand-hewn chestnut logs with some type of whitewash and then eventually, when paint was available, to cover them with a variety of colors over the years. The most recent paint jobs looked like they were done in the first half of the twentieth century; the choice of pink and light green was probably determined more by price and availability than any decorating skills of the inhabitants. The next phase of remodeling had included covering the log walls with cheap fiberboard, then adding some grotesquely-patterned wallpaper over it. Finally, the whole place was covered in sheetrock and painted a putrid green.

The previous owner had started to restore one of the houses by ripping off the sheetrock and fiberboard and sanding off the paint to expose the beautiful dark chestnut log walls. He had varnished and chinked the logs with white plaster, which created a stunning effect. This house was habitable so we unloaded all our stuff and set up a makeshift kitchen in the downstairs room, which also served as a living room. There was no running water, but there was a well with a hand pump outside the building. In a way it was even more primitive than when we had first lived in Willits because there we'd had a trailer with a hot water heater and a sink with faucets. The only source of heat was an old, inefficient stone fireplace. Fortunately the weather would be warm for the next few months, and then in January we would be leaving for teacher training until late the following spring.

While the living conditions were not as comfortable as our home in Willits, we enjoyed being within walking distance of so many of our old friends. We would often share meals and help each other with building projects and harvesting fruit and vegetables from the gardens and orchards nearby. In many ways it was the best of both worlds: living with friends who shared the same values and still enjoying the privacy and freedom of living in our own home. After we made ourselves comfortable in the remodeled house, we started planning the large room that would connect the two houses, which were about twenty-five feet apart. The new room would have a high cathedral ceiling and a sliding glass door that provided a grand view of the pond and the rugged Old Rag Mountain. Within a few weeks of our arrival in Virginia we had the footings poured and started framing the new room. Fortunately for us Martin's two sons, Doug and Jim, didn't share their father's passion for traveling around the world in search of "teachers of truth." Instead they enjoyed living on the farm and offered to build our new room.

Although our reason for moving to Virginia was to escape the isolation of Willits and to be close to our friends living on the nearby land, we found ourselves spending much of our time with folks from the TM community in Washington, D.C. The TM center was in a stately townhouse near DuPont Circle, not far from where we had lived in Georgetown just two years earlier. Now we were no longer disgruntled government workers anxiously anticipating the day when we could quit our jobs and leave the city for a life of freedom, but eager participants in a movement that hoped to bring more fulfillment to anyone, regardless of their religion or politics. Every Saturday, twenty-five to fifty people would learn meditation at the center. We would often help out with the initiations by registering the participants and preparing their trays of fruit and flowers to be given to the teacher as an offering to the Holy Tradition of meditation. Not only were students and hippies learning TM, but now more professional people were taking up the technique. Some of them were obviously uncomfortable with the fruit and flowers and were apprehensive as we escorted them to the dim room with candles and incense where the teacher was waiting. Most people looked visibly transformed when they came out of the initiation room. The change in their faces was remarkable. They looked totally relaxed and as though a great weight had been lifted from their shoulders.

The atmosphere in the TM center was sublimely silent even though it was located in the midst of a busy city. We enjoyed just hanging around soaking up the good vibes from all the initiations and meditation. When the initiations were finished for the day, all of the teachers and volunteers would usually go out to dinner and celebrate. It was a great opportunity for us to get to know many of the meditators and teachers. Most of them shared our natural-living lifestyle and were spiritual seekers like Linnea and me. The conversations at the dinners usually revolved around Maharishi and meditation. Everyone looked up to the teachers because they had this seemingly magical ability to transform their students from uptight and busy to mellow and lighthearted.

It was hard for us to imagine that in a few months we would be embarking on our own journey to become initiators. The actual procedure of initiating someone in meditation seemed shrouded in mystery. I tried to remember what had happened when I was initiated over a year ago but it was all a blur. I remembered going into the room with my offering of fruit and flowers, standing next to the teacher while he performed the puja ceremony, then receiving the mantra from the teacher, but I couldn't remember much after that. It was as if I had gone away somewhere for a while, then heard the teacher whispering to me to open my eyes. It was intriguing and intimidating to think that we would be learning how to enable someone to transcend!

The irony didn't escape us that, less than two years before, we were living in the city and had escaped to the mountains whenever we had the chance. Now we were living in the mountains and escaping to the city whenever we had the chance. We loved our new homestead, but the charm of being around the TM center and so many friends who were actively involved in the movement was irresistible to us. After years of alienation from mainstream America and disillusionment with the counterculture we finally felt as though we had found what we'd been looking for. After about a month, the center was notified that Maharishi's representative, Brahmacharya Satyanand, was coming to the Washington center to teach advanced techniques for people who had been meditating for at least a year. Maharishi described these techniques as fertilizers that aid and stimulate growth toward enlightenment, just like adding fertilizer to a plant at a certain stage of its growth contributes to its development.

Intrigued by the prospect of learning a new technique, Linnea and I signed up and offered to help Satyanand with the initiations. Weeks before his arrival, the center was abuzz with rumors and preparations for his stay at the center. This was the first real live holy man to visit the center and everyone was concerned with how to treat him. Satyanand stepped out of the car dressed in the traditional white silk dhoti and sandals worn by monks in India. To ward off the nippy November air he wore a gray wool shawl over his shoulders. He seemed impervious to the thirty-degree chill and I thought to myself, *His outfit is like stepping outside in a pair of pajamas with a towel on your shoulders in the winter.* I would have been shivering, but he was oblivious to the cold. He had a stern and fatherly air about him as opposed to Maharishi, who seemed more like a jovial uncle, yet he was very similar to Maharishi; without ego or pretension and appearing to have no personal needs. The selflessness that both Maharishi and Satyanand displayed was an inspiration to those of us who were seeking spiritual development.

Once Satyanand was set up in one of the initiation rooms, it was our job to usher people into the room with their fruit and flowers. After each person received their technique, we went back into the room to see if Satyanand was ready for the next person. I didn't quite know what to expect the first time I went into the room to check with him. I knocked on the door, half-expecting him to be in some mystical state of consciousness, and was a bit surprised when I opened the door and found him reading the *New York Times*. He was wearing wire rimmed bifocals and sporting a huge gold watch on his wrist. He greeted me in a detached, perfunctory manner, as though he had been working in an office rather than imparting esoteric knowledge and performing the ancient puja ceremony. He asked me how many more people there were to teach and, apparently realizing that he was running behind schedule, asked me if we could bring in the people a little faster. As we picked up the pace, he sped up his initiations. At times it seemed like an assembly line, but we finished by 5 PM. Then it was time for the teachers and volunteers to be instructed.

Satyanand asked me a few questions then started the puja ceremony. Although I knew it was some sort of an expression of gratitude, I didn't have a clue as to what he was chanting or why he was placing the fruit and flowers on the brass tray in front of the big picture of Guru Dev. After about thirty seconds I could feel the effects of the puja pulling me down into a deep state of silence while I was standing next to him. I felt as though I was transcending, even though I was standing and not actually meditating. He then asked me to sit down and gave me some instructions on how to direct my awareness when falling asleep, which would result in a more profound and effective use of the sleep state. This wasn't nearly as dramatic as when I first learned to meditate, but it seemed like something certainly worth giving a try. I tried it for a few days and it had some noticeably positive effects on my sleep, but not nearly as impressive as some of the people in the class who'd had difficulty falling asleep or had been waking up in the middle of the night with insomnia.

15

MEDITERRANEAN MEDITATIONS

The drive across the island of Majorca to the small resort village of Cala Major revealed a classic Mediterranean landscape of small farms, olive groves and almond orchards. The town was a deserted strip of ten hotels along a sandy beach. Behind the hotels, away from the beach, was nothing but almond orchards and olive groves. Our group filled up three of the nearly identical hotels, which were basic two-star resorts catering to budget-minded tourists from England, France and Germany. Linnea and I each had a small single room with a little balcony overlooking the ocean; the cold and sometimes angry winter waters reminded us of the California coast in January. Most days were sunny and mild, with an occasional storm. Although the staff and management were delighted to have the hotel filled with guests in the middle of winter, they soon realized that we were not the average tourists eager to get up every morning and start spending money. They couldn't understand why the guests stayed in their rooms all day and only came out for meals and meetings with Maharishi. The waiters were particularly distraught because all our meals were included in the cost negotiated by the TM movement, so they had little opportunity to earn tips at the meals. But what probably bothered them the most was that none of the young women on the course would go out with them. They couldn't understand why the women didn't want to go out to the nightclubs and hardly ever left the hotel. Many of the waiters said that the main reason they worked for such low pay was the opportunity to meet girls, and here were hundreds of attractive young women who acted like a bunch of nuns.

In some ways the routine of the course was much like that of the summer course at Humboldt, only instead of afternoon meetings, we went back to our rooms for more meditation. The location was also more secluded and remote, leaving little opportunity to stray very far from the hotel and the beach. It was the closest thing to being in a monastery that most of us had ever experienced. Everyone had a private room and spent most of the day in silent meditation. It didn't take long for us to sink into a prolonged state of deep silence, which resulted in a whole new level of experiences during meditation. Maharishi obviously anticipated this and devoted most of the evening meetings to discussing our experiences and explaining them to us. Many people were becoming progressively detached from the cares and desires of the world around them. For some this was a blissful relief, but for others it was a little distressing to see so many of the things in life that used to seem important now appear to be a trivial waste of time. Maharishi described these feelings as having our boundaries broken down. The less we became attached, the more "unbounded" we became, which resulted in more freedom from restrictions and more possibilities for growth and progress. "It is like leaving the hut for the palace," he said. "We may be comfortable in our hut and may not want to leave, but once we are in the palace we realize it is infinitely better than the hut." He continued, "This is the nature of the expansion of consciousness. We are constantly breaking down boundaries and becoming more grounded in unbounded pure consciousness, which allows us to live a more coherent and serene life."

Most of the time the routine of meditating for half an hour, then fifteen minutes of yoga asanas and then another half hour of meditation was comfortable and peaceful. However, once in a while, I would become overshadowed by very deep stress being released. This always took a different form. Sometimes it was intense restlessness, anxiety or even a gripping physical sensation. One morning during what seemed to be a pleasant meditation, my head seemed as though it was going to explode. Suddenly I was overwhelmed by a vision of the top of my head opening up like the lid of a trash can and a mountain of trash erupting, including old beer cans, cigarette butts, Styrofoam coffee cups, stale doughnuts, half-eaten chunks of pizza and a couple of old roller skates. All I could do was lie down on the bed and let it rip. Within a few minutes the event subsided and the next thing I knew it was lunch time. I must have passed out for a few hours. Later, I felt as though some big block of stress had been released from my system and I felt much lighter and more clear-minded.

Although we were supposedly in a teacher training course, we weren't doing much training, just a lot of meditation and delightful meetings with Maharishi at night. After a few weeks we were handed printed sheets of the puja ceremony, which included the Sanskrit words that are sung during the initiation ceremony along with the English translation. Every night at the end of our meeting Maharishi would perform the puja and everyone was invited to sing along with him in order to start learning how to do the ceremony ourselves when we taught meditation. At the time we were initiated into TM, we had been told the puja was an offering of gratitude to Guru Dev and the tradition from which TM came, but we had no idea what all the Sanskrit words meant. All we knew was that it was a powerful ceremony that induced a deep state of silence for the people involved and in the surrounding atmosphere. Now we could find out what it was all about. The first part of the ceremony was an invocation or recitation of the names of all the great teachers in the Vedic tradition, going back thousands of years. These were the ancient sages who "cognized" the various aspects of Vedic knowledge throughout the centuries and passed it on to their devotees. Somehow just the act of putting attention on these enlightened beings while singing their names during the puja had a potent effect on those involved with the ceremony. Maharishi said that it had a twofold effect. First it created a profound influence of silence that created an atmosphere conducive to instruction in meditation and secondly it was supposed to culture cosmic consciousness in the teacher by performing action while established in a state of pure consciousness or deep silence.

The rest of the ceremony involved symbolic offerings to Maharishi's teacher, Swami Brahmananda Saraswati (Guru Dev), who for many years held the title of Shankaracharya of Northern India. This meant that he was the living representative of the tradition of Vedic masters in the holy tradition. The fruit, flowers, incense and white handkerchief were offered to a picture of Guru Dev as a traditional expression of appreciation to the teacher for imparting the valuable knowledge of the wisdom of life to the student. When the whole group sang along with Maharishi while he performed the puja at the end of the meeting, it had a very practical effect on the group. It induced such a profound stillness that no one felt like hanging around and talking. Everyone walked quietly to their rooms and went right to sleep. A year earlier, I would have never thought I would be learning how to perform a Vedic ceremony. I was definitely not a ceremony kind of guy and had developed a healthy disrespect for hierarchy and a strong irreverence toward authoritarian institutions like religions and governments. However, I liked the profound effect the puja had on the environment. Maharishi had said that in TM we don't "mood make;" in other words, we don't create a mood of blissfulness or transcendence, but experience these exalted states of consciousness naturally without trying to create any mood. While practically everyone on the course loved the effect of the puja, Maharishi advised us that it was reserved for special occasions like initiations. The puja, like meditation, also had a purifying effect on the physiology. The settling-down effect quickly produced a state of deep rest that allowed the body to "normalize" and release stress. During the singing of the puja every night with four hundred other folks who were already "unstressing" or releasing stress from meditating all day, the atmosphere became so intense that I felt like I was coming down with the flu whenever Linnea and I stood in the middle of the group. After a few days we discovered that standing outside on the patio during the puja gave us some fresh air and enough distance from the crowded hall of people releasing stress to comfortably enjoy the experience.

In addition to the evening puja, Maharishi invited Brahmarishi

Devarat, a Vedic pundit from India, and his son to chant the Vedic hymns for us at many of the evening meetings. Devarat didn't speak English, so after he chanted the Vedas for about fifteen minutes, Maharishi would translate the ancient wisdom into English. We would then ask questions of Devarat, which Maharishi would translate into Hindi. Devarat was truly an ancient sage. He must have been in his eighties with long, straggly white hair and flowing white robes. He always carried his favorite Vedic hymn laminated and mounted on a wooden stick, which made him look like Father Time as he walked on stage. Devarat was an expert in the Rig Veda, which describes how the unmanifest becomes manifest and creates what we know as the physical universe. This phenomenon of the manifestation of creation is systematically elucidated in the Rig Veda and has many parallels to modern theories in physics. Listening to this very elderly pundit explaining the primordial Vedic world view as we sat on the patio under the stars with the rhythmic roaring and hissing of the ocean on the beach behind us was truly a magical experience.

By the time we had been on Majorca for about two months, the daily routine of meditating until lunch time, going for a half-hour walk and meditating again until dinner had become very fluid. Minutes, hours and days were a continuous flow of inner silence regardless of what our activity was, whether we were meditating, walking or sitting in the evening lectures. We couldn't have been farther from the storm of human activity that engulfed the planet. Then one day Maharishi called a meeting after lunch and announced that the landing of the astronauts on the moon was being televised and we were all invited to watch. Here we all were in monastery mode as per Maharishi's instructions and now we were invited to watch a TV broadcast of a governmental accomplishment on the moon. Most of us had retreated so far into inner space and away from world events that a TV show about outer space seemed amusingly irrelevant. Maharishi, on the other hand, seemed pretty stoked about the event and had a bunch of TVs set up in the lecture hall.

As the landing on the moon was about to take place, the TVs malfunctioned and all we could see was a snowstorm of static. One of the technicians walked over to Maharishi on the stage and told him that the only TVs in the hotel that could receive the broadcast were upstairs in the bar. Maharishi grinned and said, "Come! We will go up to the bar." As soon as he left the lecture hall, everyone scrambled out of the hall and up to the bar, which only held about fifty people. Linnea and I weren't that excited about watching the show, so we let everyone dash past us up the stairs. By the time we got to the bar everyone was coming back out. Apparently the bar's TVs had also malfunctioned. As the crowd pushed past us to the stairs we decided to take the elevator. After waiting a few minutes, the elevator door slowly opened and there stood Devarat with his laminated hymn on a stick. The vision of this ancient pundit in white robes and long white hair appearing before us was a little bit too much for us to process right away. We just stood there staring at him in disbelief for about fifteen seconds, until the door closed and he disappeared.

By the end of February, the hills in back of the hotels had turned a dazzling pastel pink as the almond orchards came into full bloom. The weather became less stormy and the sun stronger. The transition to the glories of spring on a Mediterranean island also came with a price. The warmth and sun brought more and more tourists every day. Our somnolent seaside village seemed to erupt almost overnight with an infestation of tourists from the damp and dismal countries of Northern Europe. They were understandably celebrating their release from their dank city streets to this sun-drenched, beachfront resort. While they were just normal tourists having a good time, they seemed to us like disruptive interlopers who were destroying the peace and quiet of our private meditation retreat. The situation got really annoying when they started moving into our hotel. The bar, which had been virtually abandoned for the last two months, had now come to life with drunken howls, loud, lame, European disco music and the fetid stench of French cigarettes. Fortunately, Linnea and I had rooms far from the bar on a quiet floor overlooking the ocean. Some of the meditators, however, were right next to the bar or just above it and were constantly barraged with noise and cigarette smoke. As the atmosphere in the hotel became busier and noisier every day, more and more people started complaining to Maharishi at the evening meetings. Finally, he became exasperated and said, "What to do?"

A few days later we were told that after the evening meeting everyone should pack and get ready to board the buses to take us to Cala Antena, the new course location. The organizers proudly announced they had found a new resort up the coast that was closed to the public, and we would be the first people in the new hotels. It wasn't that easy for five hundred people who had been in silent meditation for two months to suddenly plunge into the activity of moving to a new location, but it was worth it to get away from the increasing noise and traffic. The plan was for all of us to hop on an assigned bus right after the evening meeting, quickly arrive at the new hotel, check in and go right to sleep so the disruption would be minimized. After a forty-five minute ride on a dark and winding road along the coast we came to a roadblock manned by the security police. As we drove through the checkpoint, I remarked to Linnea that this should keep out the traffic and loud tourists. As we approached our hotel, there were no lights to be seen anywhere. The entire area was completely dark and deserted. Occasionally, the headlights from our bus would illuminate some construction equipment and piles of building materials along the side of the road, but there were no signs of life. Our hotel was a brand new four-star hotel and we were its first guests. It was very eerie to be checking into a completely deserted hotel in the middle of nowhere, but at least it was silent. Our rooms overlooked a spectacular pool and a vast empty darkness that must have been the ocean. As I drifted off to sleep, I could hear the distant thump of the waves crashing on the rocks beyond the hotel and looked forward to finding out where we were in the morning.

The first explosion definitely got my attention! I was lying in my bed, half-awake about 6 AM, when a thunderous detonation shook the hotel. It rattled everything in the room and caused a fine dust of loose plaster to filter down from the ceiling. I leaped out of bed just in time to look out the window and see fist-sized chunks of rock raining down. I stood by the window, awestruck by the sight of the rocks splashing into the pool. It wasn't until the bombardment stopped that I thought to look beyond the pool at the surrounding landscape. I was stunned! There was no landscape, just a vast construction site as far as the eye could see. The only place that wasn't under construction was the ocean, which expanded out beyond the horizon from this massive three-mile-long rock outcrop. The solid limestone hillside was swarming with backhoes, bulldozers and construction workers scurrying up, down and around half-finished high rise hotels and apartment buildings. While I stood on my balcony transfixed by the scale of activity going on, I heard a funny whistle that sounded like a teapot, and then noticed a group of workers running toward a cement wall and crouching down. Another explosion ripped apart the hillside next to the hotel. As I lunged back into my room to avoid the falling rocks, I saw the concussion of the blast knock over some of the workers who were obviously too close to the blast site. When the falling debris and dust stopped, the workers started jackhammering around the blast site. Then it dawned on me that they were digging water and utility lines into the solid limestone! There was no topsoil, just rock. Every trench had to be either blasted or jackhammered!

After recovering from the shock of the explosions, I realized this place was ten times worse than the place we had left! A few tourists were nothing compared to dynamite and jackhammers. I also realized there was not much I could do about it, so I started my routine of yoga asanas and meditation. While doing my asanas, I quickly became aware that the sound of the jackhammers was so piercing I had to shut the windows and close the curtains before starting to meditate. Maharishi was fond of saying that noise was no barrier to meditation. "It's like reading your favorite book in a noisy room. If you are really enjoying the book, then distractions don't bother you, but if it's a boring book then it's hard to focus on the book. It's like that with meditation; if the mind is engaged in something charming then noise is no problem," he would often say to people who complained about noise during meditation. The jackhammers and explosions were more than noise: there was ear-splitting pain involved! The only way I could think of to escape the jackhammers was to get into the closet, stick toilet paper in my ears and cover myself with blankets and pillows around my head. The closet was a little claustrophobic, especially when I was shrouded in blankets and pillows, but it deadened the pain enough to be able to meditate. After a half hour I was deep in meditation and oblivious to the fact that I was bundled up in a closet somewhere on the coast of Majorca. I thought I heard a faint knock on the door, but it soon stopped and I continued my meditation. Then I thought I heard a woman singing in Spanish. It must have been the maid, so I figured it would be better just to stay in the closet until she left. As I continued meditation, I was suddenly engulfed in a blinding white light as the maid opened the closet door. I opened my eyes and the maid looked at me, screamed something in Spanish about evil spirits and ran out of the room in a state of terror.

After two months of being in a meditative state, the metabolism slows down and walking and other vigorous activities become a struggle. It's as though you are in a state of hibernation and you have no desire to engage in even mild activity like long conversations, shopping or sightseeing. The value of doing this is to culture a state of silence in the mind that can be permanently established even in the midst of dynamic action. This state is often referred to as self-realization. ,While undergoing this process, however, the individual should be in a peaceful retreat to avoid the stresses and strains of daily life that are difficult to deal with when in the meditative state. Performing mildly demanding physical or mental activity in this situation is like being jolted out of a deep sleep and then running at full speed before you are fully awake. When you take five hundred people who have been in deep meditation for two months, rip them away from their relatively peaceful routine and deposit them in the middle of a busy construction site with incessant explosions and jackhammering, things can get ugly. The first evening meeting with Maharishi was pandemonium. After listening to distraught participants complaining about everything from lost luggage to loud noise and lousy food, he threw up his hands in a gesture of exasperation and said, "What do to? Should we call the course off and go home?" As soon as he said that there was stone silence in the hall, then someone yelled "No!" A few more people started yelling, and then the entire group erupted in a loud "No!" Maharishi grinned and said, "OK, we will stay."

Our hotel was about a mile from the hotel where the meetings were held so we had a bus take us back and forth to the meetings. There were forty meditators staying at the hotel and after a few bus rides and meals together we all became friends and shared in the misery of jackhammer sounds and eating eggs at every meal. When the bus returned to our hotel after the evening meeting most of us would go to the hotel restaurant and have some tea or warm milk before going to bed. The center of attention was a bizarre young man named Andy Kaufman. He was there almost every night, eating ice cream and entertaining us with goofy antics and fantastic Elvis Presley imitations. This was years before he became a famous celebrity and we called him "Ice Cream Andy" because his dream was to host a TV show for kids and give them ice cream and cookies. Andy also entertained the whole group at the evening meetings by asking Maharishi weird questions. Most of us had adopted a traditional yogic vegetarian diet, with the hope of becoming more "pure" by avoiding "tamasic" foods like dead animals and anything that was stale or rancid. Tamasic foods were considered to have a dulling effect on the mind and toxic effects on the physiology. "Sattvic" foods were the opposite of tamasic; they were fresh, vibrant, and easy to digest and had a purifying effect on the mind. So when Andy asked Maharishi if he could still eat steak (a very tamasic food) after he became a teacher, everyone cracked up and waited for Maharishi's response. Maharishi chuckled for a few minutes and then asked Andy, "Why would you want to eat anybody?" The audience giggled and Andy said that he

loved the taste of a nice juicy steak. Maharishi then gave his standard
answer to those who pestered him about diet by telling Andy to eat
what his mother tells him to eat.

After a couple of weeks in Cala Antena, Linnea and I were able
to move into a small condo closer to Maharishi's hotel and away from
the noise of the "war zone." As everyone recovered from the disruption of the move, the discussion at the evening meetings turned to the
more sublime subject of higher states of consciousness. Often someone
would describe an experience of slipping into a state of self-sufficient
bliss, where the mind was completely tranquil with no desires, worries
or needs. This state of samadhi or being is often described as indescrib-
able and yet there are specific criteria that indicate one has reached the
state of transcendence. In this state of silence, there is no thought or
mental activity, just the ultimate "comfort level" with a deeper reality that is beyond the limited time and space of daily life. Maharishi
called these two aspects of life the absolute and the relative. The relative is the ever-changing flux of our daily lives and the absolute is the
unchanging eternal basis of all the waves of activity that we observe in
the world around us. One night Maharishi described the absolute and
relative fields of life in the context of the Bhagavad Gita, one of the
seminal texts of Vedic literature. He explained how the central theme
of the book was based upon a conversation between Arjuna and Lord
Krishna. Arjuna was a warrior on the battlefield who became paralyzed
by his inability to decide if going into battle was the right thing to do.
He was immobilized by a terrible dilemma. On one hand he had to defend his immediate family from an unrighteous clan of kinfolk who had
been repeatedly committing crimes against his father and brothers. On
the other hand, the aggressors were his uncles and cousins. Even though
they were criminals, he couldn't bear to fight and kill them. In this state
of paralysis he appealed to Krishna, who told him that the answer to his
dilemma was to become established in yoga and then perform action.
In this case, the word *yoga* meant union with eternal divine intelligence,
the non-changing transcendental reality that underlies the turmoil and

upheavals that can occur in the relative or ever-changing field of life. Maharishi went on to explain that in this state of cosmic consciousness, the individual is grounded in a reality that is liberated from the conflict of emotional and physical attachments. The mind is free of duality and dilemma, which allows the individual to perform right action from a level of utmost clarity and purity. This, he said, is the state of enlightenment; the goal of meditation and a state of freedom from stress and negativity that enables one to live a life of inner and outer fulfillment. The concept that enlightenment was a state of non-attachment and freedom from suffering was not new to Linnea and me. For the last few years we had listened to various teachers describe enlightenment and had read about it in many books on Eastern philosophy. We liked Maharishi's approach because of its simplicity and practical application to daily life. Even though we knew we were far from enlightened, the experience of higher states of consciousness that so many people on the course were having was enough to convince us that it was possible.

According to Maharishi, this combination of knowledge and experience was the best method of accelerating one's growth toward a state of enlightenment. Knowledge without experience is simply a matter of belief, and experience without knowledge could be confusing. However, when we have these sublime, transcendent experiences and a system of ancient wisdom to elucidate them, we create a synergy that can result in an accelerated growth toward a more enlightened state. Some people were more zealous about getting enlightened than others. They truly believed that Maharishi was the enlightened master, doted on his every word as absolute truth and planned to devote their lives to serving the master. Others were more skeptical and had no intention of actually teaching meditation, but they enjoyed the opportunity to gain the rest and rejuvenation offered by the course and were curious about what Maharishi had to say about the nature of life. The rest of us, while not true believers, were inspired about what TM had to offer and were willing, in varying degrees, to go out in the world and teach meditation.

Aware that most people in the West had misconceptions and

prejudices about meditation and gurus from India, Maharishi recognized that scientific investigation was the best way to dispel many of the myths about TM. With his degree in physics, Maharishi felt comfortable with scientists and encouraged research into all aspects of meditation, ranging from the physiological changes during meditation to studies on the behavior of prisoners. The first studies were done by Keith Wallace, a long time meditator and friend of Maharishi's. He had completed his Ph.D. in physiology at UCLA and had designed a series of studies with Herbert Benson at Harvard Medical School that measured the physiological changes during meditation. The research was published in *Science, Scientific American, The Lancet* and other scientific journals. This research, which demonstrated that a series of beneficial physiological changes took place during meditation, went a long way toward dispelling the skepticism of academics and health professionals.

Although Herbert Benson was a sophisticated faculty member of Harvard Medical School, he seemed a little befuddled as he stepped onto the stage to meet Maharishi. Obviously, the sudden transition from the laboratories and white doctor coats of Harvard to this incense-filled and flower-bedecked hotel ballroom on a remote part of the Majorcan coast was a bit overwhelming. Maharishi gave him a bouquet of flowers and the audience welcomed him with grateful applause, as if he had done his research solely to promote the TM movement. While his research with Keith Wallace had given the added cachet of Harvard Medical School to the studies, Benson himself was not a devotee of Maharishi. He was simply interested in the health benefits of the relaxation which resulted from meditation. Shortly after completing his research on TM, he went on to develop his own form of meditation called the "relaxation response." He claimed all one had to do was to repeat any word over and over again and it would trigger a feeling of calm and quiet. In his best-selling book *The Relaxation Response* he claimed that it was just as good as TM, but he apparently didn't have the research to show that the physiological changes in his technique were as dramatic as those during TM.

After almost four months of floating in a sea of silent bliss and occasional effulgence, it was time to come down from rounding. This meant a gradual easing into activity by slowly reducing the amount of time in meditation and increasing the amount of activity every few days. Suddenly plunging into activity from being in a meditative state of low metabolism would be like coming up to the surface of the ocean too quickly from a long deep sea dive. Nothing as severe as the bends would occur, but it could be very jarring to the physiology. It was also time to start serious training in teaching meditation. Up to now we had learned to recite the puja and study its meaning in English and had some fun lecturing on TM to some mock hostile audiences, but we were clueless about the fine points of initiating someone into the technique.

The "steps of initiation" were much more precise than anyone thought. Every word of instruction had to be memorized and delivered in a prescribed sequence. We divided up into groups of four and started practicing the steps of instruction on each other. This activity was an easy re-entry into the outside world. We also had more time to wander along the limestone cliffs above the sea, which were occasionally interspersed with small sandy beaches. It was late spring in the Mediterranean, the days were balmy, and the air was filled with the enchanting fragrance of rosemary blossoms. Most of the time we practiced our steps of initiation outside at the beach or on some sunny rosemary-covered hillside. At times it seemed as though we were in a celestial realm after spending so much time in meditation. The senses seemed enlivened and cleansed after months of purification through meditation, yoga asanas and Vedic knowledge.

As we continued to reduce our time of meditation, we had more free time to explore the island. Cala Antena was at the end of a relatively secluded peninsula, so after a few days we had explored most of the trails along the shore. A few of the more adventurous individuals decided to rent cars and see the rest of the island's scenery. Most of us felt as though our minds and bodies were still more in a meditative state than action mode, so we decided to wait a while before attempting to drive. We realized this was a good decision when we saw some of the first group of drivers returning to the hotel with smashed up rental cars. After a couple of weeks, we succumbed to Majorcan spring fever, rented a car with another couple and headed off into the blossom-filled hills. About half way across the island we drove up to a T intersection and pulled into the right turn lane. Next to us on our left was a large tractor trailer rig that had apparently not seen us pull into the right turn lane next to him. When the light turned green the huge truck slowly started turning to the right. I leaned on the horn as the truck slowly and relent-lessly started crushing the driver's side of the car as it turned. There was nothing to do except to watch in horror as our little Fiat was squashed between the truck and a stone wall. When the driver finally realized why the truck was not turning the corner very easily, he looked in his mirror and slammed on his brakes. He then jumped out of the truck and started screaming at us in Spanish as though we had crashed into him.

As the situation became more tense, the police arrived, and I felt relieved that I could explain to them in English what had happened. They impatiently listened to me, then claimed I had hit the truck and ushered us off to the police station. They had no interest in hearing my side of the story and began making out a report stating I had hit the truck. I couldn't understand why they claimed I had hit the truck. Then I remembered that Spain was still a police state ruled by the dictator Franco and it really didn't matter what I said. It was a creepy feeling to be at the mercy of the police with no rights at all, but there was no alter-native but to accept their ruling and get out of there. Although the car was substantially smaller than when we started out, it was still drivable, so we decided to continue on to Palma, the main city on Majorca.

Walking around the bustling streets of the ancient city was more of a contrast than we had expected. It was one thing to ease into activ-ity with a few walks and practice sessions, but throwing ourselves into the maelstrom of crowded streets packed with tourists and traffic was overwhelming to the senses, and yet we all felt a delightful detachment from the buzz of activity. It was as if we were in two separate worlds at the same time. The inner silence and connectedness with a timeless, unchanging reality of the last four months was still with us as we delved into the ever-changing world of traffic, shopping and sightseeing. It was a total joy to be out of the ashram having fun and at the same time enjoying the stillness and peace of meditation.

During the last few weeks of the course we were meditating the usual twice a day; we devoted the rest of the time to learning how to teach meditation. This involved learning the puja, the steps of initiation, and the three days of "checking" which followed the first day of instruction. After we became proficient in all these aspects of teaching TM, the only thing missing was to receive the mantras we would give to the people learning TM. According to Maharishi, mantras were to be kept private to avoid confusion. The sound quality or vibration of the mantras were quite powerful and supposed to be very life-supporting. Also there were different mantras for different types of people and it wouldn't be a good idea to share a mantra with someone else. He explained how the word "OM" was used by monks and recluses because it had the effect of making the person more withdrawn from society. This was good for monks who didn't want to be tempted by worldly pleasures, but for most people engaged in daily life, becoming withdrawn could be problematic. The mantra was also not to be spoken out loud because it was more effective at deeper, more subtle levels of thought. Maharishi said the mantra was like a seed planted in the ground; we don't keep digging it up every few days to see how it is doing, we keep it to ourselves and use it only during meditation.

The mantras were given by Maharishi personally to every aspiring teacher after a brief interview with him to determine if one was qualified to become a teacher. On the night before we were to leave to go back to the States, Linnea and I had our first private meeting with Maharishi. In person he seemed even more compassionate and selfless, as though he had no personal needs. He had probably met with a few hundred individuals earlier that day and seemed tired, but he was genuinely interested in us and asked us a lot of questions about our background. He liked the fact that we had college degrees and asked us to get master's degrees. We were a bit taken aback by this request, so he explained that TM teachers would have more credibility with advanced degrees. He performed a puja with us as though he was initiating us, then whispered to each of us in private what mantras we were to use in teaching. As Maharishi whispered the mantras to me, I suddenly realized that the mantra that I was given when I was initiated into TM was incorrect. Maybe I had distorted it or maybe I was given the wrong one by mistake. I didn't know what to do, so when we stepped outside Maharishi's room, I told Linnea what happened and we decided to ask Maharishi's assistant what to do. By the expression on his face we could tell the assistant had never encountered a situation like this before. After conferring with some of the more senior staff members, he suggested we see Maharishi later that night after he finished with the new teachers. We sat outside his room for what seemed like an eternity as the new teachers came and went from their meetings with Maharishi. Finally, at about 2 AM he was finished, and one of the aids went in and explained my situation to him. Maharishi asked us both to come in and decided to initiate each of us with a new mantra, which was considered an advanced technique. He seemed so exhausted that he was stumbling, but he was so gracious to us that we felt blessed to be personally initiated by him. When we boarded the plane the next morning we were still high from our meeting with Maharishi and felt it was an auspicious way to start our new careers as meditation teachers.

16

BIBLE BELT MEDITATORS

The TM center near DuPont Circle in Washington, D.C. seemed like an oasis of good vibes after traveling from Majorca to New York and then driving down to Washington. There were ten or so new teachers who had just arrived and we were going to teach a few courses with some of the more seasoned teachers before going out on our own. It was hard to imagine that we had the skills to actually instruct someone in the delicate art of meditation after just a few months of memorizing what to do. The opportunities to screw up seemed endless, not just by making fools out of ourselves, but also fouling up someone's first experience with TM. It was comforting to know that we would be giving our first lecture with some old hands, but once we were alone in the initiation room with the person learning meditation for the first time we were on our own. What if we forgot part of the puja or even forgot the mantra during the initiation ceremony? This could seriously mess up the initiation experience, which should be smooth and flawless to produce the effect of total relaxation. It seemed that no amount of memorizing and practice could prepare us for every contingency.

The procedure of teaching Transcendental Meditation was exactly the same throughout the world. First, there was an introductory lecture where the benefits of meditation were discussed. The next night there was a second lecture that focused on the mechanics of the technique. At the end of the second lecture anyone who wanted to learn TM stayed behind for a brief interview with a teacher and made an appointment to be initiated the following weekend. On our first course there were three new teachers including Linnea and me and the TM center chairman, who had years of experience. Twenty-five people wanted to learn that week, which meant that each one of us would individually initiate about six people. The group was a typical cross-section of folks who lived in the D.C. area: college students, high-powered businessmen, low-powered bureaucrats and hippies. In general the younger people were easier to teach, probably because they were a little more receptive and not wound as tightly as some of the older professionals who were under more stress.

As soon as they filled out a brief questionnaire, the prospective student was ushered to a room for an interview with a teacher. This meant that we just waited in our little interview room for whoever was next in line. There was no choice of who we would teach. My first interviewee was an eighty-year-old deaf man named Harry, who had been sent by his relatives to learn TM. He was a nice sort of avuncular old guy. He hadn't paid much attention during the lectures and wasn't quite sure what he was getting into, but was willing to give it a try. I had to yell quite loudly for him to hear me and had to explain TM to him all over again, which seemed to take forever. The hardest part of the interview was to ask the student to bring a few pieces of fruit, some fresh flowers and a clean new white handkerchief to the initiation. Most people usually replied to this request with, "Where am I going to get a new handkerchief?" Fruit and flowers were easy to obtain, but nobody used handkerchiefs anymore and they were hard to find. We explained that the fruit, flowers and handkerchief were used in the ceremony performed by the teacher as an expression of gratitude to the tradition of meditation. The student would just stand next to us and watch. After the ceremony we would kneel down, ask them to join us and at that time we would whisper their mantra. After they had the correct pronunciation of the mantra, we would ask them to sit down and say it softer and softer. Then they would just think the mantra and they'd be off into meditation.

The next morning the volunteer ushered Harry into my initiation room with his fruit, flowers and handkerchief. This was to be my first initiation and the irony that it would be an eighty-year-old deaf guy didn't escape me. He seemed to understand what was going on, but the fact that he could hardly hear made me nervous about whispering the mantra to him. Also, the rest of the instructions were given in a quiet voice that would be difficult for him to hear. Harry sat down next to me in the chair facing the white linen-draped table with the big picture of Guru Dev propped up against the wall. I placed his fruit, flowers and hanky on the table and began explaining to Harry what we were going to do next. I could feel the atmosphere in the building sinking down into a deep silence from the initiations taking place in the other rooms next to us. Also, I could hear the other teachers singing the puja during the initiation ceremony in the rooms next to us and wondered what was going to happen when I tried to initiate old Harry. I invited him to stand next to me while I performed the ceremony. He stood up and placed his arm around me like I was a little kid. It was a tad too intimate for waving incense and flowers around while performing the ceremony with this big guy hugging me, but there was nothing I could do!

When I finished the ceremony, I placed the bouquet of flowers on the offering tray, knelt down and motioned for Harry to join me. As we knelt in front of the picture of Guru Dev, I whispered the mantra to him. He just continued kneeling there with his head bowed and his eyes shut, so I whispered a little louder. No response from Harry! This was the most subtle and delicate part of the initiation process and I couldn't just grab him and shake him, even though he seem really zonked out by the ceremony and the atmosphere in the room. The only thing I could think of was the unthinkable. I yelled "Harry!" as softly as I could and tapped him on the shoulder. He lifted his head slowly and opened his eyes as though he had been far, far away. Now that I had his attention, I looked him in the eye, whispered the mantra as loud as I could and started making wild gestures with my hands for him to repeat what I was saying. He seemed to understand what I was saying and started to say something that I hoped would be the mantra, but instead he said

"HUH?" Even though we were both in an altered state of consciousness of semi-meditation from the puja, the situation was getting awkward, to say the least. Here I was, kneeling down next to this eighty-year-old deaf gentleman, yelling this strange word at him and gesturing as though I was playing charades. This was not the way it was supposed to happen when we were practicing in Majorca. We were told to follow the initiation procedure exactly, to not change even one word. I thought to myself, *I have really got this fouled up now. What am I going to do with this nice old man kneeling on the floor?*

I concluded that I was just going to have to forget about the instructions and wing it. I got up off my knees and motioned to him to sit down. Then I said, "This is your mantra," and yelled it so loud that I knew they could hear it in the rest of the building, but I had no choice. He finally seemed to understand what I was saying and he started to repeat it. The next challenge was to get him to say it softer. Every time I yelled "softer" he said it imperceptibly softer. This was beginning to take an excruciatingly long time. Finally, he stopped shouting his mantra and started repeating it to himself without speaking out loud. Once he started thinking the mantra instead of saying it, he was gone. After someone is meditating for a few minutes, the procedure is to whisper, "Slowly open your eyes," so as not to jolt them. I knew that Harry couldn't hear a whisper, so I said loudly and firmly, "Slowly open your eyes." Nothing happened! I could tell from the expression on his face and his totally relaxed body language that he was having a pleasant, blissful experience. I hated to jolt him out of his deep meditative state, but we were told not to let anyone meditate for very long the first time. This is because sometimes the experience is so charming that the person might have a hard time coming back to the waking state. I reached over and gave Harry a gentle shake on the shoulder. He slowly opened his eyes as though he instinctively knew that was the way to come out of meditation. I asked him if it was easy. He gave me a big grin and said, "Yup - you did a good job, young feller." The next step was for him to meditate on his own for fifteen minutes in another room. A volunteer ushered him to the meditating room. She asked me if everything was okay. "It was so loud and took so long, I began to worry. You're behind schedule; are you ready for the next person?"

The next five initiations went remarkably smoothly. Everyone easily took up the mantra and slipped effortlessly into meditation. By the end of the day, I was floating in a celestial cloud of delight. Teaching meditation was the most fulfilling thing I had ever done. Sometimes, even after a few minutes of meditation, the faces of the people who were learning became transformed. A lot of stress and tension seemed to dissolve from their physiology and they looked like different people. To be able to help someone release stress from their life and function more effectively fulfilled an inner desire for public service that I had had for a long time. Not only was it rewarding to help others, but the effect of all the teachers performing pujas and meditating created a powerful atmosphere of pure consciousness that was felt by everyone in the center. A profound silence penetrated the building and yet the atmosphere was charged with a radiant glow that enlivened us with a joyful, sparkling energy.

Linnea and I lived in the center for the next week while we taught the course in TM. Even though we were living in the middle of Washington, D.C., the center was like an oasis of calm in the midst of the roar of traffic and the wail of sirens. It was also fun hanging out with the other new teachers. We shared meals and swapped stories of our successes and foul-ups while teaching for the first time. One of our friends recounted how he had finished initiating a nice older woman and escorted her to another room where she could meditate on her own. As soon as he had closed the door behind her, he'd realized with horror that he had inadvertently locked it. The normal procedure for taking someone out of meditation was to quietly go back into the room and sit and meditate with the person for a few minutes and then whisper to them to slowly open their eyes. For their first meditation people only meditate for about fifteen minutes to make sure they don't go too deep and feel disoriented when they come out. Also, it's important for them to take a few minutes after they stop meditating to just sit quietly and then slowly open the eyes to avoid shocking the system as it goes from one state of consciousness to another.

So now he had a ticking time bomb locked in the room and had only fifteen minutes to defuse the situation. If he pounded on the door to get her out of meditation before she meditated too long and "fried" herself, he could scare the bejesus out of her and definitely shock her system, resulting in a massive headache. If he just waited until she eventually stopped meditation and came out it could be even worse. It was possible that she could meditate for hours because people often lose awareness of time and space, especially when they first begin meditating. She could become seriously disoriented and have a difficult time adjusting to the usual waking state of consciousness.

This wouldn't be good if she returned home to her family staggering around with a glazed look in her eyes. The only solution Tim could think of was to go into the room next door, step out onto the fire escape and crawl into the window of the room where the woman was meditating. He crept up to the window, peered in and saw the woman peacefully meditating. Slowly, he slid the window open, crawled in, sat down next to her and started to meditate. After a few minutes, he asked her to slowly open the eyes. He then asked her if her meditation was easy and fortunately everything had been fine. Her experience had been very silent and restful and she felt refreshed. After he gave her a few more instructions, he asked if she had any questions and she asked him why he had come back into the room through the window! He explained what had happened and she replied, "Oh, I thought crawling in through the window was part of the normal instruction."

Bob Cranford, the center chairman, was a mellow, shiny-haired and refined devotee of Maharishi, probably in his late twenties. He was responsible for all the TM activity in the greater Washington area and Virginia. Most of the new teachers lived around Washington and planned to teach at the center. However, Bob thought it would be a great idea if Linnea and I could start a new TM center in Charlottesville, Virginia because we lived nearby. We felt a little intimidated by the prospect of starting a new center, but Bob had confidence in us and offered to help us with the project. Our new careers as TM teachers had turned our lifestyle completely around. The laid-back rural life we had been living was no longer our highest priority. Now, out of necessity, we would be living in a city and devoting our time to teaching meditation; returning to our farm in the Blue Ridge Mountains only on weekends.

Returning to our homestead in the mountains was not without its bittersweet moments. The balmy June air was perfumed with the intoxicatingly sweet aroma of honeysuckle that seemed to cling to every fence, rock pile and old building. The forests and fields were overflowing with lush green plant life and teeming with raucous insects and melodious birds. Sitting on our half-finished deck, watching the lightning bugs while being caressed by the warm, sultry air felt like paradise. Whenever we had to pack up to leave, we felt a little wistful but in our hearts we knew that teaching meditation was the right thing for us to do.

Charlottesville and the University of Virginia were the polar opposites of Berkeley and the University of California. It was quite a contrast to go from the hippie capital of the United States to a traditional city of the old South grappling with its new relationship to the black underclass. The university was also steeped in Southern tradition and exuded an archaic formality long gone from the more progressive campuses across the country. Most of the students were southern good ol' boys belonging to fraternities. However, there was a small group of students who were cosmopolitan intellectuals and there were even a few hippies. The South was the least active area of the country for practitioners of meditation. Most of our friends who had been in teacher training with us had gone back to the West Coast or the Northeast to teach in active centers. Not only did we have to start a new center from scratch, but it was in one of the most conservative and anti-new age parts of the country. Fortunately there was a small core of dedicated meditators living in Charlottesville who were willing to help us get a center started.

Just as we were about to start looking for a site for a TM center, we received an invitation from our friends at the Washington, D.C. center to attend a conference with Maharishi at the University of Massachusetts in Amherst. Maharishi had spoken at Harvard and had conducted a symposium on creative intelligence (this was his new name for Vedic philosophy) at MIT. He felt that the ancient knowledge of the Vedas should be investigated by modern science to see if there could be an objective way of validating the subjective experience or "direct cognition" of the sages and mystics in the world's great philosophies and religions. This concept had struck a chord with many of the philosophers and scientists who had accepted the invitation to join Maharishi at the MIT symposium. The conference in Amherst was a further opportunity to satisfy their curiosity about Maharishi and his Eastern philosophy. After listening to their presentations, Maharishi would provide a commentary from his Vedic perspective, integrating their Western scientific and philosophical ideas with his own viewpoint in a very warm and charming manner. This had a disarming effect on many of these powerful intellectuals who were used to a more combative and competitive academic discourse. In addition to his commentary, Maharishi would always give them a bouquet of flowers and sometimes ask them to sit next to him. This would invariably throw them off guard and their entire demeanor would change from intense seriousness to a delighted and liberated repose.

General Franklin Davis, Commandant of the U.S. Army War College, was definitely the most unlikely of all the guest speakers at the symposium in Amherst. It had certainly required a lot of courage on his part not only to come to Cambridge, but to appear at MIT with an Indian guru. The summer of 1971 was the height of anti-war sentiment and college campuses were the most hostile environment in the country for any military representative. When the general was introduced to the audience at Amherst, the applause was underwhelming, but at least there was no violent protesting. The audience was probably astonished not only to see a general with a bunch of long-haired hippies and tweedy academics, but also to see such a high-ranking member of the military praise the benefits of TM. He claimed that it had lowered his blood pressure ten points and, according to his wife, had improved his disposition. Davis also wanted TM to be taught in the military as an antidote to stress and to increase creative thinking in military education. After the general finished his presentation, the suspicious discomfort of the audience was palpable. For many of the students in the auditorium, General Davis represented the enemy. They were mystified as to how and why he was invited to speak to such an anti-war crowd. As soon as Maharishi started to speak the tension dissolved. "Such a beautiful hope for the world—when the military rises in creative intelligence, world peace will be a reality. The purpose of the military is to keep war from happening—or to end it quickly if it does happen." The concept of an enlightened military was something most people in the audience had not considered. These comments went a long way to warm up the audience and General Davis left the stage beaming as he was showered with genuinely affectionate applause.

Some of the speakers demonstrated a profound and sometimes eloquent understanding of Maharishi's concept of creative intelligence, while others didn't quite get it. Buckminster Fuller seemed to get it when he declared, "Contact with the great design: this is the most mysterious of all experiences we know. Science at its beginning starts with *a priori,* absolute mystery, within which there loom these beautiful behavior patterns of the physical universe where the reliabilities are eternal." Maharishi really liked what Buckminster Fuller had to say and it seemed as if this meeting of Eastern mysticism and Western science was a very auspicious occasion.

A few days into the conference at U. Mass. Maharishi closed the morning session by announcing that he had some great news for us when we returned after lunch. The dining halls were abuzz with the usual rumors about famous people starting TM or beautiful properties in California or Switzerland to be purchased by the movement for our own retreat facility. When we all returned to the meeting hall, Maharishi asked a young TM teacher named Nat Goldhaber to come up to

the microphone and tell everyone the good news. Nat had a big grin on
his face as he casually announced that "we" were going to start our own
university. The audience erupted in a standing ovation. This had been
the dream of both students and teachers who were bored and frustrated
with the conventional university model. The new university would have
TM and the Science of Creative Intelligence as its basis, which would
enhance both the quality of life and the quality of education for the
students. The goal of the university was to develop more enlightened
individuals as well as provide an integrated education in which all disciplines were examined in the light of universal principles discovered both
by the ancient Vedic sages and modern science. Maharishi had often
said that modern education was baseless and there were no underlying
principles common to all disciplines. When Nat finished with his presentation, he was deluged with questions, mainly about where, when
and who. Apparently the paperwork was well underway, a committee
was actively looking for a site and there were dozens of brilliant faculty
members from distinguished universities like Harvard, Yale and Prince-
ton who were eager to start teaching. Finally, someone asked an obvious
but overlooked question. What was the name of the university going to
be? Nat suddenly appeared uncomfortable and looked at Maharishi for
some kind of signal or guidance. Maharishi smiled at Nat and gave him
an approving nod. Nat grinned and said, "Maharishi International University." My first reaction to this name was bewilderment. I thought to
myself, *Why would they use a name that sounded weird and foreign?* Quite a
few people around me seemed to think the same thing and started talking amongst themselves. Eventually a tepid applause gained a critical
mass as folks in the audience got over their initial reaction and warmed
up to the idea.

It took only two weeks for us to find a small one-bedroom cottage
for a TM center, set up an introductory lecture at the University of Virginia student union and organize our first course on TM. We really had
no idea what we were doing. There was some minimal guidance from

the TM center in Washington, but for the most part we were on our own, including covering all the expenses of renting a house and setting up a center. The financial arrangement was a definite challenge. Our only source of income came from the fees collected from the people who learned to meditate. Students paid $35 and working adults paid $75. All the money was sent to the TM headquarters in Los Angeles, and then half of all the fees collected were sent back to us to pay expenses. The rest was used by the movement for administrative expenses, including a fund set aside to pay for us to spend one out of every six months with Maharishi meditating and learning more advanced knowledge. The concept was great, but teaching twenty-five people a week only brought in enough money to pay our expenses, with a few hundred dollars left over each month for salaries. We never knew from month to month if we were going to make enough to meet expenses. It all depended on how many people signed up to learn TM that month. Most of the TM teachers in the country were in a similar situation. There was a certain uncomfortable pressure to get more people to start TM in order to bring in enough money to survive. This meant one had to really get out and hustle by setting up a lot of lectures to bring in more people. This created a Darwinian situation for new teachers like us. The more aggressive, motivated teachers survived, while the less determined teachers lasted only a few months before they had to get jobs to support themselves and teach part-time. Everyone loved teaching meditation, but only the most aggressive or those without financial obligations could continue as full-time teachers.

We soon learned that our charming little cottage near the campus was a perfect place for us to live, but as a meditation center it was totally inadequate. After our introductory lectures at the student union, we were surprised that twenty people wanted to learn TM. It was when we were making the appointments for individual instruction the next day that we realized there was only enough room in our cottage to teach one person at a time. At the Washington center there were at least six rooms available for initiating, while the only room we had was our bedroom.

This meant only one of us could teach at a time instead of both of us teaching simultaneously in separate rooms. It took us from 8 AM to 6 PM to teach twenty people non-stop. Not only did we learn that the house was too small, but the room layout made it very awkward for optimal instruction. After a person was initiated in the bedroom we had to escort them through the miniscule living room, past the folks who were waiting to be instructed, and into the tiny kitchen where they would meditate on their own. It was much better to avoid any contact between the person being instructed and those who were waiting. Normally the people waiting to be instructed were in a reception room away from the initiation area.

Among the first group of people to be instructed that day was Mike, a classic New York hippie (there were hardly any indigenous hippies at U.Va.) who, with his long hair and fringed leather jacket, looked more like Wild Bill Hickock than a U.Va. student. As soon as I gave him the mantra during the initiation ceremony he was gone! After letting him meditate for about five minutes, I had a hard time getting him to come out of meditation. Finally I was able to get him to understand that he was going into the kitchen to continue his meditation. He was so zonked out he could hardly walk, so I had to gently take him by the arm and lead him through the living room to the kitchen. As he stumbled out of the initiation room on my arm, I thought, *This is not going to look good to the people waiting to be initiated.* As we entered the living room, Dr. Brawley, a physiology professor, looked up at us with an expression of confusion and panic on his face. He had read about the physiological benefits of TM in *Scientific American* and thought he would give TM a try. He had concerns about bringing fruit, flowers and a handkerchief to this little cottage and participating in a Sanskrit ceremony, but we had reassured him this was a simple physiological technique for gaining deep rest and clarity of mind. We also convinced him there was nothing weird or flaky about the initiation ceremony.

As the incense billowed out of the initiation room, I helped Mike stagger into the kitchen under the wary eye of Dr. Brawley. I left Mike on his own to meditate in the kitchen for fifteen minutes, and returned to the living room. While I was waiting for Mike to finish meditating in the kitchen, I made small talk with Dr. Brawley, who looked as if he was about to bolt for the door. I tried to create the impression that everything was normal and there was nothing unusual about Mike's difficulty with walking after being initiated. Finally, after what seemed like an eternity, Mike's fifteen minutes were up. I returned to the kitchen, sat down and meditated with him for a few minutes. I then whispered to him to slowly open his eyes and to be sure to take plenty of time coming out of meditation so as not to jolt him with an abrupt change from the deep rest of meditation to the activity of the waking state. After a few minutes went by, I noticed that Mike was still in a state of deep meditation so I whispered again for him to slowly open his eyes. Again no response! I knew if I raised my voice in my increasingly desperate attempts to bring Mike out of his meditative state, Dr. Brawley in the living room would hear and probably run out the door.

Finally, I was able to get Mike to come out of meditation, handed him a questionnaire to fill out about his experience in meditation and told him I would be back in a few minutes to discuss it. I zipped out the kitchen door to see if Dr. Brawley was still there and found him all set to go into the initiation room with his little basket of fruit and flowers. Suddenly the kitchen door slammed open and Mike staggered out with his questionnaire in his hand and began mumbling, "Man, this is too much - I can't handle this!" I could see Dr. Brawley's facial muscles tighten up, but before he had the chance to bail out, Linnea ushered him into the initiation room and off he went into the transcendent. By now there were a couple of typical U.Va. students in the waiting room/living room who were doing fine until they saw Mike burst into the room wearing his Wild Bill Hickock costume with his disheveled long hair covering his face. Sensing the fear and tension building up in the room, I grabbed Mike in a manner that was wholly inappropriate for a peaceful meditation center and sort of pushed him back into the kitchen. He explained that he just couldn't focus on answering the questions and that he felt disoriented. I asked him if he had taken plenty of time coming out of meditation and he replied that as soon as he heard me ask him to come out of meditation, he opened his eyes and picked up his questionnaire. I then explained to him that it was very important to take at least two or three minutes to come out of meditation—if we come out too fast we can become disoriented and feel "rough." We then sat and meditated for five minutes and then I made sure he came out slowly. He was like a different person: clear minded, energetic and feeling very relaxed.

After initiating all day, Linnea and I felt as though we were in a bubble of bliss. Performing the puja ceremony and meditating with so many people as they sank into a state of deep meditative relaxation had the powerful effect of maintaining our awareness in a transcendental state while we were engaged in activity. Over the next few days it was gratifying to see that most of the students were already experiencing some good results like more energy, clarity of mind and less tension. Dr. Brawley not only felt less fatigued, but he was getting along much better with his wife and kids and wanted the whole family to meditate. In almost every course, however, there were folks who experienced nothing and sometimes felt worse after starting meditation. Those people who felt worse after meditation usually didn't take enough time to come out of meditation. The level of rest during TM was much deeper than sleep and jumping into activity too fast could cause a headache or dizziness. Another common complaint was that some folks actually felt fatigued and sleepy for the first few days. We soon learned that these people had been very tired or exhausted before learning meditation and now that they were more relaxed the body was normalizing and getting the rest it needed. Within a few days these folks also began to experience good results. Linnea and I were amazed that teaching such a simple and effortless technique could help so many people to relieve stress in their lives and become more relaxed and clear-minded.

If it wasn't for the rewarding work, we would never have chosen Charlottesville as a place to live. The sticky, stultifying summer heat and humidity were unrelenting. There were many beautiful homes, handsome estates, and large, well-manicured horse farms, which reflected a social atmosphere that was stratified and calcified. Even the university exuded a formal stiffness that seemed antiquated and out of touch with the waves of anti-establishment fervor sweeping college campuses across the country. Fortunately there was a small group of dedicated meditators at U.Va. who had set up an official chapter of the Students International Meditation Society on campus. In addition to reserving rooms for TM lectures and helping to publicize them, they found a great house for a TM center. It was a fairly large, traditional two-story brick house with six rooms downstairs and a separate two-bedroom living quarters upstairs that we rented out to some of the meditators to help pay the rent. We soon found ourselves teaching or lecturing six nights a week. The only time we had off was after the initiations on Saturdays until we met with the students on Sunday evening. As soon as we finished teaching on Saturday, we would jump in our car and head out of town for our farm in the mountains.

The summer quickly went by with this hectic but fulfilling routine. As the students began returning to the various colleges in the central Virginia area for the fall semester, our mentor from the Washington center, Bob Cranford, suggested that we travel around to all the colleges within a hundred mile radius and teach TM to the students. Most of the schools were embedded deep in the Bible Belt and had a reputation for being bastions of traditional southern conservatism. Almost every week we traveled to small colleges in central Virginia, ranging from Sweet Briar College near Lynchburg to Madison College in Harrisonburg and as far west as Washington and Lee in Lexington. We even lectured on TM at Virginia Military Institute. By the fall of 1971, TM had gained national recognition and even at these small southern schools there were always a few students interested in learning meditation.

Most of the time there were only ten or twenty students at our lectures and usually about half of them would want to actually learn TM. The biggest challenge was to find some private rooms on campus for initiations. The average southern college was not equipped for private ceremonies of gratitude to Guru Dev, the Shankaracharya of Northern India. One time we had to initiate in the ballroom of the student union at Washington and Lee University. There were four entrances with glass doors, so we covered them with paper and had students standing outside each door to keep people from wandering in. Unfortunately, this particular weekend was parents' weekend and they were swarming all over campus. At one end of the cavernous room we covered a table with a white sheet and set up for the puja ceremony with the picture of Guru Dev. It definitely looked like an altar with the big picture, burning incense, lit candles, basket of fruit and pile of fresh flowers. As the first person was ushered in, it felt a bit surreal to walk the length of a basketball court to greet them and then walk all the way to the other end of the room to a little table and perform the puja. About halfway through the ceremony, one of the doors burst open and a bunch of people dressed in jackets and ties came bounding into the room. Apparently it was a student giving a tour of the campus to his parents and some alums. My first instinct was to run, but I knew I couldn't just leave the person I was initiating standing there all alone. Also, it would have been weird if I just stopped the ceremony or went over and tried to explain what we were doing to the interlopers. I had no choice but to continue and hope they would leave before it was time to give the student her mantra and start meditating. When the group first came into the room, they were talking loudly, but as soon as they noticed us, their faces froze, they stopped dead in their tracks and stood there speechless for about a minute with a bewildered expression on their faces, then silently exited the room. They were probably horrified that a pagan ritual was taking place on the hallowed grounds of their beloved alma mater. As soon as they left, the atmosphere settled down and we sank into the deep silence of meditation.

Sweet Briar College near Lynchburg, Virginia was the most beautiful campus where we taught TM. It was a small, exclusive women's college in a bucolic setting about ten miles out of town. The combination of brilliant fall foliage, gorgeous landscaping and charming older buildings created an idyllic ambiance perfectly suited for teaching meditation. One of the students from a major city in the Northeast had learned TM over the summer. She wanted her friends to learn, so she set up a lecture in the student union and a small group of students decided to learn meditation. When they offered a room in the student union for the initiations, Linnea and I looked at each other, remembering what had happened at Washington and Lee, and asked for the most secluded room on campus. A woman named Jennifer said, "I've got it—the Rare Book Room at the top of the library." As we walked across the campus to the library, Jennifer enthusiastically described the Rare Book Room as a vault-like sanctuary where the most ancient books and other valuable antiques were kept. It was a very secure location and required a special pass from the head librarian, who was naturally suspicious when Jennifer requested the room for a meeting of the Students International Meditation Society. Finally, after we explained in great detail why we needed the room, she relented and took us up to the locked room in the tower of the library. As the door swung open, I was almost blinded by brilliant golden light! Then, as my eyes adjusted, I realized the sunlight beaming in the window was shining directly on a huge, magnificent golden harp. I had expected a dank, musty room filled with decaying books, but the room had a bright airy quality to it. There were as many attractive antiques as there were books in the room, which also had a few very comfortable chairs that would be good for meditating. This silent sanctuary became our favorite place to initiate among all the various campuses where we taught meditation.

Even though all the schools where we taught TM were conservative and in the heart of the Virginia Bible Belt, the students who came to our introductory lectures were genuinely enthusiastic about the possibilities offered by meditation, or at least they were politely skeptical. Often when we traveled to one of these colleges, we would also set up a lecture in the community, usually at the local public library. The atmosphere at the public lectures was very different from the ones on campus. Most of the people attending these lectures had read an article about us in the local paper and were curious and suspicious about these outsiders coming into their community with foreign notions from some long-haired, bearded Indian guru. We always dressed in a professional manner in an attempt to overcome any prejudice toward meditation. It usually helped to appear "normal" to the audience. There were always a few people at every lecture, however, who avoided looking us in the eye, and sat through the lecture seething with hostility. They appeared stoked with adrenalin, as though there were ready for a fight at any second. After a while we learned to spot them as soon as they walked in the door. At the end of every lecture we would open up the meeting for questions and inevitably these folks would accuse us of a variety of blasphemous sins, including worshiping false gods during meditation and not accepting Christ as the only way to salvation. At the end of one lecture, a sweet young couple came up to us and offered to help us carry our literature out to the car. After helping us load up our stuff, they asked us if they could pray for us. We both said sure and they began the prayer by asking Jesus to forgive Larry and Linnea for their sinful ways. After the prayer they shook our hands and we all said goodbye like old friends.

The routine of traveling around the state almost every week left us very little time to enjoy our farm in the mountains. We would usually arrive at the farm late Saturday afternoon and then pack up and leave Sunday afternoon for the first meeting with the new meditators that evening. Although we could work as little or as much as we wanted, there was a tacit assumption in the movement that full-time teachers were "one-pointed." We were to become very familiar with this term over the next few years when discussing the level of dedication a teacher had to the movement. Some of the teachers we knew were totally de-voted to Maharishi and committed every waking moment to movement activities. They usually lived in TM centers and had no private life, shar-ing meals and housing with other devotees and rarely taking a day off. Other teachers had more normal lives, pursuing careers and teaching part-time on weekends. Linnea and I were somewhere in the middle of this spectrum. We loved teaching meditation more than anything else, but we also loved spending time at our mountain homestead, remodeling and gardening.

Although we earned barely enough money to pay our expenses, we were able to teach enough people to qualify for a month of rest and meditation with Maharishi in Majorca. January is not the best month to be on a Mediterranean island. The weather can be stormy and rainy, but we didn't care. For us it was a blessing to be in the presence of Maharishi and all of our fellow teachers. We were back in Cala Antena where we had trained to be teachers the year before. All the construction and jackhammering was finished and the town was deserted for the winter season. The entire group stayed in a modern hotel built right on the cliffs above the roiling winter Mediterranean Sea. It was even more enjoyable than the year before because we were already teachers and didn't have to take classes or practice teaching. We were there just for rest and rejuvenation. After about a week of meditating during the day and meeting with Maharishi at night, it was time for him to go into his annual week of silence. This time he asked the entire group of four hundred teachers and trainees to join him. The purpose was to go deep into a state of meditative silence, uninterrupted by gross activity like talking and eating. We would spend the entire week meditating in our rooms, coming out only at noon to have some juice or fruit, then returning to our rooms. The only way we were supposed to communicate was to write notes to each other.

Everyone on the course had a private room, whether they were married or not. This monastic retreat was geared more for single people than married couples, who were used to sharing their lives with each other. When the week of silence began, Linnea and I kissed each other good night and agreed to slip notes under each other's doors to communicate. The next morning, the hotel was eerily silent. The normally raucous Spanish hotel staff must have been told to be quiet as they went about their daily chores. After a couple of rounds of pleasant but not unusually powerful meditation, I heard Linnea open her door and step out onto her balcony next to mine. I couldn't resist going out on my balcony to greet her. We smiled and waved at each other without speaking then returned to our rooms to continue meditating. Around noon she slipped a note under my door inviting me to lunch, to which I wrote an acceptance and slipped it under her door.

It felt a little weird when we greeted each other with a hug without speaking, but we were willing to see what effect a week of silent meditation would have. The normally elegant dining room had been transformed into what could best be described as an industrial fruit juice factory. The floor of the huge dining room was covered with plastic to protect the carpet from dripping or spilled fruit and veggie juice and the front half of the room was set up with long tables on which sat about ten commercial juicers. There were piles of fresh fruits and veggies for juicing and giant vats for the pulp left over from the juice extraction. The staff kept busy cleaning up around the juicers and hauling away the pulp while the gaunt-looking meditators silently went about their business of juicing their apples, oranges and carrots. The Spanish waiters, who would normally be serving drinks and delectable dinners with a charming flourish to appreciative Brits and Germans, were now unhappily relegated to the demeaning job of "hospital orderlies" as they cleaned up after hundreds of spaced-out-looking "patients" who seemed to ignore them.

After lunch Linnea and I returned to our respective rooms with a few pieces of fruit to tide us over until we reemerged from our rooms twenty-four hours later. The afternoon passed as a normal rounding course of meditating and doing yoga asanas until it came time for dinner. Instead of breaking for dinner we were to just continue rounding all night and into the next day, only sleeping when we felt like it. As I continued meditating into the evening, I didn't necessarily feel like I was going deeper into a meditative state, but my frame of reference was changing. It wasn't that unusual to have the experience of "witnessing" oneself during these long meditation courses. Maharishi called this identifying with one's "big" self rather than the "small" self. The small self was one's ego, identified with its activity and desires; the big self was the universal self that transcended time and space. It was the eternal oneness described in the mystical writings of practically all religions. He often referred to witnessing or a sense of separateness from the buzz of activity in and around us as "cosmic consciousness." This was a precursor to a state of unity consciousness, in which one no longer feels separate from the transient nature of the world, but feels at one with everything. It is often described as the goal of yoga, which means "union." As I sat there alone in my room, I kept drifting into a state of oneness with not only my immediate environment of the hotel and the vast, rhythmic ocean below, but the entirety of creation. This was not an intellectual epiphany, but more of a physical connectedness that might be described as the "ultimate comfort level." This state of awareness was beyond all desires, worries, ego, time and space. Just having the awareness of being part of this gloriously diverse and yet unified universe evoked a supreme happiness and gratitude that was beyond description.

As I drifted in and out of this transcendent state of consciousness, I realized this was why monks would spend years alone in caves in the Himalayas. How could one experience anything better than this! What's the point of doing anything else when one can just soak in a warm bath of bliss! At some point during the night I fell asleep, woke up a few hours later and reflected on what Maharishi had said about the solitary life of a monk. He said that most people are not meant to be monks, but rather "householders," that is, people who have families and jobs. The life of activity was just as valid a path to enlightenment as was the life of a recluse or monk. From one perspective, sitting in a room alone day after day with nothing to eat but fruit would be a form of punishment or confinement; however, when one transcends the puny bounds of time and space, solitary confinement can be the ultimate liberation. While the opportunity to enjoy these exalted experiences was a great gift from Maharishi, the goal of meditation was to gradually bring about a transformation or purification of the individual's nervous system that would result in the ability to maintain a higher state of consciousness not only during meditation, but also while engaged in activity. Maharishi was constantly reminding us that the alternation of meditation and activity was the best way to stabilize, or make permanent, a more enlightened state of consciousness. So after four or five days of sublime silence alone in my room, I really missed my precious wife Linnea and was ready to start talking again. Apparently many others were also getting ready to talk. The silence in the dining room was gradually being degraded by an occasional whisper or laugh. The note-writing was also getting out of hand. Instead of handing a short note to someone once or twice a day, people were sitting down next to each other for long periods of time with large note pads, feverishly scribbling notes back and forth to each other. Later that evening, as I sat alone meditating in my room, I experienced the ultimate degradation of the atmosphere of silence in the hotel when the guy in the room above me frolicked with a giggly young woman almost all night. The tile and stucco rooms acted like echo chambers in the completely silent hotel, revealing every human sound except the most discreet whisper. The next morning I went up to the room to slip a note under the door to ask them to check into a motel somewhere else for their conjugal visits, when I noticed that the name on the door was Jim Donaldson, one of the movement leaders!

When the week of silence and fasting was over, it was the consensus of most of us that it was an enlightening and inspiring week, but that we wouldn't want to do it for a living. For some people it was a week of intense "unstressing," or purification, that was quite uncomfortable at the time, but after they got through it, they felt lighter and more clear-minded. An even smaller group liked the week of silence so much they decided to stay in silence the whole course. They wore "silent" signs pinned to their chests and communicated only through notes. For these folks the silent life was quite natural and it was no hardship to avoid talking to others. Not all of them were monks at heart; some of them were what Maharishi called "mood-makers." These were folks who were caught up in the mood of the moment, who seemed to enjoy the attention they received when they walked around with a name tag that had the word "silent" written across it. Maharishi felt that, in most cases, mood-making was a waste of time. He said it was more important to engage in activities that could bring about transformation rather than just create a transitory mood, no matter how exalted it was.

The rest of the course was a sheer delight: relaxing mornings, meditating on our balconies overlooking the ancient Mediterranean Sea, enjoying tasty lunches followed by leisurely strolls along the cliffs above the thumping surf, followed by afternoon meditation and spending the evenings asking Maharishi questions. Often he would ask people to come to the microphones set up in the aisles and share their experiences during meditation. Listening to people describe their experiences was always entertaining. Sometimes there were weird hallucinations that were probably the result of stress being released. Occasionally there were descriptions of bizarre physical sensations like legs jerking or the head snapping back and forth, which were also due to normalizing of the system. The most inspiring ones were descriptions of higher states of consciousness. These experiences were frequently clear experiences of one's awareness being grounded in an unbounded, eternal state of bliss while observing the transitory world as distinctly separate from one's own essential nature. Other people would explain that, while they were witnessing the relative world around them, everything seemed bathed in golden light and seemed to radiate a wondrous sacredness. Maharishi described these experiences of refined perception as "god consciousness." The state of seeing the divine in everything represented a further development of cosmic consciousness. In the beginning stages of cosmic consciousness the experience of being separate from the relative, ever-changing field of life is rather flat. However, as one's awareness continues to expand or grow, the perception becomes more refined, which results in the individual experiencing the finer, more "celestial" aspects of the relative field of life. In this state of god consciousness, the material world is appreciated as an expression of the divine creator, and is often experienced at the finest level of creation as golden light.

The state of "unity consciousness" is an even higher state of con-

sciousness than god consciousness, according to Maharishi. In this state
there is no duality. The observer and the observed are one. This is the
state of yoga or union. The worshipper and the worshipped become
one. This is the highest state of enlightenment and is the natural result
of living in cosmic consciousness (CC) for some time, which grows into
god consciousness (GC) and then unity consciousness (UC). Although
there is a progression of expansion of consciousness from one state to the
other, one can have experiences of CC, GC or UC at any point in one's
development toward enlightenment. This explains why meditators on
long rounding courses have these great experiences even though they
are not permanently established in one of the higher states. Maharishi
often referred to the dialogue between Krishna and Arjuna in his commentary on the first six chapters of the Bhagavad Gita, in which Krishna
explains the development of cosmic consciousness in the individual and
how it progresses into god consciousness then unity consciousness. For
most of us on the course, just a taste or glimpse of these higher states
of consciousness was enough to convince us that the state of enlightenment was a distinct possibility.

Larry Cornish was the embodiment of the talented, anti-establishment academic of the early 1970s. He was in his mid-thirties, had a
Ph.D. in physics from an Ivy League school and taught at an exclusive
New England liberal arts college. He always wore a tweed jacket with
no tie and had long hair tied in a ponytail. Maharishi, who also had a
degree in physics, loved Larry's straightforward and elegant compari-
sons of quantum physics with Vedic philosophy. Often when someone
described an experience of a higher state of consciousness, he would
ask Larry to comment on the experience from the perspective of the
Unified Field Theory. He compared the absolute or eternal, unbounded
source of life to the ground state in physics, which is also a limitless field
from which matter becomes manifest. This is also the "transcendent," a
state where one experiences the source of all thought, which is beyond
thought. Experienced yogis eventually become established in this state
of inner silence, even during activity. Another one of Larry's analogies

that Maharishi really liked was his description of the brain wave coherence created during meditation in terms of the laser phenomenon. He compared the "incoherent" light of a regular incandescent light bulb to the "coherent" light of a laser. In a laser, the light waves are synchronized, which creates a pure form of light more powerful than the incandescent light, which is chaotic and weak in comparison. This was analogous to the experience of pure consciousness during meditation, in which the brain waves become coherent like the light waves of a laser resulting in more coherent activity and more clarity of mind. Maharishi loved to use objective, scientific principles and established theories to explain the purely subjective phenomenon of meditation. While there was a growing body of scientific research on the physiology of TM and its beneficial results, the concepts of enlightenment and higher states of consciousness were difficult to quantify. The use of analogies from quantum physics seemed to be the most effective way to understand abstract concepts such as the absolute and the relative fields of life. Maharishi also believed that knowledge gained subjectively by the ancient sages was just as valid as modern objective scientific knowledge. His goal with the Science of Creative Intelligence was to demystify the ancient wisdom of the Vedas and make it more acceptable and accessible to the average person.

Kurt Rivers didn't look like the average University of Virginia professor. He had long scruffy hair and extra-shabby clothes that made him look more like a West Coast radical than an English professor at a distinguished southern university. His Ph.D. thesis had examined the creative intelligence of Edgar Allenn Poe, who had attended U.Va. in the 1800's. He is probably considered to be the second-most-famous person associated with the university after Thomas Jefferson, the founder. Poe is so revered at U.Va. that his room on campus was turned into a shrine viewed through a thick Plexiglas wall. When Kurt Rivers heard the term "creative intelligence" used in a TM lecture on campus, he became intrigued by the possibilities offered by meditation and decided to learn

TM. He was quite comfortable with the concept of a unified field of creative intelligence as a source of all creation from both an intuitive and a scientific perspective. He didn't have much patience with some of the more soft and squishy jargon of the TM movement, however, like "support of nature" or referring to someone as "highly evolved."

At the time, many of the more progressive universities were starting free universities. This was an attempt to satisfy the demands of students for courses that were not part of the mainstream curriculum and university structure of exams and credits. A group of meditators at U. Va. decided that it would be a great idea to have a free university course in the Science of Creative Intelligence and Kurt agreed to be the faculty sponsor. Most of the students were already meditators and familiar with most of the concepts. However, Kurt would often sit in and play devil's advocate whenever he detected fuzzy thinking or weak arguments on our part. I actually enjoyed his merciless criticisms and ruthless attacks on our assumptions and belief systems and decided to take his two-semester history of science course.

My motives for taking his classes were not just for the joy of knowledge, but to satisfy Maharishi's request that those of us with B.A. degrees should get master's degrees. Also, I could have my tuition and some living expenses paid by the new G.I. bill. I applied to attend graduate school in political science and scheduled a meeting with the dean of the political science department. As I stepped into his handsomely appointed office and greeted the impeccably dressed dean, I felt more like an applicant at a Fortune 500 company than a potential graduate student. After he looked at my mediocre grades and asked a few questions about my present employment as a meditation teacher, we both knew I was not the type of person he wanted in his graduate school. However, he did agree that if I took post-graduate courses for a year he would reconsider my application. Fortunately, all the courses I took were taught by meditating professors or by faculty who were interested in applying Vedic philosophy to their particular disciplines.

After another semester of teaching TM in Charlottesville and at various universities in central Virginia, we had earned enough advanced training credits to spend another month meditating and studying with Maharishi, this time back at Humboldt State University in Arcata, California. The cool summer fog of the northern California coast was a welcome respite from the heat and humidity of Charlottesville. Also, returning as teachers was just pure fun, with no other responsibilities other than helping the people who were taking the teacher training program, much like the teachers who had helped us two years earlier at Humboldt. Maharishi had also developed a thirty-three lesson videotape course on the Science of Creative Intelligence. In 1972 the use of videotape in education was cutting-edge technology. For the previous few years Maharishi had had all his lectures videotaped and the Students International Meditation Society had amassed a huge library of his lectures from all over the world. The video cassettes themselves were two or three times the size of the cassettes used later in the 1980s and 90s, and the video players were huge clunkers that weighed about sixty pounds. The plan was for every center to have a player and a library of videotapes. The centerpiece of the library was the Science of Creative Intelligence course, which was a stultifying attempt to explain Vedic knowledge in a systematic, simple and standardized way that could be taught by even the most inexperienced TM teachers.

Toward the end of our stay at Humboldt, Linnea and I borrowed a friend's car and drove down to Willits to see the mountaintop homestead we had sold two years earlier. When we pulled up to the building site, we were both stunned! Linnea gasped, "Oh no!" Our lovely landscaped property had been decimated! The natural cedar wood of the chalet had been painted a grotesque green and our two favorite fruit trees, Dave and Gladys, which we had planted and carefully nurtured, were reduced to a couple of half-dead, scraggly sticks used for tying up a couple of mangy animals. Before I could jam the car in reverse and get the hell out of there, the proud new owners called us over to see the house. Apparently they had been waiting all day for us and had probably spruced things up. As we walked up to the house we saw there was no living plant matter within fifty feet of the building. All the plants had either been eaten by the tied-up goats or been driven on by the motorized dirt bikes leaning up against the house.

As we entered the house, we noticed that the stench of greasy hamburgers and stale cigarette smoke seemed embedded in the walls and furniture. What they had done to the inside of the house was even more hideous than what they'd done on the outside. The natural cedar paneling had been covered with putrid-looking wallpaper and the oak and tile floors were covered with tacky church basement-style linoleum. We were truly amazed at how they had been able to transform a charming wood and tile cedar chalet into a seedy mobile home. After congratulating them on their great remodeling job, Linnea and I jumped into the car and sped off to our meditation haven in Arcata.

About a week after we had returned to Charlottesville to prepare for another semester of teaching, we received a call from Allen and Peggy, who had just completed teacher training and were now living in Charlottesville. Allen was a Ph.D. student in literature at U.Va. and they wanted to help out at the TM center with teaching. We were enthusiastic, not only to have someone helping with the center activities, but also to have some fellow teachers to share our experiences. After a delightful Indian dinner at the center with Allen and Peggy, we sat down to discuss the business of running the center. They were both sweet, lighthearted people and we were happy to have them join us. We mentioned that we were getting a bit weary of traveling so much to teach at the various colleges in central Virginia and were really looking forward to sharing the workload with some other teachers. As soon as we mentioned this, both Allen and Peggy gave us a blank stare, as though they didn't know what we were talking about. Allen then reminded us that he would be very busy working on his Ph.D. and wouldn't have time to travel. He continued, saying that it would be better for him and Peggy, who was working full time, to do the teaching at U.Va. and we should continue to travel to the outlying areas!

My first reaction to this idea was, *Whoa, wait a minute, that's not fair!* Teaching at U.Va. was the plum of all the teaching jobs because it was the most rewarding for the amount of effort required to set up a course in TM. The smaller, more conservative schools in the outlying areas required overnight travel and usually only a handful of people learned to meditate. At U.Va. there were usually twenty students who would sign up after the introductory lectures and they would all come to the center for the course, which was a lot easier on the teachers than spending four days a week on the road. After working hard for a year developing a center and traveling almost every week, we felt the newcomers shouldn't be able to come into the area and just do the best jobs while we continued slogging down the highway every week. They just couldn't see it that way and both couples dug in their heels. Finally, after much long discussion, we agreed to call the regional office in Washington for advice.

Alex Brown was a lanky, slightly seedy academic-looking guy. He was sent to Charlottesville by the Washington office to arbitrate our dispute with Allen and Peg. Even though he had advanced degrees in philosophy and seemed a little spaced out, he listened intently to both sides of the dispute and asked a lot of practical questions about the daily activities at the center. He obviously had a lot of experience dealing with sticky situations like this and exhibited a sensitivity and instinct that belied his somewhat geeky appearance. His solution to the impasse was a compromise that we all could live with. We would continue to travel, but we would also teach at U.Va. along with Peggy and Allen. Within a few weeks we were all sharing in the joy of teaching at the center and became good friends, enjoying each other's company as fellow teachers and meditators. It was a good lesson for Linnea and me not to get attached to the little niche we had carved out for ourselves! Now that there was more activity at the TM center, it became increasingly difficult to have any privacy living on the main floor of the center so Linnea and I moved to a small cottage on a classic Virginia horse estate on the outskirts of town. This gave us the privacy we desired as well as the quiet and beauty of living in the country.

Santa Barbara was like the Mediterranean in January. Frequent storms would blow in from the Pacific and disrupt the brilliant sunshine for days at a time. We had expected to spend our winter meditation retreat with Maharishi at some secluded off-season resort overseas. However, the TM movement had purchased a five-hundred acre ranch on the top of a mountain above Santa Barbara for a retreat facility and had found a new student housing building near U.C. Santa Barbara that was vacant. Always on the lookout for bargains, the organizers of the movement were able to lease the facility for the month of January for a great price. Most of us were a little disappointed when we arrived to find the six-story dormitory in a semi-urban area on a busy street. Maharishi hadn't arrived yet and no one seemed to know when he was coming. The course began with a week of silence and fasting. Somehow, remaining silent and not eating just wasn't the same in a vibrant, progressive California college town in the 1970s as it was on a remote island in the Mediterranean. Just outside our "hotel" were dozens of tempting natural and ethnic restaurants that were not easy to ignore on our noontime walks before returning to our long meditations alone in our rooms.

On the third day of the course, I was jolted out of meditation by a brawl that erupted in the courtyard below my window. A bunch of rowdy TM teachers had finished meditating early for the midday "lunch break" and were playing a wicked game of street hockey with brooms, mops and any other sticks they could get their hands on. The hockey game was the defining moment of the course. After that everyone except the true believers started talking and going out to restaurants, movies and shopping centers. The organizers tried to entice the errant yogis to stay in the facility for evening meetings with less-than-spellbinding videotapes of Maharishi. Most people didn't show up, or left after fifteen minutes. After a few days the four hundred teachers developed their own routine of extended meditations in the morning, and then a nice long break for hockey and lunch followed by a leisurely afternoon of meditation, then out to dinner with friends at a restaurant. Everyone was happy except the organizers, who had lost control of the group.

About a week before the end of the course Maharishi arrived. Within an hour everyone was transformed from irreverent hedonists to pious, Bhagavad Gita-toting devotees. At the end of our first meeting with Maharishi, someone got up and asked him the inevitable question, "What about advanced techniques?" Maharishi, who had just arrived from overseas, was obviously tired, but couldn't say no to anyone who asked him for something and as usual he answered, "Come to my room after the meeting." Before he finished his sentence, a horde of people had bolted for the door in order to be the first ones in line for the advanced techniques from Maharishi. Despite the fact that, just a few hours earlier, most of these folks were living a lifestyle that could hardly be considered that of a monk or renunciate, their desire for growth toward a state of enlightenment was irrepressible. The advanced techniques had been designed to enhance the existing practice of meditation after someone had been meditating for a few years and had met certain criteria and, of course, what could be better than receiving the technique directly from Maharishi?

Linnea and I hadn't received a new meditation technique since Maharishi gave us new mantras in Majorca two years previously and weren't really sure if the technique was an advanced technique or not, so we decided to join the crowd and try to get a new technique. Not as aggressive as the folks who ran out the door, we ended up near the end of the line outside Maharishi's room. After about half an hour, only one person had been initiated by Maharishi. We looked at my watch. It was 11 PM and we did the math. With roughly twenty-nine people in front of us it would take ten hours to get our techniques. Maharishi was known to stay up all night initiating people, but 9 AM was pushing it, so we bailed out. The next night, after the meeting, we stood near the back of the room and charged out the back door with a dozen other people a few seconds before Maharishi ended the meeting. Our strategy was to run up the fire escape stairs and not have to wait for the elevator with the rest of the crowd. As we rushed toward Maharishi's room, we couldn't believe the long line in front of us so we turned around and went back to our room. After a few more futile attempts, we realized our only remaining hope was to see Maharishi on the morning of the last day of the course, before our flight left at noon.

When we arrived at 8 AM Maharishi's waiting room was packed with other teachers who needed to see him on an urgent basis before they left. We took our place at the end of the line and started our wait. By 10:30 there were still quite a few people ahead of us, so I went downstairs to tell Leslie, our friend who was going to drive us to the airport, that it didn't look like we would be able to see Maharishi, so we would meet Leslie with our bags in the front lobby. He looked at his watch and said, "The flight doesn't leave until noon and it only takes fifteen minutes to get to the airport, so you still have an hour and fifteen minutes." In those days there was no security at airports and all you had to do was show up a few minutes before the flight left, so I said okay and went back upstairs. Another hour went by and we were getting closer, but we had less than half an hour to wait. I went up to Maharishi's assistant and told him our flight was leaving at noon. I asked him what the chances were of getting in to see Maharishi. He said, "Oh, I didn't know your flight was leaving right away; you can go in next." Everyone else in the room, including the people we cut in front of, said, "Go for it," so we moved up to the seat just outside Maharishi's door. After another half-hour of anxious waiting, everyone in the room was getting itchy as we all were looking at our watches. Just then, Leslie burst into the room looking for us and said, "Let's go—the flight leaves in twenty minutes." Everyone in the room yelled out, "Wait—you still have five minutes! Don't go!" Leslie's eyes lit up. He said, "Give me the key to your room. I'll get your bags and wait in the car." Before he finished his sentence, Maharishi's door opened and his assistant pushed us into the room, to the cheers of our support team in the waiting room.

Maharishi's room was like a cool cocoon of silence and sweetness. He greeted us softly and calmly looked over the notes his assistant had given him. He began asking us questions about our teaching activities in Charlottesville and seemed pleased that I was working on going to graduate school. The sense of urgency and, for that matter, any sense of time, faded away from our awareness as we sat in the delightful silence of Maharishi's presence and chatted away. After what seemed like a pleasant eternity, he asked us if we wanted the advanced techniques. We nodded yes and he asked us whether we were using the first or second advanced technique. Linnea and I looked at each other for the answer. We really didn't know! I explained to Maharishi that he had given us a new technique in Majorca, but we didn't know if it was considered an advanced technique or not. He then asked us about our experiences in meditation and whether we had a lot of "clear transcending" (the experience of no thought and no mantra, just silence). We both replied that we had clear transcending occasionally, but not often. He then smiled and said, "Better to wait until next year for your techniques." We were too blissed out by being there with Maharishi to even care about the techniques. We sensed it was time to leave so we thanked Maharishi and opened the door to what seemed like a blinding maelstrom. The crowd outside was cheering and congratulating us on getting our techniques so quickly, while Leslie grabbed our arms and whisked us off to his car. We had less than ten minutes to get to the airport as Leslie roared across town. After a few minutes in the car, he asked how everything went with Maharishi. When we told him what had happened, he laughed all the way to the airport.

Life in the little cottage on the horse farm only served to sharpen our desire to live at our own farm in the mountains. It was a perfect example of the phenomenon that Maharishi often referred to as "the mind always seeking a field of greater happiness." It seems that soon after we achieve a goal or fulfill a desire, the mind moves on to something else to find more satisfaction. For example, we may have a desire for a new car and, for a few months after we acquire the car, we are delighted with the pleasure of the new vehicle. Then we move on to another desire, perhaps a new house. Soon after we get the new house, we start desiring improvements and after each improvement we soon want to upgrade or change something else. This is similar to the psychologist Abraham Maslow's "hierarchy of needs" theory. At first we need to satisfy our basic needs of food and shelter. From there we go on to many levels of needs or desires that require fulfillment, depending on our degree of self-actualization, or enlightenment. These desires could be for wealth and fame or spiritual growth, depending of the state of consciousness of the individual. The phenomenon is the same for the greedy business-man or the monk sitting in a cave practicing austerities; they both want more. This is a perfectly natural process and is the basis of all progress and evolution. Maharishi was fond of saying, "Nobody gets up in the morning and says 'I hope something bad happens today;' we all want progress and growth."

Our desire to live on our own land and have a garden never went away; we just supplanted it with what we thought was the more impor-tant and more fulfilling activity of teaching meditation. Now that, in addition to Allen and Peggy, another teacher was teaching at the center, we felt we could live at the farm for the summer and commute a few days a week to teach meditation and the slack could be taken up by the other teachers. As soon as the spring semester was over, we rushed out to our farm and began rototilling and fencing a large site for our garden. It was hard to imagine a more idyllic place to live. For over two years we had relished our short visits on weekends and holidays to remodel and restore the old houses. Now we were finally fulfilling our desire to spend more time in the country. The lush fragrance of honeysuckle and the chorus of crickets was a wonderful antidote to the noise and traffic of Charlottesville. Our fifty-seven acres was on a quiet mountain road and there were no visible neighbors. This created a great sense of seclusion and serenity that we thoroughly enjoyed.

It was also a treat to finally live in the spectacular chestnut log houses that we had spent two years restoring and connecting with a huge, open-beamed living room. For the first two weeks we delighted in planting our dream garden: tomatoes, corn, peas, beans, lettuce, squash, broccoli, chard and carrots. Then one steamy afternoon the phone rang as we walked up to the house after a refreshing swim in our pond. It was the Washington TM center. They had some exciting news for us. Maharishi International University (MIU) had been accredited as a real university and the TM movement had developed an M.A. program in interdisciplinary studies. The purpose of the program was to train people to be teaching assistants, who could then help the MIU faculty teach the first-year core courses at the new MIU. The program was to start in two weeks in Santa Barbara at an apartment complex they had leased as a temporary campus. Although I was enjoying my classes on science and religion at U.Va, the thought of earning a master's degree in a meditation environment and studying Western disciplines from the perspective of ancient Vedic knowledge seemed like a wonderful opportunity. As we lay in our chaise lounges on the deck that night, engulfed by a vast universe of sparkling diamonds, glowing fireflies and the uplifting aroma of June in Virginia, Linnea and I decided to leave our mountain paradise once again and pursue a field of even greater happiness.

17

MASTER'S DEGREES from the MASTER

Two weeks later we were greeting old friends around the swimming pool in a typical California apartment complex just a short walk from the ocean. About a hundred TM teachers from around the country had just arrived and we were all eager to find out what we would be doing for the next two months. The next morning we gathered in a makeshift lecture hall to hear how the master's program was to be structured. It sounded more like a Vedic vacation than a graduate school! We could meditate until 10 AM, then we would all be together in one big class-room for a two-hour lecture, have a two-hour break for lunch, then meet in small discussion groups for an hour before returning to class for another two hours. We studied one subject at a time, with teachers from the best universities in the country who had quit their prestigious jobs to participate in the creation of a totally new kind of university. Both the students and the faculty enjoyed the absence of hierarchy and the informality of the program. Everyone was on a first name basis and the fact that we were all meditating created an atmosphere of peaceful, lively affection.

The entire program was a delightful surprise for all of us. After the morning lecture we would sit around the pool in our bathing suits and discuss what seemed to be a more profound and universal under-standing of the great literature of the world from a perspective that none of us had experienced in our "normal" college educations. When the discussion became too heated we would jump in the pool for a swim and continue the conversation. After a great natural food lunch around the pool, Linnea and I would often go for a stroll along the beach before returning to class. This was truly the way to go to college and we were thrilled that we had decided to drop everything and participate in this great educational experiment. After a few weeks Linnea was experiencing some discomfort in her lower abdomen that didn't go away, so we made an appointment with a chiropractor who was recommended to us by some of our friends. She had a funny grin on her face when I picked her up at the doctor's office. "I am pregnant!" she declared. We had been married for five years and had been thinking that it would be nice to have a child but hadn't exactly been planning on it, so it was definitely an exciting surprise for both of us. Our lifestyle was definitely what one would call flexible and carefree. We were living on student loans and had no current source of income, but that didn't bother us. We figured that we would just take the kid along with us wherever we went and it would all work out.

It was announced at the end of the summer program that the next session would start in January in Switzerland with Maharishi; we knew that the baby was also due in January. A few of the students and faculty had kids and were planning to take them along so we thought maybe we could take our new baby with us. In the meantime we had to find a place to live and a way to make some money, as well as make arrangements with a pediatrician who would support a home birth. Before leaving Santa Barbara, we gathered at a meeting to discuss the next phase in the development of MIU. The plan was to set up satellite campuses in major cities across the country; we would all go out to these areas and teach the core courses supported by videotaped lectures by the MIU faculty. Washington, D.C. was the closest big city to us, so we made arrangements with the TM center there to teach the courses.

It felt good to be back at the Washington TM center. It was a much more dynamic environment than our small center in Charlottesville. There were thirty or forty TM teachers in the area and lots of exciting projects going on involving TM in government, education and business. The only problem was that big city living was not for us; we just couldn't live in some high-rise apartment near the center. Finally we found a small, attractive basement apartment near Mount Vernon, Virginia that was far enough out of the city to provide some peace and quiet. The response to the new MIU courses was less than overwhelming. Even in a large metropolitan area like Washington, D.C., the potential for recruiting students for the program was limited to the community of meditators. Many of them didn't have the time to spend every Saturday in classes. As a result only about ten people signed up for the courses. Even though it was disappointing, we were able to keep busy teaching TM at the center.

Dr. Brewer was one of those rare, open-minded medical doctors who was enthusiastic about home births and had delivered hundreds of babies in a non-hospital setting. He was probably in his mid-50s and looked a little worn out (probably from staying up too many nights delivering babies). His humility, humanity and knowledge were an inspiration and we felt it was our good fortune to have found him. Finally, after months of excited anticipation, Linnea started having contractions around midnight on a dark and stormy night in early January. Good old Dr. Brewer dutifully arrived about 1 AM and a few hours later our dear son Ryan was born. There is no exhilaration and fulfillment quite like having a child. After Dr. Brewer left, Linnea and I just lay there with Ryan in a sea of blissful gratitude for hours. We felt so fortunate that we didn't have to subject our son or ourselves to the weird environment of a hospital. After three weeks our little family of three had settled into a comfortable routine and we began making arrangements to go to Switzerland in a few weeks for the next session of the MIU master's program. Then one night Ryan was getting really fussy so I picked him up and tried to distract him from his discomfort, but nothing worked. He was breathing hard and looked almost blue. Even though we hated the idea of calling a regular doctor we were scared, so we called a pediatrician and he told us to bring him right in. He took one look at Ryan and said, "This is serious; take him over to Georgetown Hospital right away and see Dr. Hufnagel." We were stunned by how fast our joyful family life was turning into a nightmare. How could this happen to us? We were so proud that we were able to avoid a hospital birth for Ryan and now we were helplessly being sucked into a vortex of fear, anxiety, medical tests and smoky hospital waiting rooms. Worst of all, we had to give up our dear son to strangers in white uniforms who were going to perform unbearably invasive procedures on him.

The two hours of anxious waiting in the hospital lobby was pure agony. We tried meditating to calm down, which helped somewhat to reduce the overwhelming fear that was gripping us both, but we knew from what the doctors had already told us that the situation was severe. Finally, the somber-faced Dr. Hufnagel and his assistant came into the lobby. I could tell from their body language that the news was not going to be good and felt a surge of fear and adrenalin rip through my body. It was almost as painful for them to tell us the bad news as it was for us to receive it. Ryan had a narrowing of the aorta that choked off his blood supply. It was a fatal condition. There was a small chance that a heart operation could save him, but at that time such an invasive surgery on such a young infant had not been successful. The operation was a long shot, but we had no alternative.

The sight of our beautiful three-week-old baby after the surgery was heartbreaking. He was in an incubator with a big cut in his chest and tubes and wires all over his tiny body. We sat for hours and meditated next to him. Around midnight the doctors urged us to go home and get some sleep. The TM center was much closer to the hospital than our apartment in Mt. Vernon so we decided to stand by there. In just a few short hours our idyllic life had been turned into a nightmare. Even though we were exhausted it was hard to sleep in such a state of fear and apprehension. A few hours later we were awakened by a knock at the door. It was a policeman. He said the hospital had tried to call us but couldn't get through. Apparently one of the other teachers had been disturbed by the phone ringing and had turned it off. I knew that Ryan had died even before returning the call to the hospital. When we got the official news Linnea and I tried to meditate, but we both sat there and cried. The death of a loved one is a universal experience, but the death of a child has to be the most heart wrenching.

Our apartment seemed so empty and hollow without our little buddy. His baby stuff was everywhere, reminding us of our three sublime weeks with him and the hopes we had for our newly formed family. We kept wondering why this had happened to us and to Ryan. From the perspective of Eastern philosophy, every soul enters the earthly plane for a finite number of years to continue their growth or evolution to a higher state of development and to work out any unresolved issues that might be blocking their growth, or to pay off any "karmic debts." We asked a number of people why a soul would be alive for only three weeks and the most common answer was that apparently that was all the time he needed to accomplish what he had to do. This was hard to accept, but we remembered the verse from the Bhagavad Gita that Maharishi was fond of quoting, "Unfathomable are ways of action." Intellectually we realized that it was fruitless to try to figure it all out and that it was better to just accept it and get on with our lives. Emotionally we were still in a black hole and still stunned by how fast the whole event had ripped our lives around.

The Hotel Jungfrau in Interlaken, Switzerland was a grand old Victorian five-star hotel dripping with gold-plated everything. The furniture was gold-plated, all the fixtures and wood trim were gold and the walls and ceilings were covered with wallpaper and murals that had a golden glow. It seemed odd to be checking into such an opulent hotel for a TM course after years of staying in modest but adequate two-star resorts. The town of Interlaken was a summer resort and apparently the owners of the hotel thought it would be a good idea to lease it to the TM movement for four months in the winter. Somehow Linnea and I ended up in a palatial-sized room with a large balcony overlooking the city. The bathroom was bigger than an average hotel room, with massive early 20th century fixtures. Greeting all of our old friends who were in the master's program was a bittersweet experience. On one hand it was a joy to see them and on the other hand it was difficult to see the pain on their faces when they asked about our new baby and we had to tell them what had happened.

Although we still wanted to have a family, the people on Maharishi's personal staff led a celibate, monkish lifestyle and devoted their entire time to serving Maharishi. Even some married couples had given up the "householder" lifestyle, living in hotel rooms and traveling with Maharishi. We weren't sure if we should give up our aspirations for a family and a more normal lifestyle to devote ourselves entirely to working for the TM movement. We were discussing our dilemma one day with some friends and they suggested that we talk to Maharishi about it. We approached Maharishi's personal aide and told her our story. She suggested that we nab Maharishi when he stepped out of the elevator after the evening lecture. Linnea and I scooted up the three flights of stairs before the lecture was over that night and waited by the elevator for Maharishi.

The door opened and Maharishi was standing there with a small entourage of devotees. As we made eye contact with him he seemed to sense that we had some urgent question to ask him. He gave us his full attention for a moment as we told him about the death of our child. His large, brown, compassionate eyes moistened and his facial expression looked unusually pained as we explained our dilemma to him. His entourage started closing in around him, and he quietly said, "Come to my room." As he made himself comfortable sitting cross-legged on a couch draped in white silk, the small sitting room quickly filled up with the entourage of followers who sat on the floor around him. We sat on the floor directly in front of him as he asked a few details about our obvious tragedy. We felt a little uncomfortable asking him such a personal question in front of his entourage—whether we should have any children or lead the celibate lives of monks, which some other married couples had chosen. He sat silently for what seemed a long time after we asked him, as if he realized what a profound effect his answer could have on our lives. Then, without much change of expression, he calmly

said, "Maintain celibacy for two or three years. This will help you get
stronger; then have children." We both instantly felt a flood of relief
because we knew in our hearts that we wanted to have a family. In the
rarified presence of Maharishi the idea of being celibate for a few years
didn't seem to impact us much.

Then I had what seemed at the time to be a brilliant idea! Now
would be a great opportunity to ask Maharishi for our advanced techniques. It had been over three years since he had given us our new meditation techniques in Majorca. When I asked him, he hesitated for a moment, as though he wasn't expecting this kind of request. Then he asked
us if we were using the first or second technique. We both hesitated for
a moment. We still didn't know if the technique that he had given us
in Majorca was a first technique or second technique, because we had
received just one advanced technique from Satyanand, Maharishi's associate. We could tell from Maharishi's body language that he was getting a little impatient. The vibe that we were getting from the devotees
surrounding us and from Maharishi was that we had taken enough of
his precious time; now it was their turn to have his attention. I knew
that the meter was ticking away and there was no time to explain why
we didn't know what number technique we had. I finally realized that
if Maharishi knew what my mantra was, he would know the answer to
his question. Before I could think any more about what to say, I blurted
out the mantra. I could feel a collective mental gasp in the room. How
could I have done such a stupid thing? If there was anything sacred in
the TM movement it was the privacy of the mantra! There were many
reasons why it was a bad idea to share your mantra with others, not the
least of which is that it could cause confusion if people kept trying different mantras. As soon as I said it, Maharishi winced as though he felt
a sudden pain, then looked at us as though we were naughty kids and
said in a fatherly, reprimanding tone, "No need to say the mantra—now
go to your room and rest!"

"I can't believe I did that," I said to Linnea when we got back to
the room. She looked at me and said, "If you hadn't said it, I was just

about to say the same thing." I replied, "Maharishi must think we are a couple of idiots!" We both realized that the whole incident was a signal that we had better take his advice seriously. The purpose of celibacy in the Vedic tradition is not that of sacrifice, but a matter of energy conservation. Every individual is endowed with a certain amount of life force or "kundalini." According to this tradition, sexual activity expends the vital force, while celibacy conserves this energy, which can then be used to strengthen the individual and raise the level of consciousness to a higher state. On long meditation retreats the metabolic rate is reduced and the individual tends to remain in a meditative state even during activity. The attention is more inner-directed toward a state of silence and the desire for sex and most other activity is greatly subdued. In a state of detachment from activity, the suggestion of remaining celibate to hopefully become physically and spiritually stronger seemed acceptable. Later that evening when we climbed into bed to go to sleep, I looked at this beautiful woman lying next to me and realized that it wasn't going to be as easy as I had first thought.

The four months of hanging out with our friends in the lovely Swiss town of Interlaken and studying fun subjects like religion and world history from the perspective of Vedic science went a long way toward helping Linnea and me recover from the pain of losing our child. The relatively mild and short winter quickly erupted into a glorious, flower-filled spring. We often strolled along the lake and mountain paths, soaking up the warm sun and enjoying the fragrance of the tulips and daffodils that covered the valley floor. Life in our presidential room at the Victoria-Jungfrau was wonderful. Along with delicious meals and studying with old friends, we explored the magnificent Swiss countryside as the warm spring crept up the mountainsides, replacing the snow with flowers. It was hard to believe that we had to leave in less than a week and had no idea of what we were going to do when we returned to the States. By 1974, TM had become a household word and thousands of mainstream Americans all over the country were learning to meditate. New TM centers were opening in every major city and there were plenty of teaching jobs available for people who could live on room and board and a small stipend, so we figured that we would return to the Washington area and see what was available.

The northern Virginia TM center wasn't nearly as elegant as the DuPont Circle townhouse that served as the D.C. center. It was a large, rambling, suburban ranch house that was scheduled to be demolished to make room for one of the many new highways that were transforming Falls Church from a sleepy bedroom community to a modern maze of shopping malls and expressways. Linnea and I moved into one of the bedrooms and joined six other dedicated TM teachers who had forsaken the benefits of real jobs in order to devote their full time to teaching meditation. The national consciousness had been awakened to the benefits of meditation and there were daily requests coming into the center for presentations on TM to businesses, schools and government organizations. Shortly after I started teaching at the center I got a call from Lieutenant Commander Rob Pensky, a naval psychologist, who was in charge of the alcohol abuse unit at the Quantico, Virginia Marine base. He had read some studies that indicated that TM reduced drug and alcohol abuse and he wanted me to give a presentation to a group of alcoholic Marines under his care.

Driving up to the Marine guard at the main gate to the base evoked a flood of memories of both guarding gates at military bases and entering them as an intelligence analyst. The spartan, old wooden buildings with military acronyms plastered all over them and the swarms of uniformed men marching up and down the sterile streets seemed at once familiar and alien. Building Number 4569 with its insipid green walls and gleaming linoleum floors was just like every other military building I had ever been in. The only difference was me! I was now in my third incarnation in my relationship with the military. This time I was coming back as a practitioner of yoga to share my knowledge of meditation with a bunch of grizzly old Marine sergeants. As Commander Pensky welcomed me into his office, I couldn't believe he was an actual naval officer. He seemed like a young, bearded graduate student (at the time the Navy wanted to appear more progressive and allowed men to wear beards). His demeanor was totally unmilitary and extraordinarily casual. Because his rank was Lieutenant Commander, I was expecting a much older career officer who had been in the navy for ten or fifteen years. Then I realized that because he was a psychologist, he was probably given the rank when he entered the Navy.

One of Rob Pensky's duties was to oversee the alcoholic rehab unit at the base. The treatment consisted of counseling, the use of Anabuse (a drug that induced vomiting when alcohol was ingested) and various punishments ranging from demotion in rank to discharge from the Marines. Rob had done his homework on TM and, because he was perhaps more open-minded than a typical naval officer, he felt that if TM could reduce stress and tension in the lives of his patients they could reduce or eliminate their dependence on alcohol. After I gave my presentation to him and his assistant, an affable, young guy named Jim in a naval lieutenant's uniform, they seemed impressed and wanted me to set up a course on TM for their patients and themselves. On the drive home, I was starting to get excited about the possibilities of bringing meditation to the Marines, when the reality of the logistics of teaching TM on the Marine base suddenly struck me. The vision of these no-nonsense Marine sergeants sitting in the clinic with their boots off and holding a bouquet of fresh flowers, fruit and a little white hanky as an offering to Guru Dev seemed ridiculous, but I couldn't see any way around it.

The tough old sergeants were more attentive and compliant during the first part of the TM lecture than I had expected, probably because they had been struggling with alcoholism for years and were pretty desperate. When it came time to talk about the day of initiation and the fruit and flowers, I wasn't sure if they would get fed up and walk out of the lecture or think the whole thing was crazy, but they sat dutifully through the whole lecture about mantras, gurus and offerings without rolling their eyes or groaning. Then the moment of truth came when I asked those who would like to take the course to stay behind to set up an appointment. I half-expected all ten of them to get up and leave as fast as they could, but almost all of them stayed behind. A few days later, I had Commander Pensky's office turned into a meditation room with some comfortable chairs and his desk covered with a white sheet. It looked like an altar, with a large picture of Guru Dev and a shiny brass puja set for the initiation ceremony. Seeing the stress dissolve from the faces of these battle-hardened warriors as they sank deep into meditation for the first time was intensely gratifying and poignant and served as a powerful reminder of how universal the process of transcending was. By the time the course was over they were all having good results. I encouraged them to keep regular in their meditation, even though people would often learn meditation and start to feel so much better that they would lose the incentive to continue. If anyone needed the benefits of meditation, these guys certainly did. Now it was up to them to continue. All I could do was to offer follow-up "checking" (a simple procedure for insuring continued, effortless practice and maximum results) and hope that they would take advantage of the continued program.

After two months of communal living at the center, Linnea and I were ready for more privacy. The only problem was that we couldn't afford to rent an apartment with the small salaries we made teaching TM unless one of us got a job. Again we were faced with the dilemma of living in a stuffy high-rise apartment near the center or living farther out of town and commuting long distances. Fortunately we found both; a job for Linnea and a quiet garden apartment that opened up onto a golf course and miles of hiking and biking trails in Reston, Virginia. The entire town of Reston was a planned community designed to provide an environment of quiet semi-rural living. Linnea got a job a short bike ride from our apartment, working for someone who had an office in his home. It was easy office work that paid well, so I could continue teaching meditation. We soon settled into a pleasant, peaceful summer routine of hiking and biking the myriad trails that wound through the semi-forested community. Often on weekends we would drive out to our farm and enjoy the true silence, clear skies and sweet air of the Blue Ridge Mountains.

18

FRAT HOUSE ASHRAM

We knew by now not to get too settled into a routine. As the steamy days of summer began to get shorter and cooler, marking the transition into fall, we realized that the time and place of the next session of the MIU master's program had not yet been announced. There were rumors that the TM movement was looking at a bankrupt college in Iowa as a permanent location for MIU. Thousands of people across the country were learning TM and the organization was generating enough funds to buy its own facilities for meditation retreats. The beautiful land in the mountains above Santa Barbara proved to be too remote to build a large facility. Instead, the movement decided to buy old semi-rundown resorts in rural locations like the Catskill Mountains in New York and a rustic resort near Clear Lake in northern California. Then one day in early September, we got the inevitable phone call. The bankrupt Parsons College in Fairfield, Iowa had been purchased and classes would be starting in a few months, as soon as they could get the facility up and running and find some students. This was the most exciting development in the short but fast-paced history of the TM movement. A university by and for meditators was a dream come true! In the mid 1970s many students had become disillusioned with what seemed to be the anachronistic, medieval, hierarchical structure of most universities. They were looking for a more relevant and flexible structure for gaining knowledge. With its primary focus on the development of human consciousness, MIU provided an attractive alternative to the conventional system of higher education.

Hundreds of volunteers were needed for everything from food service to faculty members. The program offered room, board and $75 per month plus credit for tuition at MIU. Linnea and I sent in our applications and prepared to move to Iowa. This was a great opportunity to finish our master's degrees without taking out any more student loans, and also to take part in this historic endeavor with hundreds of our meditation friends. Within a week we received a call from Dave Kramer, an old friend who had been working on the MIU project and was now the dean of students. Even though MIU was still a family of old friends, where everyone was on a first name basis, they were required to set up a traditional structure in order to get student loans and accreditation. Instead of offering us a job at MIU, Dave thought we might be interested in teaching the MIU core courses at the Cobb Mountain facility in northern California. Although we had been looking forward to going to MIU, teaching in California also sounded enticing, so we quickly accepted his offer. He suggested we stop at MIU on our way to Cobb Mountain to discuss the details of the program and pick up our teaching materials.

The midwestern Corn Belt in late October is not quite as bleak as it is in winter. While most of the fields showed brown stubble and the leaves were gone from the few trees around the farmhouses, there were still occasional patches of green grass and stubborn ornamental bushes refusing to give up their colorful leaves until the bitter end. Every college campus we had ever been to, including ones in the Midwest, were jewels of delightful landscaping that set them apart from the mundane residential and commercial neighborhoods surrounding them. Parsons College was different. It looked like an abandoned military base. There was no landscaping! The only plants on the campus were weeds and two-foot-high grass that had not been cut for at least a year. Most of the buildings (except for a small cluster of traditional stone buildings) had been constructed in the 1960s out of the cheapest possible materials. It didn't take very long for them to look like neglected army barracks, with faded paint and boarded-up broken windows. The roads were full of potholes filled with muddy water, which made it impossible to determine how deep they were before attempting to drive through them. In spite of the derelict state of the campus, there was excitement in the air as hundreds of meditators from around the country arrived to create an alternative educational universe.

Dave Kramer's office was in the small enclave of traditional stone buildings that included the president's office, the chapel and an old abandoned library. After meeting with Dave to discuss the details of our plan to teach the freshman core courses at Cobb Mountain, he suggested we stay at MIU for a week and take advantage of the book and tape library in order to develop our curriculum for the courses. We were assigned a room in one of the newer but still creepy dorms. There were about fifteen of these two-story, six-sided housing units in one section of the campus. Each unit had been a fraternity or sorority house in the heyday of Parsons College. Parsons had had a reputation as a party school, known as "Drop-out U." Apparently many of the students had flunked out of other colleges and Parsons had employed a loose admissions policy, which made it very popular during the Vietnam War. It gained a national reputation as a great place to party hard and get a deferment from military service. This resulted in an explosion of enrollment and the need to build new housing fast and cheap for all the new students. By the end of the war, the boom had turned into a bust and the school went bankrupt. It just sat there empty in the Iowa cornfields until MIU bought it for a rock bottom price. As we entered our dorm, the first thing we noticed was the old togas and other frat party paraphernalia lying around on the beer-stained carpets. Each floor had a large central room. The walls were covered in generic, sleazy paneling with one of those goofy circular metal fireplaces in the center, surrounded by a few threadbare couches and beat-up lounge chairs. Eight private rooms opened onto the central room and there was one industrial-sized bathroom serving all the rooms on the floor. Fortunately our building was reserved for staff and faculty and many of our old friends from the master's program were already living on our floor. A month earlier we never would have dreamed that we would give up our delightful garden apartment for a beat-up room in a fraternity house in Iowa.

For the next week we prepared for our teaching assignment in California and enjoyed meeting our friends over tasty natural food meals in the campus cafeteria. The enthusiasm of everyone involved in creating a university based on developing one's full potential mitigated the fact that the place was a dump in the middle of nowhere. We were actually sad when it came time to leave. Dave Kramer suggested we meet with him one more time, so we scheduled a meeting with him just as we were all packed up and leaving for California. It was a little surreal seeing so many of our friends playing the role of university faculty and officials. It was almost like the inmates taking over the prison. Here were all these high powered, well-appointed executive offices that had been inhabited by middle-aged men with official titles and Ph.D.s taken over by a bunch of counter-culture "kids" in their twenties. Although they were young, they were well educated, bright and adaptable and displayed a lighthearted competence not found at a traditional university. Dave's office exuded gravitas: the walls were real cherry paneling and the expensive walnut and oak furniture made the office look like the chambers of the Supreme Court. As we sat in plush leather seats in his waiting room, we could hear him talking on the phone to the director of the Cobb Mountain facility. At one point he became very agitated and said, "I can't do this to these people! They are great people and have driven all the way from Washington, D.C." Linnea and I looked at each other and rolled our eyes with that "oh no" look we were so used to in our short careers in the movement. Dave emerged from his office, his neck and entire head beet red from a combination of anger and embarrassment. Apparently Mel, the director of the Cobb Mountain facility, had precipitously changed his mind about offering the MIU courses, which meant that Linnea and I were out of a job!

Dave felt really bad for us and suggested that we stay at MIU for a few more days while he would see if he could find some jobs for us. It was less than an hour since we had hugged all of our friends goodbye at the dorm, so it seemed a little funny to be moving back into our room, but most of them were veterans of working with the TM movement and were used to last minute changes. Linnea and I weren't very disappointed either and we were confident we would find jobs at MIU. We were excited about participating in such an extraordinary educational adventure. For the next few days we explored the campus and the town in the bright, brisk air of October in Iowa. The town of Fairfield was classic Middle America, with a small square with a bandstand in the middle of the downtown shopping area. Most of the stores were there to serve the basic needs of a typical farming community, but there were a couple of higher-end clothing stores that must have been there to serve the wealthier Parsons College students. The townsfolk seemed a little befuddled by the sudden invasion of "hundreds of followers of the Maharishi" as the local newspaper described the newly arrived meditators. On one hand they liked the increase in economic activity that the reopening of the college would bring, and on the other hand they were nervous about having so many weird members from an Eastern cult in their decent Christian town. The Chamber of Commerce guys were bending over backwards to welcome the new university, even though they were probably thinking to themselves, "Who in their right mind would call a small midwestern college in the middle of nowhere Maharishi International University?" Neither the campus nor the town was a match for the quaint small college towns of New England and Virginia. The kindest way to describe them was characterless and boring. At least they weren't gruesome and dangerous.

Dave Kramer had some good news for us. He had been talking with Alex Brown, who had come down to Charlottesville from the Washington TM Center to mediate our disagreement with Peggy and Alan the previous year, and Dave had mentioned to him that we wanted to work at MIU. Alex was now the director of the "forest academy" program and needed two more teachers. Over lunch at the MIU cafeteria the next day, Alex explained the program to us. Unlike any another university, after every three months of academic courses, the MIU students attend a one-month residence course called a forest academy. So instead of gathering fatigue and stress from the rigors of college life, MIU students would go deep into meditation and Vedic knowledge for a whole month. The daily routine consisted of a few rounds of meditation and yoga asanas in the morning. Then the students would meet with the forest academy instructors for a discussion or videotape of Maharishi describing the ancient Vedas. The students would also gather for a meeting in the afternoon before meditation and again in the evening. Not only was this a unique opportunity for the students, but it was also a great opportunity for the forest academy instructors. There was nothing most TM teachers enjoyed more than diving into the vast and deep ocean of ancient knowledge from the multitude of Vedic texts commented on by Maharishi. Even though we were technically instructors we were more like facilitators and Maharishi was the teacher. This made our job that much more enjoyable: no lectures to prepare or papers to grade. In addition to our dream jobs we were given room and board, a stipend of $75 a month and, for every three months of working as teaching assistants, we received one month of free tuition for our master's degree program.

Most of the students at MIU had been to other universities and were older and more mature than the average freshman. They were all enthusiastic about spending a month on the forest academy course, meditating and soaking up Maharishi's knowledge. Each instructor was assigned a group of about fifty students. It was our job to make sure that everything was going okay with their meditation and that they attended the daily videotaped lectures of Maharishi and the discussion that followed. Many of the lectures focused on the Vedic texts such as Rig Veda and Sama Veda. Maharishi described the Vedas as the "blueprint of creation" and claimed that this knowledge of how creation manifests is just as valid as the knowledge of the universe we have gained through modern objective science. The only difference was that one method was subjective and the other was objective. Apparently the ancient Vedic seers had directly cognized this knowledge through their higher states of consciousness and had passed it on to their students orally for thousands of years. Sometimes Maharishi would spend hours commenting on just one word of the Rig Veda, for example the word *Agni,* which contains the mechanics of the origin and expansion of the universe. Then he would call on one of the MIU physicists to compare the Vedic description of the manifestation of the physical world to the theories of quantum mechanics. Most of the time these discussions were fascinating and kept the attention of the students; at other times they were so arcane and abstract that our hair would begin to hurt.

After about two weeks of long meditation some of the less dedicated students started getting a little restless and began skipping the daily meetings. Due to the delicate nature of the nervous system during long meditation courses it was our job to closely monitor all fifty students in our class. If someone was missing, they might be experiencing some intense "unstressing," which could affect their sense of mental and physical well-being. Some people can make rash decisions and exhibit weird behavior when their minds are clouded by the release of stress. To prevent any regrettable incidents caused by someone experiencing heavy unstressing outside of meditation, the forest academy students were restricted to campus and weren't allowed to drive. As soon as someone was missing from a meeting we had to find them to make sure they were okay. Most of the time, we would find the missing students either asleep in their rooms or just hanging out in the dorm. Their usual excuse for not going to a meeting was that they were feeling a little rough from release of stress. Usually we were able to remedy this by checking their meditation and giving some instructions on how to handle any intense thoughts or emotions that might come on during meditation.

Ted Redick was definitely not the typical MIU student; he was in his 30s and was a veteran who had recently been in a drug rehab program. He was quite overweight and had only been meditating a short time when he heard about MIU and decided to attend on the G.I. bill. While most of us at MIU had been part of the counterculture for years and had been exposed to natural food, yoga and Eastern philosophies, Ted was a mainstream, midwestern ex-drug addict. To his credit he liked everything about MIU except the food. He really missed eating lots of steak every day so he purchased a small freezer and a hot plate for his dorm room so he could have his daily steak. When he didn't show up for a meeting I went to his room and he invited me in. It smelled like a Bonanza Steak House and was littered with the remains of many partially devoured steaks. Ted explained that he was on a weight loss program and was only eating steak and lettuce three times a day. As a result he had a severe case of gout and was unable to leave his room. It didn't take much convincing to get him to cut back on the amount of daily steak and to add some fruit and veggies to his diet. He felt better in a few days and was back at daily meetings.

Saturday night was the most challenging time for finding truants. For some reason we had the highest rate of absenteeism on Saturday nights and we couldn't figure out where the truants were going. They weren't in their rooms or in the library. Then we realized they were at the Saturday night movie in the student union. Every Saturday evening they played an old classic 35mm film for the students and staff. After some undercover reconnaissance we raided the theater by suddenly flipping on the lights and nabbing all the forest academy escapees. The raids were so much fun for everyone that it became a regular Saturday night ritual.

Every three months we had a month off to work on our master's degrees. This also gave us more free time to get out of Fairfield and explore the countryside of southeastern Iowa. It was virtually impossible to find any forests or interesting land for hiking. In less than one hundred years, almost every acre of land in the Midwest had been disturbed, much of it contaminated with chemical fertilizers and pesticides. Many of the wells on the local farms were so toxic the farmers had to haul water for their cattle, while the municipal water in the town of Fairfield was an abomination. After a few trips to some local parks, we reconciled ourselves to walking around the campus, which was bleak and windswept most of the time. We missed our beautiful farm in the Blue Ridge Mountains, but the exhilaration of taking part in the development of this remarkable university was worth the relatively minor hardships of living in such a harsh and austere environment.

Around the end of February, rumors that Maharishi was coming were flying around the campus. The rumors became confirmed when one of the dorms became an around-the-clock construction site. Usually Maharishi would stay in a comfortable home when visiting an area, but in this case they wanted to create a spectacular luxury residence for him, probably out of gratitude and devotion. Every few days we would walk by the eviscerated dorm and peek at the stunning white wool carpeting, expensive hardwood furnishings and golden fixtures in the bathrooms and kitchen facilities. The transformation of the shabby dormitory into an exquisite VIP residence in the middle of the dirty snow, gooey mud and dead weeds of an Iowa winter was truly surreal.

A few days before Maharishi came the entire campus lost its academic focus and began preparing for his arrival. The anticipation was similar to Santa coming to greet a bunch of five-year-olds. Everyone from the true believers to the curious but skeptical students was keyed up about his visit. Even the national media and major TV networks were beginning to show up on the campus. During the previous months, Maharishi had appeared on the Merv Griffin show (probably the most popular talk show on TV at the time) with Clint Eastwood, who extolled the benefits of TM. The sight of a tough guy like Clint Eastwood bantering and joking around with the diminutive, chuckley monk from India captured the imagination of the American public and thousands of people began flocking to centers around the country to learn TM. Instead of the usual ten or fifteen people learning TM every week at the average TM center, there were fifty to a hundred now learning to meditate. This created what everyone in the movement called the "Merv Wave." This was the most exciting time to be teaching TM in local centers anywhere in the country.

The largest lecture hall on the campus was converted to what must have looked like a Hindu temple to the news media. At one end was a carpeted stage with an attractive white couch for Maharishi. Behind the couch was a large altar with a huge gold-framed picture of Guru Dev surrounded by every fresh flower available from all the florist shops within a hundred-mile radius. When Maharishi entered the hall, the entire university community was in the room waiting for him. For the first time I noticed a hierarchical atmosphere in the room with Maharishi. The seating was arranged in order of rank; the first row was reserved for high-level MIU officials, then a row for faculty, then the staff and visiting TM teachers in the back of the hall. Even though the faculty sat close to Maharishi and were basking in his lavish praise, there would be no MIU if it hadn't been for the brilliant and dedicated work of the staff that created a functioning university from scratch in a few short months. After a few hours of canned show and tell from the faculty, Maharishi opened the meeting up for questions. The questions, for the most part, were about higher states of conscious and the Vedas. This went on for a few more hours. Maharishi was known to sit in meetings for ten or twelve hours without taking a break or having a meal. For those of us whose physical constitution required more than one meal a day, it started to get real uncomfortable after seven or eight hours. Finally Linnea and I bailed out and went to the dining room to eat.

When we returned to the room an hour later, the diehard devotees of Maharishi were still in their seats clinging to every word. Now they were discussing the "Merv Wave" and its dramatic effects on the centers across the country. Some of the teachers were getting burned out from teaching so many people and were concerned that they couldn't keep up with the demand for TM. Linnea and I found this astounding! Ever since we'd begun teaching almost four years ago, TM teachers had to go out and "beat the bushes" to find people who were interested in TM. It was hard to imagine just sitting around in the center, answering the phone and trying to schedule in everyone who wanted to learn to meditate. Then the subject of what to do with all the money generated by the huge increase in teaching activity came up. Usually half the funds went to the national office for administration and expansion, like buying facilities and teaching materials, and the other half went to the centers for rent and teachers' salaries. Now there was so much extra money left over in centers that the teachers were worried about having too much money and they asked Maharishi what should be a reasonable salary for a teacher. When Maharishi said, "About $30,000," I could feel my jaw drop. There was a collective gasp in the audience. This was a huge amount of money! In 1975 the average TM teacher earned less than $10,000 a year. I said to Linnea, "What are we doing here?" Our first impulse was to leave MIU and return to teaching "in the field" as it was referred to in the movement. It didn't take long, however, for us to realize that for now MIU was the place for us to be. It was at the center of the TM universe and by far the most exhilarating and dynamic project undertaken so far by the TM movement.

Maharishi often claimed that one of the reasons why he wanted to teach so many people to meditate was to create coherence in the collective consciousness. If this were true, then at MIU, where there were about a thousand people meditating, one would expect a great deal of coherence in the group. After participating in the project for six months, it was hard to deny that the phenomenal achievement of creating a university well on its way to accreditation so quickly was the result of the collective creative intelligence of the meditators working on the project. While Maharishi was very pleased with the success of MIU, there were rumors going around that he was concerned about TM teachers not progressing toward the state of enlightenment fast enough and he was planning a new program for enhancing the development of the teachers. The most common speculation was that he was developing an advanced course in Switzerland, where he was now living. While participating in the establishment of MIU was probably the most exciting event in the movement, the thought of spending six months with Maharishi on a program of personal growth was the ultimate goal of all dedicated meditators. We all wanted to get enlightened as soon as possible! It was a no-brainer! Why wallow in ignorance and suffering when the possibility of living a life of blissful freedom was everyone's birthright? Most of us had been meditating long enough to experience a taste of this in our daily lives and it was natural to want more. The possibility of spending time with Maharishi developing higher states of consciousness was now the hottest topic at MIU.

By the middle of the summer about forty of us had completed our M.A. degrees and decided to celebrate by renting caps and gowns and conducting a graduation ceremony in the campus chapel. Even though the degrees were actually from an accredited university, we all knew that the ceremony and degrees were sort of meaningless as far as a mainstream career was concerned. In 1975 the demand for anyone with an M.A. degree in interdisciplinary studies from Maharishi International University in Fairfield, Iowa was virtually nonexistent. Everyone in the program was there for their own enjoyment and enrichment, which made the whole experience both fun and enlightening for all involved. Some members of the "Class of '75" had decided to stay on at MIU as teaching assistants and work on Ph.D.s in specific disciplines, while the rest of us were ready to move on. When the details of Maharishi's new course in Switzerland were announced a couple of months later, Linnea and I were among the first to sign up.

19

HIGHER CONSCIOUSNESS at HIGHER ALTITUDES

Stepping out of the train in Interlaken felt like coming home. The lakes, mountains and delicate October colors of Switzerland were a delightful respite from the austere monotony of Iowa. This time we were staying at the Hotel Royale, a smaller and less grand hotel than the famous Victoria-Jungfrau where we had stayed the previous year. Over the next few days more and more of our old friends from around the country began arriving. The atmosphere in the hotel seemed more like a convention than a yogic retreat. While we all waited for the program to start, there was nothing to do but get together with friends for meals and hike up into the hills, which were covered with golden European larch trees. After a few days of settling in, our entire group of two hundred was moved to the small ski resort village of Engelberg. To keep expenses down, the TM movement specialized in finding good deals on renting resort hotels in the off-season. The ski season didn't start for a couple of months in Engelberg, so they found an old, traditional Swiss-style hotel that had been transformed into a repulsive Club Med hotel for swinging singles. The inside of the hotel was stripped of every vestige of old European furnishings and painted garish colors of orange and green. The beautiful old wooden floors were covered in wall-to-wall carpet that actually went halfway up the walls to create a modern 1970s look. Despite the weird loser decorating, the hotel was situated on a hillside above the village with stunning views of the valley and the surrounding mountains.

After a few days of enjoying the new surroundings we finally had a meeting with the course organizers, who explained the structure and goals of the six-month program, which was designed to cleanse, purify and refine the physiology in order to support higher states of consciousness. In the Vedic tradition of spiritual development, the connection between physiological refinement or purity and growth toward enlightenment plays a much greater role than in most Western religions. There are remnants of the need to purify the physiology in current Judeo-Christian and Muslim traditions, like fasting and taking a Sabbath, but the true meaning seems to have been lost over the centuries. Purification seems more like a penance than a technique. In the Vedic tradition, the relatively austere practice of purification is called "tapas," which is generally practiced by monks and yogis to enhance and accelerate their development. In the Western spiritual tradition the culturing of the nervous system seems to be overlooked, with little attention paid to yoga exercises, healthy diets, herbal supplements and deep meditation techniques that produce dramatic physiological changes. Maharishi often said that the human nervous system is our machinery of perception and, just like an athlete who trains his body for excellent performance in a particular sport, those who want the clearest perception unhindered by stress and negativity need to "train" their nervous systems accordingly. For the next six months our goal was to train our nervous systems to support a more enlightened perception.

The exact methodology of this "training" was explained by the course directors and it was not what most of us had expected. We were looking forward to Maharishi arriving and spending a pleasant six months meditating during the day, then meeting with him at night. The new program was a lot more austere than we had anticipated. To start off, we would be fasting on fruit and vegetable juices for two weeks and then gradually ease back into solid food for another week. Then, after eating solid food for one more week, we would begin fasting again. The purpose of this was to detoxify and purify the system. Fasting is an old yogic technique and is also the basis of the European school of "nature cure," which is the foundation of naturopathy. This approach to health had been adopted by many naturopathic physicians and chiropractors. Apparently Maharishi thought it would be a good idea to assign a chiropractor and a naturopathic doctor to design the cleansing part of the program to enhance the growth of the course participants. Besides fasting, another important aspect of this "natural hygiene" method was colon cleansing. According to this system, the colon is the key to health. Without proper digestion and absorption of nutrients, all systems in the body are negatively affected, which can result in a multitude of ailments. The conventional wisdom of nature cure is to rid the colon of the toxic materials accumulated over the years. The preferred method of cleaning the colon is an enema, which fills the colon with water and then is flushed out. The doctors in charge felt that fasting and daily enemas were the best way to purify the system, which would result in a more purified consciousness.

Although we all had fasted for various lengths of time in the past, the daily enema routine was new to most of us. After some rudimentary instruction on how to take an enema, the doctors sent us all into the little village of Engelberg in search of enema bags. The only place in town selling enema bags was a small pharmacy, which was quickly overrun by hundreds of starving Americans from the Club Med hotel looking for enema bags. The kind old Swiss pharmacist was dumbfounded by what appeared to be hordes of tourists overrunning his little shop in pursuit of enema bags. Within minutes he sold the only six "irrigators" (the German word for enema bag) in stock. Faced with a crowd of desperate people who were unable to purchase an irrigator and therefore were going to lose out on their opportunity to get enlightened, he quickly explained through an interpreter that he would order some more and put a big sign in the window when they arrived. Every day for the next two weeks people on the course ran down to the little shop during our midday break to see if the irrigator sign was in the window. The more aggressive folks would always get there first and buy out all the irrigators within minutes. For some reason the pharmacist could only get twenty at a time so it took about two weeks for everyone to get an irrigator. At first the pharmacist was intimidated by so many skinny people dressed in suits and ties demanding irrigators, but after a while he seemed to get into the spirit of the whole event and as soon as we walked in the door he would greet us with a big grin, proudly say "irrigator," and usher us over to his latest selection.

The snow started falling soon after we arrived and seemed to continue almost every day, blanketing and obscuring everything in a cold, grayish-white fog. Beginning every day with an enema lying on the cold tile floor, followed by a cold shower then sipping a small amount of cold, watery fruit juice in a cold room during a constant blizzard evoked a sense of being in a medieval monastery. As the snow got deeper and deeper day after day, the village became more and more silent, as hardly any vehicles could drive through the six feet of snow that showed no sign of letting up. Just as the constant snow gradually reduced the noise and activity in the village, the fasting and long periods of meditation reduced the noise and collective metabolic rate of the two hundred dedicated TM teachers cloistered in the snowbound hotel. The lack of food being digested in the system slowed down the metabolic rate and facilitated the process of transcending during meditation. As our physiology settled down, our experiences in meditation became deeper which resulted in the release of deep-rooted stress. In traditional terms this process is called purification, which is an integral part of most mystical traditions. In practical terms, most of us experienced a growing inner directedness and silence along with a blurring of the line between activity and meditation. Maharishi's hope was that this intense combination of meditation and fasting would enrich our experiences of cosmic consciousness and even higher states of god consciousness and unity consciousness. He also hoped this purification and refinement of our nervous systems would accelerate our growth toward a permanent state of enlightenment.

In the meantime quite a few people on the course were having trouble giving themselves enemas. There were a number of accidents and injuries that were not only a concern to the directors of the course but also to the hotel manager, who found out that every one of his two hundred guests was taking daily enemas in their rooms. For some reason this upset him more than the usual drunken hell-raising that took place during the ski season. A few weeks earlier, the whole group had watched a videotape on how to do the yoga asanas by one of Maharishi's dedicated assistants, a skeletal young guy named Johnny Gray. Johnny later became an expert on male-female relationships and wrote the bestseller *Men are from Mars, Women are from Venus*. As I sat in the daily group meeting listening to a barrage of complaints from the course participants about problems with their enemas, I thought of Johnny Gray's yoga asana tape and decided to announce to the group that he was making an enema video that would address many of the questions about proper enema procedures. My intention was to provide some comic relief from all the complaining and grumbling. About half of the two hundred people in the group started howling with laughter while the other half thought I was serious and wanted to know when it would be available. I was caught off-guard by the gullibility of the folks who actually believed there would be a tape of someone taking an enema, so I announced that it would be shown in three days. This seemed to mollify some of the more disgruntled folks and get the heat off the course directors, who knew they were no replacement for Maharishi.

About three days later, the atmosphere at the daily meeting was getting a little testy, so I decided to present an update on the status of the enema video. I explained that instead of using graphics with an audio voiceover, they decided to film someone taking an enema live in order to more effectively elucidate how to achieve the best results. After a few gasps and sniggers from the audience, I then announced that unfortunately the tape, which was made in France, was confiscated by the Swiss border police. They claimed it was a porno flick and arrested the mortified young movement volunteer who was trying to deliver the tape. He tried in vain to explain in sign language that it was an instructional video, but it was useless. The Swiss police sent him to Interpol headquarters for questioning, where he finally broke down after a brutal interrogation and confessed to trafficking in pornography. As usual about half the group finally caught on that I was jerking them around while the other half groaned in shock and disappointment that they wouldn't be getting the proper enema protocol.

Most of the people on the course were experiencing deeper and clearer transcending as a result of the fasting and longer periods of meditation. However, they were also experiencing the symptoms of physical purification, including headaches, GI tract disturbances and short flare-ups of various diseases and physical traumas from their past. Occasionally, someone would experience the pain and swelling from a broken leg or another traumatic injury from the past. It would usually last only a few hours or a day and then go away. Maharishi often explained that sometimes we actually experience the physical and emotional symptoms of the original stress or trauma as it is being released. In the past on long courses, Maharishi was always there to answer questions and provide inspiration and humor when we were unstressing. This made the discomfort much more tolerable. However, on this course Maharishi was not available, except by the occasional conference call. As the weather got colder and the days grew shorter, the morale of the group began to suffer without the presence of our much-loved teacher.

In response to the growing complaints about the course, Maharishi decided to send Satyanand, his devoted associate, to spend a few days with us answering questions and giving talks. Everyone loved Satyanand and looked forward to hearing his stories of life in Guru Dev's ashram with Maharishi. The only place in the hotel for a large group meeting was the bar/nightclub which had grotesque, creepy carpeting covering the walls, and a long bar and dance floor at one end of the room. The nightclub was always dark and reeked of stale beer and cigarette smoke, which was anathema to a group of yogis seeking spiritual development. It seemed particularly weird to have a meeting with a holy monk dressed in a white dhoti in such a "tamasic" setting. The organizers of the course did their best to transform the barroom into a sort of temple. They placed a couch covered with white sheets and some clean oriental rugs on the dance floor and surrounded it with fresh flowers.

As soon as Satyanand sat down, dozens of people started raising their hands to ask questions. Everyone knew that he was much more willing to tell personal stories than Maharishi, who always avoided talking about himself. He started out telling us about the time that he, Maharishi and a group of other monks had to travel to a distant city to organize a speaking event for Guru Dev. When they arrived Maharishi made sure that everyone else had a place to stay and was comfortable before he himself went to bed. Satyanand described how Maharishi worked tirelessly and always looked after others before taking care of himself. Then someone asked him about his first meeting with Guru Dev. Satyanand explained that he was not a lifelong monk like Maharishi and that he had been a "householder" who worked for the government of India and that sometime after his wife died, a friend of his invited him to hear Guru Dev speak. At first he was skeptical of gurus and didn't want to go, but his friend prevailed and so he agreed. At one point during his talk, Guru Dev made eye contact with Satyanand and he realized that Guru Dev knew what was in his mind at that moment. He also felt that Guru Dev knew exactly who he was and projected a sense of unconditional acceptance toward him that completely dissolved any skepticism and melted away any pretensions that he had. He felt at one with Guru Dev and a profound inner peace came over him that he had never experienced before. When he finished telling this story, he closed his eyes and all two hundred of us instantly closed our eyes and fell into a deep, blissful state of transcendence. It was as if we were all stuck in a state of samadhi, until someone decided to ask another question, which seemed to jolt the audience out of such a profound state of silence that quite a few of us groaned in disapproval of such a rude interruption.

By early December, the snow was deep enough to open the ski runs around our classic alpine village and the hotels started filling up with holiday skiers. This meant that it was time to move back to Interlaken where it was now off-season and hotels were available at discount rates. Our new hotel was right on the main street in Interlaken. The busy sounds and diesel fumes from passing vehicles provided a sharp contrast to the monastic silence of our snowbound hotel in Engelberg. After a few weeks we all adjusted to our city environment and found a new benefit at our hotel that had been unavailable in Engelberg. We discovered quite by accident that if we pressed number one on the elevator, it took us directly to the basement supply room where all the food was stored, including cases of pineapples, bananas, apples, oranges and avocados. This was a true gift from the gods. Many of the gaunt folks on the course were tired of fasting and craved some delicious fruit; they began sneaking it up to their rooms and privately indulging in some extracurricular ingestion. The avocados were the most relished of all the food. People would hoard them in their rooms, wait until they were perfectly ripe and then add them to some contraband bread and cheese for an illicit dining thrill.

Eventually the hotel manager noticed that most of his produce was disappearing almost as soon as it was delivered and he complained to Bradley, the course director, who made a stern announcement about pilfering the produce. Bradley was a nice guy, but he was a bit of a prima donna. He seemed to have injured his back, so I thought it would be fun to start a little rumor about how he hurt his back to see how far it would go. Whenever the opportunity arose, I would tell people the story of how Bradley was caught in a very embarrassing situation by the hotel manager. It seemed that he had also been hoarding avocados not only for eating, but also for use as a skin moisturizer. The hotel manager, like many of the Swiss hotel owners and staff, appreciated filling his hotel with paying guests during the off-season. However, he was mystified and at times annoyed with the behavior of the reclusive, skinny Americans who stayed in their rooms all day eating fruit and burning incense that left burn marks on the furniture and carpets. The hotel owners became so concerned about damage from the incense and accumulating fruit peels in the rooms that they insisted on spot inspections. One day, when everyone was in a meeting, the manager randomly selected

Bradley's room for inspection and knocked on his door. Bradley was in the bathroom, naked, busily rubbing perfectly ripe avocados over his entire body. Either he didn't hear the knock on the door or he was too embarrassed to go to the door covered from head to toe with the green slime of a dozen avocados. The manager, assuming that no one was in the room, unlocked the door and entered just as Bradley was running out of the bathroom, green and naked. They made eye contact, Bradley slipped and fell on the floor ending up in an indecent position, and the stunned manager turned around and ran out of the room. For the next few days, whenever Bradley made announcements to the group, there would be sniggers and giggles as he approached the podium.

Although almost everyone in the group was settled into a sublime routine of meditation during the day, the evening meetings were just not the same without Maharishi. Then, about halfway through the six month course, Maharishi arrived and began meeting with us every afternoon and evening. He was very interested in our experiences during meditation and wondered if the three months of purification had resulted in any changes in our ability to experience deeper levels of consciousness, both in and out of meditation. One memorable afternoon he asked us to arrange ourselves according to our experience of transcending during meditation. The first two rows were for those who had "clear" experiences of pure unbounded awareness with no thoughts, just total absolute silence. The next few rows were for those who had "hazy" experiences of the transcendent. This meant that the unbounded bliss of transcending was not experienced all the time, but was broken up with thoughts and other sensations during meditation. In the back few rows were the "nils." These were the people who almost never had clear transcending and had lots of thoughts or discomfort during meditation. This arrangement created a fascinating dynamic. The people with the clearest meditations sat up front close to Maharishi, which created an uncomfortable hierarchy. Everyone wanted to sit close to Maharishi, resulting in an interesting observation about the need for people to be close to the source of power whether it's a guru, politician or rock star.

As soon as everyone was arranged by category, Maharishi began asking each individual in the front section very specific and detailed questions about their experiences. This caught many of them off-guard and revealed that perhaps they weren't having such profound experiences after all. They were often banished to the back of the room while the hazys and the nils moved up. This bizarre game of "mystical" chairs had a fascinating, humbling effect on almost everyone as Maharishi spent the next four hours constantly shifting everyone around from one category to another. The only conclusion that Linnea and I could come up with from this apparent waste of valuable time with Maharishi was that he was breaking boundaries of so many people by shaking up their beliefs and behavior patterns.

Winter seemed to be the best time to go on long meditation retreats. Nature was asleep; the busy tourist town of Interlaken was bereft of summer tourists and blanketed with a layer of snow that added to the silence. The daily routine became greatly enriched by meetings with Maharishi and concerts of delightful and soothing Ghandarva Veda music played on the sitar and tabla drums by an accomplished family of musicians from India. After a few weeks of discussing experiences during meditation, Maharishi decided to initiate everyone in some new techniques that were aimed at enhancing the expansion of awareness from our localized consciousness to a state of oneness with the entire creation. He decided to do this electronically by gathering all two hundred of us in the meeting room and hooking us up to earphones through which he would give us our techniques privately. It was a little weird, but it was a very efficient way for one person to privately initiate a couple of hundred people in a few hours. I really enjoyed my technique, which seemed to connect my consciousness with all of creation. I enjoyed it so much that I didn't want to bring my awareness back to my own individuality. I was a little concerned that I didn't want to come back from this expansion and mentioned this to Maharishi during our checking session. He replied, "Expansion is good!"

After four months of deep meditation and purification Linnea and

I felt like we could just stay there in Switzerland and meditate forever. However, this was not to be. After returning from our lunchtime walk one day, we saw a note for us to check at the front desk of the hotel about a phone call from the States. In the mid-70s international phone calls were a big deal, usually involving several operators, and were very expensive. The news that my father had suffered a heart attack and was in the hospital sent a flood of adrenaline and anxiety through my system. After arranging a call to my mother and hearing about his condition, we had no choice but to go to Lorain, Ohio as soon as possible. Leaving our blissful cocoon in beautiful Switzerland and traveling to the frozen, grimy rustbelt of the Midwest was like being kicked out of heaven. Also, on a practical level, it was definitely not a good idea to immediately plunge into activity after being in a meditative state for so long. It usually took a minimum of three weeks to come down from long rounding to avoid jarring the nervous system. Before we left, one of Maharishi's assistants recommended that we try to do as much of our meditation routine as possible while we were in Ohio to avoid the effects of coming down from rounding too quickly.

By the time we arrived in Lorain, my father had already had bypass surgery and was in a coma in the ICU. In the 1970s this procedure was in its infancy and there were lots of complications and an unknown prognosis. After a few days of waiting anxiously to hear from the doctors we fell into a daily routine of long meditations in the morning, then driving from my parents' house in Lorain, about twenty-five miles west of Cleveland, to the Cleveland Clinic on the east side. As many people know, it is not easy to see a loved one unconscious and clinging to life with the aid of a bunch of beeping and whirring machines. Every day we would anxiously meet with the doctors who were trying to keep him alive, but were not sure if he would make it. During one meeting with the doctors, I convinced them to let me sit and meditate for an hour every day with my father. I figured there was nothing else we could do and meditating with him would at least provide a soothing, coherent and hopefully healing atmosphere.

When we arrived in Ohio from Switzerland, we were both quite emaciated from all the fasting. Linnea was down to about ninety pounds and I was about ninety-five pounds. Because we were still doing long meditations while at my parents' house, it was difficult to participate in the typical American meat-and-potatoes diet with the rest of the family and gain any weight. They were very tolerant and never said anything about how skinny we were or about our weird diet of fruit and nuts. After about three weeks of doing whatever we could to support my mother, we got a call from the hospital asking us to come right away. They wouldn't tell us if my father had died, but we all knew that was the reason they wanted us to come immediately. The general understanding we had gained from all of our new-age reading and conversations with our meditating friends was that when someone dies their soul hangs around the loved ones for a while before moving on to another level of existence. I didn't sense my father's presence until we were at the gravesite and his casket was being lowered. I then sensed his presence very strongly. It seemed that he was in a peaceful, blissful state and that he was liberated from all suffering and going on to a higher realm.

If leaving our meditation retreat in Switzerland for the Midwestern rust belt seemed like being kicked out of the Garden of Eden, returning to Switzerland in early spring seemed like going back to heaven. As we rode the train from Zurich to Interlaken, we saw the green meadows flanking the snowcapped peaks filled with yellow and pink wildflowers and the fruit trees in full bloom. Everywhere there was newness and freshness, a far cry from the blighted decay of industrial northern Ohio. Our friends greeted us with applause as we rejoined our meditation group. We immediately began soaking up the heavenly atmosphere of peace and profound silence created by all the meditation that had taken place in the hotel. This joyful reunion was to last only a couple of short weeks because the course was ending and everyone was returning home. Fortunately we were able to join a new course and make up for the month we were away. It was also time for the seasonal migration of the TM movement. The tourists were returning to Interlaken and the ski season was winding down, so it was time to return to the higher elevation resorts. This time we ended up in Arosa, a fairly remote ski village high in the Alps. Although it was colder and spring hadn't quite begun at this high elevation, the views from our delightful old wooden hotel were magnificent and the pure mountain air was wonderful. This new course also began with a long period of fasting. However, because Linnea and I were there for only a month to make up for the time we missed, we didn't have to participate in the austerities of fasting and enemas. We had our own cosmic vacation of meditation, eating full meals and taking long walks in the mountains.

About a week before we were scheduled to leave, we heard that Maharishi was coming in two weeks. Unfortunately this meant that we would miss him by only one week. We asked the course directors if there was any way we could stay for another week. They said if we agreed to go on staff they could justify us being around for another week. That was fine with us. We had come down from long rounding and were doing our normal routine of meditating once in the morning and once in the afternoon and were looking for some activity. They needed help in the kitchen and because everyone was fasting, we helped put the fruit and juice out for a few hours a day and had the rest of the time off to hike on the mountain trails. At the end of the fast, the doctor in charge of the fasting program decided it would be a good idea if everyone on the course ended the fast by sipping a small glass of fig juice to get their bowels working again before they resumed eating solid food. We looked around the kitchen for some figs and noticed wooden crates of dried figs that were strung together with twine and packed in straw mixed with rat droppings. Before we could decide what to do, the Yugoslavian kitchen workers emptied the boxes of figs into large aluminum vats and added water without paying much attention to the turds that were falling in the vats. The next morning they put the large vats of fig juice and some small juice glasses on tables in the dining room for the folks to take small amounts of juice for sipping slowly. As the crowd of starving course participants descended on the vats, they ignored the small glasses and grabbed some big mugs and started gorging on the feces-laden fig juice. Linnea and I were shocked at the ferocity of the starving juice drinkers, who gulped down multiple mugsful. We thought they were only going to take a few sips and that a few rat turds probably wouldn't make much difference but this was so out of control there was little we could do.

A few days later, as most of the over-indulgers were recovering from their excess intake of fig juice, Maharishi arrived and we all crowded into the hotel ballroom to hear his words of wisdom. Linnea and I thought this would be a great opportunity to receive our advanced techniques from Maharishi. After using the same technique for a number of years, the nervous system becomes cultured to be able to handle a more powerful technique, which is supposed to accelerate one's growth toward a higher state of consciousness. Maharishi always waited until the end of a course when people were ready to go home to give advanced techniques. Linnea and I were the only ones going home and we thought the lack of competition for his time would improve our chances of finally receiving our techniques. The last two times we tried, once in Santa Barbara three years earlier and once in Interlaken two years earlier were fiascos, so this time we hoped it would work out. As soon as the evening lecture was over, Linnea and I rushed to the lecture hall door to see if we could nab Maharishi before he became mobbed with people asking him questions. For some reason the crowd surrounding Maharishi was smaller than usual and we were able to approach him rather effortlessly. The usual protocol was to ask him to give the advanced technique right after the evening lecture. It was almost impossible during the day because he was so busy. As his entourage approached us we sidled up to him and asked for our techniques. He stopped walking and looked at us as though he was contemplating what to do. Then, after what seemed like a long silence, he said, "Not tonight. It's better that I do it first thing in the morning when I come to your hotel for the meeting." Both Linnea and I felt a wave of disappointment. To us this meant no! The chance of Maharishi coming to our hotel early in the morning was highly unlikely. He usually got so wrapped up in important projects that we would be lucky if he even came back the next evening.

As Maharishi and his entourage drove off to his hotel, I turned to Steve, the course director, and asked him if we should follow Maharishi up to his hotel and try again. Maharishi usually met with people until one or two AM and often, if one could get his attention, he would initiate them if they asked at the right time. Steve discouraged us from trying again and said, "Come down to the hotel desk first thing in the morning and I will call up to Maharishi's hotel to see when he is coming." We were skeptical, but figured it was worth a try. When we went down to the lobby the next morning there was no one at the desk. We looked in the lecture hall. There were quite a few people sitting in there doing their morning meditations with the hope that Maharishi would show up and they would have great seats up front. A few minutes later, Steve appeared in the lobby and offered to call Maharishi's hotel to find out if he was coming down to our hotel. After a very brief conversation, he quickly hung up the phone and said, "They'll be here any minute! Here's what we'll do. As soon as Maharishi enters the hotel, I will remind him that he was going to give the advanced techniques to you and Linnea. Let's get everyone out of the lecture hall and we'll set up a puja table so he can initiate you in there and when he is done everyone can come back in." We gave each other a skeptical look. There were only a few minutes before Maharishi would be walking in the door and it seemed unlikely that they could set up everything to work as smoothly as Steve so confidently suggested.

Maharishi caught everyone by surprise as his entourage came through the lobby headed for the lecture hall. It was very unusual for him to appear this early because usually everyone spent all morning meditating in their rooms and then he would meet with us after lunch. Before he could enter the lecture hall, Steve intercepted him and reminded him that he was going to initiate us before the meeting. Maharishi looked pleasantly surprised and motioned to us to come with him into the hall. The hall was completely empty except for a puja table and three chairs set up in front of the stage. Linnea and I were a bit astounded that it was just the three of us walking down toward the stage and yet it seemed perfectly natural. It was as though we were with our best friend, and Maharishi, who usually had a tight twenty-hour-a-day schedule, seemed like he had all the time in the world. Everything seemed completely effortless. After he asked us a few questions about our meditation, he motioned to us to join him in the puja. As the three of us performed the puja ceremony, I felt all the boundaries slipping away as I settled down into a state of oneness with all life. After he gave us our new techniques, we sat for a while and meditated blissfully with Maharishi. He seemed to thoroughly enjoy teaching us and seemed to be in no hurry to leave, so the three of us just sat in the lecture hall chatting while hundreds of people were waiting outside the doors to come in. We told Maharishi that we loved teaching, but that in order to continue teaching full time we would have to sell our property, which we could no longer afford to maintain on the small income of TM teachers. When we asked him what he thought we should do, he sat quietly for a long time; his large brown eyes seemed like pools of kindness. He said, "Don't sell your property, but find a way to teach full time." We both felt relieved as he spoke those reassuring words. Teaching was what we loved to do, but we didn't want to live a communal life in a center with a bunch of single teachers. We still had a strong attachment, or desire, to have our home in a quiet, rural area. Somehow we had to reconcile this with our desire to teach. It seemed like we could have sat there all day, but we could hear the restless crowd outside the door. The three of us got up. Maharishi headed for the stage and we found a couple of seats in the audience.

The drive to our farm in the late September sun was even more dramatic than we had remembered. The house had been rented for the last two years and we had forgotten how uniquely beautiful the property was. The white pines that lined the driveway had been only a few feet high a few years before; now they were towering over the road and covering the ground with a soft blanket of aromatic pine needles. As we drove down the winding road, across the dam and up the other side of the hill to our welcoming house, we felt as though we had finally come home after a two-year odyssey of living in dorms and hotel rooms. As soon as we unpacked our bags, we ran down to our pond for a refreshing swim in the mountain water, then sat on our deck for hours soaking up the sun, sounds and smells of our mountain paradise. We felt as though we never wanted to leave, but we knew in our hearts that teaching meditation was our first love and that it was not possible to live in such a remote location and teach TM. The previous summer, we had taken a trip up to New England and noticed how much more progressive and open-minded it was than rural Virginia. There were so many TM centers in Massachusetts and New Hampshire that we realized we could live in the country and teach at one of the TM centers without commuting forty miles each way. As much as we loved our farm, we knew we had to sell it and move to Massachusetts, where we could find a rural, but not too remote, small homestead. The decision to sell was actually quite easy. We had owned the farm for over five years and had only lived there a few weeks at a time. The prospect of actually living full time in our own home and being able to teach TM was an exciting prospect.

It was mid-November by the time we sold our farm and moved into Carl and Nora's spare bedroom in Beverly, Massachusetts. The house was built in the 1600's and, while it was in good repair, the floors listed to one side so severely that it was like being on a ship in a storm. We had met Carl and Nora on our six month course and they asked us to look them up when we came to Massachusetts. They had the same goals that we had of teaching meditation and having their own home. Carl had a good job as an engineer, but was interested in starting a mail order business selling imported sweaters from Iceland, Scotland and Ireland. They offered to share the business with us so that we all would have more time to teach meditation and yet earn a living. This sounded like a good plan so Linnea and I started working with Nora and Carl to get the business off the ground.

The Beverly TM center was in a delightful location of large expensive homes about two blocks from the ocean. Carl and Nora had been teaching there part-time and we joined them in teaching and helping out at the center. The more we explored the North Shore area, (about thirty miles from Boston), the more we liked it. It was far enough away from the density of Boston to find a rural home that appealed to us, so we began making appointments with real estate agents to look at houses. It didn't take long for us to find a wonderful, traditional, New England Cape Cod-style house with five acres and access to a pond. After only one look, we decided to make an offer. The next day the real estate agent called us up and said someone had beaten us to it and signed a contract on the house right after we looked at it. We were disappointed, but continued looking. Over the next few months, every time we found a place we liked, it would be sold out from under us. The real estate agents said they loved to show us property because it almost guaranteed the house would be sold that day. In spite of our frustration at not being able to find some property, we were thoroughly enjoying our new life in Massachusetts. Our new business with Nora and Carl was progressing well and teaching at the TM center was, as always, a joy. Even as the New England winter started to turn bitter cold, walking on the beach in our bare feet was a daily delight.

About two weeks before Christmas, wild rumors began circulating among the teachers at the various TM centers around Boston that Maharishi was planning a new six-month course for TM teachers. This was the flashiest course ever offered! In the past Maharishi had been mildly dismissive about the more flashy aspects of higher states of consciousness like reincarnation, kundalini and yogic powers like levitation. He always used the analogy of "capture the fort" to describe how we should treat all those special abilities described in yogic literature. In other words, focus on gaining enlightenment first and then automatically have control over all these abilities. With this new course, he seemed to be saying that we had been meditating long enough to have some success with the powers described in the *Yoga Sutras*.

According to Maharishi, somewhere around 200 BC, a great yogi named Patanjali developed certain formulas or practices that, when performed while established in a state of samadhi or transcendental consciousness, resulted in the ability to see and hear things at a distance and even to levitate or become invisible. The goal of practicing these Yoga Sutras was not to gain mastery over these special abilities (known in the Vedic literature as "sidhis"), but to train the mind to function while established in a state of pure consciousness. In other words, by introducing these thoughts or intentions during deep meditation, we gradually culture the ability to function from a deeper, more silent or coherent level of consciousness. In the state of enlightenment we function from that level all the time, which ideally eliminates stupidity or what Maharishi called "mistakes of the intellect."

Our first reaction when we heard about this new course was to drop everything and go back to Switzerland. The course was starting in two months. Then we realized that we were just getting our new business started and looking for a home to buy so we decided to wait until the next course started in the fall. Over the next few days we settled back into our comfortable, fun lifestyle of combining teaching TM, looking at real estate and developing our business with Carl and Nora. Then one day Carl called and said they decided not to do the business. We were a little shocked at how suddenly they hit us with the news, but we had become used to precipitous changes in our lives ever since we had begun working for the TM movement. Within a few days we realized we now had no reason not to go on the sidhis course. Our business venture had fallen through, every house that we liked was sold before we could buy, and we now had the finances from the profits of selling our farm to pay for the course.

As soon as we walked into the lobby of the small, modern hotel situated on a hillside overlooking Lake Lucerne, we realized that we had made the right decision and were perhaps not so crazy after all. Almost all of our good friends from the last six month course were there to greet us. It was like a hometown family reunion, even though we had never even heard of Weggis, Switzerland. Every room in the hotel had a spectacular view of the lake and the surrounding snow-covered mountains. The small town was a quaint lakeside summer resort that was now deserted for the winter months. The weather in the winter was too mild for snow so all the tourists were up in the mountains skiing and we had the town all to ourselves. After about two weeks of hiking and sharing meals with many of our old friends, we started into a routine of silence and all day meditation in preparation for Maharishi's new sidhis program. This course was a lot less austere and more fun than our previous six month course. Nearly every day we would have a conference call with Maharishi, who was across the lake in the town of Seelisburg. Finally, after we had been there almost a month, Maharishi called and initiated the whole group of us in the sidhis program over the conference phone. He gave us a few yoga sutras to start with to see what kind of experiences we had. After settling down in meditation for a half hour, we would introduce one of the sutras while in a very subtle state of awareness. The principle behind the technique was that the deeper we were in meditation when we introduced the sutra the more success we would have with that particular sutra. For example, if we were enlightened and grounded in pure consciousness then we would have total success with a particular sutra, such as seeing something from a distance. Naturally none of us on the course were enlightened, but we had been meditating for quite a few years and it was hoped that we would get some noticeable results.

After a few days of practice most of us were experiencing what Maharishi called "flavors" of the sutras. There was definitely something to it. While a few people probably let their imaginations get the best of them and thought they had become invisible or partly invisible, the rest of us were pretty level-headed and simple enjoyed the sensations the sutras evoked during meditation. One of my favorite sutras was the navel sutra. I had often heard the term "contemplating your navel" when people discussed yoga and dismissed it as a misguided concentration technique. Now I had a new understanding of the significance of the navel in yogic practice; by directing one's awareness to the navel while in the state of samadhi, "one gains knowledge of the bodily systems." When I practiced the sutra, I became aware of the kundalini or energy spiraling up my spine and filling my head with sublime effulgence. The rise of kundalini is one of the quintessential indicators of experiencing higher states of consciousness and offers an experiential verification of the philosophy of yoga. Everyone on the course seemed to be having such good experiences with the sutras that every two weeks Maharishi would give us a few more to do. There was nothing tedious or ascetic about this new practice. We considered it "spiritual recreation," which defied the conventional wisdom about the severity of monastic life.

On previous long courses we stayed in our rooms and meditated alone morning and evening, but on this course Maharishi had all the furniture taken out of the lecture hall and had the floor completely covered in foam rubber mattresses. Instead of chairs, all one hundred and twenty of us sat in the lotus position and practiced our meditation and the yoga sutras together morning and evening. There were all kinds of rumors flying around about why Maharishi had us meditating together on the foam. Then, on one of our conference calls, he explained that a large group meditating together created a powerful atmosphere of silence and coherence that enhanced the experience of meditation for everyone, which in turn created a positive influence in the collective consciousness of the world. When someone asked about the purpose of the foam, he chuckled and casually replied that it was for the practice of the flying sutra, also known as levitation. About half of us in the audience gasped and the other half let out a noisy howl when we heard him say this. After a few days of wild speculation and anticipation, Maharishi gave us the instructions for the flying sutra and explained that in the beginning stages of levitation, yogis started hopping around. The foam mattresses were there to make our landings soft, or more comfortable.

The first time we tried the flying technique was hilarious. After meditating in the lotus position for an hour in order to settle into a state of deep silence, we began the flying technique. According to Patanjali, the enlightened yogis can levitate because they can function on the fin-est level of creation. This is analogous to the advanced physicist who can create a powerful laser beam as a result of his mastery of the laws of physics, whereas a caveman would only have enough knowledge to start a fire by rubbing two sticks together. So the enlightened yogi who has mastery over the laws of nature should be able to levitate. For the rest of us who were not enlightened, but had some degree of pure awareness, something else happened that was pretty amusing to look at.

The amazing thing was that something happened at all, consider-ing that no one in our group of over a hundred seemed to be enlight-ened. The first thing that happened to most of us when we introduced the flying sutra while in a deep state of meditation was to feel a surge of energy and a strong urge to lift up off the ground. While in the lotus po-sition with our legs folded under us we couldn't just jump up like Super-man. Most people started rocking back and forth while some people just sat there twitching and shivering. Then, like popcorn in a popper, a few people would start hopping up and down on the foam, then suddenly a large group would start hopping almost simultaneously and then, like the last few kernels of corn in the popcorn popper, the rest of the people in the group would finally pop. Everyone had a different style of hop-ping; some made subtle delicate hops while others made aggressive and very large, athletic leaps. Hopping while sitting in the lotus position is not an easy feat, but the fascinating thing about this was that we were in a deep state of meditation when we did the flying sutra. Normally any sudden physical movement while in such a deep state of rest would be very jarring to the system and probably result in a headache. However, when we practiced the flying technique we felt a blissful exhilaration that seemed to energize the whole body. It sure looked weird to see over a hundred people hopping around in a room covered in foam, but the experience was indescribably pleasurable.

While this was not levitation in the classical sense of effortlessly flying around the room, it was more than just a physical act of hopping around on the foam. For some reason when the flying sutra was introduced during meditation, there was a surge of energy that became even more enlivened as we continued. After fifteen minutes, most people felt infused with blissful energy rather than fatigued from what would normally be strenuous physical exercise. When someone asked Maharishi what the purpose of this rather unusual practice was, he replied that it was a powerful technique for integrating the mind and the body that greatly accelerated one's development toward enlightenment. He also explained that, during the flying sutra, the brain becomes very coherent and when a large group of people are flying together, it creates a powerful effect not only in the immediate atmosphere, but in the collective consciousness of the world.

Herr Brunner, the owner-manager of our hotel, was like most Swiss hotel managers: happy to have his hotel filled during the off-season, but also nervous about the odd behavior of his guests. He had just become used to the idea that we were spending all morning and afternoon locked in our rooms, coming out only for lunch and dinner. Removing all the furniture from his elegant meeting room and covering the floor with three truckloads of foam rubber mattresses seemed to be too much for him to process. Now we were walking to the meeting hall in our loose-fitting meditation clothes that looked like pajamas. Most people also carried the pillows from their rooms to sit on while meditating on the foam. It was hard to imagine what Herr Brunner was thinking when every one of his guests went into the meeting room in their pajamas and locked themselves in for two hours every morning and evening. During our meditation sessions there was a deep silence in the room. Meditating with a hundred and twenty other people definitely enhanced the silence and enriched our experiences. It was easy to understand Maharishi's theories about creating more coherence in the collective consciousness where large groups of people were meditating. While the silence was palpable in the hotel full of meditators, the concept that the coherence created by our group of meditators in the hotel could radiate out to the rest of the planet was not so easy to accept. However, almost everything else that Maharishi had said about meditation and the Vedas was vali-

dated by our own experiences, so it seemed reasonable to give him the
benefit of the doubt.

Although Maharishi hadn't come to our hotel, we had inspiring
conference calls with him almost every day, during which he would ask
us about our experiences with the Yoga Sutras. He was especially interested in the flying sutra and seemed delighted that we were all hopping
around the room with ease. He felt that the flying technique was the
most powerful of the sutras for purifying the physiology and developing a more enlightened state of consciousness. He kept increasing the
amount of time we would spend practicing the flying sutra, from five
minutes to ten and then fifteen minutes. The longer the group spent
flying, the more intense and wild it got in the meeting room, which was
now called the flying hall. Some people were hopping their brains out by
hopping really fast and working up a sweat while others started emitting loud sub-human barking sounds. Sometimes it looked like a nine-
teenth century English madhouse, with people hopping and screaming
all over the room. Most of us assumed this weird behavior was the result
of very deep stress being released during the flying program.

As we continued the long flying program day after day, the yelp-
ing and screaming increased to an intolerable level for most of us, who
just hopped along silently and easily. It got so bad that a number of us
complained to the course leader, who promised to ask Maharishi if it was
necessary to have all this screaming during the program. Also, we knew
the noise and floor shaking in the flying hall could be heard not only
throughout the hotel, but also outside the hotel on the street. The louder
the strange, demented sounds were, the more distant and agitated the
normally phlegmatic Herr Brunner became. When we first arrived at
his hotel, he was a very gracious host. Then, as the situation in the hotel
went beyond his comfort zone, he avoided making eye contact with anyone in the group and his normally gregarious bulldog, who always hung
out at the front desk greeting everyone, became aloof and unpredictable. As the days went by without hearing a definitive word about the
screaming from Maharishi, the entire group divided into two camps, the

screamers and the non-screamers. The folks who did the howling said that they couldn't control themselves and that it was a strain to try to suppress the urge to yell out such primal sounds. Those of us who were not screamers found it difficult to understand why someone sitting next to us while we were meditating would let out a blood-curdling scream and scare the bejesus out of us. Finally, after two weeks of meditating with what seemed to be a bunch of lunatics jumping and screaming around us, Maharishi brought an end to the madness by softly uttering a few words when someone asked him about the screaming during the conference call. He simply said, "No need to scream."

For half the group, the silence in the meditation hall was a welcome relief, but for the other half it was an uncomfortable challenge to suppress the urge to screech during the flying sutra. Whenever he talked about the flying sutra, Maharishi emphasized how important it was to practice the program in a large group. He kept reminding us that when we were practicing the sidhis, we were not only becoming more enlightened individuals, but we were reducing the stress in the collective consciousness of the world. It was hard to believe that a few hundred people practicing this rather bizarre technique could have such a far-ranging influence. Although many of us were skeptical, we figured, what the heck, it doesn't do any harm and seems to be a great tool for individual growth.

After a few months of flying together morning and evening, the novelty began to wear off and it seemed to become a normal routine until one morning when I was merrily hopping along on the foam. I suddenly felt a snapping sensation in my lower back, which immediately seized up in intense pain. I could hardly walk back to my room, where I collapsed on the bed, unable to move. This had happened a few times over the years and had been diagnosed as a slipped disc. Usually after a week of lying on my back it would gradually improve enough to get out of bed, and then I would be stiff and sore for another week before it went back to normal. Unable to sit up, I had to meditate lying down, which is not ideal because there is a great tendency to fall asleep in that position. After a day of meditation in the prone position, I felt my awareness being drawn to my lower back. As this happened, I began to witness excruciating physical and emotional pain radiating from that spot in my lower back. It felt like some deep agony was being released from my body that was so dark and painful that it was hard to believe it could have happened in my present lifetime. All I could do for the next week was lie in bed feeling this intense stress being released from my back. It wasn't much fun, but I didn't have any choice. It reminded me of the "dark night of the soul" that so many mystics referred to in their accounts of meditating alone in some secluded monastery.

Maharishi's model of stress being "deposited" or "stored" in the physiology seemed to make a lot of sense. In the scientific literature unrelated to TM, some scientists of questionable judgment had actually installed a "window" in the stomach of some volunteer of equally questionable intelligence to observe the physiological reaction to emotional stress. When the volunteer was insulted or threatened, there was a distinct and observable biochemical reaction in his stomach. Physical sensations associated with emotional release of stress were common during these long meditation courses and seemed to validate this theory of stress actually being deposited in the nervous system. Anyway, the model worked for me and after being out of commission for two weeks I was back on the foam and hopefully freed from a big block of stress.

The goal of all this purification and release of stress was to get enlightened ASAP. The tricky part was measuring or quantifying how much progress we were making toward that goal. Although there were numerous physiological and psychological tests that indicated a certain degree of growth, the ultimate test was the subjective experience of the individual. There were two ways of evaluating one's progress. One was the experience during meditation and the other was the experience outside of meditation in activity. The problem was that having great experiences during meditation and even during activity were not a reliable indicator of permanent transformation. After years of listening to people on these long rounding courses get up to the microphone and tell

Maharishi and the audience about some truly astonishing experiences, I noticed that some of the folks who had these celestial visions and very clear experiences of being at one with the universe were not the most stable or integrated individuals I had ever met. According to Maharishi, the true test of enlightenment is when one is always grounded in that state of the eternal bliss consciousness described in the Bhagavad Gita and other spiritual texts.

The most common experience of many of us who attended these long meditation retreats was a gradual dissolution of boundaries or restrictions in our awareness that translated to a steadily increasing comfort level or identification with everyone and everything on the planet. In other words, a constantly growing appreciation of all individuals, cultures, religions and races. As this expansion of awareness continued, negativity was replaced with delight, joyfulness and an increased sense of being grounded in a transcendent reality. It seemed that for most of us it was definitely not a fast or sudden transformation but a slow, inexorable, almost imperceptible shedding of restrictions and limitations being replaced with a growing fullness of life. Maharishi had often said that everyone was evolving toward a state of higher consciousness whether they knew it or not, however, some were evolving faster than others. One of the most common questions that meditators asked Maharishi was how long it would take to achieve cosmic consciousness or enlightenment. In the early days of the movement he used to say, with a certain degree of casualness, three to five years. Then, after so many of us had been meditating for over five years he realized that, while we had made some progress, we were nowhere near enlightened, so he then started talking about an individual having "mountains of stress." According to Vedic philosophy, we were born into this life with certain *samskaras*, which can be described as tendencies, unfulfilled desires, stress or baggage from our past life. These samskaras also tended to restrict us from gaining liberation and needed to be dissolved or resolved in order to progress to enlightenment. Most of us had no idea when we first started meditating that it would take so long or involve so much work to make even a modest amount of progress in the direction of enlightenment, but at least we were having fun with the new sidhis program.

As the days became longer and the retreat of the snow up the mountains gained momentum, the tourists returned to Weggis to sit in the outdoor cafés, soak up the sun and rent hotel rooms. This was a great relief for Herr Brunner, who couldn't wait to liberate his hotel from the weird and reclusive meditators. In a few days his contract with the TM group would be up and he could start renting to normal, beer drinking, cigarette smoking tourists. For us it meant another move in the middle of a deep meditation course. Usually it was a strain to pack up and move out of our rooms while in a state of such low metabolism. However, this time it was much easier than on previous courses. Apparently the practice of hopping around on the foam resulted in a greater ability to function while the mind and body were in a meditative state. Maharishi had often said that in the state of enlightenment, the awareness was always established in the state of inner silence, or samadhi, while performing activity. One of his favorite quotes from the Bhagavad Gita was "yogasta kuru karmani," which means "established in yoga perform action." This is the essence of enlightenment. In that state of yoga, or union, one is in a state of eternal bliss consciousness and any action performed in that state is free of mistakes and is often termed "right action." Hopefully all our meditation and purification and practice of the Yoga Sutras resulted in being able to function from a more silent and effective level of the mind.

There were still large patches of snow on the ground when we arrived in Arosa and the rarified air was chilly, but it felt good to be back in this remote high altitude village now that all the skiers were gone. There was already a small sidhis course of European TM teachers going on in our hotel so we were able to join them in the flying room without any delay. After about an hour of silent meditation and yoga sutra practice, the flying commenced. Within a few minutes the person next to me scared the crap out of me with an ear-piercing screech and took off hopping. Seconds later, almost all of the Europeans started howling. Then the members of our group who had been "cured" of screaming started whooping it up. I felt sorry for the older, more dignified members of our group, who had to put up with what appeared to be deranged behavior. Two of the couples were in their seventies and had been devotees of Maharishi for decades. Everyone on the course admired them and loved them, but this did not stop the people sitting next to them in the flying room from erupting in the most hideous screams imaginable.

As the course entered its final weeks, some of the participants had to return home to the States early. Maharishi asked them to give public presentations about the sidhis program when they returned to their areas. It was one thing to talk to the public about the obvious and practical benefits of TM, but to give a lecture on levitation and its benefits seemed a bit daunting. Our group practice of the sidhis program was always done under strict security. The door to the room was locked when we began the practice and no one was allowed in the room until the program was over. It was probably a good idea to keep it private because it got pretty bizarre at times and the image of humans hopping around screaming their brains out could be distressing to the uninitiated. Maharishi said that in numerous ancient texts there were references to yogis hopping around in the beginning stages of levitation. His grand new plan was to have large groups of "sidhas" practicing the technique in every country to bring coherence to the whole world. He called this the "World Plan" and restructured the movement to bring it about. He even gave the TM teachers who were practicing the sidhis the title of "Governors of the Age of Enlightenment." The TM centers were now to be called "Capitals of the Age of Enlightenment." From each capital, the governors would be responsible for creating coherence in their area by organizing large groups of people who would be practicing the yogic flying program together.

According to movement scientists, it was possible to transform an entire physical system from a state of entropy or incoherence to a state of coherence by creating coherence in only the square root of one percent of the system. Maharishi felt this model could be applied to the collective consciousness of the world and that if only the square root of one percent of the population was generating coherence by practicing yogic flying (or hopping), it would create greater coherence in the collective consciousness. The practical result would be less negativity like crime and violence and more positive developments like peace and prosperity. It was our job to go out into the world and convince people to become sidhas and to get leaders in society like congressmen and governors to support the program. On one level there was a certain logic to the whole scheme and on another level there was a certain wackiness to it. While most of the teachers in our group experienced a marked increase in bliss and enlivenment of the physiology as a result of the program, the idea of promoting group levitation to the general public as a solution to the world's problems left some of the teachers uncomfortable, while others couldn't wait to tell the world all about it.

A few weeks after some of the teachers went back to the States to introduce the sidhis program to the public, those of us still on the course started receiving letters (this was before email and cell phones) from the "brave" pioneers who were giving public presentations in major cities across the U.S. Those who received the letters often read them to the rest of the group at the evening meetings. Most of the letters were reports of polite but skeptical responses from their audiences.

After a while the letters became a little boring and predictable so I decided to spice things up by concocting a fake letter that I pretended to receive from some friends back home and read it at the evening meeting. The letter started out with the typical scenario of four returning teachers renting a large auditorium in the Boston area and generating a wave of publicity with newspaper articles and radio and TV interviews about their ability to levitate and its benefits. A much larger crowd than expected showed up and, because they had rented an inexpensive union hall in a working class district of Boston, the group was raucous from the beginning; it took some effort to quiet them down in order to start the lecture. Apparently, many in the audience were expecting to be entertained by some mystical-magical yogis who were going to levitate for them. They seemed disappointed when the two young couples who looked like the accounting team from a discount chain store walked onto the stage and sat down in folding chairs next to a large blackboard. The situation on the stage was completely devoid of glamour or glitz and the four boring-looking people sitting next to the dusty chalkboard created an aura of excruciating boredom.

This might have been acceptable at one of the universities in the area or at a public library, my fake letter continued, but not a union hall where people were paying ten dollars to find out the secrets of levitation. (By the time I started reading this part of the letter everyone in the room became stone silent and those who were chatting outside the meeting room came in and quietly took a seat.) The devoted teachers, Peter, Joan, Wendy and Ron, were a little rattled by the rowdy crowd, but they started out with a standard TM lecture as instructed by Maharishi. At first the audience was surprisingly polite, probably because the skinny TM teachers looked so sincere and because what they had to say was so simple and universal. After about forty minutes of lecturing, the audience started getting a little itchy, and finally a burly man in his fifties stood up and said, "Look, I paid my ten bucks. When do we get to see you guys levitate?" While the four teachers looked at each other wondering what to do or say, more and more people in the audience began demanding to see them levitate. Joan was the first to get a little panicky and suggested they turn off the microphone and make a quick getaway out one of the back doors. Then they realized this was a private union hall and there were no public security personnel to help them get away. While they were huddled on the stage trying to figure out what to do, the crowd started throwing paper cups and food wrappers on the stage and began chanting, "We want levitation." (By now I could hear people in my audience beginning to gasp as I noticed Linnea and some of my close friends trying to suppress their laughter.)

Maharishi had given all the returning teachers firm instructions to practice the sidhis in strict privacy and never to let anyone who was not practicing the program observe the levitation technique. This made a lot of sense because, without the inner experience of the sutras, it might look really weird to the uninitiated. As the four teachers described in my letter tried to quickly discuss their options, the situation was becoming uglier by the minute. Then another rough-looking dude stood up and yelled, "If you guys don't start levitating, I am going to levitate you right through that window!" The crowd howled in approval. Finally Ron looked at Wendy, Peter, and Joan and uttered the unthinkable: "We gotta do it!" They all instantly knew they had no choice. It was their only chance. Ron flipped the microphone back on and motioned for everyone to sit back down. As things began to quiet down he announced they would give a short demonstration, but they needed about ten minutes to prepare and asked for volunteers to bring up all the large seat and couch cushions they could find in the hall. The mood instantly changed from hostility to enthusiasm as audience members began covering the stage with thick cushions.

As I continued reading my fake letter, the members in our group were sitting on the edges of their chairs staring at me in disbelief. I told them the four teachers then made a valiant attempt to look dignified as they sat down on the cushions and tried to sit in the lotus position in their business suits and skirts. The audience remained remarkably quiet as they meditated for about ten minutes. It was as if they could feel the effects of the meditation. Then gradually, one by one, the speakers began hopping around on the cushions as their business ties and scarves flew up in their faces during liftoff. The crowd was mesmerized. They were either stunned that these folk had the audacity to charge them ten dollars to watch them hop around on a bunch of cushions or perhaps they were settling down to a meditative state as a result of the coherence generated by the yogic flyers. Then suddenly, someone sitting in one of the front rows started hopping up and down in his seat. Within a few minutes, most of the people in the audience were twitching or hopping in their seats. This went on for ten minutes. Then, when the teachers stopped hopping, the "yogic seat hoppers" in the audience just sat back in their seats, grinning from ear to ear. After a few moments of silent bliss, everyone got up and gave the four bewildered teachers a standing ovation. As I finished my fake letter, most of the folks had figured out that it was a hoax and started howling, while a few sat there in awe and started asking me more details of the extraordinary event.

20

The ACCIDENTAL ASHRAM

By the time we returned to Massachusetts a few months later, the genie of unrealistic expectations had been let out of the bottle. The entire meditating community in the greater Boston area was abuzz with rumors about levitation and various other yogic powers. The reality was that we never saw anyone actually levitate or become invisible. The closest anyone came to experiencing any of these powers, or sutras, was what Maharishi called "flavors or tastes" of the sutras, like seeing things at a distance. Linnea and I were among the first group of teachers to return from the course and were asked to give presentations to the meditators on Maharishi's new program to make the sidhis available to all the meditators, not just the TM teachers. The first question we were asked at our presentations was, "Do you levitate?" The best answer we could give was, "Sort of." We tried to downplay the flashy aspects of the sidhis program and instead emphasized the goal, which was to accelerate one's growth toward a more enlightened state of consciousness. Maharishi realized that the average person couldn't take six months off to go to Switzerland to learn the sidhis, so he developed a program where people could take a series of one week in-residence "preparatory courses." After attending six of these one-week meditation retreats, meditators would then take another two week course, where they would actually learn the sidhis.

In order to accommodate these courses, the TM movement began an aggressive campaign to find facilities to be used for meditation retreats in every area of the country. In the meantime local retreat facilities were rented for these courses, which became wildly popular all over the country, especially in New England and on the West Coast. Linnea and I realized that teaching these one-week preparatory courses presented us with the possibility of fulfilling our desire to teach meditation full time and also have our own home to live in. Our plan was to use the money from the sale of our farm in Virginia to buy a ten-acre parcel of land in a rural area of Gloucester, Massachusetts. The secluded property was close to the ocean and had been converted into a Montessori school. There were about ten classrooms attached to a large, six-bedroom house that could be easily converted into a retreat facility. The only drawback was the cost: about four times more than the money we had from the sale of the farm. We asked Linnea's father, who was an experienced business-man, if he knew of any way we could borrow the rest of the money to pay for the property without any income. He suggested we make up a business plan based on the projected income from the preparatory courses, which would generate enough funds to pay the mortgage. We had no idea how much income the courses would generate so we just made up a figure that looked good on paper and met with the president of a local bank recommended by the realtor.

As we sat outside the president's impressive cherry-paneled office with our hokey one page "business plan," Linnea and I felt like these hard core capitalists were going to laugh us out of their office when we presented our plan to teach "levitation prep courses." For some reason they warmed up to us as soon as we entered the room and when we told them we were TM teachers they didn't bat an eyelash. Fortunately, east-ern Massachusetts was a very progressive area and everyone either had heard about TM or knew someone who was a meditator. Our meeting with the bankers seemed more like a social visit than a business presen-tation. The officials said they would let us know in about a week if the loan would be approved and we left the office a lot more confident than when we went in. A few days later, we were stunned to find out the loan had been approved, but it would be months before we could move in, so we started to look around for a short term rental.

The town of Manchester was a classic, small New England coastal village with a delightful harbor and a stunning sandy beach. Many of the homes were large mansions and the rents were exorbitant, but we saw an ad for a smaller contemporary house right on the ocean that intrigued us. The owners were going away for the winter and wanted someone to live in the house and take care of the cats and plants. As a result the rent was very reasonable and the owners were fine people who were understandably very picky about who would be living in their house. After an hour-long interview they decided they liked us and agreed to rent their lovely home to us. They would be leaving in about three weeks. We would then move right in and enjoy the fully furnished house with its magnificent ocean view. In the meantime we were living at the Beverly TM center and enjoying teaching meditation. About two weeks before we were to move into our seaside dream home, Shawn and Karen, the TM teachers who were assigned the job of looking for a retreat facility, announced that they had found a ski resort named Swiss Meadows on two hundred beautiful acres in the Berkshire Mountains near Williamstown, Massachusetts. All the TM teachers in New England were invited to meet on the property to decide if they liked it.

The drive out to Williamstown in the brisk October air was like sailing through a sea of red and gold. The half-mile driveway up to the facility meandered through a series of emerald green meadows ringed with white birch and sugar maple trees showing off the finest fall colors imaginable. While the buildings at the top were underwhelming, the view of Mt. Greylock and the surrounding Berkshire hills was dazzling. There were several older chalet-style buildings, two newer motel-type units and a minimally maintained swimming pool and tennis court.

After an hour of vigorously debating the pros and cons of the site, the fifty or so TM teachers present voted in favor of purchasing the property. In practice this didn't mean very much; TM teachers had been meeting with Maharishi for years and voting on all kinds of construction projects from Switzerland to Santa Barbara and usually nothing ever happened. After the meeting, Linnea and I got together with Shawn

and Karen and swapped funny stories. We had met them in Arosa earlier that year and had an instant connection with them. They were both
irreverent and didn't take the movement too seriously, but had devoted
their lives to working for Maharishi. Now that the area TM teachers had
voted on Swiss Meadows, Shawn and Karen were free to go to Switzerland for the sidhis course. They asked us if we could monitor the facility project for them while they were away. Shawn pointed out that all
we had to do was fill out a monthly report. They would be back in six
months to manage the project in case the movement really decided to
buy the property.

Shawn and Karen started regaling us with stories of their adventures representing the movement in search of a New England retreat
center. After looking at a number of private schools and making in-
sanely low offers, as instructed by the movement officials, they found
a magnificent, brand-new resort on the coast of Maine. The movement
had a reputation for buying property at bargain prices regardless of its
condition. The resort in Maine wasn't some worn-out hotel, but a luxury resort in excellent condition. For some reason it wasn't making the
money the investors had hoped for and they were ready to unload it at a
reasonable price. Shawn and Karen received word from Valerie, who was
directing the movement's search for property from Switzerland, that
they would be contacted by Jim Dressler, a local meditating lawyer who
had the details of the movement's offer. They were instructed to meet
with the investors and make an offer as soon as they heard from Jim. A
few days later Jim called and said he had the movement's offer, but it
was only half the asking price and he didn't think it would be accepted
by the sellers. Shawn reassured him: the movement always made low offers and they would arrange a meeting in Maine with the investors, who
had to fly in from various locations including the Virgin Islands.

The meeting with the investors went just as Shawn and Karen
thought it would. The investors were angry and insulted that they had
flown in from around the country and were only offered half what they
thought was a rock bottom price. Shawn and Karen took the awkward

situation in stride, but Jim the lawyer was embarrassed to make such a ridiculous offer. A few weeks later Shawn and Karen got an urgent message from Valerie in Switzerland saying the movement had reconsidered and they were going to make an offer the sellers couldn't refuse. It wasn't easy, but they convinced the investors to meet again in Maine for the new offer. As they were waiting outside the office of the resort owners with Jim the lawyer, Jim decided to go over the numbers of the complicated new offer. He assumed, because Valerie had said it was an offer they couldn't refuse, that it was much more that the original offer. The offer was complicated with multiple payments, so he borrowed a calculator. After a few minutes of punching in numbers and mumbling to himself he suddenly looked as if he was going to be sick! Shawn asked if he was okay and Jim could hardly talk. After sitting there unable to speak for several minutes, he finally muttered, "My God! This offer is less than the original one." Just then the investor's secretary opened the door and invited them in for the meeting. Needless to say, the movement didn't buy the property and Jim the kindhearted lawyer refused to have anything to do with the movement's real estate deals in the future.

Shawn assured us the Swiss Meadows deal was different. The price had already been agreed upon and the contract would be closed in about six months. We explained that we were really busy with our own real estate venture and couldn't devote much time to the Swiss Meadows project, but if all we had to do was file a few reports we could do it. A week later, Shawn and Karen went off to Switzerland and few days after that we received a call from George Newhouse at the movement headquarters in New York. He was in charge of all the programs at the TM residence facilities and wanted to know why we weren't out at Swiss Meadows finalizing the sale of the property. I explained that we thought it was going to take at least six months to close and that Shawn and Karen were going to take care of it. As I continued to explain our situation to George, Linnea began to roll her eyes with that "here we go again" look. He sounded slightly desperate as he tried to talk me into dropping our plans and going to Swiss Meadows as soon as possible. Apparently the movement was ready to buy it right away and the owners were anxious to sell as soon as possible. Now that Shawn and Karen were in Switzerland there was no one to represent the movement at the sale and to get the facility and programs up and running. Our first reaction to his plea was to say no because of our other commitments, but we hated to let the movement down, especially when we were asked to take on this important project, so we told George that we would have to think about it for a day and get back to him.

The next day we took a long walk on the beach to try to sort out what was the right thing to do. Maharishi had often talked about "spontaneous right action" as one of the qualities of an enlightened individual. When one is grounded in the deep silence of pure consciousness, the mind is not clouded with emotions, stress and a fuzzy intellect. The enlightened person's actions are in accordance with natural law and are supported by nature. Although we felt closer to the state of enlightenment as a result of all the meditation we had done in the last few years, we certainly were not enlightened enough to spontaneously know the right thing to do in this situation. On one level it was obvious that it was more important to get this regional facility up and running than setting up our own small local facility, especially when we were being asked by the national director. However, that meant we would have to weasel out of our rental agreement with the nice people who chose us over many other potential tenants and we would have to find some way to back out of our real estate contract and loan with the bank. We walked up and down the beach for hours in the brisk fall air in our bare feet. The cold sand and icy water were clear signals of the impending winter, which would bring dramatic changes to the beach in a few short weeks and which were also a harbinger of the dramatic changes that would take place in our lives in the following weeks.

After considering all the ramifications and consequences of each course of action, we finally concluded that we should abandon our plan to develop our own facility and take on the Swiss Meadows project.

This was definitely the harder of the two choices. We felt terrible about breaking our rental agreement with the sweet older couple who were all set to go south for the winter. After offering to give up our deposit and to find someone else to rent their house, they were somewhat mollified, but still very disappointed. The poor real estate agent's jaw dropped when we told him that our plans had suddenly changed. He just couldn't believe that after all our effort to convince the bank to give us the loan we would just walk away from the project. We felt awful that we had disappointed so many people, but we also felt a sense of relief that we had made the right decision—hopefully!

Art Cronin was waiting for us as we drove up to the caretaker's cottage. He walked up to our car before we could open the doors and get out. I rolled down the window and introduced Linnea and myself. When I explained that we were there to represent the movement at the upcoming sale, he gave me a hostile look and said, "I know," in a weary and cheerless tone of voice. In the next few minutes we quickly found out why Art was so contemptuous. For the past ten years he had put his heart and soul into creating an attractive resort for groups and families who would come back year after year for skiing in the winter and tennis and swimming in the summer. He and his wife lived in the caretaker's cottage and did all the work themselves; from taking reservations to all the maintenance, including plumbing, wiring, carpentry and snow-plowing. Now that the owners were selling, he was losing his job and his housing. On top of that, many of his clients who came to Swiss Meadows every year were calling daily to make reservations and because the movement had given him the impression that the sale would take place a few weeks ago, he had turned them away. Now, three weeks later, everything was still up in the air and he didn't know whether or not to start taking reservations again and get the facility ready for another season. He kept hearing from the movement that the check for the property was in the mail, but almost a month had passed and no check. He was distraught, disgruntled and at the end of his rope when I stepped out of the car and offered to shake hands. He glowered at me and muttered in a gruff whisper, "Larry, if I don't get that check by the end of the week, I am going to shoot your ass."

The administrators of the TM movement had made an arrangement with the owners of Swiss Meadows for Linnea and me to stay in one of the motel units for a few days until the sale was finalized. Art had been notified of this plan and grudgingly showed us to one of the newer motel suites. As we unpacked our bags, I realized how suddenly our lives had changed in just a few short days. Less than a week earlier, we were on the verge of fulfilling our dream of buying a beautiful rural property near the ocean that would enable us to teach TM and live in our own home. Now we were living on a mountaintop in the Berkshires with a disturbed and angry innkeeper who was threatening to shoot me! It seemed as if we were thrown into a maelstrom of events over which we had no control. We had no idea what was going on with the check. No one had told us anything about it and all we could do was hope and pray that the check would come by the end of the week. The first thing we did the next morning was to drive into town and call the movement office in New York to find out about the check. No one at the office seemed to know anything about Swiss Meadows and they assumed that we had everything taken care of. Finally, after talking to five or six people, we found out that the check for the property was being sent from Switzerland to Bill Walsh, a meditating lawyer who lived near Williamstown. We called him right away. He didn't know anything about the check but offered to help us with the closing.

As we drove back up the mountain we realized that Art was probably not going to shoot us, but he certainly was not going to be very happy if we told him we didn't know what was going on with the check. We decided to tell him that the check had been sent from Switzerland and that was why it was taking so long. Hopefully it would arrive at the lawyer's office by the end of the week and we would be able to schedule the closing right away. Art listened to our story with a skeptical smirk on his face. At least it wasn't the outright rage with which we were greeted the day before. Every morning for the next two weeks we drove into town, checked our mail and called the lawyer to see if the check had arrived. Then we would call the main office in New York to find out what was going on, but still no news. After we drove back up the mountain, we tried to avoid Art as much as possible. It was a tough situation for him and also for us. At least he wasn't threatening to shoot us anymore and seemed to realize we were doing the best we could.

Other than our daily run into town to see if the check had arrived, we had a lot of free time on our hands to explore Williamstown, the surrounding Berkshire Mountains and southern Vermont. Even though we had put our dream of living in our own house and teaching meditation on hold, we were excited about developing the beautiful mountainside property into a meditation retreat. It looked as if we would be able to have our own private living space, teach the sidhis weeklong prep courses and live our idea rural lifestyle on two hundred acres of forest and meadows. After two weeks of our fruitless daily excursions into Williamstown to check the mail, I opened a generic-looking envelope and there it was! A check for $250,000 (in 1978 this was probably the equivalent of one million dollars). There was no cover letter, just the check. For some unknown reason it was sent to us instead of Bill Walsh, the lawyer. Finally, the closing was set for the following week at the office of a high-end law firm in Williamstown. On the morning of the closing day we received a call from the TM headquarters in New York that George Newhouse and a group of staff members from their office were on their way to Swiss Meadows to accompany us to the closing. I looked at Linnea and said, "What if they are late or don't show up or even get lost. This could ruin the whole deal!" We decided that if they didn't show up by 11 AM we would leave without them even though technically they were in charge of the whole project. Just as we suspected, 11 AM arrived and they were nowhere to be seen, so we left for the law offices to meet with the sellers, who had driven up from Connecticut.

The atmosphere at the lawyer's office felt more like a courtroom than a small town office. The three business partners were dressed in dark suits with power ties and sat opposite us at a huge conference table.

They perfunctorily acknowledged us without shaking hands as we sat down at the table with Bill the lawyer. Linnea and I were both wondering what we were doing there. We had no legal authority to represent the TM movement in the purchase of the property. The purchase and sale agreement had been signed by the trustees of the movement and sent to the lawyer representing the sellers. Our job apparently was to observe the shuffling of the piles of papers between the lawyers.

In addition to the standard sale agreement, there were about thirty special arrangements hashed out over the months of negotiation. These involved all the equipment, furnishings and even the two snowplows. In exchange for all these demands, the TM movement agreed to allow Art, the manager, to live in the caretaker's house for six months while he showed us how to run the facility. As they read through the special arrangements, one of business partners suddenly let out a loud moan. Bill Walsh jumped up from his seat, thinking the man was having a heart attack. As soon as he finished his moan, he yelled out in an angry and frustrated tone, "They didn't sign it! I can't believe those people in Switzerland didn't sign this!" Linnea and I looked at each other in bewilderment as Bill quickly reached across the table for the document and said, "Let me see." The businessman shoved the contract toward Bill and started yelling, "I can't believe this. If this takes another six months for them to sign this then the deal is off!" As Bill was looking at the contract, I asked him what was going on. He shook his head and muttered to me, "They didn't sign the agreement to let Art stay. This doesn't look good—you'd better sign this." I looked at him as if he was out of his mind and said, "What are you talking about? I'm not a movement trustee. It would be meaningless and probably illegal if I signed." Meanwhile, the three businessmen were getting more and more agitated. Bill gave me a desperate look and growled at me, "Just sign it—if you don't the whole deal will fall through."

Just as I was signing the document, George Newhouse and his entourage of four women dressed in Indian saris walked into the room. George came over to me and blurted out, "What are you signing?"

as he snatched the papers from my hands. The atmosphere suddenly changed from grumbling and disgust to a stunned silence as George and his entourage of ethereal women in their brilliant gold, red and yellow saris wandered in circles around everyone seated at the conference table while George looked at the contract I had just signed. As we all sat there anxiously wondering what he was going to do, the tension in the room became palpable. After what seemed like an eternity, George flipped the contract on the table, made a proclamation which sounded like "Maha Maya," turned around and walked out of the room with the ladies in the saris following in his footsteps. While the sellers looked on with a dumbfounded glaze in their eyes, Bill gasped in a panicked tone, "What does 'Maha Maya' mean?" I replied that it literally means "big illusion," which I guess meant that George didn't think it was any big deal that I had signed the contract. The tension suddenly was released from Bill's body and the color came back to his face as he quickly announced to the mystified business partners that everything was okay and the arrangement to have Art stay for six months was agreed to and signed. We all reached across the table, quickly shook hands and stampeded out of the room.

The next day we had an inaugural celebration at Swiss Meadows for all the meditators in the area. Afterward George Newhouse laid out the plan for the new facility. The first thing we should do, he suggested, was to put up a large, dignified sign with lots of gold lettering at the entrance to the property saying, "Academy for the Science of Creative Intelligence—Swiss Meadows." This was intended to give the impression that Swiss Meadows was not just another flaky hippie ashram, but a respectable educational institution. The next step was to transform what was basically a motel and ski lodge into a residential educational facility. This meant extensive remodeling and conforming to building codes that were much stricter for educational institutions than for lodging facilities. When George proclaimed to the group that the remodeling of the motel units into a dining room and meeting hall facility should only take about a month and that we should start planning to hold the first residence course next month, I thought to myself, *This is completely unrealistic*. It would probably take at least a month to have the plans drawn up and permits obtained from the state and city. After George finished describing the grand plan for Swiss Meadows, I said to him there were two important details missing: who was going to do all this construction, and how were we going to pay for it? He replied rather cavalierly, "No problem. Just make sure you get at least three estimates for materials and we will send you the money you need. Then get meditator volunteers to do as much of the construction as possible." Just as he was leaving, I reminded him that we had no people to administer and teach the programs and also no staff to take care of the facility. "Oh yeah, I forgot," he replied. "Just get two more Governor Couples (this was the latest title for TM teachers who were married) to help you run the place and about six volunteers to do the cooking and cleaning. Good luck and call us if you need anything." As George and his entourage roared off down the drive, Linnea and I looked around at all the buildings and two hundred acres of mountain meadows and woods that had just been handed to us and wondered, *how did this happen?*

Alan and Dorothy had been our good friends since we lived in the same dorm at MIU a few years earlier and, like us, they were dedicated to serving Maharishi and the TM movement, but were not zealous true believers. We shared a love for the outdoors and often took hikes together when we were in Switzerland on various courses. When we invited them to join us at Swiss Meadows, they jumped at the chance. Alan came from an upper class British family, had a Ph.D. from MIT and worked at the Stanford Research Institute before giving it all up to become a TM teacher and teach physics at MIU. In spite of his formal British background, he behaved like a wild and crazy American. Dorothy had a great sense of humor and an enthusiasm for the simple country life offered by living at Swiss Meadows. Now they had agreed to join us and we felt that, not only was some of the burden of creating a meditation retreat from scratch lifted, but we would also be able to have a lot of fun with our buddies. Then a few days later we were delighted to learn that Shawn and Karen were coming back from Switzerland to join us in the project. Over the next few months, the six of us were able to get the permits, complete the construction on the meeting hall and dining room and begin teaching the one-week sidhis prep courses for meditators.

Winter in the northwest Berkshire Mountains was much like Vermont—lots of cold and snow. Most nights the temperature was around zero and during the day it rose to about fifteen degrees. Every new snowstorm would simply pile on the existing snow pack and we were constantly busy plowing snow to keep the steep road up the mountain open. The two old snowplows were our lifelines to the outside world. Soon after the serious snows began, we were reduced to one plow when Donnie, one of our overly confident volunteers, blew up the engine of the 1940 Dodge power wagon by plowing the snow uphill instead of downhill. The old plow was Art Cronin's pride and joy and the first thing he taught us about snowplowing was to always plow downhill, especially with the power wagon, which was near death. Art was livid when he saw Donnie roaring up the hill with the old truck smoking and steaming. He came running out of his house just in time to see the truck shudder and give its last gasp. Donnie, who seemed clueless about the seriousness of the situation, gave Art a sheepish grin and asked where the other plow was so he could finish his plowing job. Art felt a little better after we told him that this was going to be Donnie's last day at Swiss Meadows, but he warned us that the other plow was not much better and that if we had a serious blizzard it probably wouldn't be able to handle a deep snow. He suggested we get a new snowplowing vehicle right away, before we were all trapped on the mountain in the snow.

The only way we could get a new snowplow was to request it from the TM main office in South Fallsburg, New York. Even though Swiss Meadows was generating significant income from the one-week prep courses now being taught, all the money was sent to the main office to be strictly accounted for because of the non-profit educational status of the facility. This meant we were at the mercy of a slow-moving bureaucracy for anything we needed, from snowplows to shovels. Before we could get a response to our request for a new plow, the great blizzard of 1978 buried us, and most of the rest of New England, under many feet of paralyzing, heavy snow. Our worn-out Jeep snowplow was now buried in a drift and wouldn't even start. It was simply overwhelmed with snow and cold. Fortunately there was no immediate need to have contact with the outside world. The weekly retreat had already started and the participants were all in their rooms, meditating and enjoying the beauty and silence of waist-deep snow, brilliant blue skies and vibrant mountain air. The Swiss style of many of the buildings, constantly falling snow and isolation from the basic American culture in the valley below created an atmosphere of a remote alpine village that seemed to enchant even the most urbanized guests. No one complained about wading through the deep snow to get from building to building. In fact, we all thought it would be great to be snowbound for the rest of the winter.

Linnea, Alan, Dorothy and I had the added pleasure of cross-country skiing our way around the facility instead of walking. This was the best of both worlds—every morning we would have a long group meditation program in the lodge at the top of the hill, and then enjoy the exhilaration of zipping down the hillsides in fresh deep powdery snow on our way to our daily activities of teaching, office work or taking care of the physical facility. Next to teaching the meditation courses, the favorite activity of the guys was snowplowing. Shawn and I had engaged in various forms of physical labor like mowing lawns, working on cars and trucks and using basic tools like hammers and power tools. Alan, on the other hand, coming from a privileged upper-class British background, was somewhat lacking in basic working-class skills. After he suggested we take the heating elements out of the electric stove, hook them up to an extension cord and place them on the snowplow engine to keep it warm at night, Shawn and I thought it would be better if we did the snowplowing while Alan confined his activities to the office. He had the misguided impression that operating a snowplow was just like driving a car and was very disappointed that we wouldn't let him plow.

A few days after we hired a contractor to bulldoze our road open, there was still a lot of snowplowing left to do around the buildings. Shawn and I were walking around, planning a strategy to clear the snow from the motel-style units, when we both realized the buildings looked funny, as though something was missing. Then we looked in the snow drifts that were up against the building and observed quite a few smashed-up boards in the snow. Suddenly we noticed that the entrance decks had been sheared off every single unit, so when the course participants wanted to leave their rooms they had to jump out the door into three feet of snow. Shawn and I were dumbfounded. We walked over to the snowplow and discovered a bunch of smashed-up boards jammed in the plow mechanism and even on the hood of the vehicle. Just as I was wondering out loud who could have done this, Shawn interrupted me and said, "Let's have a little chat with Sir Alan." As soon as we walked into his office, Alan looked up with a sheepish grin and said, "I suppose you noticed that I got a little close with the plow this morning."

The contractor's bill for plowing our road up the mountain was a little over $1,000, which we immediately sent to the main office in South Fallsburg for payment. This really got their attention and they agreed to give us a new snowplow, sort of. They had just purchased a new heavy duty pickup truck with a new snowplow for themselves, and offered their older truck to us. It was only a few years old and was infinitely better than ours, so Alan and I immediately drove to South Fallsburg to pick it up. We were also going to have a meeting with George Newhouse, the national coordinator of the capitals project. The South Fallsburg "Capital" was a 1950s style, tacky, borscht belt resort hotel in the Catskill Mountains. The movement had a knack for buying has-been hotels for very low prices and, instead of pouring lots of money into them for rehab, they kept them on life support by doing minimal maintenance—usually with volunteers. The main lobby looked like an old casino that had been taken over by monks. Even the pictures and posters of Maharishi and Guru Dev, which were plastered everywhere, couldn't disguise the fact that we were in a former nightclub.

As Alan and I stepped into George Newhouse's suite of offices on the top floor of the hotel there was a dramatic transformation from seedy hotel to stunning ashram. The entire suite was carpeted in brilliant white wool. The couches and chairs were covered in a radiant gold material perfectly accented by warm peach-colored walls. George sat on the gold couch in a modified lotus position dressed in a white linen suit, which was the latest style of dress for TM teachers. Dark and especially black suits evoked a tamasic, or impure, quality compared with very light colored suits which were more sattvic, or pure, and apparently preferred by Maharishi, who always wore a white dhoti. George conducted the meeting much like Maharishi would, with a kind but firm authority that demanded a coherent progress report on our activities at Swiss Meadows. He seemed satisfied with our progress, but wanted us to expand our activities even further. As he described how we could increase the enrollment in our programs, the other couples in the room, who were dressed in whitish suits and saris, added additional advice and comments in a gracious and supportive manner, as though Swiss Meadows was their younger brother. Alan and I returned to Swiss Meadows with the "new" truck and were greeted like heroes by the rest of the staff.

A few weeks later we received a call from George Newhouse, who said that we had too many staff members at Swiss Meadows and we should let all our staff go except for the three Governor Couples: Alan and Dorothy, Shawn and Karen, and Linnea and me. This latest pronouncement was a shock to all of us. We were already working long hours every day with hardly any time off and now the six of us would have to do the work of twelve people. Even worse, we would have to fire all of our wonderful, dedicated and hard-working staff. They had given up their jobs or interrupted their educations to work for room, board and seventy-five dollars a month just to be in the silent atmosphere of Swiss Meadows. This was definitely the hardest thing we had to do in our entire careers with the movement. At times we felt that the folks at South Fallsburg were obsessed with corporate efficiency by giving us such a tight budget and small monthly stipends of only $125 a month. The six of us agonized over how to give the staff the bad news. We decided to invite them to a nice dinner and tell them afterward. Finally, after a long dinner and a great dessert, there was nothing else to do but drop the bombshell. At first the staff couldn't believe it, and then everyone started crying when we explained that we had nothing to do with the decision and that it came from headquarters. We explained that it was probably some bean counter sitting in an office with a spreadsheet, concluding that six people should be enough to run such a small facility and that, by reducing the staff, it would be more cost effective.

Although we were relatively isolated from the outside world, and had a long group meditation program morning and evening, the pace of life was intense now that we had no staff to help us. From the time we finished meditation in the morning until late at night we were busy with administrative, teaching, cooking, cleaning and maintenance responsibilities. There was a lot of pressure to fill the facility every week in order to have more people learn the sidhis. Maharishi was restructuring the entire TM movement to have as many people as possible practice the sidhis and yogic flying in large groups to create coherence in the collective consciousness of society. By now thousands of TM teachers, or Governors of the Age of Enlightenment, had learned the flying program and were traveling to trouble spots in the Middle East, Central America and Eastern Europe to practice the group flying program to reduce crime, violence and war. With each group of several hundred yogic flyers assigned to a country, a team of research scientists was dispatched to monitor the crime rate and war intensity before and after the group practice of the sidhis program. As crazy as it sounded, the research showed measurable drops in crime and other negative events in the areas where large groups were practicing the program. This encouraged Maharishi to create the World Government of the Age of Enlightenment, with a parliamentary structure similar to Great Britain and other European governments. He wanted to have Capitals of the Age of Enlightenment all over the world, radiating coherence from the group practice of the governors and sidhas. They were practicing the sidhis program in large groups that were equivalent to the square root of one percent of the world's population, the magic number of coherent particles needed in a quantum mechanical system to shift the whole system into a state of coherence.

The movement hierarchy with ministers, governors and citizen sidhas seemed a bit wacky, but we felt gratified by the work we were doing at Swiss Meadows. Even if all the people who were coming for the week-long experience of deep meditation, rest and exposure to Maharishi's Vedic knowledge were not going to become sidhas and save the world, at least they would go home after a week or two of meditation refreshed and much freer of the stress and tension they had arrived with. As the days became longer and warmer, the blanket of pristine white snow that had covered the buildings and grounds was becoming frayed at the edges, revealing lost mittens, dead mice and pieces of frozen trash. Even though the weather was getting warmer, I missed the tranquil purity of the deep snow, which had concealed all the blemishes that were now popping up as the snow receded from the roads and lawns. Then, as the last drifts of snow transformed into liquid, the long-forgotten swimming pool and tennis courts appeared like magic. Of course, there was no money in the budget to get the pool up and running. Swimming was not an integral part of a meditation retreat where people sat quietly alone in their rooms all day, and certainly not necessary for the six dedicated Governors of the Age of Enlightenment who couldn't waste their time on such trivial activity. I guess we weren't dedicated enough. As soon as the ice in the pool melted we all chipped in our own money, purchased the pool supplies and spent what little free time we had painting and repairing the pool for swimming. Between swimming, tennis and our teaching of the meditation programs, we had nothing to complain about, in spite of the fact that just we three couples had to do everything, from teaching to cleaning bathrooms.

One of the glories of Swiss Meadows was the meadows themselves. As spring arrived they were filled with vibrantly colored wildflowers, which provided a perfect backdrop to the surrounding mountains. By the end of May the wildflowers had faded to brown and we realized that we had acres of mowing to do and only one junky old mower. We appealed to South Fallsburg for a new mower. They told us to send in a report explaining why we couldn't use the existing mower. Rather than write a long report, Shawn took an axe and smashed the old mower to smithereens, took a couple of pictures from different angles and sent them off with our request for a new mower. As the weeks went by with no word about a new mower from South Fallsburg, the whole facility became overgrown with weeds and looked like it had been abandoned. Finally we decided to hire a mowing service to do the lawn and send the bill to South Fallsburg. As I emerged from the lodge after the morning meditation in my loose-fitting yoga clothes, the mowing contractor was waiting outside the door. I wasn't expecting him so early. I was on my way to put my suit on to start the daily meeting in the lecture hall, so I greeted him in my pajama-looking outfit and quickly walked around the property showing him what needed mowing. Then I hustled over to our apartment and changed into a suit, picked up my briefcase and ran over to the lecture hall as the bewildered contractor stared at me, wondering why I had suddenly changed my clothes.

   When the morning meeting was over, Shawn and I would always take a swim while the course participants were having lunch. As I walked out of the changing room in my bathing suit, I noticed the mowing contractor look up from his mower. Then Shawn came running over to join me for a quick dip before lunch. He couldn't find his bathing suit and, thinking that all the course participants were at lunch, he had slipped into his wife Karen's bikini and was prancing around the pool performing some very hilarious and suggestive body movements. In the middle of his performance the door to the Brook House opened. Twenty would-be sidhas filed out late for lunch much to the surprise of Shawn, their Governor of the Age of Enlightenment. As he scooted back into the changing room, I noticed the contractor staring at us from behind his mower. By now I was becoming a little self-conscious about changing my clothes so often and began wondering, *why AM I changing my clothes so much?* Of course Shawn and I put our suits back on after our swim, under the watchful eye of the contractor. Then, as soon as the afternoon meeting was over, we both changed into old work clothes to finish a painting job. Apparently all the clothes-changing was too much for the contractor. As soon as he finished mowing, he roared off down the road without giving us a bill or saying goodbye.

The summer weather in the Berkshires was delightful: not too hot during the day and always cool at night. In spite of our intense schedule we did manage to go on a few hikes and even attended some outdoor symphony concerts at Tanglewood. Life at Swiss Meadows was perfect for a monk who wanted to get away from the outside world and live a simple life of devotion and meditation. However, Linnea and I and the other two couples were what Maharishi called householders. He often said that very few people were cut out to be monks and that most people were householders. However, the householder path to enlightenment was just as valid as that of a monk. The monk's path was considered that of *gyana yoga* or the yoga of knowledge, while the householder's path was that of *karma yoga* or action. While the renunciate may gain enlightenment through the study of the Vedas, the householder can also grow toward a more enlightened state by performing right action. We were definitely action-oriented so, after being at Swiss Meadows for almost a year, Linnea and I were ready for a trip to the Maine Coast.

21

ISLAND PARADISE

Ted and Carla had attended a number of the sidhis prep courses at Swiss Meadows and we had become good friends. They often talked about a piece of property they owned on an island near Acadia National Park in Maine and how uniquely beautiful the area was, with a combination of mountains and seashore. This sounded like a perfect place to get off the ashram for a couple of weeks. We stopped at L.L. Bean and bought a large tent with lots of room to do our meditation and "hopping" program and found a stunning campsite overlooking Somes Sound, the only fjord on the East Coast. In 1978 Acadia was one of the more heavily used parks, but once we got on the trails the crowds melted away. We spent every day discovering new lakes, mountains, breathtaking ocean vistas and beaches with invigorating, icy water. Toward the end of our visit, we decided to take the ferry out to the island Ted and Carla had talked so much about. When we arrived at the ferry terminal there was no room for our car, so we decided to walk on and explore the island on foot. The boat ride alone was worth the price of admission. There is a certain inexplicable joy that people who love the ocean receive from being at sea. We were enchanted by the cool salty air, the primal aroma and swelling of the sea. Often there were porpoises and seals swimming alongside the ferry boat, which added to our delight.

By the time we walked off the boat, all the cars and people had sped off to their destinations. We were suddenly left alone on the road leading from the ferry terminal to the rest of the island. We looked at each other and asked, "What now?" As a car approached us, I instinc-

ISLAND PARADISE   381

tively stuck out my thumb and a nice lady named Nan from New Jersey
picked us up. We mentioned we had some friends from New Jersey who
owned some land nearby. She replied that she knew Ted and Carla and
their land was close to where she lived. Not only did she take us there,
but she gave us a tour of the island, which included a trip to the magnificent lighthouse at the entrance to the main harbor. Ted and Carla
owned two and a half acres of shorefront property on a magical little
cove and our new friend Nan dropped us off in front of an adjoining lot
with a for sale sign. She suggested we look around and enjoy the wild
blueberries and raspberries. As we meandered down the sloping fir and
spruce-studded property toward the water, we were overwhelmed by
the purifying scent of sun-drenched evergreens combined with the cool
briny sea breeze that wafted through the trees from the rocky shore. We
sat on a large rock that protruded into the water like a dock and marveled at the crystal clear turquoise water that looked like the Caribbean,
but felt like the Arctic. I looked at Linnea and said without hesitation,
"We should buy this." She instantly replied, "Yes!"

On the ferry ride back to the mainland, we discussed the wisdom
of buying property on a remote island off the coast of Maine. Ever since
we had sold our farm in Virginia a few years before, we had been trying
to buy some property to call home. Even during our stay at Swiss Meadows we looked at real estate in Vermont and coastal Massachusetts, but
nothing seemed to work out. This oceanfront land was the most beautiful property we had seen, but it was ridiculously remote. However, we
were aware that our lives with the movement would be very unsettled,
and no matter where we owned property, we would not be able to live
there for very long before we would be off on some project somewhere in
the world. So why not buy a beautiful piece of land on the ocean, build
a little house and enjoy it whenever we got the chance? Also, we knew
that if we didn't buy soon we would have to pay capital gains taxes on
the property we'd sold in Virginia. Beneath the various rationalizations
for buying the land was our mutual deep-seated urge to own our own
home. On one level we recognized that the highest priority was to be-

come enlightened and live a life of true freedom from "mistakes of the intellect" as Maharishi often called them. However, we are all born with samskaras or tendencies, which are often called baggage. For us, living in a communal ashram, although a very powerful way toward enlightenment for some people, was not the path for us. Our ideal was to live in our own home and teach meditation, but our last attempt at that in the Boston area hadn't worked, so perhaps having an oceanfront home in an area of spectacular beauty where we could spend summers might be a great way to fulfill our desire to be near the ocean and live in a remote forested area.

Eastern philosophies often describe life as a process of fulfilling desires, and that the goal of spiritual life is to be free of desire and attachment. There is, however, an evolutionary or natural process in desire that seems to move all life in a forward direction toward self-actualization. Whether it's a person living in poverty trying to gather enough food to keep alive or a corporate executive intent on becoming a CEO, the process is the same. Everyone wants more and when they fulfill a certain desire, they quickly move on to the next desire. Where Maharishi departed from other philosophers on the concepts of attachment and desire is that he felt it was not necessary to lead an ascetic lifestyle to be free of material attachments. On the contrary, it was possible to become detached from the activities and possessions of the world and still enjoy them. This view resonated with Linnea and me and many of our friends in the TM movement. In effect, one could lead a normal lifestyle and still be a yogi. This was the two hundred percent of life that Maharishi always talked about. It seemed to manifest itself in our ability to enjoy the glories of the natural world and also to enjoy the inner silence and bliss of meditation. We realized the rate of growth toward enlightenment depended not only on how much meditation and spiritual practices one performed, but it was also greatly influenced by one's samskaras and how deeply rooted they were. According to Maharishi, some people had "mountains of karma." This left open the possibility that it could take many lifetimes to reach enlightenment.

The day after we looked at the land we decided to try the TM movement technique of offering half price for the lot. This would give us time to think about it a little more before making a more serious offer. The asking price was $18,000 for two and a half acres, which was very reasonable for shorefront property. We finally settled for $14,000. It felt really good to own some property again and we immediately started making plans to build a house with the rest of the proceeds from our sale of the Virginia property. Over the next six months we explored different options for spending more time at our beautiful island property. Our goal was to be able to spend most of the summer in Maine and teach meditation for the rest of the year. The longest vacation we could take off from Swiss Meadows was about one week a year, so we realized that, as much as we loved our life there, we would have to leave. At first it was hard to consider leaving, but then as our second winter at Swiss Meadows turned into spring, our thoughts turned to the salty ocean air and the wonderful smell of the sun-drenched balsam fir trees on our secluded cove.

Our arrival on the island in late April was a bit of a rude awakening. When we left the mainland on the ferry it was a lush spring day, with temperatures in the 70s and seemingly every plant and tree in bloom. However, when we drove up to our land and stepped out of the car this time, we were hit with a gust of cool, damp air about twenty degrees colder than the mainland. Nothing seemed to be in bloom and it felt like March at Swiss Meadows, right after the snow melted. We quickly found out the advantages and disadvantages of living on a Maine island surrounded by the cold water of the Gulf of Maine. The ocean tended to moderate the temperature so that it was warmer in the winter and cooler in the summer. Spring didn't arrive until late May or early June due to the influence of the cold water surrounding the island, and fall lasted a long time because it took longer for the surrounding waters to cool down.

Our plan was to build a small one-room cabin to live in while we were building the house, then move into the house as soon as possible. We quickly found a contractor who was willing to let us supply all the materials and finish the inside of the house once he had completed the shell. The house was a simple 24' x 32' Cape Cod-style two-story house with lots of sliding glass doors and windows looking out over the ocean. In contrast to our other attempts at buying real estate in New England, this project seemed to have a lot of "support of nature" as meditators say when things go smoothly. All we had to do now was figure out a way to earn enough money to live on so that we could teach meditation during the winters and be able to spend summers at our island home.

As we became more familiar with the area around Acadia National Park we met a number of people in the tourist business who earned enough money in the summer to last them the whole year. We decided to start a summer tourist business that would allow us to teach TM the rest of the year. While the Bar Harbor area and Acadia National Park were tourist hot spots, our remote island had little to offer tourists. It was mostly a small, year-round fishing community with a few summer homes, one take-out restaurant and a small general store. There were definitely more business opportunities on the mainland, but we didn't want to commute by ferry every day. The island take-out restaurant was for sale and appeared to be our only option. We definitely did not want to sell hot dogs, hamburgers and French fries, so we considered turning it into a soup and salad restaurant and to also rent bikes to the tourists. After working in the TM movement we knew how to generate publicity and cook natural food for large groups. We thought if we could produce a lot of flyers and brochures and distribute them to all the tourist infor-mation spots on the mainland, we could bring tourists to the island to enjoy delicious natural food and rent bikes to explore the island. This plan worked out well, sort of. We opened the restaurant on Memorial Day weekend and for the month of June, business was excruciatingly slow. Although we did extensive publicity on the mainland, the tour-ist season didn't really start until July. And it ended after Labor Day in September. Even though we did a good amount of business in July and

August, we only earned enough money to last a few months, until the first of the year.

After we closed up the restaurant in September, we spent a couple of enjoyable months working on the house and enjoying the mild and protracted fall on the island. Much of the island was undeveloped and we were able to take long hikes along the dramatic shoreline of smooth pink and gray granite cliffs that were occasionally interrupted by small, white, sandy beaches. The white sand under the water at the beaches turned the color of the water from a dark blue to an inviting light turquoise that looked tropical and beckoned one to jump in for a swim. It didn't take too many plunges into the frigid water to figure out that it was an illusion. Even on the hottest days of summer the water temperature stayed in the fifties. In spite of the cold water, we cherished living on this secluded silent island surrounded by the sparkling and ever-changing ocean. The vast, seemingly unbounded sea was ceaselessly welling up into individual waves and then dissolving back into the infinite sea. It was a constant primal reminder to us of the eternal nature of unbounded consciousness and how individual human life was rooted in a sea of infinite consciousness while maintaining its individuality.

The TM center in Wellesley, Massachusetts, just outside Boston, seemed like a great place to spend the winter. It was a large, rambling semi-mansion in an exclusive area of large homes. We were able to rent a small room and participate in various teaching activities and the daily group meditation and flying program, which was now called the super radiance program. It was a busy and dynamic center, serving the western suburbs of Boston, and had a large, enthusiastic group of sidhas who came to the center every day to practice the group sidhis program. The flying hall was a large converted garage divided into women's and men's sections. By now thousands of meditators across the country had taken the sidhis course and were practicing the group program. It was relatively easy for those of us who were living at the center to get together twice a day for group meditation, but it took real dedication for all those meditators who commuted to jobs all over the Boston area to come to the center every day to participate in the group program. Everyone loved the deep silence and bliss created by the program at the center, and even though there were a number of scientific studies that seemed to support the theory of super radiance, it took a real leap of faith to believe that we were also saving the world by meditating and hopping around the room together.

Although we no longer had the privacy and seclusion of our beautiful oceanfront home, Linnea and I thoroughly enjoyed the silent atmosphere of the center and all the group activities with other meditators. Almost every night after the evening program, we got together for dinner with the other teachers who were living at the center and the meditators who came from all walks of life, ranging from students to older professionals. Deepak Chopra's brother Sanjiv and his wife Amita, who were also physicians, were enthusiastic and warmhearted supporters of the center. Deepak, who lived closer to the Cambridge Center, attended the programs there until Maharishi asked him to travel around the world extolling the health benefits of TM.

As soon as spring was in full bloom in the middle of May, we returned to Maine to get our restaurant ready for another, hopefully more profitable, season. To generate additional income, we also began selling gifts: a friend of ours made jewelry out of semiprecious stones and Linnea started to paint small watercolors of the wildflowers and birds of Maine. By the end of August, however, we realized the additional income generated by the sales of gifts wasn't very much and we would have to figure out a better way to earn a living. One day, shortly before the end of the season, we received a call from one of the directors of the TM headquarters in South Fallsburg. He wanted to know if we would go back to Swiss Meadows as caretakers. Apparently the TM movement was being restructured into teams of ten governors called "Vedic Atoms" who would operate out of a capital in each area and would be responsible for the TM activities there. Each one of the ten governors, as teachers were now called, was also responsible for different areas of society such as health, education and government. They even had titles like "Minister of Information." Swiss Meadows was not part of this plan but they needed someone to live there and take care of it until they decided what to do with it. As much as we liked serving the movement, it was easy this time to say no to both the caretaker job and the Vedic Atom program.

September is often the most delightful month of the year on the coast of Maine. The tourists and fog of the summer months are gone and the air is crisp and clean, with warm, sunny days and cool nights. With the restaurant again closed for the season we spent September and October finishing the inside of the house. We used native white pine to finish the walls and floors, complementing the many large windows and sliding glass doors that offered brilliant ocean views from the front and one side of the house. This was by far the most beautiful house we had ever built and we felt fortunate to have found such a magnificent waterfront setting for it. We could have easily lived the whole year there, but we had used up the last of our money on the house and had to find a way to earn a living over the winter. Linnea's watercolors of the flora and fauna of New England received a lot of compliments and we thought that, if we could sell them wholesale to gift shops around New England, it would be an ideal business we could do from our home. The response to our paintings was not earth shattering, but we began to sell enough of them to pay our living expenses and spend most of the time at home painting, framing and shipping orders.

22

NEW DELHI and the SACRED INDUSTRIAL PARK

On one of our selling trips we stopped by the Wellesley TM Center to visit old friends and do the group meditation. We were surprised to find that our old friends who had been teaching there were replaced by a Vedic Atom team of ten single women, who were now running the center under much stricter security. This left us feeling slightly unwelcome and surprised at how much the movement had changed in just the few months since we'd left. As soon as we arrived back home in Maine, we learned about an even bigger change in the TM movement, perhaps the biggest change yet. Maharishi had asked every governor and sidha in the movement to drop what they were doing and come to India as soon as possible. Our first reaction to this news was that we didn't have enough money to go to India for a month. The airfare alone was in the thousands! If we had been working for the movement at the time our expenses would have been paid, but now we were private citizens and had to pay our own way. A number of friends kept calling us to tell us how great the course was going to be. Maharishi was inviting renowned Vedic scholars, yogis and Ayurvedic doctors from all over India to speak to thousands of meditators from around the world, who would be practicing the group flying program together in a huge facility in Delhi.

This opportunity was too good to miss, so we racked our brains trying to figure out a way to get the money for the trip. If we could get a loan on our house we would have the necessary funds, but that would take at least a month and the course would have already started. However, if we used our credit card to buy the tickets and to get a cash advance from the American Express office in Delhi, we could pay off the card later from the proceeds of the loan. The only catch was that our income was rather sketchy, to say the least, and the bank might not approve our loan. Then we would be in trouble. We couldn't wait a month to find out if the loan would be approved, so we decided to take a chance, go to India, and deal with the consequences when and if we returned. By the time we did all the paperwork for the loan and had the bankers come out to appraise the property, all the movement charter flights for India had left, carrying with them thousands of teachers and sidhas from the U.S. There was a skeleton crew at the movement headquarters in South Fallsburg arranging a charter for some last-minute people like us, but they weren't sure when it was going to leave from JFK Airport in New York. After spending a couple of days trying to get through to the office in South Fallsburg with no luck, we decided the best thing to do was to go there in person and find out what was going on.

The tacky Catskills hotel, now the Capital of the Age of Enlightenment, evoked an eerie feeling. This was in sharp contrast to the sweet and silent vibrations we had experienced when we had visited the year before. Normally three or four hundred people were there on meditation courses with about fifty staff members who administered the TM programs for the whole country. Now the place was abandoned, with stacks of cardboard boxes in the halls and piles of luggage in front of the reception desk. After wandering through various offices we found the nerve center of the India project and asked them if our names were on the list for the charter to India. After some searching they found our names near the bottom of the list, which meant that a few more planeloads of meditators would be leaving before us over the next day or two. They suggested we stand by in New York City and they would call us when the plane was going to leave. Ted and Carla, our friends whom we'd met at Swiss Meadows and who owned the property next to us on the island, lived in New Jersey just across the river from Manhattan. They graciously offered to put us up until our flight to India left. For the next few days we waited near the phone for the call. Finally one morning it came; our flight was leaving later that night. Suddenly I remembered it was Linnea's birthday and dashed out to the nearest store to buy a gift. The only thing I could find that would be appropriate for India was a large, beautiful rubber snake that looked like the real thing. Linnea was used to weird gifts from me and didn't want to hurt my feelings, so she packed it in our luggage and we dashed off to the airport. While we were waiting for our plane, I decided to call our bank in Bar Harbor one more time before we left the country. We had tried repeatedly over the last week, but couldn't get through to the loan officer. This time when I called the main number of the bank, for some inexplicable reason, instead of the usual receptionist answering the phone, the loan officer himself answered. I asked him if our loan had been approved and he said, "What a strange coincidence. The board just approved it about five minutes ago." The news couldn't have come at a better time. We were completely broke and would have had a lot of overdue bills to pay when we returned from India if we hadn't received the loan.

The Delhi airport was pure mayhem. The mobs of colorful, chattering and yelling people constantly surging and receding made it impossible to find our way out of the terminal or even to find out where our luggage was. After being pushed back and forth aimlessly across the terminal, someone from the course office tracked us down, helped us get our bags and got us out of the riotous terminal. Once we were outside it was even more chaotic, with carts, cars and cows wandering around in all directions. The TM representative found a place outside the terminal that was relatively free of confusion and traffic and informed us that, due to the shortage of available hotel rooms, men and women would be separated. The women were to stay in hotels and the men would be camping in a huge field outside of town, supposed to have been the ancient battleground where Krishna spoke to Arjuna. As the women were loaded onto a van, I gave Linnea a kiss goodbye and wondered when and if I would see her again. By then we had been awake for almost twenty-four hours and, after an hour of waiting, most of us lay down on our bags and fell asleep. Another hour went by as our group of fifteen men grew increasingly uncomfortable in the hot sun and dusty air. Finally a van pulled up and our guide explained that we would be going to the Indian Express building where the course was being held. As the van driver forced his way through the teeming streets with his horn blasting, I realized that in the midst of all the chaos, there was a lot of laughter and lack of hostility in the social interactions among the throngs on the streets. Even though the conditions were wretched, the people seemed more happy and engaged than in New York or other crowded U.S. cities.

After another miserable hour weaving through the swarming masses in the streets, the van drove up to a large office building under construction. We were stunned when the driver said, "Here we are at the Indian Express building." Back in the States we had heard that the owner of one of the largest newspapers in India, *The Indian Express*, was a friend of Maharishi's and had offered his new building for the course. No one mentioned that the new building was just an unfinished, four-story cement shell. There were no windows installed, just giant square holes in the walls with rebar sticking out all over the place. The first floor was a massive, makeshift dining hall crammed with long folding tables and rickety old chairs. The floor was covered with shiny metal military mess hall trays. About a dozen Indians were busy wiping the food from them with greasy old rags and then stacking them on the floor to dry. As we walked past them, I noticed they were also using the same rags and buckets of dirty water to clean the floor. The second floor was turned into a lecture hall and huge flying room, with every square inch covered in foam. At one end was a stage filled with flowers, some big overstuffed chairs and a couch for Maharishi. As we passed by on the way up to our temporary quarters on the third floor, Maharishi and some other monks and yogis were listening to a huge guy in a traditional dhoti lecturing in Hindi, while about two thousand people were crammed onto the foam listening to his words being translated into French, German, English, Spanish and a number of Asian languages.

The third floor was just as large as the other floors, but almost empty except for about forty cots at one end and a bunch of sheets strung up at the other end to provide a makeshift privacy screen for what we were to learn was a "clinic" for sick people. The entire 150' by 200' bare cement room was completely devoid of any furnishings except for the cots and a few light bulbs dangling precariously from the ceiling. Victor and I were the only two Americans in the group of about forty men. About half of the men had just arrived from a variety of European countries and the other half were a tight-knit and well-disciplined group of Germans who had a stern and seemingly pompous leader. We soon found out that they were the "security service" for the course and it was their job to make sure that only course participants could enter the building. Apparently they had been the security detail at the movement headquarters in Seelisburg, Switzerland. They were so efficient that Maharishi brought the whole group to India to keep order among the three thousand participants from around the world.

Victor and his wife Joan were friends from the Beverly TM center where we used to teach together a few years before. As soon as we arrived in India, the first thing we were told by the course representatives at the airport was to choose a "buddy" for the course in order to keep an eye on each other in case one of us got lost or sick. The men and women were separated, so Victor was my buddy and Joan was Linnea's buddy. Our guide didn't seem to know what was going on except that Victor and I would be staying at the Indian Express building for a few nights until there were enough tents available out at NOIDA, the big "sacred" field out of town, where the men were housed. I asked someone what NOIDA meant. They explained that it meant New Okhla Industrial Development Authority. Apparently, even though the land was supposed to be sacred, it was also designated as a future industrial park!

The next morning I was awakened at dawn by the sound of hundreds of birds flying in and out of the large window holes in the cement walls of the building. Soon after that, I could hear people chanting as they seemed to be walking closer to the building on one of the side streets. I walked over to the window and looked down at a group of people carrying a body. I learned later that this happened every morning, when the people who died in the streets overnight were taken to a funeral pyre to be cremated. In the alley in back of the building there was a makeshift kitchen set up, with about thirty people chopping vegetables and stirring gigantic pots over open fires. This was where all the food for the course of three thousand was prepared. The only water available was from a nearby hydrant that, like the rest of the tap water in Delhi, was contaminated. After observing what was going on in the streets, I looked up toward the sky and realized that the sun was hardly visible through the grimy soot in the air generated by the coal-burning power plant about a mile away. It was after I realized that I had no idea where Linnea was and had no way to contact her that I began to wonder why we ever left our beautiful island home for this refugee lifestyle. Just then, my buddy Victor came over to my cot and reminded me that there were only two bathrooms for three thousand people, so we had better run downstairs and wash up before a long waiting line developed.

There were no showers in the bathroom, just a couple of sinks and toilets. Fortunately, the thousands of people attending the course had not arrived for the meeting with Maharishi and we were able to wash up before the toilets backed up and flooded the floor with sewage. When we returned to the third floor we noticed that all the Germans were awake and doing their yoga asanas in unison under the direction of their kommandant. After they finished their asanas, they quickly jumped up on their cots, meditated and zipped off to guard the doors and check the badges of everyone entering the building. After Victor and I finished our meditation, we went down to the dining hall on the first floor, which was now packed with thousands of course participants having breakfast consisting of rice, lassi and fruit served on the greasy metal trays that had been stacked on the floor. After milling through the crowd for twenty minutes, we finally found Linnea and Joan sitting outside on a small wall eating breakfast. It felt like weeks since I had seen Linnea, even though it had only been a day. I guess not knowing what happened to her made it seem like a long time. She and Joan were assigned to a small, relatively clean hotel about a half-hour bus ride away. Their room had only one bed so they had to share it, but it was a much better situation than Victor and I had.

As the cavernous, foam-covered meeting room began to fill up with sidhas from all over the world, the air became progressively more stifling. There were nearly three thousand people packed in an unfinished cement room designed to be a suite of offices for maybe fifty or a hundred people. Most people loved to get as close as possible to Maharishi, but the closer one got, the more packed it was, and the heat generated by so many bodies and camera lights for the videotaping became unbearable except for the most devoted true believers. Linnea and I found a spot near the exit with a slight breeze, which enabled us to breathe without too much difficulty. In spite of the wretched conditions, we were both thrilled to be in the presence of Maharishi and so many great teachers on the stage with him. Seated on both sides of him on stage were famous Indian "pundits" or experts in various aspects of the Veda, which included Sama Veda, Rig Veda and Ayurveda. We had heard the melodious and soothing Sama Veda before and had often listened on other courses to Brahmarishi Devarat, one of the most famous Rig Veda scholars, recite the Rig Veda while Maharishi translated, but this was the first time we had the privilege to hear Triguna, one of the foremost Ayurvedic scholars in India.

Trigunaji, as he was fondly called by Maharishi, spent hours every day expounding on the principles of Ayurveda, which is a vast body of knowledge dealing with the health of the individual. Ayurveda is considered the oldest "energetic" health system in the world. Both Chinese and Tibetan medicine have their origins in Ayurveda, according to Ayurvedic scholars. Ayurvedic medicine, which has been gaining in popularity in the West, describes optimum health as a state of balance in the mind and body. It is not a one-size-fits-all system but rather a subtle and multifaceted system aimed at correcting imbalances in the individual through modification of diet and lifestyle. There are three main "doshas" or body types, described as vata, pitta and kapha. Vata types are usually thin and wiry with curly hair, have a tendency toward dry skin, and become cold easily. Mentally they are creative, alert and restless. They may think too much and have a tendency to worry. People with a pitta constitution are usually of medium height and build with thin brown hair and a tendency toward early graying and baldness. Pitta people are intelligent but short-tempered. Kapha folks have a tendency to be overweight, have thick wavy hair and are more calm and deliberate than pitta people. While these descriptions are extremely oversimplified, everyone is either dominated by one of these doshas or is a combination of two or three of them. A highly gifted and experienced Ayurvedic physician can detect subtle imbalances in the doshas and can prescribe herbs and dietary changes to bring a state of balance to the system. This ancient method of creating health seems to work for millions of people and is being rediscovered by Indian doctors trained in Western medicine. Triguna was considered a master of pulse diagnosis and practically every person in the group of three thousand went to him for a diagnosis.

Most days, Maharishi would be up on the stage in the hot, airless lecture hall from morning until night without taking a break. For most of us, when it came time for lunch break, we would walk downstairs, go through the serving line, pile up some pretty decent-tasting Indian food on our greasy metal trays and sit outside in the sun and relatively fresh air for an hour or so. Meanwhile, Maharishi and the pundits were continuing their discourse in front of a few hundred hard core devotees. Sometimes they would even continue right through the evening group meditation time. When this happened, about half the people in the hall would be meditating and hopping around and the other half would be listening intently to the discourse between Maharishi and the other pundits. After our afternoon group flying program, most of us would take another break for dinner and then rejoin the ongoing Vedic discussions.

One evening after the meeting I returned to our sleeping area before the German guards came back from their evening duties and decided to explore the vast empty section of the third floor with my flashlight. As I probed the far end of the building I discovered a relatively small, unfinished room that lacked a door but offered a much greater degree of privacy than sleeping with the Germans. As I continued stumbling through the bags of cement and stacks of beams and scaffolding in the dark, I found another room nearby and was astounded to find that it was a new bathroom with running water. It must have just been completed in the last few days and, judging from the cement and plaster splattered all around, had never been used. Finding a functioning bathroom that was not being used by three thousand other people was like discovering gold! I rushed back to the other side of the vast construction site, found my buddy Victor getting ready for bed and excitedly told him of my discovery. The German guards hadn't come back yet so we decided to leave some of our stuff on our cots, grab a couple of extra cots and escape to the other side of the building under cover of darkness. As soon as we got to the other side, we set up our cots next to a gaping hole in the outside wall that seemed to be a connection to the old Indian Express building. Then we joyfully washed up in our own private bathroom, put our jammies on and blissfully went to sleep in our newfound "luxury suite."

As the morning light began filtering through the various large holes in the unfinished walls of the new building, I heard a sound that was different from the birds fluttering and singing as they flew in and out of the building. It was a strangely familiar tapping sound. As I became more awake and the daylight became stronger, I realized the sound had to be coming from multiple typewriters. *How could this be?* I thought. I sat up in bed and peered through the big hole in the wall. I couldn't believe what I saw! Our "private luxury suite" was actually connected to an office in the old building and the only thing separating us from the office was a three-foot wall topped by a huge open window. All that had to be done to make it one big room was to knock down the wall and take out the window. As I gazed at the busy office in astonishment, the Indians who were only about ten feet away looked up from their desks and started giggling and waving to me. I meekly waved back and just stood there in a stupor for a minute, then realized that Victor was snoring away in the bunk next to me. After some vigorous shaking, he woke up disoriented, realized where he was, bolted out of bed and peered at the busy folks in the office. The Indians who were watching me try to wake him were cracking up at the sight of these two Americans bumbling around in their pajamas in what was soon to be their new office. Although they were bemused by our presence and sleepwear, they weren't startled or afraid, probably because they were used to seeing people sleeping in the streets and just about anywhere a person could lie down, including hotel lobbies.

The people working in the Indian Express office soon got used to us and continued on with the job of producing a daily newspaper while Victor and I washed up in our luxurious cement bathroom and headed downstairs to the meditation hall. As we walked by the German kommandant he gave us a suspicious look, as though he knew we weren't sleeping in our assigned beds. After the evening meeting Victor and I were getting ready to go to bed in our little hideout when the kommandant appeared with six of his troopers. "Not allowed," he proclaimed with a heavy German accent, pointing at our cots. "Why not?" I asked him in German. He explained that this area was going to be set up for the clinic to take care of the increasing number of sick people. He went on to say that the new tents were ready at NOIDA and we would be moving tomorrow anyway. Victor and I both had mixed feelings about moving to NOIDA. Even though it was supposed to be a sacred site, we had heard horror stories about the rough conditions there. Apparently there were about a thousand men living there in old Indian Army surplus tents. It was often described as a primitive refugee camp; cold at night with uncomfortable bedding, poor sanitation, no running water and mosquitoes possibly infected with malaria.

Victor and I, along with a few other newcomers, got off the overcrowded bus and looked over the dark, vast, dusty field partially lit by bare light bulbs strung on poles along the rows of hundreds of faded brown military tents. It looked like a turn-of-the-century British military camp. The only difference was that the thousand men living there were wearing suits and ties instead of military uniforms. It was easy to understand that the TM movement wanted to make a good impression by requiring men to wear ties and jackets and women to wear saris in Delhi, but camping in the boondocks with a tie on was absurd. Our tent, like all the others, was quite spacious for two people. It was one of those four-sided tents with a pointed roof that allowed us to stand up and walk around inside. It was also lit by a single bulb hanging in the center. The only other things in the tent besides the light were two beat-up cots with a couple of moth-eaten blankets on each cot. The floor was bare earth with a few patches of old crop stubble from the last harvest. Fortunately it was the dry season in Delhi and the weather was mild except that, out in the countryside, it was in the 40s at night and, with only a couple of blankets between us, we had to sleep in our clothes to stay warm. The hardest part was getting out of bed in the cold early morning air and walking to the well, filling our plastic buckets with cold water, and then dumping the icy water on our shivering bodies in an attempt to take a shower. The latrines were right next to the wells so those of us who were familiar with country living drank only bottled water from hopefully reliable vendors in town.

One morning, while rummaging around in my bag for some clothes, I put my hand on what felt like a snake. Halfway through my instinctive leap backwards, I remembered it was the rubber snake I had given Linnea for her birthday. I looked over at Victor meditating serenely on his bed and realized what a great opportunity it was to put the snake to use. There were rumors going around the camp of poisonous snakes crawling around on the ground and everyone was supposed to look first before jumping out of bed. I laid the snake on Victor's bed so he would be sure to see it when he opened his eyes after meditating. I returned to my cot and fell into a deep meditation. About twenty minutes later, I was almost blown off my cot by an explosive scream emanating from Victor. As I opened my eyes, I saw Victor half jump and half fall off his bed. As he lay there in a state of shock and terror I realized it was the snake and started convulsing in uncontrollable laughter. He looked over at me and screamed, "Wardwell, you bastard!" I started rolling on the dirt floor, laughing uncontrollably. It was only then that I recognized what a valuable resource the seemingly worthless snake would be. After he recovered from the shock, Victor thought it was such a great way to scare the crap out of his friends that he asked to borrow the snake. For the next few weeks, nearly every time I would see someone jump or yell during the group meditation, I saw the rubber snake at their feet. Apparently Victor had passed it on to a friend after using it and it started making the rounds throughout the population like a virus.

Taking one of the buses from the camp to the Indian Express building every morning presented only one problem: there was never enough room on the buses for everyone who needed a ride. This meant the last thirty or forty men to get to the buses were left behind at the camp with no chance to join the group with Maharishi. Once the last bus started to fill up it became a mad scramble to get on. The language barrier made it difficult to communicate with most of the other men desperately jostling for position near the door to the bus. This added to the confusion and sometimes hostility. The Europeans, Latin Americans and Asians seemed to be more aggressive and adept at pushing and shoving than the inexperienced Americans, who probably never had to fight to get on a bus or train. One morning, I found myself at the back of the pack and realized I wasn't going to make it. I noticed a couple of guys climbing up the ladder to the roof of the bus. Without thinking, I scrambled up the ladder and tried to find something to hold onto as the bus took off. The ride on top of the bus was definitely breathtaking. Not only was the unobstructed view breathtaking, but the experience of holding onto a small bar as the bus roared around corners and bullock carts at forty miles an hour was definitely enough to take my breath away. After ten minutes I found a way to wedge my body between the rooftop luggage racks and was beginning to relax and enjoy the view of the ancient huts and temples scattered among the fields of rice and wheat. Then, as the bus almost tipped into the Jumna River on a narrow bridge with no guard rails, I noticed that the other guys on the top of the bus were yelling at me in an unintelligible language. I saw them duck and instinctively lay down flat just before the bus drove under a huge banyan tree about eighteen inches from the top of the bus. The rest of the trip was a nightmare of constantly being brushed by tree limbs and electrical wires.

The daily joy of meditating in such a large group of people from around the world, then soaking up the wisdom and knowledge of the Vedic pundits, seemed worth the rough living conditions and contaminated food. The mechanics of creation expounded by the Rig Veda pundits, who could spend all day explaining one verse of the Veda, were strikingly similar to the description of the way matter behaves according to the latest theories in quantum mechanics. For the pundits, the extremely detailed and subtle "blueprint of creation" laid out in the Vedas was second nature to them because, from the time they were young boys, their whole lives were dedicated to the study of the Vedas. The science of physics seemed to be just another way of looking at the same phenomena through the process of math and scientific theories. This glimpse into the vast knowledge of the Veda awakened a hunger in many of us to know more about the Vedas.

Although it was a priceless opportunity to be exposed to so much profound knowledge, as soon as we stepped out of the stuffy lecture hall, the reality of overflowing bathrooms ankle deep in sewage and eating from filthy, greasy trays began to take its toll on the group. Hundreds of people were getting sick with dysentery, respiratory infections and other infectious diseases. The clinic on the third floor was overflowing with sick people who were lying on cots in the cavernous room with only a few sheets strung up for privacy. There was also an outpatient clinic for those of us who had relatively mild cases of the various diseases. The Ayurvedic doctors diagnosed hundreds of people every day and dispensed little black balls of Ayurvedic medicine wrapped in old newspaper. Eventually most of the participants figured out that the food and dirty conditions in the dining room were making them sick and word got out about some clean restaurants with pretty good food. The favorite place to eat was an upscale Italian restaurant on the top of one of the high-priced hotels frequented by diplomats and other refined folks. Now, at every lunch hour, it was overwhelmed by starving meditators who overran the Italian buffet, picking it clean before the less aggressive diplomats got a chance to fill their plates. The scariest part was when the staff would place a mountain of mango ice cream on the buffet table. The hapless waiters would deposit the ice cream and get out of the way as fast as possible, before the hordes of meditators descended on the mound of ice cream with the largest dishes in the dining room, and gorged themselves on huge platefuls of the wonderful mango desert.

Until now Linnea and I were among the few people who hadn't been very sick. Then one day I couldn't find Linnea at lunch. I found out from Victor that Joan was in the clinic with a high fever and that she hadn't seen Linnea. It was a strange feeling not knowing where my wife was or if she was okay. The telephone system was very primitive and there was no way to call her, so I decided to take a "cab" to her hotel to see her. The small, private hotel was on the other side of town. It took a long time to find a cab driver who knew where it was and was willing to take me there. The driver was a very affable Sikh gentleman wearing a traditional turban and driving a motorized rickshaw, which was basically a motor scooter with a two-wheeled cart attached to it. After about a mile, the cab ran out of gas and the driver was very apologetic about asking me to wait in the cab while he took an empty Coke bottle and went looking for gas. The scooter started right up with the infusion of fuel and we proceeded for another mile until it ran out of gas again. Again he apologized profusely for the delay and took his empty Coke bottle to the gas station for a refill. I was getting a little impatient and thought about getting another cab, but he seemed so desperate for the business that I just couldn't abandon him, even though I was anxious to see if Linnea was okay. After a few more refueling stops we arrived at Linnea's hotel two hours after we had left the Indian Express building.

The hotel was actually a small guest house with maybe ten rooms. Compared to the tent that I was living in, was a five star resort. Linnea was in bed with a fever but feeling a little better, so I felt relieved even though she was still sick. Joan was staying in the clinic so I decided to spend the night with Linnea. It was the first real bed I had slept in for three weeks. When I got up to go down the hall to the bathroom in the middle of the night, I almost tripped over a bunch of people sleeping on the hallway floor. Apparently they were the hotel staff and were still sleeping in the hall when I got up to take a shower the next morning. Fortunately, Linnea was feeling better and we took the chartered bus to the Indian Express for the daily program. By the time we got there, I was developing a fever and was having chills, which could have been malaria, but was probably the bug that almost everyone on the course had had by now. I was so sick that all I wanted to do was to curl up in the fetal position and go to sleep, so I went up to the clinic and they put me in a cot next to Victor, who had the same symptoms.

The clinic was divided into different wards separated by sheets draped over ropes that crisscrossed the entire third floor of the building. Victor and I were in the "moderately sick" bay; the section next to us was for the more seriously ill patients who were visited by real doctors on a regular basis. The only thing separating me from one particular critically ill person in the next section was a thin sheet and two feet of space. He sounded like he was hallucinating and burning up with a high fever. Finally a group of doctors came in and told him and his wife that he had malaria. They both gasped in shock and the wife started whimpering. Linnea and I had been considering staying for another month to take advantage of the precious opportunity to be with Maharishi and the Vedic experts. We were constantly weighing the advantages of being on the course with the disadvantages of the disease and discomfort of eating contaminated food and the degradation of hygiene when three thousand people share two bathrooms. The stomach bugs and respiratory ailments were not that horrible and we had figured out a way to get some decent food, so we had pretty much decided to stay for another month, until I heard the malaria victim's wife sobbing in the "room" next to me in the clinic. I suddenly had the realization, or rationalization, that we could soak up all this wonderful Vedic knowledge in a few months by watching videotapes of the course in the comfort of the local TM center.

Later that evening, the German security troopers came through the clinic and started kicking some of the patients out. Most of the people reluctantly packed their bags and headed back to NOIDA, except for one guy who refused to go. They had to forcibly remove him. Victor and I watched the scuffle and wondered if we would be next. Victor was in a cantankerous mood and wanted to put up a fight. When they approached us I thought about trying to talk them out of kicking us out. Instead I decided to beg for mercy in German. I told them that we were both really sick and begged them to let us stay one more night. They said they needed the space and we had five minutes to get out. Victor started to get belligerent. I reminded him that we were outnumbered and pretty sick so he finally agreed to go back to NOIDA. The bus ride back to the camp was interminable as Victor and I huddled against each other freezing, sweating and fighting nausea as the bus bumped along the potholed road to the camp. When we arrived the air was cold and damp, which intensified our misery. We grimly stumbled toward our musty tent, climbed into our cots with as many clothes on as possible and collapsed.

Once we made the decision to leave, Linnea and I started thinking about seeing more of India than the Indian Express building and the NOIDA campground. Many of the people who were getting ready to leave were going on trips and tours to the Taj Mahal and to Rishikesh, a sacred area in northern India on the Ganges River and the site of Maharishi's ashram, made famous by visits from the Beatles, Donovan and the Beach Boys. We only had time for one trip so we decided to take a bus tour to Rishikesh with David and Anna, some old friends from the couples' sidhis course in Switzerland a few years before. The bus ride to Rishikesh was more than we had bargained for. The roads were narrow, one lane wide, poorly constructed and used mainly by bullock carts. Although the roads were actually paved (sort of), the buses were too big and took up the entire roadway, forcing all other vehicles they encountered off the road. This seemed to work out until we met another bus coming from the other direction. Most of the time neither bus driver was willing to pull over to let the other pass, so they ended up playing chicken as they careened toward each other on the narrow strip of pavement with their horns blasting away. Then, at the last minute, one of them would pull over and let the other driver pass. Occasionally we saw the remains of wrecked buses and trucks tipped over on the side of the road. Apparently they were losers in the game of chicken. One time we came upon two buses that had hit each other head on and were sort of welded together by the force of the collision, with the front ends of each bus stuck together about four feet off the ground, like two horses rearing up on their back legs.

The Ganges River at Hardwar in the foothills of the Himalayas was pure and icy blue, much different from the foul, murky water that flowed through the crowded cities of India farther downstream. The "ghats" were a series of large stone terraces leading into the river for bathing. They were a site of pilgrimage for Hindus and Buddhists, who bathed in the sacred waters to wash away their sins. David, Anna, Linnea and I weren't so sure that all our sins would be washed away, but a dunk in the icy mountain river looked especially inviting after our hot and dusty eight-hour bus ride, so we decided to take the plunge along with the hundreds of other pilgrims. As we walked down the wide stone terraces toward the river, we noticed there were many small altars set up where people were performing pujas as part of the spiritual ritual of bathing in the river. One of the monks, or puja performers, came up to us and asked us if we would like him to perform a puja for us. Having experienced the deep, transcendental effects of performing and witnessing many pujas over the last ten years, we said, "Sure, why not?" Before starting the ceremony, the man doing the puja for us asked for a fee. We were taken aback that we had to pay for the spiritual ceremony but figured he needed the money, so we paid him and he started the puja. About a minute later another puja performer came over and started arguing with our puja performer. We got the impression it was some sort of territorial dispute and we had to jump out of the way when they started fighting. After a few minutes of punching and shoving, they split the money we gave them and our "spiritual ceremony" resumed. As soon as the ceremony got under way the atmosphere settled down and we could feel ourselves sinking into a state of deep silence in spite of the tension in the atmosphere a few minutes earlier.

Women don't wear bathing suits in India and instead wear their saris when they go in the water. All the men need to wear is their underpants, so David and I stripped to our underwear while Linnea and Anna wore their saris as we all stepped into the roaring river. It was shockingly cold, but the clear, clean water felt very purifying after a month of living in the dust and grime of Delhi. After a few brief minutes in the water we hauled ourselves out and lay down on the sun-baked terrace to dry off like a group of harbor seals on a rocky ledge. While the ghat at Hardwar was a far cry from the intense congestion and chaos of Delhi, it was teeming with holy men, pilgrims and vendors selling spiritual equipment like coral and rudraksha beads, sandalwood paste and puja sets. At first we were a little unnerved by this curious mix of commercial and spiritual activity at such a sacred site, but it was nothing compared to what we saw when we arrived in Rishikesh, the holy city of many saints and gurus. It looked like a miniature Las Vegas, with colored lights and garishly painted billboards advertising yoga teachers and gurus all over the town. It was spiritual tourism run amuck: even the motel we stayed in was called the Guru Dev Motel. Across the river from the town were several ashrams including Maharishi's ashram, where the Beatles and other celebrities had studied with him after they learned TM. The only way to get across the river was on a foot bridge suspended by cables that traversed a deep gorge in the river far below. As we walked along the bridge we were greeted by monkeys who were having a great time swinging on the cables and showing off their prehensile skills as they hung from the bridge by a tail or one hand over the river far below.

Once on the other side we felt as if we had entered another world where time didn't seem to matter. We were immediately drawn to the banks of the Ganges, where the four of us sat down to meditate. The silence was so deep and intense that I felt as though I could spend the rest of my life sitting by the banks of the river meditating. It was not easy to stop meditating and start walking again, but we only had a few hours before the bus returned to Delhi. Maharishi's ashram, enclosed by a high fence, was about a mile farther down the river and seemed almost deserted. There were a few one-story buildings scattered around the minimally landscaped grounds and even a few vegetable gardens scattered among the trees. After walking around the outside of the compound, we found a locked entrance and knocked on the door. A pleasant Indian man in his mid-thirties came to the door and invited us in. He immediately knew we were from the course in Delhi and offered to take us on a tour of the facility. Maharishi hadn't been there for a while because the facility was too small and remote for the large programs he was now conducting. Now the ashram was inhabited by a group of monks who were living in small one-man stucco structures that looked like beehives. They were rounded on top with a small sleeping loft and a downstairs area for meditating. On our way out we were surprised to hear children playing behind one of the buildings and asked our host about them. He explained that some of the monks were married and had their wives and kids with them. It wasn't exactly what we had expected for a genuine Indian ashram on the banks of the Ganges, but we felt grateful and inspired that we could actually be in Rishikesh and meditate in the profound silence by the river.

On our last day in Delhi, Linnea and I walked around saying goodbye to all our friends who were staying on. We felt a little wistful about leaving and missing out on the exciting new knowledge and group meditations, but our instincts told us to go. Just before we got on the bus to the airport, one of our friends came up to me and handed me the rubber snake and thanked me for all the fun that everyone had

had with it. I didn't want it and told him to keep it, but he insisted on returning it. So, rather than argue with him, I stuffed the snake in my briefcase and jumped on the bus. An hour later, we were going through the customs baggage check at the airport and the security guard asked to see my briefcase, so I placed it on his desk. As he opened it I noticed the blood quickly drain from his face as he slammed the briefcase shut and jumped back in horror. After he gained his composure, he looked at me in anger and exclaimed, "Mr. Vadvell, you cannot take this snake on the aeroplane!" I had forgotten all about the stupid snake and tried to explain to him that it was a fake snake, that I didn't want it, and that he could throw it out. He didn't seem to understand what I was trying to say. He responded in an angry and exasperated tone, explaining that taking the snake on the plane could be considered an act of terrorism, because I could possibly threaten the crew or passengers with it. Again, I said, "Fine. Just throw the damn thing away," and again he replied that he was not allowed to throw it away, that it was my responsibility to take care of it and that I would have to come with him to the supervisor's office. Linnea and I looked at each other, and then at the clock, which indicated we had less than half an hour before the flight left. The thought of missing our plane crossed my mind. As the policeman insisted that I go to the customs office somewhere in the bowels of the airport, I began to think about the possibility of getting stuck in an Indian jail on some kind of terrorism or smuggling charge.

After what seemed like an eternal trek through a warren of small offices we came to the commander's headquarters and appeared before a dignified man in the uniform of a high-ranking officer that suggested he was a general or colonel. As we entered the room, he gave me a weary look as the customs agent explained that I had a snake in my briefcase. As soon as the agent mentioned snake the colonel's eyes lit up. He jumped up out of his seat and started berating me about taking a snake on the "aeroplane." He calmed down a little when I told him that it was only a rubber snake and that they could keep it and throw it away; all I wanted to do was to get on my plane and get out of there!

"No, no, Mister Vadvell, it is your property and we cannot take it—you are responsible for it!" I started thinking that I was in some kind of insane Franz Kafka nightmare. Linnea must be freaking out, wondering what had happened to me. I looked at my watch; the flight was due to leave in fifteen minutes. My only hope was to place myself at the mercy of the colonel and beg him to let me go home. His face lit up and he said, "Follow me." Again we were winding through an endless maze of old offices and warehouse-sized rooms. Finally we came to a sealed door with a sign on it that said "Animal Quarantine Centre." The colonel barged through the door and said, "Quivickly, give me the snake," and yelled at one of the clerks behind the counter to give him a small animal cage. He ordered the clerk to put the snake in the cage and explained to me that it would be shipped with the other animals on the plane in the baggage compartment. I "quivickly" filled out a bunch of forms and the colonel said, "Okay now, let's see if we can get you on your aeroplane." This time we ran through what appeared to be some back rooms for authorized personnel only, then suddenly we appeared at the gate where Linnea and the plane were waiting for me!

During our two-hour layover in Paris, we decided it might be fun to see if our snake had arrived safely and was being transferred to the flight to New York. After asking about fifteen Air France employees where the animals were being held, we finally found a helpful young man who escorted us to the animal shipping department. He took us directly to the cage with our name on it and sure enough, the snake was resting comfortably in the cage. When we arrived in New York all we wanted to do was get through customs and get out of the airport, so we decided to forget about the snake. However, our dear friends Ted and Carla hadn't arrived to pick us up yet so we went to see if the snake had made it from Paris. We asked one of the agents at the ticket counter about our snake. He seemed so concerned that we didn't have the snake with us that he literally jumped over the ticket counter and ran down to the baggage terminal to find the snake for us. Before he could return, however, Ted came running into the terminal and said, "Hurry up! Carla is double-parked outside." We didn't want them to get a ticket so we grabbed our bags and ran for the car, never knowing the fate of one of the most popular rubber snakes in the world!

We hadn't realized how much weight we had lost until we got to Ted and Carla's place. They both remarked how thin we had become and were concerned about our constant hacking coughs. It hadn't seemed that noticeable in India, where almost everyone had some kind of affliction, but Ted and Carla noticed a big change in our appearance. We didn't feel that great, either, and decided to go to our little home on the ocean in Maine to rest and recover.

The temperature was fifteen degrees outside when we opened the door to the house. It was also fifteen degrees on the inside. It felt like we were walking into a frozen food locker. The only heat in the house was the Defiant wood stove, which took almost a week to thaw out the walls and floors as the temperature dipped below zero at night and never went above twenty during the day. For the first few days we huddled around the wood stove and avoided touching the floors or walls. Then it really got fun. As we regained our strength and we were able to sleep all night without constantly being woken up by coughing fits, we got out our cross-country skis and blissfully skied along the deserted roads near our house. The view of the ocean in sub-zero weather was dazzling. The air was so cold in contrast to the warmer ocean water that "sea smoke" was created, which made the ocean appear as if it was steaming. Then, as the cold tightened its grip on the land and sea, the ocean stopped smoking and froze solid. The ocean, which was always so dynamic with its waves crashing on the shore, was now in a state of suspended animation. The only hint of activity was when the tide came in and out of the cove in front of our house. As the tide went out the solid mass of ice would crack and buckle as the water was drained from beneath it. Then, when the tide came back in, the ice field would slowly start heaving and pushing itself up on the shore. Farther out, the frozen sea was solid enough for snowmobiles to zip along at fifty miles per hour and greet the ferry as it haltingly crunched through the ice toward the terminal.

23

MIDNIGHT MONSTER in the CLOSET

After a few weeks of arctic bliss, our thoughts turned to what to do next. Now that we had a mortgage to pay, we had to figure out how to earn enough money to pay the bills and not get tied down to nine to five jobs. A few days after we started putting our attention on supporting ourselves, we got a call from one of the local teachers at the Wellesley TM Center. The center had been virtually closed since the team of ten Vedic Atom women, who had been running the center, had left for India. The new plan from Maharishi was to have Governor Couples run the centers and the single men devote themselves to a new program called "Purusha," where they would spend their time in seclusion, meditating in a large group. The single women would do the same thing in a separate program called "Mother Divine." None of the local TM teachers could teach full time so they asked us if we would be interested in the new program. In exchange for running the center we would receive room and board plus one hundred dollars a month each. We said yes without a moment's hesitation. The Wellesley TM Center was our favorite center and, of course, teaching meditation was our favorite activity. Even though the meager wages were not enough to cover our mortgage payments on our house in Maine, we figured that if we could sell Linnea's watercolors part-time we could meet our expenses.

When we arrived in the middle of January, 1981, the elegant but not-too-formal eight bedroom mini-mansion was cold and empty. The once vibrant TM center was locked up, with no one in sight. The vibes were always sweet at the center, but with no one living there it seemed a little spooky. We quickly moved into the large master bedroom with a private bath and organized a group meditation program in the flying hall with a dinner afterwards. Within a week all the local sidhas were coming to the group program every night and we were arranging public lectures and TM courses. Life at the center was fulfilling and comfortable. We taught TM courses almost every week and came to realize that we were suited to teaching in the field more than the monastic life of a retreat facility like Swiss Meadows. In many ways it felt like we had come home. We knew all the teachers and meditators from our stay at the center the previous winter and I had grown up in one of the neighboring towns, so the area was quite familiar. Although the center was located near a busy highway, we were close to parks and the small lake at Wellesley College for daily walking.

When the "whisper writer" arrived at the center we thought it was a good idea. This was before email and fax machines. The whisper writer was a cutting-edge communication device which allowed us to receive messages over the phone line, which were printed on a dot matrix printer. Before we had this remarkable device, the main method of communication from the movement headquarters was by conference call with all the other TM centers in the country. Often it would take an hour just to get everyone on the phone while we waited on the line with the long-distance meter ticking away. Once everyone was connected each center had to report, which took another half hour. Now with the whisper writer we could receive ten, twenty and even fifty page messages from movement headquarters announcing the latest programs. Because long distance phone rates were much less expensive after midnight, we always received the messages in the middle of the night.

For some reason, the movement had become obsessed with security ever since the mass cult suicide at Jonestown a few years before. Since then, there were rumors going around that the movement had been infiltrated by CIA agents to make sure there were no more mass suicides. Apparently the government thought the TM movement was another weird cult with a bunch of brainwashed hippies following a bearded Hindu monk who might pull a stunt like Jim Jones and have everyone drink poisoned Kool-Aid. This created a wave of secrecy in the movement hierarchy that seemed bizarre at times. For example, Linnea and I were not to tell anyone about the whisper writer and we were supposed to keep it in a locked secret place. We decided that the closet in our bedroom was the best place because we could tap into a nearby phone line and lock it up.

At first we tried to ignore the whisper writer when it started printing out messages around 2 AM. One morning, when we opened the closet to check the messages, the closet was overflowing with dot matrix computer paper. Apparently the whisper writer had malfunctioned and had used up a whole ream of paper. From then on, whenever we heard it printing in the middle of the night, we felt compelled to go into the closet and check it out. Our biggest mistake was to read the messages, which were often announcements of new projects that seemed unrealistic and a waste of time. Most of the proclamations came from the Council of Supreme Intelligence of the World Government of the Age of Enlightenment. Over the past few months, the movement had been restructured into a formal hierarchy. For the first fifteen years the TM movement had enjoyed a relatively informal structure. Jerry Jarvis had been the leader of the movement in the U.S. and was known simply as Jerry. There were area coordinators for the various parts of the country and they were also known by their first names. Now the movement was run by the Council of Supreme Intelligence, a group whose identity was kept secret. Whenever I talked to the council on the phone and would recognize someone's voice, I would call them by their first name. They would never acknowledge who they were. After a while we grew to hate the whisper writer in our closet that was constantly spewing out weird plans and directives that kept us awake for hours in the middle of the night while we tried to make sense out of them.

Another wacky idea from the whisper writer was the "sidha dresses." This was a well-intentioned, but perhaps misguided, plan to generate income for various projects to make TM available in the Third

World, and to provide appropriate clothing for the ladies in the movement, especially Governors of the Age of Enlightenment. The dresses were made out of fine silk from Asia and were lovely pastel colors. The style of the dresses was elegant and formal, which made them perfect for elderly British matrons to wear to afternoon tea parties or perhaps an audience with the Queen. The marketing strategy was to ship fifty or so of these very expensive dresses to each capital, or TM center, have the Governor Couples, who were now running most of the centers, organize a fashion show and offer them for sale to the meditating community. It didn't take a fashion expert to figure out that trying to sell these Margaret Thatcher-style dresses to hip, high tech, young Boston women and organic brown-rice-eating housewives was an embarrassingly dumb idea. After our failed fashion show we received another brilliant nocturnal memo directing us to sell them wholesale to exclusive dress shops in our area. Linnea definitely didn't want to do it so she talked me into making appointments with some of the fine shops in the Wellesley area. A few weeks earlier I would never have dreamed that I would be trying to sell expensive dowager dresses to upscale fashion houses in Wellesley. When I showed the dresses to the store buyers, they were surprisingly polite and appreciative but didn't think they could sell them, so we shipped the dresses back and waited for the whisper writer to give us our next fun-filled assignment.

In spite of the electronic monster in our closet, life at the Wellesley Center was fulfilling and seemed to progress in a frictionless flow, as though we were in the right place at the right time. In addition to living in a beautiful house and experiencing the joy of teaching meditation almost every weekend, I was able to sell our pictures to area gift shops, which brought in enough money to pay the mortgage on our house in Maine. We had the best of both worlds: living in the silence of a spiritual center and yet maintaining our house in Maine to enjoy on holidays. Even the communal living at the center was fun. Within a few months the five additional bedrooms were filled with fellow TM teachers who either had jobs outside the center or helped us out with center activities.

Every night we cooked a big dinner for the sidhas, who came to do the group super radiance program in the flying room. There were usually ten to thirty people attending every evening and most stayed for dinner, which was a great way for everyone to get together and socialize. The Cambridge TM Center also had a similar program, but bigger. They usually had forty or fifty people meditating and flying at the exact same time as we did, to create an even more powerful wave of coherence or super radiance. In many ways it was an act of faith for so many of the dedicated sidhas to go out of their way and stop by the center for the evening program before going home. Even if the "creating coherence" program didn't work, there was no doubt in most people's minds that group meditations were more enriching than meditating alone.

Every few months, the midnight monster in our closet would spew out a new plan to get more people to meditate. By the early 1980s the number of people starting TM had slowed down, especially among college students. Gone were the days of disillusioned students rebelling against the status quo in search of an alternative lifestyle. It was as though the 1960s and 1970s were a fad that had run its course. Now there were more mainstream, older professionals learning TM for very practical reasons, mainly to reduce stress in their lives. However, there was also a large group of dedicated teachers and meditators who meditated for spiritual development. Most of the TM teachers were dedicated to becoming enlightened and felt the benefits from Maharishi's programs, but they also had jobs and careers outside of the movement. Another group of teachers were the hardcore true-believers. They took the new hierarchy of the Council of Supreme Intelligence (ministers, governors, sidhas and meditators) seriously and never questioned even the most ridiculous schemes and proclamations of the World Government of the Age of Enlightenment.

The next thirty-page plan from the whisper writer was to generate more interest in meditation by offering immortality through TM. Immortality seemed a little over the top, but during the last ten years there had been hundreds of studies indicating that meditation reduced both physical and emotional stress, which suggested a possible reduction in aging. The plan was to start a public awareness campaign about the anti-aging benefits of TM by contacting the media and setting up presentations by local meditating doctors and scientists on the reversal of aging. There were a surprising number of meditating doctors in the greater Boston area who were willing to give lectures on the health benefits of TM and give radio and TV interviews. Deepak Chopra was one of the most enthusiastic spokesmen for TM and was constantly giving lectures and speaking on TV shows, which helped to generate a new wave of interest in meditation. The fact that he was an M.D. gave a lot of credibility to his claims about the health benefits of meditation.

Maharishi was impressed with Deepak's knowledgeable and articulate presentations and asked him to be the national spokesman for TM. This launched Deepak into the national spotlight, where he has remained for the last twenty-five years, as a best-selling author and proponent of Ayurvedic medicine. After studying Ayurveda in India, he became the director of the Lancaster, Massachusetts Ayurvedic Health Center, located on a ninety-year-old estate that had seen better days, but still evoked the formal grandeur of a bygone era. For a few years it was used as a meditation retreat, and then turned into an Ayurvedic health spa frequented by Hollywood celebrities. Deepak ran the Ayurvedic program called "panchakarma," which included massage with warm sesame oil, aromatherapy and pulse diagnosis. Eventually he left Lancaster and decided to go into private practice with his own clinic in San Diego.

Although there was an increase in people starting meditation as a result of all the national publicity, there was also a lot of competition in the relaxation business. Dr. Herbert Benson, who had done some of the original physiological research on TM, had published a book called *The Relaxation Response.* He claimed that one could get the same results as TM by just closing the eyes and mentally repeating any word. He claimed there was no need for any initiation ceremony or the use of Hindu mantras. Some of the more competitive TM teachers complained that the research he cited to claim results for his relaxation response was actually the original TM research he did with Keith Wallace in the early 1970s. Maharishi always used to joke that you can't learn meditation from a book because the first instruction is to close your eyes! One evening, after I had finished giving a TM lecture, a nationally known author sat down with me to set up his appointment to learn meditation the next day. When I asked him how he found out about TM, he said that his friends were colleagues of Dr. Benson and they told him to learn the real thing and start TM. He seemed to get some good results. A few years later I read that he had become a Zen monk!

Sometimes teaching TM to the public in the 1980s on the basis of its health benefits seemed like living in two different universes. Ten years earlier a fair number of people had been seekers and had started TM to become enlightened. Often during lectures and meditation courses, arcane issues like experiences of kundalini rising, samadhi, unity consciousness and Vedic literature would be brought up by people interested in meditation. Now the questions were about more practical concerns related to health and job performance. In one part of the TM center we would be lecturing on stress management while in the flying room meditators would be practicing Patanjali's Yoga Sutras with varying degrees of success and hopping around on the foam-covered floor with visions of enlightenment dancing in their heads. There seemed to be a parallel universe of the Veda coexisting with the mundane world of cable TV, oil changes and dog food. When TM teachers and meditators got together at the center they could enjoy the cosmic camaraderie of the Vedic universe, and then go out into the other world of traffic jams and credit cards. Of course the hallmark of enlightenment was to be equally at home in both worlds, but being in a supportive environment of fellow meditators seemed preferable to participating in many of the activities offered by the dominant culture. This desire to live in a community of meditators had been kicking around the TM movement for years, but never got anywhere because of the diverse needs and job circumstances of meditators. Some wanted to live in an urban condo-style environment, while others wanted to live in the most pristine rural location possible.

Now that there were so many people practicing the group program together twice a day, Maharishi thought it would be a great idea for each area to find some property, which would be called the Ideal Village. The goal was to have a community where meditators could have their houses together and a central building for the super radiance program, or group meditation. In spite of the fact that the historical records are littered with the remains of deceased utopian communities, it seemed like a practical idea that would make life easier for all the dedicated sidhas who drove to the center every day. Within a few weeks every TM center in the country had a committee devoting hours of its time every week looking for a large enough piece of land to build homes and preferably a golden dome for the group flying program. Establishing the Ideal Village in our area was much more difficult than anyone had thought. First, there was very little property available in eastern Massachusetts that suited our needs and second, trying to get several hundred individuals to agree on a location and come up with a large amount of money was almost futile. The only thing that the hundreds of dedicated sidhas had in common was their commitment to the group meditation program and the Vedic philosophy associated with the technique. Otherwise they were a very disparate group with different lifestyles ranging from wine-sipping Harvard academics to beer-guzzling rural construction workers.

In other areas of the country, the movement was having more success starting Ideal Villages. In Fairfield, Iowa there was already a substantial community associated with MIU which was building a large golden dome for practicing the super radiance program. Almost two thousand people had moved to Fairfield to participate in the program and had purchased homes and started businesses. There was a lot of pressure from the movement to have as many people as possible meditating and flying together in the MIU dome. To reach the critical mass of the square root of one percent of the world's population, seven thousand people would need to meditate together in the same place. There just weren't seven thousand sidhas in the country who could pack up and move to Iowa, so the next best thing was to have all the centers in the country meditate at the same time. The hope was that seven thousand people flying at the same time would also have a beneficial effect on the collective consciousness. The movement was so serious about this that we had to report the number of people in the flying room at the center every day to see if the amount of people across the country doing the program together reached the magic number of seven thousand.

After we had been at the Wellesley TM Center for about a year, we got a call from Josh, an MIU student who had spent the previous summer at the center while he was working his way through college. During his teacher training course in Europe, he had decided to stop eating. When the course directors asked him to start eating, he refused so they told him to go out into the world for a while and get a job to become more stable. He asked us if he could stay at the Wellesley Center while he was looking for a job. He was a really nice kid and always eager to help out at the center so we figured, *Why not?* Josh seemed perfectly fine when he moved into the center. The only thing that troubled me was that he had taken a job selling cookware to young women who had just become engaged. He found his leads in the wedding announcement section of the newspaper and called them up cold to show them his wares. He was a smart kid who had almost finished college and I felt that he could have done much better. However, he felt it was a great opportunity to become a successful businessman. This sounded a bit naïve to me, but I didn't want to dishearten him so I wished him well. After a couple of weeks, he became quiet and withdrawn and seemed depressed. He finally confided in me that he hadn't made any sales and that it was almost impossible to get an appointment with the young engaged women. They seemed suspicious and hung up on him. I suggested he try another job, but he was determined to prove to himself that he could succeed.

A couple of weeks went by. Josh was becoming more depressed

but still determined to make a sale. One morning I noticed a horrible, acrid stench like burning rubber wafting into our bedroom on the second floor. I opened the door and the hall was filled with smoke. I ran downstairs into the living room and saw Josh trying to peel his burning, melted sneakers from the top of the hot wood stove. He glanced over at me and, with a pathetic and vacant look in his eyes, said, "I'm sorry Lar." I felt like calling him an idiot for trying to dry his shoes directly on the wood stove, but I felt so sorry for him I told him not to worry about it and helped him scrape the remains of his sneakers off the stove. A few hours later I happened to look out the window from our second story room and noticed Josh throwing a lot of his belongings in the dumpster, then drive off in his car. There was an air of finality in his actions and my first reaction was to run out and see what was going on. It was one of those nasty New England winter days when, after about six inches of snow had fallen, it had turned to a cold, foggy rain. Before I could get my boots on and go outside, the doorbell rang. It was someone for my first meditation checking appointment of the day. By now Josh was long gone and it was useless to try to go after him. I had about ten appointments, one after the other, and each one took half an hour to "check" to see if the person is meditating effortlessly and to answer any questions they might have about the practice.

Throughout the day, the vision of Josh throwing his things in the dumpster and then driving off kept haunting me. Every time a car pulled into our parking lot, I jumped up to see if it was Josh. Just as I was leaving Mrs. Hanson, a dignified matronly woman, to meditate on her own in the checking room, the phone rang. It was Lieutenant Warren with the Wellesley Police. They had found Josh wandering aimlessly in downtown Wellesley. He had no shoes on and wore only a shirt and pants that were soaked from the rain and slush on the streets. Fortunately Lieutenant Warren was an old high school friend from the 1950s and we had given him a Maharishi Award for his public service a few months earlier. Josh told him that he lived at the center. Lieutenant Warren was familiar with the TM center and, after talking with me, agreed to turn Josh over to me instead of throwing him in jail for further evaluation. Just as the police car was pulling into the driveway, I ran up to the checking room and asked Mrs. Hanson to take five minutes to slowly open her eyes. I told her I would be right back. I tiptoed out of the room, ran down the stairs and out the door just as Josh was getting out of the police car. He was acting like a disoriented zombie, had turned kind of bluish and was shivering violently. I quickly thanked Lieutenant Warren, whisked Josh into the house, took him up to the second floor bathroom, told him to take off his drenched clothes and take a hot shower, and that I would be back in a few minutes. I realized he had no dry clothes so I quickly threw a blanket in the bathroom for him to wear, ran down the hall and tiptoed into the checking room where Mrs. Hanson was finishing up her meditation.

As Mrs. Hanson and I were walking down the hall after finishing the checking session, Josh suddenly emerged from the bathroom wearing only the loosely draped blanket and started staggering down the hall toward me and Mrs. Hanson. I could tell she was becoming very uncomfortable as Josh closed in on us, so I excused myself, intercepted Josh before he could get any closer and hustled him into another room. I quickly got him in bed under a pile of blankets and told him not to move until I returned. I then hurried out of the room and found Mrs. Hanson standing in the hallway looking rather dumbfounded. She seemed to know that it would be indiscreet to ask questions so we walked to the door in awkward silence. When I asked her if she would like to make another appointment for the following week, she unhesitatingly declined and said that she would call back some time. Josh was sitting up in bed when I returned to the room. He seemed a bit more coherent so I found some clothes for him and we went down to the kitchen for some hot tea. He still was quite withdrawn, with a vacant stare, but not agitated or hostile.

I had no idea what to do with him so I asked him if he had any family nearby. His father lived about a half-hour away, so I called him and explained to him what had happened. He wasn't very surprised; apparently this had happened before, so he offered to come to the center and talk to Josh. When he arrived, Josh wasn't too happy to see him and his father wasn't too pleased with what Josh had done. His father was a psychologist and kept accusing Josh of "maladaptive behavior," with which Josh reluctantly agreed. After a half hour, Josh agreed to go to the hospital with his father. I felt guilty about Josh going to the hospital, but having him wandering around the center like a zombie was not good for him or the center. A few days later, I went to see him in the hospital and then I felt really guilty! He was locked up in a maximum security unit, which was just like a prison. I had to take an elevator that looked like an animal cage to his floor, which was enclosed in iron bars. Fortunately he was feeling a little better and looking forward to getting out in a few days. Some of the other TM teachers and meditators also visited him in the hospital. After his release he was offered a job as an assistant at a TM center in New York by some friends who helped him get back on his feet. A few years later he seemed fully recovered and had started his own business.

The first year at the Wellesley TM Center was so enjoyable that Linnea and I decided we would like to continue on there for at least a few more years. This was the first time we'd had a sense of stability in our movement work. We thought that it might even be possible to start a family. Within a few weeks after we decided to have a baby, Linnea was pregnant. On one hand we were overjoyed at the news and on the other hand we were anxious because of what happened with our first baby seven years earlier. Because of our ages (I was 41 and Linnea was 36) and the fact that our first baby died of a birth defect, the obstetrician became alarmed. She recommended they do amniocentesis testing to see if the baby had Down syndrome or other defects and suggested we undergo genetic counseling. The idea of puncturing the amniotic sac with a needle, which was required for amniocentesis, was just too risky, so we decided to forgo all the testing and counseling, surrender to the will of God and have a natural childbirth. We found a great natural childbirth doctor and a wonderful midwife who worked together and were both very supportive of our decision. However, we didn't think it was appropriate to have a home birth in the TM center because it was still considered a risky, counterculture way to have a child. If there were any complications it could reflect poorly on the TM movement. The idea of going to a hospital was repugnant to us, but Betty, the midwife, found a nice natural birthing room at a hospital nearby.

Linnea felt a little foolish hobbling around on crutches two weeks before the baby was due. Some of the older-generation women scolded her for hiking while pregnant, but the midwife and doctor thought exercise was a good preparation for childbirth. Except for the twisted ankle incurred while hiking down a mountain, everything was going fine with the pregnancy and as the due date of September 25th approached, Betty began to check with us more often. Around the 22nd Linnea started having a few contractions. Betty had given us her beeper number so that we could get in touch with her right away. For the next few days the contractions would come and go. On the 25th they started intensifying a little, and when Betty came over to the center to check Linnea, she told us to pack our bags and get ready to go to the hospital in the next day or so. Not much happened for the next twenty-four hours. Then, on the afternoon of the 26th, Linnea very suddenly started having serious contractions at close intervals. I called Betty. She came right over and examined Linnea while I was frantically throwing our stuff in the car in preparation for a hasty departure. After checking Linnea, Betty calmly looked at us and said, "Linnea, you're not going anywhere—you're going to have this baby right now!"

We hadn't even considered that we wouldn't make to the hospital, but by now Linnea was in full blown second stage labor and wasn't interested in logistics. Betty immediately took command of the situation and instructed me to find a bunch of towels and linens. Meanwhile, Ric and Tom, a couple of TM teachers who were living at the center, were enlisted to boil some large pots of water. They hadn't expected anything like this and were running around frantically, boiling water and trying to find whatever supplies Betty yelled out from the upstairs bedroom that she needed. In spite of the urgent and somewhat chaotic situation, I was glad that we didn't have to go to the hospital if everything was going to work out all right—and it did! In less than an hour from the time Betty arrived, our son Devan was born. It was an amazingly smooth and quick birth. As soon as he was born, he let out a scream, reached up, pulled the midwife's hair and wouldn't let go! After she pried his little fist from her hair, she exclaimed, "Watch out for this guy—he's a cowboy." It turned out to be a very prescient observation. For the first couple of nights we tried to have him sleep with us, but we would wake up in the middle of the night falling out of bed. It was like sleeping with a little helicopter! He thrashed around so much that he kicked us out of the bed on either side of him.

For the next few days we stayed in our room, basking in the bliss of being blessed with such a beautiful child and feeling grateful that we didn't have to go to the hospital. Everyone around the center felt that Devan didn't want to be born in the hospital and that was why events unfolded the way they did. Another benefit of having a home birth was the saving of about $2,500 in hospital fees. We had no medical insurance and weren't quite sure how we were going to come up with the money. We weren't even sure how we were going to pay for the midwife and the obstetrician. A few days after Devan was born we received a large order for our prints from LL Bean, which brought in enough money to pay for all our childbirth expenses.

Raising a family while living in a meditation center on a small monthly stipend was not very practical so most centers were run by couples without kids. Our situation was unique; the center was large enough to have our own private suite of rooms and we had a part-time business to pay for the extra expenses. Also, Devan had at least twenty-five "aunts and uncles" at the center who loved to hold him and play with him. He was the star of the center.

As Devan started crawling, his favorite activity was to scoot around the kitchen while Linnea was cooking dinner, open the cabinets and yank out all the pots and pans. The sound of pots and pans banging around in the kitchen wasn't the most meditative sound in the center, but no one seemed to mind and it kept him occupied while Linnea was trying to cook. When he got big enough to sit in a high chair he would join all the meditators having dinner after the evening group meditation program. Everyone loved to sit next to him, even though they had a good chance of being splattered with rice or dhal when he would indiscriminately wing a fistful of food in their direction. By the time he was a year old, he had developed the ability to flip his whole dish of food onto anyone or anything near him. This wreaked havoc on the dining room carpet and on newcomers, who were unfamiliar with his lack of proper dining skills. Eventually we spread a piece of plastic on the carpet and set his high chair up out of range of any potential victims.

24

A TASTE of UTOPIA

"A Taste of Utopia" was the heading of the twenty-page whisper writer message that rudely awakened us at 2:30 AM. The movement was never known to be shy about using superlatives to describe its various programs. Maharishi liked words like invincibility, immortality and infinite, so when I saw the word utopia, I yawned and went back to sleep without reading any further. When I got around to reading the rest of the message the next morning, instead of yawning, I yelled out, "Whoa!" Maharishi wanted seven thousand sidhas to come to Fairfield, Iowa in the next couple of weeks for a huge group flying program. My first reaction was that this was going to be a logistical nightmare. There were only about five or six thousand people in the whole town and about fifteen hundred of them were sidhas who were regularly going to the golden domes for the group meditation program. That meant that over five thousand more people would have to go to Fairfield, which would double the size of the town virtually overnight. This was December 1983, not July, which meant no camping out in friends' backyards or parks. There just weren't that many extra beds in the whole town, let alone motel and dorm rooms at MIU.

The idea itself was a noble one. Because of the apparent similarities in the behavior of human consciousness and the unified field theory in physics, Maharishi and his band of dedicated physicists were convinced that if they could get seven thousand people to practice yogic flying at the same time in one location it would have a measurable effect on world consciousness. This could be measured in a reduction of inco-

herent activity like war, crime, accidents and disease. It was surprising
how many people believed in this. It was probably a result of their good
experiences during the group flying program and their faith in Maharishi. Even if they were skeptical, why not give it a try? And that they did!
Within three weeks there were over seven thousand people from all over
the world in freezing Fairfield, Iowa, ready to fly together.

The dorms at MIU hadn't changed much in the nine years since
we had lived there. In spite of the fresh coat of nonspecific paint on the
outside of the buildings, the insides were still sort of shabby and lacked
the attention of skilled maintenance personnel. The overall impression
of the campus was that of a Third World military base on a very tight
budget. However, we felt lucky to have a room at all. Many people were
sleeping on friends' couches and sharing single rooms with three or four
others. Not only were we lucky enough to have our own room, but
we had two! Linnea's parents had offered to leave their beautiful farm
in Virginia and spend three weeks over the Christmas holidays taking
care of Devan so that Linnea and I could go to the meditation program
together twice a day. They were really good sports to spend three weeks
in the bleak, windswept plains of Iowa, trudging through snowdrifts in
below-zero temperatures. Two days after they arrived, we were moved
into a brand-new mobile home with three bedrooms and two baths in
Utopia Park.

Utopia Park was a remarkable achievement and enough to make
one believe in the power of coherence generated by a large group of
people meditating. Within three weeks, a fifty-acre abandoned field on
the north end of the campus was transformed into a subdivision with
graveled streets, water, sewer and electricity hooked up to about fifty
brand-new mobile homes of decent quality. This had all been done in
sub-zero temperatures and blizzard conditions. We were some of the
first people to move into one of the spacious furnished units, which were
much better for a family than living in two rooms in a dorm and sharing the bathroom with twelve other people. Even though most of the
units were livable, Utopia Park was a hornet's nest of construction crews

and machinery. The streets were unrecognizable; lost in a sea of frozen mud and drifted snow, while backhoes, bulldozers and trucks swarmed around the mobile homes like angry hornets. To get to the campus from our unit we had to navigate a war zone of six-foot ditches, piles of mud and snow and beeping backhoes.

Every morning, Linnea and I would venture out of our trailer, which looked like an Antarctic research station. It was blasted with blowing snow that drifted up to the windows and over the roof. The snow obliterated any of the features of the structure that distinguished it from one of those buildings the scientists lived in at the South Pole. The constant threat of being crushed by a huge bulldozer suddenly emerging out of the blinding snow only enhanced the sensation of being in an alien land. Once we found the main road to the campus, Linnea would head for the Golden Dome where three thousand women were meditating and practicing the yogic flying together, while I would join the forty-five hundred men in the newly constructed "flying shed." The shed was a massive metal industrial building about the size of a football field that had taken four weeks to construct. Its prefabricated beams and metal siding had been trucked to Fairfield and assembled with giant cranes that seemed impervious to the vagaries of below-zero temperatures and blizzards.

The shed was amazingly comfortable for a prefab metal building resembling an airplane hangar. The entire floor was covered with thousands of foam mattresses that accommodated at least four thousand men who sat and meditated in long rows. The security procedures to get into the building seemed obsessively paranoid; everyone had to have an extra-large laminated flying badge measuring seven inches long and three inches wide. This made them very inconvenient to carry in a pocket or wallet. Each badge had a large photo on one side and was color-coded; gold for governors and green for sidhas. Not only did we need the badge to get in the building, but once we were seated inside, there was another security check. Everyone had to sit in a small circle of ten people and check the badge of the person next to him. For most of us it was a perfunctory inconvenience, but every once in a while a zealot sitting next to me would take my badge and carefully examine it to make sure my face matched my picture. I couldn't figure out what they were so afraid of. Who in their right mind would want to sneak into a group of people who were meditating for a couple of hours? If some unauthorized non-meditator snuck in, they would be extremely bored! After the badge check, at the appointed time, everyone started hopping around as they began practicing the flying sutra. This was considered the most powerful sutra in terms of producing brain wave coherence and Maharishi had us spend a long time flying around on the foam to create as much coherence as possible.

The effect on the immediate environment of over seven thousand men and woman meditating together was obvious and understandable. The challenge was to find out if this large group of people practicing the sidhis program in the frozen cornfields of Iowa could create a positive influence in the collective consciousness of the world. The responsibility for this fell on the shoulders of the social scientists who were measuring statistics like crime and accidents during the three-week event. One of the first statistics to come out of the research was a dramatic drop in crime and accidents in Iowa during the event. At first everyone was excited about this, until someone brought up the point that the extremely cold weather was probably the reason for the reduction in accidents and crime. Apparently during that time far fewer people had been driving or even venturing outside; criminals were usually less active during extreme weather. However, the scientists were able to find some data that demonstrated a reduction in international conflicts and infectious diseases, plus growth in the stock market and in the U.S. GNP during the time of the course.

These were certainly not earth-shattering statistics, but Maharishi was so convinced that these large group meditations were having a profound effect on the consciousness of the world that he asked as many meditators as possible to move to Fairfield in order to maintain a permanent group of seven thousand sidhas. This marked an important milestone in the history of the TM movement. Up until then TM was presented as a simple technique for relaxation, stress reduction and a possible path to enlightenment. Maharishi's one-pointed mission in life was to eliminate suffering and bring about a more peaceful world through meditation. For many meditators, this concept was easy to accept based on the results of meditation in their own lives. Now the stakes were much higher. Everyone was asked to disrupt their lives and move to Fairfield as soon as possible to bring about world peace by meditating together. For many people, moving to Fairfield was a sacrifice. Up until then there were no sacrifices associated with TM. On the contrary, no one was asked to give up anything or change one's lifestyle. As Maharishi often declared, TM was about living 200% of life: 100% fullness in the relative field of life and 100% in the absolute field of life. Who could ask for more: blissful enjoyment of all aspects of life while grounded in an unflappable serenity?

Now there was pressure to do something that would cause a lot of people to give up their comfortable lifestyles and careers, pack their bags and leave for Fairfield. It was amazing how many people were willing to do this. Of course there were the benefits of living in a community of meditators and the joy of participating in the daily super radiance program with seven thousand other devotees. Within a few days, a chamber of commerce was set up to help people find housing, jobs and office space to move their businesses to Fairfield. One of the features that attracted a lot of families was the Maharishi School. Kids in grades preschool through high school could now go to a school where everyone meditated and the curriculum was guided by Vedic philosophy. For many of the meditators, moving to Fairfield was a dream come true; no more commuting in rush hour traffic and living in stressed cities. Now they could live a more yogic lifestyle as part of a community of like-minded people. Although we were dedicated to the movement, Linnea and I didn't really want to move to Fairfield and fortunately we had a good excuse: we were needed back at Wellesley to run the TM center.

Toward the end of the course, rumors started flying around that

Maharishi would be coming any day. In spite of the blizzard conditions and the huge meditation program that brought most activity to a standstill, the word that Maharishi was coming created a buzz of construction activity on the campus. Buildings for Maharishi and his entourage had to be remodeled and security guards posted at every entrance to the campus. There were a couple of reasons for the increased security. Apparently, a disgruntled or deranged TM teacher name Ronnie Corbin claimed that he had suddenly slipped into a permanent state of samadhi (i.e. become enlightened), and that Guru Dev (Maharishi's master) had come to him in a vision. He also claimed that Guru Dev told him that he, Ronnie, was now the anointed one to be the custodian of the Vedic knowledge. He was to replace Maharishi as the leader of the movement. Ronnie was a pretty charismatic guy and was going around the country teaching his own program that was apparently a combination of EST training (a popular personal growth program in the 1980s) and meditation, with special mantras that included his own name. The reason the movement administrators were worried he might try to disrupt the course was that he had already hired a plane to fly over the campus and drop leaflets urging meditators to defect to his new movement. Another reason for the security was that, whenever word got out that Maharishi was going to be somewhere, it brought a lot of weirdos out of the woodwork who either wanted to confront him or hug him.

As soon as Maharishi stepped onto the stage, the audience members jumped to their feet and started wildly cheering and clapping. There was something about the excitement in the room that made Linnea and me feel strangely uncomfortable. It felt like a rock concert instead of the quiet, lighthearted and dignified atmosphere typical of the meetings we had enjoyed with Maharishi in the past. There had always been grateful devotees who lined the entrance to Maharishi's speaking engagements to offer him flowers or ask a question, but there had been no cheering or yelling when he appeared on stage. Now he just stood there with a bemused look on his face waiting for things to quiet down. After a few words of gratitude and praise for all of the people who came to Fairfield under less than ideal conditions, he started taking questions from the audience. Probably most of the people in the audience had never seen Maharishi before and were obviously excited to be in the presence of the man who had made such a difference in their lives. Most of the questions seemed like superficial and somewhat inappropriate celebrity questions. This was disappointing to those of us who were hoping Maharishi would reveal some deep knowledge, which he often did when he felt the timing and questions were right. Sometimes under the right circumstances he would sit for hours, often into the wee hours of the morning, discussing a whole new level of the Veda that he had never mentioned before. Apparently this was not the right atmosphere or circumstance for a long discourse and after an hour he decided to leave. We wondered if we would ever see him again in those intimate circumstances that had so blessed our lives in the past.

A few days before the end of the course, Maharishi asked as many people as possible to stay on as long as they could to keep the coherence level from dropping precipitously. Although Linnea and I were ready to go back to Wellesley, it was expected that, because we worked for the movement full time, we would stay on indefinitely. This would have been fine, except that we had a rambunctious one-year-old to take care of. Linnea's parents had to get back to Virginia so we took turns taking care of Devan and going to the program. This was fun in our spacious trailer, but when we were reassigned to a smelly basement room in one of the nastiest dorms on campus it wasn't much fun any more. There were very few people who had kids who worked for the movement full time. Most of the couples who were full time lived like monks, with no home or family to bother with. So when they stuck the three of us in a tiny room, we felt they weren't taking the unique needs of a family into consideration. The worst part was the odor of vomit and the shabby beat-up condition of the basement area to which families were assigned.

This really hit home after we were invited to visit a couple who had high level positions in the movement. Even though they had no children, they were given a stunning three bedroom apartment on the upper floor of our dorm. It was quite a contrast from the hell-hole we were living in. We felt like second-class citizens because we had a kid. This was reinforced by the dining hall arrangements. The national leaders from around the world had a bountiful dining room set up on the top floor of our dorm, but children were not allowed. The families were relegated to eating on crates set up in a makeshift dining area in the basement. After two weeks of living like this, Linnea and I rationalized that world consciousness wouldn't suffer if there were two fewer people meditating in Fairfield. We told the directors we wanted to leave and they reluctantly said okay. The nice thing about "working" for the movement was that we were never told what to do but were always asked. Even though it was developing into a hierarchical system with funny titles like governors, ministers and the Council of Supreme Intelligence, everyone worked hard, not based on any authoritarianism, but out of a willing devotion to Maharishi.

It was surprising how many of the meditators in the Boston area were willing to give up the natural beauty and cultural benefits of New England for the cornfields of Iowa to participate in the super radiance program. Within a few months over a thousand people from all over the country had moved to Fairfield. This was a long way from the goal of seven thousand, but it was enough to transform Fairfield from a basic Midwestern farm town into a relatively upscale community. New shops were opened, an artistic community developed and new recreational activities made the town even more attractive to meditators considering relocation. Linnea and I felt grateful that we were needed at the center in Wellesley, otherwise we probably would have moved to Fairfield out of a sense of duty. After three years at the Wellesley Center, especially after the birth of our son Devan, our life was very gratifying. Living in a meditation center with a strong-willed one-and-a-half year old kid running around the building had its challenges, but it was also a rare blessing to be able to spend so much time with him. We took him with us wherever we went, especially hiking and cross-country skiing. When he was only a few months old I would carry him in a "Snugli" on my chest while skiing. When he got bigger he rode in a pack on my back. As he grew older and heavier, he would jump up and down in the pack, throwing me off balance. One day I was going pretty fast down a hill when I suddenly hit something, a rock or branch, which caused me to come to a sudden stop and fall forward. Somehow Devan was catapulted out of the pack and over my head as I was falling down into the snow. He landed about four feet in front of me in a snowdrift and crawled out laughing and begging me to do it again.

With so much of the energy of the movement focused on creating a permanent group of seven thousand in Fairfield, the whisper writer in our closet remained relatively dormant. Then, late one night, it erupted with a huge twenty-page message announcing the Natural Law Campaign. As I tore the fifteen-foot long proclamation from the machine the next morning I couldn't help but groan when I first looked at the dense copy filling every page. After I read a few pages I realized that it made a lot of sense. Maharishi had often talked about the laws of nature in a very clear and direct manner. Presenting TM to the public in the context of natural law seemed to be an approach most people could relate to. The concept was quite simple; you violated the laws of nature and you suffered, or you obeyed the laws of nature and found life fulfilling. For example, if you disregarded the law of gravity and jumped off a high building, you would suffer when you hit the ground. However, you could take advantage of other laws of nature and enjoy a smooth and comfortable ride from the top of the building to the ground floor in an elevator. The more laws of nature we understand, the less we suffer and the more we enjoy life. The goal is to be in tune with all the laws of nature. This is the state of enlightenment where we don't make mistakes and all our actions are in harmony with natural law. This is basically what Krishna said to Arjuna in the Bhagavad Gita. He said, "yogastah kuru karmani" or "established in being perform action." In other words, if we are established in a state of pure consciousness when we perform action, then our judgment will not be clouded by stress or negativity and our actions will be free from mistakes. Along with these yogic buzzwords, there is also a physiological definition of enlightenment: a permanent state of restful alertness, in which one's actions are not clouded by fatigue and stress. This physiological explanation of TM was appealing to skeptical academics in many of the universities in the greater Boston area. In an attempt to gain more credibility within the academic community, the movement set up the Institute of Natural Law in Cambridge, a few blocks from Harvard. Sam Decker, an articulate and savvy lawyer who taught government and natural law at MIU, was named director of the institute and began contacting area universities about presentations on natural law.

The Natural Law Campaign was the latest initiative to generate more interest in TM, which had been declining since enthusiasm among students had dropped off dramatically in the 1970s. Students seemed more interested in careers and achieving a comfortable lifestyle than in spiritual development and changing the world. Even though the busy professionals now learning TM had little or no interest in the philosophy, they seemed to respect Maharishi's perspective on the development of consciousness and tolerate the initiation ceremony as a requirement for learning a physiological technique for relief of stress and improved job performance. Often, the more skeptical people were the most enjoyable to initiate. They would come into the initiation room with their obligatory fruit and flowers and sit down with a mild smirk on their faces that quickly dissolved as soon as they started meditating. After a few minutes of meditation we would ask them to open their eyes. Sometimes they would be so deep in meditation that we would have to ask two or three times before they could open their eyes. We could tell by the look of total relaxation in their faces and bodies that they were experiencing a level of silence they had never experienced before. These results were completely independent of their attitudes when they entered the room to learn meditation.

Dan Burnham was a spiritual Indiana Jones. He spent his summers and sabbaticals from his job as a psychology professor at Boston

College traveling the world looking for shamans, gurus, saints and any esoteric teacher he could find. He was intrigued by the concept of natural law and spiritual development and asked us to give a presentation to his psychology class. I invited Sam Decker, the resident expert on natural law, to join me in the lecture. It was so well received that Dan asked us to develop a course on natural law and meditation for the whole semester. Sam and I thought this was an excellent opportunity to regenerate some interest in TM at B.C., so we agreed without hesitation. After a few lectures we realized that, while the students seemed mildly interested in what we had to say, their main concern was to get good grades in the class. We invited the whole class to the center for an introductory lecture on TM and only a few showed up. It was curious that, while they were somewhat interested in learning about TM and its benefits, none of them wanted to actually learn the technique. They seemed almost obsessed with what kind of exam we were going to give and how they should prepare for the quizzes. I soon realized they were under a lot of pressure to get good grades for a variety of reasons and that it would be better for them to have some fun while learning about Maharishi's approach to the philosophy of yoga. I remembered the College Quiz Bowl TV show from my youth and thought it would be fun to divide the class into two teams that would compete with each other for points based on their answers to questions I presented to them. We did this once a week or so. Everyone got their competitive juices flowing and we had a raucous time while learning something at the same time. It was a little disappointing that no one learned TM, but they certainly had fun, gained a greater understanding of what TM was all about and everyone in the class got an A.

In spite of all the public awareness campaigns to promote more interest in TM, the number of people learning TM continued to decline. Instead of an average of twenty people a week learning meditation at the Wellesley Center, there was now about twenty a month. The main focus of the movement was trending away from teaching meditation to creating coherence by getting large groups together to meditate. In addition to trying to get seven thousand meditators in Fairfield, Iowa, there was another initiative to have two thousand people doing their sidhis program together in Washington, D.C. The plan was to create an atmosphere of coherence in the nation's capital that would result in a positive effect on the decisions of the U.S. Congress and the President. The movement purchased a large hotel in downtown Washington between the White House and Capitol Hill. Hundreds of Purusha and Mother Divine members moved in and began a long daily program of meditating and flying to radiate a calming influence on the government. Most of the people who were now practicing the sidhis program were not dedicated monks like the Purusha group, but regular folks who had jobs and families, so the movement bought another facility for their practice of the sidhis program. The plan was to have as many people as possible relocate to Washington and live close enough to the facility to easily participate in the group meditation program.

Washington was a lot more attractive and practical place for meditators to relocate than Iowa. Many people who didn't want to go to Fairfield because of lack of jobs or aversion to the isolation and brutal winters of Iowa moved to Washington. They either rented or bought houses near the meditation center, which was an old veteran's nursing home just off 16th street in the northwest part of D.C. The property had a nondescript brick building on two acres of minimally landscaped grounds surrounded by a high steel-spiked fence, which gave the impression of either a neglected estate or a minimum-security institution with limited funding. It was surprising how many intelligent and successful sidhas from the greater Boston area packed up and left for Washington. There were a lot of benefits to living in a community of people whose lifestyle was so different from the mainstream. Most meditators liked group meditations, whether they believed in the super radiance effect or not. Every night after the group program dinner was served at the center, which provided an opportunity for socializing and networking. Within a few months there were almost five hundred sidhas living in the area and meditating at the new center.

25

BACK to WASHINGTON, AGAIN!

The pounding on the door was louder and more urgent than the usual gentle knock or deep bong of the doorbell. I was settled deep into my morning meditation and was mystified why anyone would be trying to get into the TM center so early. We usually scheduled meditation checking sessions late in the morning and there were none scheduled that day until late afternoon. The incessant pounding was sending a not-so-subtle-message that whoever was out there was not going away. When I opened the door the first thing that came to my awareness was a large golden star glinting in the brilliant morning sun. Then I noticed it was attached to a sheriff's uniform worn by a clean-cut man in his twenties. He asked if I was the owner of the house and when I said no, he explained that the bank had foreclosed on the property due to failure to meet the mortgage payments and that an official notice would appear in the local paper announcing a public auction of the property! I was surprised, but not stunned. After working for the movement for fifteen years I had seen more than my share of weird real estate events unfold. I quickly agreed to sign the receipt for the stack of papers the deputy offered up to me. Later that morning I called the Council of Supreme Intelligence and asked what was going on. They glibly told me "not to worry" (one of Maharishi's favorite sayings) and to continue with the center activities.

This dismissive answer didn't exactly instill a lot of confidence in me, especially in light of the recent closings of many TM centers around the country due to lack of activity. Even at the Wellesley Center, which had been one of the more dynamic centers in the country, the number of people learning TM had continued to drop significantly. Also, many of the meditators who had been the most active supporters of the center had moved to Fairfield or Washington, D.C. The situation in the Boston area was unique, since most major cities had only one main TM center. However, Cambridge and Wellelsey were two major centers only fifteen miles apart. Rumors had been going around for a few months that the Wellesley Center was going to be sold, but the council kept assuring us it would stay open.

A few days after the sheriff delivered the foreclosure papers there were more early morning knocks on the front door. This time they were less demanding and almost timid. I also heard a lot of cars pulling into the driveway. When I opened the door, half a dozen people asked, almost in unison, "What time does the auction start?" I replied, "Sorry, I don't know anything about it." Then they started getting aggravated. One of them shoved a newspaper in my face with a big ad in it announcing the sale and said, "I took a day off from work. You can't do this to me." In the meantime more cars were pulling into the driveway for the auction and the situation started getting chaotic. All I could do was to tell them it was a mistake and to call the number listed in the ad. I retreated into the house and immediately called the council. They reassured me it was all taken care of.

In spite of these reassurances Linnea and I knew the end was near. We had worked for the movement for fifteen years and knew that when change came about it was usually precipitous. Despite all the public awareness campaigns and Deepak Chopra's appearance on major talk shows promoting the benefits of TM, the public seemed to have moved on to new self-improvement trends like jogging, weight-loss diets, fitness centers and antidepressant medications. Teaching meditation was the most rewarding and joyful work we had ever done and we felt blessed that we had been able to live and teach for five years at such a wonderful center. Two months after we were reassured that the center was not going to be sold, we received a midnight message on the whisper writer informing us that the center was going to close. Linnea and I had been ripped around so many times by the movement that it didn't bother us that much. The hard part was breaking the news to so many of the dedicated meditators who had supported the center over the years. Now they were losing something that had become an important part of their lives.

Linnea and I weren't exactly sure what we were going to do next. The local meditators would be able to go to the Cambridge Center, but we were out of a job and a home. Most of the jobs in the movement were done by single people and a few couples without children who lived a monkish lifestyle. Instead of being one-pointedly dedicated to the movement, we now had another priority, which was raising our son Devan. He was the main focus of our lives now and we were having a blast with him as he was emerging from the "terrible twos" into the age of reason. Now that he was almost four years old, he could hike along with us instead of being carried in a backpack. Also, because he was now too big and unruly to ride on my back while cross country skiing, he would ride in a sled tethered to a rope tied around my waist. This was fine when going uphill or on level ground, but skiing downhill was wild, especially when the sled started going faster than me and started pulling me behind it. The three of us treasured our time on the island in Maine. We contemplated living in our beautiful little home on the ocean, but we also felt a duty to the movement to at least participate in the super radiance program. This meant moving to Fairfield or Washington, D.C. and finding a way to support ourselves. Our hand-painted picture business had provided us with enough income when we received room and board at Wellesley, but now we would have to pay for food and housing, which would require a lot more money.

Spring is by far the most celebrated season in Washington. The Tidal Basin is awash in cherry blossoms and nearly every street is lined with flowering dogwoods, crab apples and redbuds. Even the dingiest parts of the city are inhabited by fragrant vines and flowering shrubs. It was a relief to escape from the grip of a gray and dying New England winter and luxuriate in the warm sun and lavish colors of April in Washington. Tom and Julie were generous to let us stay in a house they had purchased in Silver Spring but had not yet occupied. The house was only ten minutes from the meditation center so we were able to participate in the super radiance program every day. It was exciting to be part of a dynamic community of old friends who were moving to Washington.

Despite the good fortune of finding a house waiting for us and the headiness of joining our friends from around the country in such an inspiring project, Linnea and I came to the conclusion that urban living was not for us. This posed a unique dilemma; on one hand we felt obligated to dedicate ourselves to the movement, and on the other hand we knew that finding a regular nine to five job to earn enough money to live in the city close to the meditation center was abhorrent to us. After a few days of trying to figure out what the right course of action was, we decided that we just couldn't join the rat race and live and work in the city, even though we wanted to join the super radiance program.

Our ideal was to live in the country and still join in the group program at least once a day, even if we had to drive an hour to get there. To us it was worth it to raise our son in a rural and relatively pristine environment. We decided to buy an inexpensive house in the country near Front Royal, Virginia, about an hour from Washington. Our plan was to fix it up, sell it for a profit and continue to buy or build houses until we could afford to live in a rural area closer to Washington, where real estate was more expensive. Within two weeks of our intention to buy a "handyman special," we found a cute little two-bedroom ranch house on a quiet country lane less than a mile from the Shenandoah River. The house was ten years old, but the owner had never finished the inside or installed a well or septic. The price of $14,500 was a good deal and we talked the bank into giving us a construction loan to finish the house. Our first priority was to install the plumbing and septic and get a well drilled. Within a few weeks we had the plumbing and septic hooked up and I had made arrangements with a local well driller to drill a well as soon as possible. In the meantime we were able to haul water from our neighbors for washing, and we drove down to the Shenandoah River to scoop up five-gallon buckets of water for flushing the toilet. We had expected the well to be drilled within a week, but the well driller never showed up, even though he kept promising us we were next on his list. After a few weeks, I gave up on him and made arrangements with another driller. For Linnea and me, hauling the water was becoming a tedious chore, but for Devan it was the highlight of the day. He couldn't wait to drive down to the river. As soon as we approached the low-water bridge (a ford with about a foot of water running over it), he would beg me to roar across the bridge as fast as possible. This caused the water to splash up so high that we could hardly see out the windshield. Devan loved this and howled with delight as the water sprayed us through the open windows, simulating an amusement park ride. By the time we returned home, the inside of the car was completely drenched and we were both so waterlogged our shoes made squishing sounds when we stepped out of the car.

After working on the house for about six weeks, most of the remodeling was completed and we were ready to put the house on the market, make some profit and then build another one. The only glitch was the well. By now I had contacted every well driller in the area and they all told me the same story. I knew there was a building boom going on, which meant the drillers were probably behind schedule, but two months seemed way too long to wait for a well. One day I was talking to one of the neighbors about the well situation and he explained that the well drillers didn't like to drill in this area because there is no bedrock, just loose river boulders. When they drilled into the loose rock, the walls of the shaft caved in around the drill bit and it could be impossible to pull it back out. Losing a drill bit can be very expensive so the drillers always dug the easy wells before they took a chance in our area. Not only did this mean continued water hauling, but it meant that we wouldn't be able to sell the house until we found a way to supply it with water.

We had already put a down payment on a mountaintop lot nearby with a dramatic three hundred and sixty degree view of the Blue Ridge

Mountains and had a contract to have a custom modular home set on the lot. This property was also in Front Royal, but was closer to Washington and I-66, a high-speed freeway. Driving into Washington to do the group meditation every day was not as easy as we had thought, but at least we were getting closer to Washington. The only thing holding us up now was the damn well. Finally, after a few more weeks of research, I located a well driller about a hundred miles away who specialized in drilling in difficult areas. He had special equipment for spraying a material to cement the sides of the well and keep it from caving in. What we had expected to be about three weeks of hauling water was now turning into three months! At least the house was finished and was a very pleasant place to live. The main section of the house was one large room with a cathedral ceiling, lots of large windows overlooking the distant meadow and sliding glass doors with new decks that made the house seem more spacious than it actually was. There was nothing more to do to the house to make it more attractive, so we put it on the market and guaranteed a well in the sales contract. Within a few weeks we found a buyer who agreed to our price if we could have the well drilled within thirty days. By now it was the end of November and the well driller said if he couldn't get out to our site within the next few weeks we would have to wait until after Christmas, assuming the weather would cooperate.

The situation was turning into a nail-biter. If we couldn't get the well drilled within the next few weeks, we would lose the sale of the house. This meant that we wouldn't have the money to pay for the modular house and its foundation. It all depended on the well. Two more weeks went by and no sign of the well drilling rig. After we repeatedly called the well driller, he finally agreed to come out some time in the next few days. Within a few hours of his arrival with his monster rig it started snowing heavily, making all the roads in the area impassable. At least now I was able to tell the buyers who had been badgering me almost every day that we were actually drilling the well. The conditions for setting up the drilling rig were nasty; the ground was covered with two feet of snow and the soil under the snow was soft, gooey clay. Every time they maneuvered the forty thousand pound rig around to drill at the spot where the dowser had found water, it sunk about two feet into the mud. Well drillers don't like to drill wells that have been dowsed. They would much rather drill in the easiest location for their giant machines. After two hours of cussing and spinning tires in the mud and snow, they had the rig lined up over the spot marked by the dowser. According to the well driller, if we found water at a hundred and twenty-five feet as predicted by the dowser, we would be in luck; if not, it was highly unlikely there would be any water until they drilled down to the bedrock, which was at least another six hundred feet. There was also a greater risk of losing the drill bit before hitting bedrock, which would add thousands of dollars to the very high cost of drilling so deep.

About this time I was beginning to realize this was not as much fun as I had thought it would be. Remodeling and building spec houses on borrowed money was fraught with more dangers that I had anticipated. It was hard to believe that less than a year ago, Linnea, Devan and I were living a stress-free life in the blissful cocoon of the Wellesley meditation center, engaged in the fulfilling work of teaching meditation. Now we were out in the world, working to make a living, with all of its attendant hassles. At least we were able to participate in the big meditation program in Washington a few days a week, and working for ourselves offered us more free time, especially in the evenings.

During this time, the focus of the movement continued to change from teaching meditation to the public to offering new programs to people already meditating. In addition to the sidhis program, there were Ayurvedic health consultations, Sthapatya Veda building recommendations and Maharishi health supplements. A number of meditating M.D.s had gone to India, including Deepak Chopra, to study Ayurveda and were now apparently qualified to evaluate people and give them lifestyle and herbal recommendations. All of these programs were relatively expensive and must have generated a lot of operating funds for the movement. Sthapatya Veda was the newest program and seemed to be the most dogmatic. In some ways it was similar to traditional Chinese feng shui and in other ways it contradicted it. The basic premise was that the design, location and direction of one's house had an influence on one's consciousness, which could be negative or positive. Many people in the movement seemed to take Sthapatya Veda a little too seriously and began blocking off the south-facing entrances to their houses, fearing that "negative influences" would come in through the entrance. Some people remodeled their houses to incorporate east-facing entrances or actually built new houses according to the rules of Sthapatya Veda. Even at the MIU campus in Iowa the south entrance to the university was blocked off. There were so many people afraid that if their house was "out of vastu" (not in compliance with the principles of Sthapatya Veda) they would suffer grave consequences. After reading a few books on Sthapatya Veda and feng shui, I concluded that the design recommendations probably had some influence, just like a poorly designed house made one feel a little weird and a coherently designed house evoked a comfortable and peaceful feeling. The obsession with the bad influences of south-facing entrances seemed over the top to me, which prompted me to call the program the "architecture of fear." In spite of our discomfort with some aspects of the movement, Linnea and I were still dedicated to driving into Washington as often as possible for the group program. It seemed like the least we could do for Maharishi, who had given us so much knowledge and so many great experiences.

With just a few days to spare, the drillers hit water at a hundred and twenty-five feet, exactly the depth our dowser had predicted. He was also right in his prediction that it would produce five gallons per minute, which was the minimum amount required by the bank to give the buyers a loan. Once the sale of the first house was completed we started building the foundation for the new modular house. We ran into Jake, a charming and affable ex-convict, who talked me into giving him the job of laying the cement block for the foundation, which had to be the exact size of the modular home. After impressing me with his professional job of laying the block for the foundation, he asked me if he could have the contract to pour the concrete basement floor. The floor required a different set of skills than block work and had to be properly reinforced with rebar to meet the building code, and it had be perfectly level and smooth. Jake admitted he had never done that kind of work, but he had seen how it was done many times and was going to have two experienced cement workers helping him. So, based on the good work he had already done, I gave him the job. He calculated the amount of cement needed for the floor and we arranged for the cement truck to come to the site that afternoon and start pouring. It was crucial that we order enough cement for the entire floor to be poured all at the same time. If part of the floor was poured and then hardened, the cement that was poured for the next part would not adhere to the existing cement and the floor would be ruined.

After two-thirds of the floor was poured, the mixer ran out of cement. Jake had miscalculated the amount needed! It was too late to try to get another load of cement and the floor, which looked like a lava flow from a volcano, was starting to harden up. Jake knew I was not pleased with the outcome, so he assured me that he and his crew would get some special bonding material and stay up all night, if necessary, to fix the floor. The next morning, the first thing I did was to check the basement floor to see how the repair job had come out. As I entered the walk-out basement, I was assaulted by the overwhelming aroma of newly dried cement, stale beer and cigarettes. Then I noticed the floor! It was just like I had left it the night before except now it was covered with empty beer cans and cigarette butts. I walked next door, where Jake was staying with his sister's family, to have a little chat with him and pounded on the door for five minutes before he opened up. It was obvious that he had slept in his work clothes and he still had blotches of cement splattered on his face. Even though he was visibly hung-over, he seemed to remember that something he did last night was regrettable. "Hey man, sorry about the floor," were the first words out of his mouth. When I asked him what had happened, he thought for a moment and casually said, "Oh yeah, we were really tired and went out for something

to eat and a few beers and when we got back to the job, we had a few
more beers and before we knew it we were really loaded so we went
home." Assuming he knew more about cement work than I did, I asked
him what he was going to do about it. Without hesitating, he replied,
"Yeah man, that floor is really screwed up, man. I don't know what you
can do about it."

After three grueling days of removing the tops of the frozen waves
of cement with a monster grinder and mixing bags of special cement
with bonding materials, I began to wonder if this line of work was my
"dharma." In the Vedic tradition, if you are following your dharma, the
work or career you have chosen will be naturally fulfilling and there is
little resistance to achieving success in your field. On the other hand, if
you are not following your dharma, there are obstacles and the work is
not enjoyable. Maharishi has often said that the father's genetic tendencies or skills are passed on to the son in the "Y" chromosome, so it's
often easy and natural for a son to follow the family tradition and join
the family business or career of the previous generations. In India, strict
adherence to this tradition has had both positive and negative results.
Some families have produced generations of great scholars, doctors, musicians and tradesmen, while others have been stifled or restricted from
following their dreams due to an ossified caste system. I knew it wasn't
my life's path to have a normal nine to five job like the rest of my family and that pursuing the path of yoga was my dharma. However, I was
very definitely a "householder," as Maharishi described those of us in the
movement who had families and responsibilities. He was fond of saying
that most people were not monks and that it was actually easier to get
enlightened through the path of karma yoga or activity than living the
life of a monk. The question is: what is the most suitable activity for a
particular individual? I was beginning to think that construction was
not my dharma and that I was a "closet yogi." None of the construction
people I worked with knew that I spent three hours a day practicing
meditation and yoga. In the world of two by fours, Sheetrock, half-inch
copper elbows, and twelve/two Romex, the Vedic terms samadhi, asanas

and kundalini were not part of the operative lexicon. Although there was a certain degree of fulfillment in building and remodeling houses, it wasn't a "frictionless flow" of successful activity, as Maharishi described life in accordance with the laws of nature.

Fortunately the rest of the building project turned out to be relatively easy and within two months the house was finished and ready to be placed on the market. Although there were numerous small ranch houses similar to ours offered by other contractors in the huge subdivision, ours seemed to be the most attractive. As a result of finishing off the walk-out basement, there were five bedrooms, three baths and lots of decks and large glass doors, which offered the best mountain views on our street. The inside featured cathedral ceilings and a large open floor plan with a sliding glass door and deck off the living room, plus a kitchen with French doors opening onto another deck with a sweeping view. Even the master bedroom had its own deck with a great view. Spring was considered the best time to sell a house so after some landscaping, which added another layer of charm to the house, we put it up for sale. We assumed it would sell within a few weeks in the hot local market, but after a month with no offers, we began to wonder why our house was not selling while all the other smaller, more mundane houses in the neighborhood were quickly sold and occupied. This prompted me to walk around and look at the other houses to see what they offered that ours didn't. At first I was baffled! The other houses were sterile and banal. There were no large windows to capture the mountaintop views, no decks for outside living and no landscaping, with just a gravel driveway for a pickup truck and a short path to the door to bring in the groceries. After a few days of checking out the other houses, I noticed a pattern of activity that suggested a lifestyle very different from ours. These folks were working people who came home at 6 PM, turned on the TV, kept the window curtains closed, went to bed at ten and left for work at 7 AM, repeating the pattern almost every day. They had no time to sit around on decks enjoying the views and the evening stars.

After a few more months, with no interest in our attractive house while almost all the others were sold, Linnea and I began to realize that, instead of building a house that reflected our own values, we should have just built a little boxy ranch house that would have sold in a few weeks. Although we enjoyed living in the house, the mortgage payments were eating up all the profits from the sale of our other house and we were unable to start our next building project. All we could do was hope for a buyer to come along and find a way to earn some money until the house sold.

Now that Devan was five years old and enjoyed traveling, we decided to develop a new line of Florida bird and flower prints and take a long camping trip south. The trip was a great combination of splashing on the Florida beaches with Devan and opening new accounts for our prints. When we returned a few weeks later, the house had still not sold and we realized it was time to reconsider our goal of rapidly building and selling houses until we could afford to build a house closer to Washington. Our only option was to sell our lots in Front Royal and the one in Haymarket. Fortunately, the lots all sold quickly and we earned enough profit to keep us afloat for another five or six months, until the house sold. In the meantime we had to figure out what to do now that Plan A was not working out. Linnea and I both felt that perhaps nature was not supporting our efforts and that maybe we should try something else that would allow us to be supportive of the movement and live a comfortable life, plus find a school for Devan. He was now five years old and, although he was not in school, he was receiving a great education traveling with us and participating in many of our business activities. But now it was time for a more structured educational experience. A few weeks after we made our decision, we found out about Radiance, a community of meditators in a rural area outside of Austin, Texas. About a hundred people had gotten together and purchased two thousand acres in the hill country fifteen miles southwest of Austin. They built a beautiful golden dome in a wooded setting for the super radiance program, had their own Age of Enlightenment elementary school, a few hundred acres of hiking trails, a swimming pool and even an equestrian center.

This sounded much more attractive to us than either the frozen plains of Fairfield or the urban congestion of Washington, so we decided to visit Radiance as soon as we sold our house.

Finally, in the spring of 1988, a little over a year after we had put the house on the market, we found a buyer. A week after signing the contract on the house, Linnea's brother, who was active in the TM movement in England, invited us to the inauguration of the Ideal Village, a community of meditators, which was built around a golden dome for the group meditation program. The Ideal Village was located in Skelmersdale, a relatively pleasant town a hundred and fifty miles north of London on the west coast. There were a few hundred meditators from all over England who had moved there and started building their homes. When we arrived on a soggy, gray spring day, the village looked like any other typical European construction site, with lots of tall brick row houses clustered together on small plots of land. However, in the midst of all the construction confusion was a cute little round brick building with a dome-shaped roof. The color of the roof wasn't exactly gold; it was more a beige color. We found out later that the British building code would not allow any wild and crazy colored roofs so the meditators had to settle for beige. The inside of the dome was not quite finished, but the floor was covered with foam mattresses for the group flying program and provided a great opportunity for those living around the dome to walk from their homes twice a day for group meditations. In essence this is what Linnea and I were looking for in the U.S. Skelmersdale was much more appealing than Fairfield, had decent weather and it didn't have the urban sprawl of Washington, D.C.

The grand inauguration of the dome was scheduled a few days after our arrival. Maharishi was always urging meditators to have lots of celebrations and inaugurations, which was okay except that most of the time they involved excruciatingly long speeches by a multitude of people with official titles like governor, minister and doctor. The format for the inaugural celebration in the dome was to have the movement leaders of countries throughout the world give speeches honoring and blessing the new dome. Unfortunately, there were no movement leaders from the U.S. attending the grand event. It would be rather awkward if the country with the largest number of meditators was not represented at such an auspicious celebration. In desperation, the organizers of the event turned to me, the only available American. My reputation as a wise-cracking satirist had preceded me and the organizers were worried I would say something inappropriate for such a dignified occasion. Although I was incapable of giving a long-winded speech full of true-believer propaganda, I actually was impressed by the accomplishments of the meditators who were creating a community based on meditation and the knowledge of the Veda. I agreed to give a "straight" presentation as a representative of the United States.

The dome was extra-stuffy that evening, both literally and figuratively. The atmosphere was stifling because the British didn't want to open the windows and let any damp, cold air inside. Their tendency to embrace formality added to the oppressive atmosphere. The leaders of the Ideal Village had invited every government official in the area to the inauguration to make a good impression and to allay any fears that a weird cult was moving into their peaceful little town. The movement had become quite adept at being represented by people who had impressive degrees and were comfortable and skilled at presenting Maharishi's philosophy to civic leaders. They had convinced Sir Edmund Weston, a Member of Parliament who represented the district that included Skelmersdale, to deliver the keynote address. This made the movement leaders a little nervous because they weren't sure what his reaction to a large dome filled with people lounging around on foam mattresses would be. As a result, they over-compensated by erring on the side of pompous formality. In addition to the predictable speeches from the national leaders of the TM movement and some lame entertainment, the highlight of the evening was to be Sir Edmund's address.

Up until Sir Edmund's speech, the evening was going as planned. He was introduced by Dr. Gerald Brentworth, the leader of the Ideal Village, with the utmost aplomb and obsequiousness and with the assumption that Sir Edmund would give an equally formal and mind-numbing speech. Instead of a mind-numbing speech, he delivered a mind-blowing account of the sexual enthusiasm of his wife. It all started with the story of his first contact with the TM movement. Apparently he was invited by some representatives of the movement to attend a performance of the world-famous magician Doug Henning, who was a dedicated proponent of TM. One of Doug's most famous tricks was to turn a woman into a tiger by putting her in a large box and sealing the door. When he reopened it a live tiger would jump out. After recounting the story of turning the woman into a tiger, Sir Edmund looked up from his speech notes and said with a devilish grin, "While turning a woman into a tiger may look impressive, it's not that unusual—why, I turn my wife into a tiger almost every night in our bedroom." The movement officials sitting on the stage with Sir Edmund were stunned and paralyzed while the audience started sniggering and then broke into howls and applause. After a few moments of awkward silence and a fit of uncontrollable coughing, the evening's speeches by the remaining national leaders continued as though nothing had happened. I went back to sleep on my comfortable piece of foam in the back of the hall, knowing that the United States was the last country to offer its congratulations, which would allow me to sleep for another two hours. The next thing I knew, someone was shaking me and telling me to get up on stage. As I quickly jumped up and headed for the stage I realized my suit was all rumpled up and my tie was loose and flapping behind my neck. When I hopped up on the stage to deliver my speech, the officials who still hadn't recovered from Sir Edmund's outburst looked at me apprehensively. I was too sleepy and didn't have the heart to say anything off-the-wall, so I delivered a mercifully short and sincere speech praising the folks in the Ideal Village and quickly stumbled off the stage, much to the relief of the movement officials.

26

GOLDEN DOME in the HILL COUNTRY

The rugged and rolling limestone hills southwest of Austin were a welcome relief after driving all day through the flat agricultural prairie of east central Texas. As we approached the turnoff for Radiance about twenty miles southwest of Austin, we were filled with anticipation. Based on our positive experience at the Ideal Village in Britain, we had decided to rent a condo sight unseen, with the hope that it would live up to our expectations. According to their slick brochure, Radiance seemed to offer a lifestyle of daily group meditation in a beautiful dome and affordable property, where we could buy a house or land to build on. Other than reading the promotional brochure, we had no idea what it was really like. It could be creepy or blissful, but we felt compelled to give it a try. The entrance to the two thousand acre subdivision seemed like a typical development of middle class higher-end homes. There was a large, attractive sign that said "Goldenwood" with limestone pillars on each side of the turnoff from the main highway. The group of meditators who developed Radiance purchased the original two thousand acres and split the property into two sections: Radiance and Goldenwood. Lots in Goldenwood were sold to the general public to help pay for the Radiance project, which was only for meditators.

We started up the entrance road, winding our way up a fairly steep ridge dotted with small juniper and oak trees. As we approached the turnoff to Radiance, the landscape became scrubby and rock-strewn, which evoked a feeling of Southwest ranch land rather than a manicured suburban subdivision. We found this very alluring as we drove in. After a half-mile we began seeing some eye-catching houses tucked in among the junipers and oaks. We came into the main section of Radiance where the condos, townhouses and single family homes were clustered near the golden dome, which sat in a grassy meadow graced with lovely oaks. Behind the dome was a large open space with a creek and a fairly steep hill, creating a dramatic backdrop for the entire development. If it wasn't for the golden dome at the end of a short lane, Radiance would have looked like any middle class Texas subdivision. There were generic townhouses, a cluster of one-story small condos nestled near the creek and single family homes ranging from modest limestone and wood ranch houses to over-the-top, ostentatious "McMansions." The most appealing aspect of the small development was its silence and seclusion. There were no through roads and, except for the winding entrance road, the area was completely surrounded by rolling tree-covered hills.

After settling into our small but adequate two-bedroom condo facing the creek and meadows, Linnea and I took a leisurely stroll over to the dome for evening meditation. We were amazed at how warm it was for late November and how quick and easy it was to simply walk out our door and be in the dome in less than three minutes. For me the dome was love at first sight; it was brand-new and had a spacious, light and airy feeling to it, with a high-domed wooden ceiling. It certainly was much more pleasant than the musty, damp basement in Washington, D.C. where the group program was held, and much less crowded than the huge domes in Fairfield. Radiance seemed to offer the living situation we had been looking for and we were relieved and delighted that we had decided to try it out. It was amazing to be living in a community of meditators again after being in rural Virginia for almost three years. Every morning and evening people could be seen coming out of their houses and walking to the dome to meditate; not your usual suburban scene. Austin was about fifteen miles away and more pleasant and progressive than Washington. There was a Whole Foods store on our side of town and the winter weather was warm and balmy compared to Virginia. It was almost like living in California.

The Age of Enlightenment School was in a converted farmhouse next to a small compound of cottages at the base of the ridge leading up to Radiance. After living such a carefree life of traveling around the country and playing on the rocky coast of Maine every summer, Devan wasn't that excited about going to school. However, riding his bike down the steep, slightly treacherous rocky trail to school made it worth his while. Linnea and I were happy to see him in a school where the kids started every day with a group meditation and studied a curriculum based on Vedic knowledge. There were about thirty kids attending the school from kindergarten through the sixth grade, with only two teachers. Within a few weeks of our arrival in Radiance we had met almost everyone in the community. Some folks were actually old friends from MIU and courses in Switzerland. Most were about our age with school-age kids. There were lots of potluck dinners and meetings in the dome, which engendered an atmosphere of mutual support and familiarity. The community school board soon found out about Linnea's teaching skills and asked her to teach at the school. A short time later she became the director. We were both surprised at how fast we became integrated into the community and how much we enjoyed the modified ashram life of going to the dome every day and then having the rest of the day free to do anything we wanted, as opposed to the more structured program typical of most ashrams.

After a merciful mini-winter of a few days below fifty degrees, the Texas bluebonnets livened up the sleepy countryside and we were out exploring the nearby state parks and lakes in our trusty VW camper. On longer holidays we hiked the vast desert areas and mountains of West Texas and eastern New Mexico. We were less than a day's drive from Padre Island National Seashore, where we could drive our camper onto the beach and spend the night parked as close to the surf as we dared. It didn't take us long to decide to buy some land in Radiance and build a small adobe-style house with a courtyard. We had always admired the Santa Fe Spanish-style architecture we had seen in New Mexico. This was more appealing to us than the showy Texas-style houses common in the Austin area. Although the lots in Radiance were close to the dome, they were small and had too many restrictions against things like clotheslines and wood stoves. We soon found a lot in the adjoining (non-meditator) subdivision of Goldenwood that was much larger and was only a few more minutes from the dome by bicycle. It was located next to our old friends Terry and Marion, from our days of teaching in Charlottesville. They enjoyed the same country lifestyle we did and had a large garden, horses and even a half-wrecked car in their rocky, unpaved driveway.

After teaching at the school for a few months, Linnea began to realize that the students were not all little meditating angels. In fact they were no different from kids found in public schools. Some were "latchkey" kids who obviously needed more parental care and supervision; others were angry and hostile. One of them even stabbed Devan in the hand with a pair of scissors in a dispute over a crayon. Linnea found she was spending as much time trying to help the problem kids as she was teaching. By the end of the school year she realized that she couldn't be a mother to so many needy kids and still devote time to her own family so she decided not to return in the fall. Both of us were gradually beginning to realize that a meditator community was merely a microcosm of the rest of society. There was a representative sample of divorces, affairs, disputes, integrity lapses and even some minor illegal activities. After being involved with the TM movement for twenty years, however, we certainly didn't expect a utopia, and found there were definitely more coherence and less stress in a community of people who were meditating. We both loved to meditate in the dome every day and, even if it didn't bring about world peace as claimed by the movement's true believers, we experienced the positive results in our own lives. Although Radiance was not "heaven on earth" as claimed in the glossy brochure, it still had a lot to offer including our favorite place to meditate, a delightful haven of natural beauty in the hill country outside Austin, and lots of meditating friends who shared the same interests and values.

Even though the metastasizing suburban sprawl of shopping centers, subdivisions and freeways was devouring the countryside south-west of Austin, Radiance was fortunately surrounded by a ten thousand acre ranch on one side and a two thousand acre property called Friday Mountain Ranch on the other. The rolling hills had occasional dramatic limestone outcroppings and mini-canyons with seasonal creeks. Our favorite place to hike was Friday Mountain. There were well-traveled horse trails beside a creek that ran along the base of a small mountain and ended up in a secluded fertile valley occupied by the original Friday Mountain homestead. Most of the ranch outbuildings were falling apart, but the original L-shaped farmhouse built out of large limestone blocks was well maintained and listed on the Texas register of historic buildings. At one end of the valley was an idyllic swimming hole at the base of a cliff, which provided a welcome relief from the intense Texas sun. The ranch would have made a great park, but it was under a sales contract with some of the meditators from Radiance who wanted to de-velop it into an upscale golf and retirement community. We would have preferred that it remained undeveloped for hiking and swimming, but the relentless juggernaut of backhoes, bulldozers and real estate sales-men was spreading out from Austin in all directions and gobbling up every speck of land it could get its hands on.

    Winters in Austin and summers in Maine were a great plan. By the middle of May it was getting hot in Texas and starting to thaw out in Maine, so we returned to our island home for a refreshing summer of swimming, boating and hiking. This was an ideal life for Devan. He spent his days hopping rocks along the shore, jumping into the ocean whenever he felt like it and messing around with small homemade wa-tercraft that were always doomed to sink to the bottom as a result of being bombed by powerful, explosive boulders. Before heading back to Texas in late October, we decided to take a road trip in our rusty and somewhat trusty VW camper to visit some of our old customers and open up some new accounts for our print business. By the time we got to southern Maine the engine sort of blew up, which was not uncommon in air-cooled VW campers, so we had to abort our trip and limp back to our island home on three cylinders. Rather than spend thousands of dollars for a new engine, we decided to buy a Toyota mini-motorhome that included a bathroom with a shower, a kitchen with larger refrigerator, plus heating and air conditioning. Not only did this make traveling much more fun and comfortable, but when we arrived in Texas in January, we decided to live in the camper on our land next to our buddies, Terry and Marion. The weather was so mild that we set up a tent for an extra bedroom and were able to hook up to the water and electricity from our willing neighbors. Living outdoors on our own five-acre campground was infinitely more enjoyable for us than even the most luxurious house or condo, and we were only a five-minute bike ride from the golden dome in Radiance.

After tromping around our land for a few weeks, we finally de-cided on an ideal site for our adobe-style house. Now all we had to do was to figure out a way to pay for it. Our print business paid the bills but we didn't earn enough money to get a loan for a second house. We were reluctant to sell our oceanfront home in Maine, which was becom-ing increasingly more precious to us. During the few months we'd been away in Maine, the urban sprawl around Austin had made significant advances toward our rural meditation enclave. The freeway system was getting so close that, in order to go to the health food store, we had to get on and off a bunch of freeway ramps and overpasses, which dramati-cally increased the amount of time and hassle it took just to buy food. This decreased our enthusiasm for living in Austin and we started to have second thoughts about trying to build a house. A few days after we arrived back in Radiance, we decided to take one of our favorite hikes on the Friday Mountain ranch. As we clambered up the steep limestone ridge separating Friday Mountain from the Radiance property, we were stopped in our tracks by a massive chain-link fence stretching as far as the eye could see. Usually we don't let fences stop us, but this fence was about ten feet high and every tree within fifteen feet on each side of it was cut down and removed, making the fence just about impossible to scale. We were astounded that such an ominous-looking barrier had been erected in the short time we had been away. Our fence-climbing skills were no match for such an impenetrable wall of wire.

A few days later we learned that Friday Mountain had been purchased by the supporters of Swamiji, a spiritual teacher from India. Apparently they were planning to build a mega-ashram with an enormous Hindu temple and hundreds of acres of flower and vegetable gardens. The huge fence was built to protect their gardens and flocks of free-range peacocks from deer and predators. A small group of folks from Radiance had defected to the other ashram. They had invited Linnea, Devan and me to take a tour of the massive new Hindu temple and to meet Swamiji, who was in residence for a few weeks. As we drove past the security guard and into the ashram we were amazed at the transformation that had taken place on the ranch in such a short time. Near the entrance was a small industrial park with three or four new metal warehouses containing a mail order business owned by their movement, apparently to generate income for their ambitious projects. After passing by the industrial park, the main road meandered farther into the ranch. We could see the colossal temple rising out of the small secluded valley. It completely dwarfed the original two story ranch house that was now connected to it. The folks at the ashram wanted to tear the ranch house down, but because it was a registered historical building, it had to remain where it was and in good repair so they just incorporated it into the temple. This created a surreal vision as one approached the site. From one angle the magnificent temple had this humble ranch house attached to its side, and from another perspective a classic Texas hill country ranch house had a giant Hindu temple added on to it. Any illusion of being in Texas was quickly dissolved once we entered the temple. Marble floors, piles of flowers in every corner, intoxicating aromas of incense and imposing statues of Hindu deities transported us instantly to India. There were even hundreds of real Indians from the Austin area wandering around the beautiful gardens surrounding the temple. They were delighted with the progress of what was to become the largest temple of its kind in the United States.

After soaking up the good vibes of the temple, we were asked by one of the members of the ashram, who looked vaguely familiar, if we would like to meet Swamiji. As we entered the room, Swamiji was sitting on a couch garlanded with flowers and surrounded by a band of busy zealots buzzing around attending to his needs. While we were sitting on cushions waiting to meet him, I noticed why everything seemed so familiar. Most of the people bustling around Swamiji were ex-TM teachers whom I had seen around the TM movement for years! When I asked a few of them if they were ex-meditators they seemed a little embarrassed and were reluctant to acknowledge their involvement with the TM movement. After a surprisingly short wait, we were ushered into a small private room used for meetings with Swamiji. Linnea, Devan and I were the only ones in the room with him. Sitting in the presence of a holy man reminded me of the times we had spent with Maharishi. The profound silence radiating from a person who is so grounded in a state of transcendental pure consciousness is not only palpable, but tends to put things in perspective in one's own life. Even after a short visit of exchanging pleasantries with a spiritual teacher, one can realize how unenlightened one is and at the same time be uplifted by the possibilities of growing toward a more evolved state of consciousness.

Our visit to the beautiful temple and meeting Swamiji was a real inspiration, but Linnea and I had no desire to join their movement. Even though the TM movement had become structured into an inexplicable hierarchy and lacked the intimacy, ceremony, iconography and a more accessible guru or master offered by Swamiji's program, we liked our meditation program and didn't feel the need to be in the presence of a guru. Actually, the last few times we had seen Maharishi in the dome at MIU left me feeling uncomfortable with the way he was treated like a rock star. The crowds often went wild with cheers and standing ovations that lasted an embarrassingly long time. I felt a lot of love, affection and gratitude toward Maharishi, but for me he wasn't an enlightened savior whose every word was the utter truth. Obviously he was considered a great sage and wise man, but he was also an imperfect human like the rest of us, capable of making mistakes, and would have been the first to admit it with a chuckle.

There is something primal in human nature that seems to engender the need to have a savior or great leader to direct our lives. The increasing remoteness of Maharishi and the quasi-governmental structure of the TM movement left a lot of meditators feeling a lack that was fulfilled by Swamiji's movement. Here was an accessible spiritual teacher with a dynamic movement that was unabashedly Hindu, offering a beautiful temple and religious ceremonies that were more appealing than the secular and sterile ceremonies offered by the TM movement. Linnea and I felt perfectly comfortable with our friends who had joined the other ashram, but there were others in Radiance who felt that the folks who had left were defectors; they even felt a sense of competition with the other ashram. This sense of competition must have been conveyed to some of the teenagers in Radiance who stole Swamiji's golf cart and drove it off a cliff!

There were aspects of both movements with which we felt uncomfortable, but we enjoyed meditating in the dome twice a day even though the number of people participating in the program had steadily declined over the last year, from an average of about thirty to maybe ten. Most people seemed to get caught up in the daily pressures of work and raising a family and probably found it easier to meditate at home than go to the dome before and after work. Linnea and I were fortunate because we didn't have to roar off to the office every day and could plan our activities around meditation time. Although we lived on the edge financially, with no benefits like health insurance, we loved the freedom it afforded us. Now that we had our new motor home, we were able to take extensive trips to the Southwest during late winter and spring for a combination of business, exploring and home schooling Devan.

27

LOST on the MOUNTAIN

The Chihuahuan Desert extends for a thousand miles, from West Texas to eastern Arizona, where it merges with the Sonoran Desert, which is famous for its saguaro cactus. About halfway through this seemingly endless desert of chaparral on the New Mexico/Arizona border are the Chiricahua Mountains, one of our favorite places in the Southwest. After six hundred miles of windswept desert basin, the Chiricahuas offer a refreshing treat of live oak and pine filled canyons with rushing streams and spectacular, steep-sided gorges of pink rhyolite. This is an area where the Indian leader Cochise hid from the cavalry, often luring them into the narrow canyons and ambushing them from above. Our goal was to complete a hike we had started a few years before but had never finished. We planned to hike up a canyon to the mountain ridge, then along the ridge and back down via another trail, which would make a loop of about fifteen miles; a nice day hike of six or seven hours. As we were leaving the RV, Devan insisted we bring our hats and gloves. It was a balmy spring day and hats and gloves seemed ridiculous, but rather than argue with him, we walked back to the camper to pick them up. As I was going out the door, I noticed a pack of matches and instinctively picked them up.

The flora at the beginning of the trail seemed more like Florida than Arizona, with moisture-loving plants and lots of water flowing in the stream beds. As we climbed higher, the plants changed to the more familiar species of Arizona desert canyons: cactus, alligator juniper, yucca and pinyon pine. The pink rhyolite sides of the canyon became steeper and more dramatic, revealing many caves and bizarre formations. Usually when I am hiking in such a pristine and spectacular landscape, I am blissfully enjoying the exercise, clear crisp air and the great scenery, but as we hiked deeper into the canyon, I began to have the strange sensation that there was a presence guiding us up the mountain and that in a past life I had participated in chasing the Chiricahua Indians up into the canyon as a member of the U.S. Calvary. Maybe it was my imagination, maybe not!

By afternoon we had reached the higher elevation of large evergreen trees and a few patches of old snow. After hiking along the mountain ridge for a few miles, the trail simply disappeared without a trace. We knew the general direction we wanted to go, so we continued along the ridge hoping to pick up the trail again. The forest along the ridge became thicker and full of blown-down trees and boulders, making it difficult to continue. After an hour or so, we stopped and considered going back the way we had come. It would be a long hike, but at least we would know the trail. We calculated that it would be dark well before we could get down the mountain and, without flashlights, it was not a good option.

Looking back down into the canyon we could see where we had come from. If we could bushwhack or climb directly down the canyon wall we could probably get back by nightfall. So we proceeded directly down the canyon wall, which became steeper and steeper. There were many sheer cliffs that looked as though they had been waterfalls in the rainy season. After trying to climb down two or three of these dry waterfalls, it became apparent it was too difficult without rock climbing equipment or risking serious injury. By now it was almost dark and we realized that we would have to spend the night without tents, sleeping bags, food or warm clothes. We started hiking back up the mountain until we found a small ravine that seemed to offer some protection from the wind. As the pitch-black night descended upon us, we quickly gathered pine needles and logs for a makeshift shelter and bedding. The temperature dropped below freezing quickly, but we were reasonably comfortable as long as we kept feeding wood to our fire. We also felt lucky that Devan had suggested we return to the camper to pick up our hats and gloves and that I had grabbed the matches on the way out the door.

I realized I would need to keep awake all night in order to keep the fire going, so I decided to meditate for a half hour to gain some rest, then add more wood to the fire and meditate some more. Around midnight I noticed a few snowflakes drifting down, which increased in volume and intensity, soon becoming a full-scale blizzard. We quickly fashioned a crude lean-to shelter facing the fire where Linnea and Devan could get some relief from the driving snowstorm. As I sat toward the fire my face and hands were fairly warm, but my back was drenched with cold, wet snow, so I turned my back to the fire to dry it out. After about ten minutes I smelled something different burning and saw that the back of my jacket was smoldering. I quickly rolled in the snow to put it out and faced the fire again. This time I saw that my hiking boots were catching on fire!

Suddenly I was enveloped by an exceedingly comfortable, brilliant, golden sunlight. There was a vague feeling of being in the past rather than in the present; then I must have passed out. When I woke up it was about 4 AM, the fire was almost out and I was covered with frozen snow. As I tried to get warm and dry, it seemed like daylight would never come. Linnea and Devan were sleeping soundly in the lean-to, but the snow was still coming down and there was now more than a foot accumulated on the ground. The temperature was well below freezing and we were completely lost in a high elevation wilderness. The deep snow obliterated any trails and the only way back was to find the trail we had taken up here. For the first time, the thought of not making it out alive entered my mind. I wasn't frightened or panicked but, although I knew that freezing to death was not a bad way to go, I definitely didn't want to die.

As soon as the oppressive, pitch-black darkness of night began to give way to a welcome, dull, gray dawn, Devan and Linnea woke up.

Devan was raring to get going and continue with the expedition. Linnea was beginning to turn blue from hypothermia and I was exhausted from being up all night trying to keep from either freezing to death or catching on fire. Despite the deep snow our only option was to hike back up to the top of the mountain and try to find the way we had come. As we trudged up the mountain Devan ran ahead and yelled at us to hurry up. We had no food left and the water in our canteens was frozen into icy slush. This didn't seem to bother Devan, who was always hungry anyway. We realized that we could last quite a few days without food, but the cold and snow were beginning to take their toll. Linnea was turning even more bluish and I wasn't sure how much longer she could last. Then she noticed a piece of candy in her jacket pocket and started chewing on it. Within minutes the color returned to her face and she stopped shivering uncontrollably. It must have been the glucose that restored her vital signs. After an anxious one-hour trek through the deepening snow we made it to the ridge where we had lost the trail. The mountaintop was plastered with snow and there were no recognizable landmarks that would help us find the trail.

We were getting increasingly colder and wetter as we searched in vain for any sign of the trail. Hiking through deep snow in soaked hiking boots and heavy, wet clothes required at least twice as much energy as hiking on a warm sunny day. If we started down the mountain without finding the trail we could get sidetracked for hours, which could be fatal. It was extremely discouraging in the almost white-out conditions to try to find even the slightest hint of a trail, but it was the only option we had. As we stood in the middle of a small clearing, scouring the terrain for any sign that would lead us in the right direction, there was a sudden crashing sound in the brush to our right that sent chills up my spine. Linnea turned in the direction of the sound and got a quick glimpse of a deer bounding away from us. "That's it—the trail!" she yelled out. "As soon as I looked at the deer, I recognized the spot and the large yucca where it jumped out," she exclaimed. In ancient Vedic literature there are references to deer showing the way. Was this some kind of cosmic sign or just a coincidence? It looked a lot like the lost trail and it was our only hope so we started down the snow-covered path. The longer we stayed on the trail the more confident we became that we were on it. After an hour we finally started descending down out of the snow zone.

Farther down the trail it got warmer and dryer and we became more energized and giddy. For the first time since the ordeal began we looked at each other and half cringed and half laughed. Our faces were covered with soot and our clothes were burned and singed from being too close to the fire. We looked like we had just crawled out of a burning plane crash. As we continued down the mountain and out of the snow, we started to thaw out in the increasingly warm sunshine. Despite the long trek down the mountain and the lack of sleep, food and water, we felt almost normal, until we encountered a hiker in shorts who was climbing up the mountain. As we greeted him, we noticed that he seemed a little frightened and quickened his pace up the mountain as if to get away from us. Then we realized that we must have looked pretty scary to someone who was so clean and well dressed.

Opening the door to the camper and stepping onto the warm, dry carpet was like entering heaven. I was overcome with waves of gratitude that we had escaped from the mountain alive. Just being in our humble camper seemed like the most blessed luxury. All the usual comforts of daily life, food, shelter and dry clothes, which we take for granted, now seemed like precious gifts bestowed on us by an almighty benefactor. After we washed up and savored the most delicious hot soup of our lives, Linnea and I settled into a blissful meditation while Devan went roaring off on his bicycle.

EPILOGUE

It's been over twenty years since that event in 1991 and Linnea and I continue to meditate twice a day and practice our yoga asanas. We have a truly blessed life and it's hard not to attribute it to living a yogic lifestyle. The simple message of Maharishi's, balancing silence and activity in daily life, seems to work for us. While we love to practice our daily meditation, we have become less connected to the TM movement, which has become a bit too dogmatic and hierarchical for our comfort level. We still have many wonderful friends in the TM movement; some are still true believers and some are cynical about all the claims and programs offered by the movement. Many, like Linnea and me, still meditate, but have no interest in the latest projects of the movement. There are still a couple of thousand people in Fairfield meditating in the domes to bring harmony to world consciousness. Hopefully it is having a beneficial effect on the planet, but after all these years we feel free of the compulsion to drop everything and join them in the dome.

It took a few years for us to realize that living in a meditator community was not our dharma. At least we tried, out of a sense of duty, for almost ten years after we stopped teaching TM full time. It never seemed to work out, which we finally took as a sign to do what we really wanted to do: live a quiet life in the country and find a way to work from our home so we wouldn't have to live in the city or spend a lot of time commuting. After a few years of traveling in the Southwest during the winters to sell our pictures, we were asked by a friend to organize conferences on herbal medicine. This allowed us to live and work at our island home most of the time, while traveling to the conferences only a few times a year. It was a great experience for Devan, who loved the travel and freedom from the routine of going to school every day. The older he got, the harder it was for us to home school him as the lessons became more advanced, so we decided it might be a good idea for him to go to a real high school.

Devan wasn't too keen on leaving his idyllic life on the island to attend a high school. Somehow he used his excellent bargaining skills to get Linnea and me to agree to buy him a snowmobile if we moved off the island. We had visited Linnea's relatives in southern Oregon every spring and marveled at the mild weather and natural beauty of the area. Devan wasn't as impressed and was still holding out for a snowmobile if he was required to move. One fall day when we were camping in the mountains near Ashland, Oregon, Linnea had to do some work, so Devan and I went for a hike on some trails above the campground. We stopped to rest in a clearing and were both stunned at the unexpected sight of a massive snow-capped mountain. We were both sitting there silently gazing in awe at the mountain when Devan turned to me and blurted out, "Dad, this is amazing—we ought to buy some land here and build a house!" Within a couple of years we found some land and Devan helped us build a beautiful cedar chalet about five miles from where we'd sat in the clearing. He didn't even demand his snowmobile. By the time we finished building the house, he only had two years of high school left. He didn't want to get up early every morning for school so we continued to home school him. Then he went to college, joined the Peace Corps after graduation, and now works for a humanitarian aid organization.

Linnea and I often reflect on the fact that we have been meditating for forty years and the effect it has had on our lives. If someone had told us in 1968 that we would still be meditating forty years later, we would have thought we would surely be enlightened by now. Maharishi used to say a person would reach a state of cosmic consciousness after about five years of meditation. One thing we know for sure is that we are definitely not enlightened, using the criteria that an enlightened person is permanently established in a state of unbounded bliss consciousness and never overshadowed by the vagaries of daily life. Also, the enlightened individual is supposed to be so in tune with the laws of nature that they don't make any mistakes.

While most yogic literature claims that it takes many lifetimes of trial and error to become enlightened, it seems plausible that we can accelerate our progress by practicing the techniques of meditation and yoga. The concept of the evolution of consciousness described in the Vedas is a useful model for measuring the growth of an individual or society toward a higher state of acceptance, appreciation and even love of the diversity expressed on our planet. On a continuum of evolution from a lower level of consciousness to a higher level, an individual or society can be viewed as evolving from a state of operating from the amygdula, or lower brain stem, to functioning from the cerebral cortex, which is considered the higher level of the brain. Recent research has shown that when people experience negative thoughts toward someone from another race, ethnic group, tribe or team, the amygdula is activated. This phenomenon is also called "pack mentality" and is expressed as unquestioned devotion or allegiance to one's country, political party or religion.

Enlightenment can be described as the opposite of pack mentality and perhaps is indicated by activation of the higher brain. The enlightened individual spontaneously has the experience of oneness with all of creation, which transcends the boundaries of race, religion and national identity. This experience can result in a sublime comfort and a joy in diversity that greatly enriches the experience of daily life and eliminates the fear, anger and anxiety associated with lower brain stem functioning, or lower levels of consciousness. As one evolves or grows toward a state of enlightenment, there is a quantifiable increase in bliss and serenity that is infused into daily life. It is this growth toward a more evolved state of consciousness that Linnea and I have experienced over the last forty years. It has enriched our lives and has motivated us to "come out of the closet" and tell our story. Our hope is that, just as the evolution or growth of an individual's consciousness can be accelerated, so can the evolution or progress of the collective consciousness of society be accelerated so that the negative aspects of lower brain stem activity can be eliminated or dramatically reduced. Demonizing people outside our own pack, or group, whether it's our religion, political party, ethnic group or nationality, is the most destructive expression of a less evolved, or unenlightened, state of consciousness.

Not everyone has the time, motivation or discipline to develop a higher state of consciousness, so how can we as a society evolve out of this behavior that seems structured in our DNA? At one point in the evolution of mankind the ability to recognize as a threat someone from a different tribe was a useful survival mechanism. Now we have to calm down the part of the brain responsible for this instinct and enliven the higher functions of the brain responsible for love and understanding of our fellow humans. In my own lifetime I have seen this country evolve from a state of institutionalized racism to a dramatic improvement in the legal rights and social acceptance of African Americans. It is by no means a perfect situation, but after hundreds of years of oppression it was a relatively fast transition. This was brought about by legal enforcement, education, and a new generation of Americans unhindered by the prejudices of their parents. Hopefully we can accelerate our evolution out of our fundamentalist, fanatic and fascist tendencies by becoming aware of them and having the intention to rise above them when we are tempted to succumb to these natural but obsolete and destructive instincts. We certainly can't punish this behavior by sentencing offenders to two years in the state ashram, but we can educate the next generation about the possibilities of raising their consciousness to a higher level.

Yoga is often translated as "union" or "unity." The aspiration of the yogi for a state of unity consciousness described in the Vedas is more than an abstract philosophical concept. It is a pragmatic paradigm that can be directly experienced. It is both useful and fun, and is probably the reason why so many highly evolved holy men (and women) have such a great sense of humor. A spontaneous love and appreciation for all mankind without making a mood of it is a great stress reducer. It provides a perspective for making decisions that are the most likely to be enlightened, or life supporting, as opposed to life damaging or negative. There is no doubt about it! This is a great way to live. The trick is to operate from that state of consciousness all the time. After forty years of meditating, I realize how far I have to go to reach that enlightened state, but considering where I started, I am able to live close enough to that state of consciousness to be eternally grateful to Maharishi for bringing the knowledge of the Vedas out of the Himalayas to wacky westerners like me. Of course there are other great teachers and systems of knowledge available that offer this ancient wisdom in many forms. Let's hope that we are in the last throes of intolerant lower brain stem activity and there will be a rapid transition to the enlivenment of the cerebral cortex, or higher brain function, that will allow mankind to experience a state of union, or yoga, within an individual's own religion or philosophy.